Impact of Globalisation on Accountancy Education

Promoting educational exchange and facilitating educational development

Gert H. Karreman

For additional copies of this publication or copyright enquiries please contact:

International Accounting Standards Committee Foundation (IASCF)
Publications Department
1st Floor, 30 Cannon Street, London EC4M 6XH, United Kingdom
Tel: +44 (0)20 7246-6410, Fax: +44 (0)20 7332-2749,
Email: publications@iasb.org.uk Internet: www.iasb.org.uk

EI ASM

NETWORKING SINCE 1971

EUROPEAN INSTITUTE
FOR ADVANCED STUDIES
IN MANAGEMENT

Impact of Globalisation on Accountancy Education

Research Publication 2002

Promoting educational exchange and facilitating educational development

Gert H. Karreman, project director

EIASM, www.eiasm.be
Place De Brouckère plein 31
1000 Brussels – Belgium
Telephone + 32 2 511 9116
Fax   + 32 2 512 1929

Gert H. Karreman
Sportparklaan 59
2103 VS Heemstede
The Netherlands
Telephone   +31 23 528 0063
E-mail g.karreman@inter.nl.net

To all committed experts and staff
who were willing to share their expertise
and the support of their organisations.
Their contributions made the project
possible, their friendship made it
worthwhile !

Gert Karreman

ACKNOWLEDGEMENTS

In the acknowledgements due regard is given to the individual experts, institutes and sponsors who make the research project possible by contributing their expertise and support.

Steering Group (* Management Committee)

Prof. Ian F. Y. Marrian*, chairman, Institute of Chartered Accountants of Scotland, United Kingdom
Gert H. Karreman*, project director, European Institute for Advanced Studies in Management, Belgium
Prof. C. Mark Allison*, Institute of Chartered Accountants of Scotland, United Kingdom
Prof. Alain J. M. Burlaud*, Conservatoire National des Arts et Métiers, France
Anthony Carey, Institute of Chartered Accountants in England and Wales, United Kingdom (until end 2001)
Gerry van Dyck*, European Institute for Advanced Studies in Management, Belgium
Prof. Hans Kuijl*, Leiden University, The Netherlands
Michael J. Walsh*, Association of Chartered Certified Accountants, United Kingdom
Prof. Klaas Wezeman, Royal NIVRA, The Netherlands
Liaison with the IFAC Education Committee: Prof. Gary L. Holstrum, University of South Florida, USA
Liaison with the International Association for Accountancy Education and Research: Prof. Belverd E. Needles Jr., DePaul University, USA

International advisor: Prof. Charles C. Calhoun, University of North Florida, USA
International advisor: Prof. Adolf J. Enthoven, University of Texas, USA
Scientific support: Economic Social Institute, Free University, The Netherlands
Database support: KPMG Qubus Competence Center, The Netherlands

Participating Professional Bodies and Contacts

American Institute of Certified Public Accountants (AICPA), Bea Sanders, USA
Association of Chartered Certified Accountants (ACCA), Michael Walsh, United Kingdom
CPA Australia, Ann Johns, Australia
Fédération des Experts Comptables Européens (FEE), Henri Olivier, Belgium
Institut der Wirtschaftsprüfer in Deutschland (IDW), Prof. Kai-Uwe Marten, Germany
Institute of Chartered Accountants in England and Wales (ICAEW), David Cairns, United Kingdom
Institute of Chartered Accountants of Scotland (ICAS), Prof. Ian F. Y. Marrian, United Kingdom
International Accounting Standards Board (IASB), Kurt Ramin, United Kingdom
Koninklijk Nederlands Instituut van Registeraccountants (Royal NIVRA), Gert Smit, The Netherlands
Ordre des Experts-Comptables (Ordre), Hélène Michelin, France

Sponsoring Accountancy Firms and Contacts

Arthur Andersen, Jeremy Jennings, Belgium
Deloitte & Touche, Gregor Kruijssen, The Netherlands
Ernst & Young, Richard Findlater, United Kingdom
KPMG, Andrew S. Jones, United Kingdom
Moores Rowland International, Jérôme Adam, Belgium
Pricewaterhouse Coopers, Jens Røder, Denmark
Education and Training Task Force, Hans Verkruijsse, The Netherlands

Education Contacts

Australia, Institute of Chartered Accountants in Australia (ICA Australia), Gillian Cappelletto
Australia, CPA Australia, Ann Johns
Canada, Certified General Accountants Canada (CGA-Canada), Lynda Carson
Canada, Society of Management Accountants of Canada (CMA-Canada), Richard Benn
Canada, Institute of Chartered Accountants of Alberta (ICA Alberta), Steven Glover
Czech Republic, Chamber of Auditors of the Czech Republic (CACR), Prof. Bohumil Kral
France, Ordre des Experts-Comptables (Ordre), Hélène Michelin
Germany, Institut der Wirtschaftsprüfer in Deutschland (IDW), Wolfgang Böhm
Hong Kong, Hong Kong Society of Accountants (HKSA), Georgina Chan
Hungary, Chamber of Hungarian Auditors (CHA), József Roóz
India, Institute of Chartered Accountants of India (ICA India), C.R.T. Varma
India, Institute of Cost and Works Accountants of India (ICWAI), Swapan Dey
Japan, Japanese Institute of Certified Public Accountants (JICPA), Nobutake Hipposhi
Kenya, Institute of Certified Public Accountants of Kenya (ICPAK), John K. Njiraini
Lebanon, Lebanese Association of Certified Accountants (LACPA), Munir D. Sidani
Malaysia, Malaysian Association of Certified Public Accountants (MACPA), Tan Shook Kheng
Malaysia, Malaysian Institute of Accountants (MIA), Albert Wong Mun Sum
Mexico, Instituto Mexicano de Contadores Públicos, A.C. (IMCP), Salvador Ruiz de Chávez
The Netherlands, Royal NIVRA (NIVRA), Jeroen Buchel
New Zealand, Institute of Chartered Accountants of New Zealand (ICANZ), Bill Robertson
Pakistan, Institute of Chartered Accountants of Pakistan (ICAP), Yusuf Siddiqi
Pakistan, Institute of Cost and Management Accountants of Pakistan (ICMAP), Z.M. Zafarullah
Poland, Association of Accountants in Poland (SKwP), Zygmunt Korzeniewski
Poland, National Chamber of Statutory Auditors (KIBR), Danuta Krzydwa
Russian Federation, Institute of Professional Accountants (IPA Russia), Oleg Moiseevich Ostrovski
Saudi Arabia, Saudi Organisation for Certified Public Accountants (SOCPA), Ahamad Almeghames
South Africa, South African Institute of Chartered Accountants (SAICA), Adri Kleinhans
Spain, Instituto de Auditores-Censores Jurados de Cuentas de España (IA-CJCE), Enric Vergés
Sweden, Föreningen Auktoriserade Revisorer (FAR), Björn Markland
Turkey, Union of Chambers of Certified Public Accountants (TURMOB), Prof. Recep Pekdemir
United Kingdom, Association of Chartered Certified Accountants (ACCA), Michael J. Walsh
United Kingdom, Institute of Chartered Accountants in England & Wales (ICAEW), Michael Payne
United Kingdom, Institute of Chartered Accountants of Scotland (ICAS), Prof. C. Mark Allison
United States of America, American Institute of Certified Public Accountants (AICPA), Bea Sanders, Prof. Charles Calhoun.

Introduction

The research project on the Impact of Globalisation on Accountancy Education was conducted at the European Institute for Advanced Studies in Management (EIASM) in Brussels. For the purpose of the research project a Steering Group has been formed to overview both academic rigor and professional relevance. Professional accountancy bodies participated in the project, shared their expertise and gave a financial contribution towards the coverage of the costs of the research project. Major accountancy firms have agreed to sponsor the project, which was executed on a no-fee basis for participating experts. Co-operation has been established with the Education and Training Task Force initiated by the Global Steering Committee of the big firms.

A close co-operation was maintained with the IFAC Education Committee and with the International Association for Accounting Education and Research (IAAER). Essential for the project are the education contacts in the selected countries, who were willing to make local knowledge about accountancy qualification, education and training available in a comparable way. The European Federation of Accountants FEE has agreed to be a liaison organisation to the project. Contacts have been established with the European Union, the Organisation for Economic Co-operation and Development (OECD), the World Bank and the United Nations Conference on Trade and Development (UNCTAD).

The participating institutes and sponsors were invited to special functions connected to the project. This started with the conference that was organised by EIASM together with the Centre for Business Performance of the Institute of Chartered Accountants in England and Wales (ICAEW) in London on 29 September 2000. This conference focused on the global challenges for accountancy education in the 21st century. Intermediate results of the research project became available after each separate part. The professional results were presented at the 9th World Congress of the IAAER that took place in November 2002 in Hong Kong preceding the 16th IFAC World Congress of Accountants. The research results are made available in print and possibly electronic form.

Due to the cooperation with accountancy education experts the necessary expertise was available on a worldwide scale. This ensured that the objectives of the research project were addressed effectively. During the project there has been an unexpected growth in the network of participating experts, professional bodies and accountancy firms with excellent contacts with international organisations. The voluntary contribution of the experts involved illustrates the importance of the project for the general advancement of accountancy education.

The worldwide willingness to share information about the professional bodies and about accountancy qualification, education and training is very important for the research project. We appreciate the fact that this was only possible through collecting data in the format of the questionnaire. In many cases this made translation in the English language also necessary. This study reflects the information available and reviewed by the education contacts.

Ian F.Y. Marrian, Chairman of the Steering Group
Gert H. Karreman, EIASM Project Director

Scope of the Project

All over the world major developments in accountancy education are taking place. These are a result of local, regional and global developments of the accountancy profession in an emerging global economy. The developments take place in countries and regions, which show great differences in cultural background, legal and educational system and in economic position. Accountancy education is influenced both from the accountancy profession and by the institutes of higher education in the countries involved. Governmental regulation and directives from regional bodies set standards for professional and higher education, which may differ from country to country.

The specific contribution of this research project is a comparative analysis using a model developed for the classification of accountancy education systems which links accountancy education with the development of the accountancy profession and with relevant general characteristics of the countries included in the study. International guidelines and directives on accountancy education are compared in order to provide benchmarks for the qualification, education and training of professional accountants and auditors. A comprehensive definition of accountancy education is used, which includes qualification, professional education, practical training and general education. Contrary to the usual procedures a top-down approach was chosen, starting at the qualification level, as this is the only way towards comparability. The respective roles of standard setting bodies, professional organisations and educational institutes have been analysed for their influence on accountancy education.

Country characteristics include legal system and economic position. The research method is inductive, from observation to theory. Professional bodies worldwide have been selected in view of the coverage of all possible relevant distinguishing factors. Information was gathered through the use of a comprehensive questionnaire, augmented by interviews and the study of literature. The analysis of the data shows that it is possible to use one model for accountancy education worldwide, which still does credit to local and regional differences. Results are given on various levels of abstraction.

A descriptive review of accountancy education worldwide follows the analysis of the country profile. This is the basis for an overall analysis of the characteristics of accountancy education. The model for accountancy education is tested for relevance and interdependence of its variables. The resulting model is instrumental in the discussion of local and regional differences in accountancy education. Effectively a classification of accountancy education, with its elements of regulation, qualification, education and experience, can be described in four steps. The four steps identify the hierarchical levels of the classification model: regulation, final examination, professional education in combination with practical experience and education background.

The recommendations are based on the results of the research project in relation to a review of international developments. Attention is given to the scope and influence of international guidelines on accountancy education, the promotion of the international development of accountancy education including the furtherance of mutual recognition and harmonisation and to the influence of regional and local characteristics on accountancy education. Finally recommendations are given for future research. Cooperation between standard standards, the accountancy profession, universities and other institutes of higher education can be instrumental in advancing accountancy education in the setting of rapid international development and increasing demands on knowledge, skills, competences and professional values.

CONTENTS

EXECUTIVE SUMMARY

Chapter 1   Introduction

All over the world major developments in accountancy education are taking place. These are a result of local, regional and global developments of the accountancy profession in an emerging global economy. The developments take place in countries and regions, which show great differences in cultural background, legal and educational system and in economic position. Accountancy education is influenced both from the accountancy profession and by the institutes of higher education in the countries involved. Governmental regulation and directives from regional bodies set standards for professional and higher education, which may differ from country to country.

The specific contribution of this research project is a comparative analysis using a model developed for the classification of accountancy education systems which links accountancy education with the development of the accountancy profession and with relevant general characteristics of the countries included in the study. Accountancy education in selected countries is described and compared. The results contribute to the understanding of the present position and the possible future development of systems of professional qualification, education and training of accountants and auditors.

A comprehensive definition of accountancy education is used, which includes qualification, professional education, practical training and general education. Contrary to the usual procedures a top-down approach was chosen, starting at the qualification level, as this is the only way towards comparability. The respective roles of standard setting bodies, professional organisations and educational institutes have been analysed for their influence on accountancy education. A distinction is made between developed market economy countries, countries in transition from a planned economy to a market economy and emerging countries with developing economies. Major legal systems in the world as well as cultural background are considered for their possible influence on accounting and auditing and on accountancy education.

The research project started in September 1999 with finalisation in 2002. Intermediate results became available after each separate part of the project. Education contacts worldwide were approached in the first half of April 2001. The data gathering in the selected countries was followed by analysis and publication of country results in December 2001 and March 2002. The final results were presented at the 9th World Congress of the IAAER in 2002 in Hong Kong preceding the 16th IFAC World Congress of Accountants. Intermediate and final reports have been made available to the participants in the research project. Without their continuous support and without financial contributions by professional organisations the project would not have been possible.

Chapter 2   Development of Accountancy Education

International Guidelines and Directives can be used as benchmarks for the comparative analysis of national systems of accountancy education. As part of this research study a review was undertaken of the IFAC International Education Guidelines, the relevant Directives of the European Union and the Guideline for a Global Accounting Curriculum by the United Nations Conference on Trade and Development. International Accounting Standards by the IASB and International Standards in Auditing by IFAC directly influence accountancy education programmes. Their necessary coverage is included in the IFAC guidelines.

The education guidelines and directives focus on the content of programmes for the qualification, education and training of professional accountants and auditors. Relatively little attention is given to regulation, structure, recognition and expertise. It can be concluded that on content there is a major overlap between the various recommendations (IFAC, UNCTAD) and requirements (EU, GATS). Further convergence becomes more urgent as IFAC decided to move from International Education Guidelines to International Education Standards, which will be mandatory.

The analysis shows that the main elements of any system for the qualification of accountants and auditors should be a final examination of professional competence, supervised practical experience before certification and a programme of professional and general education. As there are no major differences between the various Guidelines and Directives the following summary is based on the IFAC International Education Guideline IEG 9. A critical review of the requirements follows later.

- Objective. IFAC defines as the goal of accountancy education and experience to produce competent professional accountants with the necessary knowledge, skills and professional values and with an attitude of learning to learn.
- General Knowledge. Arts, sciences, humanities for the development of general knowledge, intellectual skills and communication skills. Two years of a four-year degree (or equivalent).
- Organisational & Business Knowledge. Economics, quantitative methods and statistics for business, organisational behaviour, operations management, marketing, international business.
- IT Knowledge. IT concepts for business systems; internal control in computer-based systems; management of IT adoption, implementation and use; development standards and practices for business systems; evaluation of computer-based business systems.
- Accounting & Accounting related Knowledge. Financial accounting and reporting, management accounting, taxation, business and commercial law, auditing, finance and financial management, professional ethics.
- Practical Experience. Prior to recognition a minimum of three years approved and properly supervised practical experience primarily in the function concerned and in a suitable professional environment.
- Qualification. Final examination of professional competence assessing theoretical knowledge and the ability to apply that knowledge competently in a practical situation

Emphasis in the requirements is shifting from knowledge to the intellectual, interpersonal and communication skills, professional values and competences that are necessary for a career as an accountant in an environment of constant change and life-long learning. The history of accounting education change gives important indicators for future approaches. In general two areas have to be distinguished. The first relates to programme development on the level of institutes that are involved in education and training. Continuous attention is necessary for course content and curriculum, pedagogy, skill development, use of technology, development of expertise and strategic planning. The second covers activities of standard setting bodies and global activities of professional bodies and major accountancy firms.

Exposure Drafts of the proposed International Education Standards were published on the IFAC website at the beginning of July 2002, with an exposure period of six months. The Standards are due to be implemented by the beginning of 2005. They cover: entry requirements, professional education, professional skills and general education, professional values and ethics, experience requirements, assessment of professional competence, continuing professional education and development. The Compliance Committee of IFAC will need to monitor compliance with these Standards by the member bodies of IFAC. The Standards have adopted a 'competence-based approach' following the publication of IFAC's revised Discussion Paper on Competence, which defined competence as 'being able to perform a work role to a defined standard, with reference to real working environments'.

Chapter 3   Classification of Accountancy Education

The development of a conceptual model for the classification of accountancy education systems in various parts of the world is a key element of the research project. Classification is chosen as an efficient way of describing and comparing different systems for accountancy education. One important observation however has to be made. Traditional classification is permanent in time, which would make it difficult to cope with rapid developments in both the accountancy profession and in accountancy education. Major changes in legislation, regulation, world trade and in the accountancy profession during the last decade and results of globalisation to be expected in the next period make it essential to develop a flexible model with well defined parameters, which in themselves are constant in time, but allow systems of accountancy education to move from one state to another by changing the values of the parameters.

The selection of the possible distinguishing factors was based on a study of the literature available. These factors, mentioned below, were tested on their relevance for accountancy education.

- The influence of differences in cultural background.
- The present economic position of the countries involved.
- The effect of the legal system on accountancy education.
- The contribution of higher education to the qualification of accountants.

The final selection of countries is based on a preliminary analysis of the differences in the main characteristics that can be expected to influence accountancy education. In this way a comparative study in a limited number of countries can lead to an effective way of comparing different systems. The country profile is further analysed in Chapter 5. Professional bodies in the following geographical regions and countries have been approached.

- European Union: France, Germany, Netherlands, Spain, Sweden, United Kingdom
- North and Middle America: Canada, Mexico, United States of America
- Central and Eastern Europe: Czech Republic, Hungary, Poland, Russian Federation
- Africa: Kenya, Senegal, South Africa
- Middle East: Lebanon, Turkey, Saudi Arabia
- Asia: Pakistan, India, Malaysia, China, Hong Kong
- Far East: Australia, New Zealand, Japan
- South America: Argentina, Brazil

Country information about Senegal was not available. Neither was sufficient information available about accountancy education in Argentina, Brazil and China to include them in the analysis.

To achieve comparability a core model for accountancy education was developed. In its centre are the main components of accountancy education, surrounded by the various influences that have to be considered. Content, structure and recognition are included in the review.

	Influence of the Accountancy Profession on Accountancy Education	
Country Characteristics	**Accountancy Education**	**International Developments**
Cultural background Legal system Economic position Higher education	Professional qualification objective Qualification standards, final examination of professional competence Professional education Practical experience General education	Standards Guidelines Directives

In the Global Accountancy Education Questionnaire the following subjects are covered: respondent, country profile, profession, professional qualification, programme requirements and future developments.

Chapter 4   Research Questions and Method

The Central Research Question is to develop, test and evaluate a conceptual model for accountancy education in various parts of the world and to use the results to contribute to the understanding of the present position and the possible future development of systems of professional qualification, education and training of accountants and auditors. For operational use the following partial research questions are distinguished.

- Research Question 2.1: Analyse International Guidelines and Directives that are relevant for accountancy qualification, education and training in a format that makes it possible to use the results as benchmarks for the comparative analysis of national systems of accountancy education.
- Research Question 2.2: Analyse the factors that make change of accountancy education necessary and that influence the requirements regarding the professional qualification, education and training of accountants and auditors.
- Research Question 3: Develop a conceptual model for the classification of accountancy education systems in various parts of the world that can be used for evaluation and comparison.
- Research Question 4: Analyse the data relevant for accountancy education as a basis for decisions on the final model of the professional qualification, education and training of accountants and auditors.
- Research Question 5: Describe country characteristics and accountancy education as a basis for classification, comparison and analysis.
- Research Question 6: Develop a classification of accountancy education based on a conceptual model and evaluation of distinguishing factors.
- Research Question 7: Analyse regional and local differences of accountancy education in the selected countries.

The model of accountancy education has been specifically designed for the project. At the core of the model is the system of accountancy education. Two assumptions are central in the approach that has been chosen.

(1) It is essential to use a definition of accountancy education, which does not only include the content of accountancy education and training – the usual approach – but also its structure and recognition. Although the content of education and training programmes is important to judge the present abilities of professional accountants and auditors, it does in itself not indicate the potential that is available for further development. This is largely decided by the structure of accountancy education, including the allocation of responsibilities and the available expertise in a national setting.

(2) Accountancy education cannot be considered as a closed system, but is influenced by outside actors. Based on a field study and existing literature a distinction is made between international requirements and developments in the accountancy profession and in accountancy education, influences from the accountancy profession on accountancy education and the influence of country characteristics.

The research method can be characterised as an inductive (from observation to theory) classification of accountancy education, using a system of parallel processing (theory development and country studies combined in a step-by-step approach) with input from selected academics and professionals as database. The supporting literature review was both theory oriented and country oriented. Classification in comparative accounting studies should be based on four fundaments.

- The *characteristics* of a chosen classification should be adhered to consistently.
- The subsets of a given universe should be *exhaustive*, i.e., they should jointly cover the whole field.

- The subsets should be *pair-wise disjoint*, i.e., be mutually exclusive.
- There should be a preservation of *hierarchical integrity*, i.e., elements of one hierarchical rank should not be confused or mixed with elements of some other ranks.

In Chapter 8 the final classification model in four hierarchical levels is described in relation to general classification criteria.

Chapter 5   Global Country Studies

To decide on country characteristics the indicators for cultural background, legal system and economic position were compared. Cultural background can be described by 'power distance' and 'uncertainty avoidance'. The two major legal systems, especially when considering business implications, are 'common law' and 'civil law'. An overview of cultural background and legal systems for the selected countries is shown below.

Small Power Distance and Weak Uncertainty Avoidance
Common Law	Australia, Canada, New Zealand, UK, USA
Civil Law	Netherlands, Sweden
Common Law with Civil Law	South Africa

Small Power Distance and Strong Uncertainty Avoidance
Common Law	Not included in the selection
Civil Law	Argentina, Germany, Hungary

Large Power Distance and Weak Uncertainty Avoidance
Common Law	Hong Kong, India, Kenya, Malaysia
Civil Law	China

Large Power Distance and Strong Uncertainty Avoidance
Common Law	Pakistan, Saudi Arabia
Civil Law	Brazil, Czech Republic, France, Japan, Lebanon, Mexico, Poland, Russian Federation, Spain, Turkey

At the start of the project a preliminary distinction was made between industrialised countries with a market economy as the overall system, countries 'in transition' from a planned economy to a market economy and developing countries with emerging economies. In addition the following indicators with a possible relevance for the comparison of the economic position of countries were considered.

- Country population in millions
- Total labour force in millions
- Female percentage of the total labour force
- Gross National Product in millions of US $
- Gross National Product per capita in US $
- Number of personal computers per 1000 people

Based on the analysis in Chapter 5 a dichotomy was found between on the one hand countries that in general can be classified as 'industrialised' and on the other hand countries that in general can be classified as 'in transition/emerging'. This is based on a comparison of Gross National Product per person and Number of Personal Computers per 1000 Inhabitants. A graphical representation is given in Table 510.5. Although there are important differences, especially in the second group, the two-way classification is included as a possible distinguishing factor in the research analysis presented in Chapter 6.

Statistical analysis showed legal system and economic background as independent variables. There is however, at least for the group of countries considered in the research project, a correlation of cultural background with legal system and economic background. For that reason cultural background is not included as an indicator for the country profile.

Professional bodies and countries in relation to country characteristics and regions are given below.

Professional Body	Abbreviation	Country
Industrialised, common law		
Certified General Accountants Canada	CGA Canada	Canada
Society of Management Accountants of Canada	CMA Canada	Canada
Institute of Chartered Accountants of Alberta	ICA Alberta	Canada
American Institute of Certified Public Accountants	AICPA	USA
Association of Chartered Certified Accountants	ACCA	United Kingdom
Institute of Chartered Accountants in England & Wales	ICAEW	United Kingdom
Institute of Chartered Accountants of Scotland	ICAS	United Kingdom
Institute of Chartered Accountants in Australia	ICA Australia	Australia
CPA Australia	CPA Australia	Australia
Hong Kong Society of Accountants	HKSA	Hong Kong
Institute of Chartered Accountants of New Zealand	ICANZ	New Zealand
In transition or emerging, common law		
Institute of Certified Public Accountants of Kenya	ICPAK	Kenya
South African Institute of Chartered Accountants	SAICA	South Africa
Institute of Chartered Accountants of India	ICA India	India
Institute of Cost and Works Accountants of India	ICWAI	India
Malaysian Association of Certified Public Accountants	MACPA	Malaysia
Malaysian Institute of Accountants	MIA	Malaysia
Institute of Chartered Accountants of Pakistan	ICAP	Pakistan
Institute of Cost and Management Accountants of Pakistan	ICMAP	Pakistan
Saudi Organisation for Certified Public Accountants	SOCPA	Saudi Arabia
Industrialised, civil law		
Ordre des Experts-Comptables	Ordre	France
Institut der Wirtschaftsprüfer in Deutschland	IDW	Germany
Royal NIVRA	NIVRA	Netherlands
Instituto de Auditores-Censores Jurados de Cuentas de España	IACJCE	Spain
Föreningen Auktoriserade Revisorer	FAR	Sweden
Japanese Institute of Certified Public Accountants	JICPA	Japan
In transition or emerging, civil law		
Instituto Mexicano de Contadores Públicos, A.C.	IMCP	Mexico
Chamber of Auditors of the Czech Republic	CACR	Czech Republic
Chamber of Hungarian Auditors	CHA	Hungary
Association of Accountants in Poland	SKwP	Poland
National Chamber of Statutory Auditors	KIBR	Poland
Institute of Professional Accountants	IPA Russia	Russian Fed.
Lebanese Association of Certified Accountants	LACPA	Lebanon
Union of Chambers of Certified Public Accountants	TURMOB	Turkey

The main characteristics of the systems of accountancy qualification, education and training are discussed in Chapter 5.

Chapter 6   Characteristics of Accountancy Education

This chapter is dedicated to the classification of accountancy education based on comparison and analysis of the country data that have been collected through the use of the global accountancy education questionnaire. The results concerning the most important indicators are described here.

Country Profile
The two major parameters for the country profile are economic *position* and *legal system*. Legal system is divided in common law and civil law. economic position is divided in industrialised and in transition or emerging.

Regulation and Recognition
A measure to distinguish between *government regulation* and *professional self-regulation* is based on the following indicators.

Regulation of the accountancy sector: by law, by professional self-regulation or by both.
Recognition of the accountancy profession: as a regulatory body, as a disciplinary body, or as both.
Responsibility for qualification standards: the government, the professional body, or both.
Recognition of professional education: by the government, by the professional body, or by both.
Recognition of practical training: by the government, by the professional body, or by both.

The resulting *regulation index* can take the following values: high professional self-regulation, emphasis on professional self-regulation, emphasis on government regulation and high government regulation. Overall common law countries have higher professional self-regulation and lower government regulation than civil law countries. Industrialised common law countries score somewhat higher in professional self-regulation than common law countries with economies that are in transition or emerging. For civil law countries the situation is reversed with high government regulation for industrialised countries. This may well be an effect of EU regulation as five out of the six industrialised, civil law countries that are considered in the research project are members of the European Union.

The results are a measure for government and professional influence on accountancy education.

Professional Body
In view of qualification objectives and the existing or necessary systems of professional education and training a particular importance has to be attached to the employment sector of members and of new members. Most professional bodies have members in all four sectors: public practice, industry and commerce, government and other areas.

All professional bodies in common law countries have less than 50% of their members in public practice. Most professional bodies in civil law countries have more than 75% of their members in public practice.

For most professional bodies the percentages of members in public practice and new members in public practice are comparable. For some professional bodies the situation is quite different for new members. The clearest examples with all or almost all new members in public practice while membership is spread over all employment sectors are ICA Alberta in Canada, AICPA in the USA and ICAEW in the UK. For ICA Alberta and ICAEW the explanation can be sought in the requirements for practical training, which are explored later. For AICPA however practical training is not a requirement for qualification, although it may be required for licensing dependant on State regulation.

Professional Qualification and Background
The main qualification objectives mentioned in the questionnaire are accountant and auditor. Clear definitions for general use are not available. IFAC defines 'accountant' as a member of a professional body that is a member of IFAC. For the majority of the professional bodies the qualification objective is accountant and auditor. There is no clear classification distinction. Specialisation is disregarded as in most cases, if mentioned at all, there was no visible differentiation in programme requirements.

The admission requirements to the profession in general include a final examination of professional competence. Admission requirements for professional education and practical training are discussed as part of the education system. It was not possible to use the information on the qualification level in the categories postgraduate, graduate and undergraduate because of differences in the definitions that were used by the respondents. University entrance level is almost always requested.

The education background of candidates can be divided in possession of a general university degree, an accounting, finance or business university degree, general higher education and accounting, finance or business higher education. The results show that most professional bodies have either a high percentage (75-100%) of new members with an accountancy, finance or business university degree or emphasis (50-75%) in that sector. Four professional bodies have either a high percentage of new members with a general university degree or emphasis in that sector. Three professional bodies do not fit in one of the above categories.

Examination, Education and Training
In order to distinguish between possible kinds of examinations the core programme, the objectives, the methods and the entrance requirements have been compared on a scale between 'theory oriented' and 'practice oriented'. The total for theory and for practice determines the relative position of the examination on the scale between 'theory oriented' and 'practice oriented'. Overall most professional bodies have a mixed approach in their final examination with comparable attention for theory and practice. A theoretical orientation exists at nine bodies, a practical orientation at three bodies. Two of the professional bodies do not have a final examination.

All professional bodies in common law countries are provider of their own examination, in the case of AICPA in the USA together with the State Boards of Accountancy, who are the official providers.
The situation in civil law countries is more mixed with often a dominant role of the government. The Netherlands and Hungary are the only two countries with an official responsibility of the universities in the final examination. In all countries university experts participate in the examination.

The final examination can be recognized by the government or by the professional body itself, or in a combination. There is no principal difference between the two systems, as the professional bodies, who recognize their own examination normally do so under government charter. Direct government responsibility is concentrated more in civil law countries than in common law countries.

The majority of the professional bodies is involved in professional education, in many cases in cooperation with universities and/or commercial companies. Recognition of professional education can be a (joint) responsibility of the professional body or rests with the government. In many cases practical experience must be combined with professional education, sometimes it is possible but not required, while in three cases it is excluded. Two professional bodies do not have specific requirements on professional education and practical experience.

For most professional bodies practical experience is for more than 75% offered in public practice or in a combination of employment sectors. Only CMA Canada has a majority of more then 75% of its candidates in industry and commerce. The normal duration is three years or more fulltime. In situations where part time practical experience is allowed the usual condition is that the total amount of time spent on practical experience stays the same. Recognition of providers of practical experience almost always rests with the professional bodies or with the professional body in combination with the government. Sole government responsibility only occurs twice.

Chapter 7   Differences in Accountancy Education

The research project has resulted in the classification of accountancy education systems worldwide. Overviews of accountancy education are available for 34 professional bodies in 25 countries. Overviews for each professional body are given in Annex 3. Three countries, Argentina, Brazil and China, are included in the country analysis but for these countries there is no information on accountancy education available.

Region in itself may be less relevant than other factors like historical background and international associations. First attention is given to the region, the legal system, the regulation index for government regulation compared with professional self-regulation, membership of regional organisations of professional accountants and professional self-regulation of mandatory membership and mandatory CPE according to the membership regulation index.

Based on economic considerations some changes were made in the regions that were introduced in Chapter 3. As a result the comparison is given in the following groups.

- America: Canada and USA have a common law background; Mexico has a civil law background.
- European Union: The United Kingdom has a common law background; France, Germany, the Netherlands, Spain and Sweden have a civil law background.
- Central and Eastern Europe: The Czech Republic, Hungary, Poland, the Russian Federation and Turkey have a civil law background.
- Africa: Kenya and South Africa have a common law background. In South Africa this is combined with a strong civil law influence.
- Middle East: Lebanon has a civil law background and Saudi Arabia has a common law background.
- Asia: India, Malaysia, Pakistan and Hong Kong have a common law background; China and Japan have a civil law background.
- Australia and New Zealand: both countries have a common law background.

Membership categories, education background and qualification objective are discussed in regard to their possible relevance for accountancy education. The qualification objective, accountant and/or auditor, could be expected to be significant for the education and training system. The same applies to the education background as this decides the starting level for additional professional education not included in the system of higher education. Membership categories, especially for new members, possibly reflect practical training requirements.

In general for common law countries a higher emphasis on practice can be expected then in civil law countries. On the other hand the actual situation may very well depend on the actual contribution of higher education to accountancy education, both in content and in number of students. In industrialised countries with a high participation in higher education, prospective accountants will in general start their professional education and training after they have already reached a certain expertise. As a result it becomes possible to concentrate additional professional education and the final examination more on the practical aspects of the accountancy profession. In emerging countries and countries in transition it may presently be necessary to concentrate more on knowledge.

Worldwide the majority of new accountants and auditors has either an accountancy, finance or business university degree or a general university degree. Higher education has a relatively higher importance in countries that are in transition or emerging. In general it can be concluded that the education of accountants and auditors is at the same level as the education of other professionals in their country.

It may well be that the content of university and higher education programmes does not fit the general knowledge as described in IFAC IEG 9. In fact it can be expected that only in countries like the USA with a very high participation in university education two years of a four year degree will be devoted to arts, sciences and humanities in general. This is not necessarily a problem. It is quite logical that general knowledge of accountants is developed on the highest country level. Furthermore in countries where a high participation in university education has not yet been achieved intelligent, young people should find opportunities to become accountant in a work-study combination. This is not only to their advantage but also to the benefit of the accountancy profession, which has to attract the best candidates in competition with other employers.

The conclusions about the subjects in the various programmes of accountancy education can only be general. If subjects are included this is only a first step towards, for example, mutual recognition of qualifications. Separate content analysis is outside the scope of this research project. Conclusions however have been reached about subjects in the programme and the relation between knowledge, skills and professional values.

In Organisational & Business Knowledge economics, quantitative methods and organisational behaviour are covered in almost all programmes. This is not the case for operations management, marketing and international business. IT Knowledge and all subjects in Accounting & Accounting Related Knowledge are at least covered. In respect to ICT applications it makes a vast difference whether candidates follow full time education or have the opportunity to combine professional education with hands-on experience during practical experience.

Skills get increasing attention in professional education, for the moment with emphasis on intellectual skills. The systematic integration of skills in practical experience is at the beginning.

Mutual recognition is ruled by the GATS, by IFAC and regional directives and by agreements between countries. The GATS as a general agreement does not relate to content, but to the procedures that should be followed. The GATS requires that all countries have procedures to verify qualifications of professionals from other countries. Though GATS is multinational in scope it does provide for bilateral implementation. Rules set out by GATS are meant to ensure the same privileges for foreign providers and domestic counterparts, to remove discriminatory obstacles and to provide transparency.

Comparison has shown that we are only at the beginning of mutual recognition agreements between professional bodies and countries. Interest in cross border recognition is certainly increasing and results are being achieved, but at the moment these are still limited and on an individual basis. Limited in the sense that most agreements only give access to examinations, sometimes with exemptions, and there is no systematic coverage of relations between countries. A specific problem is that mutual recognition may not yet be possible because a system is further developed than its counterpart.

The Introduction by the IFAC Committee of draft International Education Standards is an important step towards further harmonisation and mutual recognition of the qualifications of professional accountants because the standards give additional guidance and, depending on local legislation, implementation will be mandatory for the member bodies of IFAC.

Chapter 8 Conclusions

The objectives of the research evaluation are to conclude whether the objectives of the research project have been reached and to see what lessons can be learned from the results. Effectively a classification of accountancy education, with its elements of regulation, qualification, education and experience, can be described in four steps. The four steps identify the hierarchical levels of the classification model: regulation index, final examination, professional education and practical experience, education background. This provides the structure to evaluate the overall results of the research project in relation to its original objectives.

Existing guidelines and directives focus on content with an emphasis on the theoretical side. Attention for skills and competences is increasing with much work still to be done on instructional and assessment methods. There are major differences between professional bodies in the realised and systematic contribution of practical experience to professional expertise. In guidelines and directives relatively little attention is given to requirements for providers and recognition. This is easily understood as a result of the wide range of approaches that exist worldwide. On the other hand it must be realised that possibilities for future development depend largely, not on existing programmes, but on a structure that is open for necessary change, is flexible in time and has access to expertise.

This is clearly shown by the demands on the accountancy profession and on accountancy education. It will be well to bear in mind that choices have to be made and that accountancy education can not be expected to achieve for its students understanding of all the complexities related to modern corporate activities. For accountancy education to be able to concentrate on skills and competences it is necessary to differentiate between core knowledge that must be included in the mandatory programme and knowledge that can be acquired when needed after qualification. The most important issue is not 'how to become an accountant' but 'how to be an accountant during the whole career'.

In general professional bodies in common law countries show a tendency towards professional self-regulation compared with a tendency towards government regulation in civil law countries. This is particularly true for common law countries with a historical UK background. The USA on the other hand shows a rule-based approach and a tendency towards government regulation. It is also clear that regional regulation can alter regulation patterns, as is shown in the European Union where EU Directives have to be implemented in the legislation of the member states. There is no overall distinction in regulation as a result of economic position.

Qualification standards were defined as admission requirements to the profession. They can include: a formal final examination of professional competence, a prescribed programme of professional education and a prescribed programme of practical experience. The results show that all three elements are almost always included. A final examination is always part of the qualification requirements. Professional education is always available in one form or another, mandatory or voluntary, post higher education or included in higher education. Practical experience is generally included in qualification or licensing requirements. There is however a clear distinction between professional bodies in the requirement to have practical experience before the final examination. This is the main reason that the final examination was selected as a classification parameter.

Professional education and practical experience are part of almost all qualification programmes. The interesting distinction for the classification of accountancy education is their respective position. To this end the combination of professional education and practical experience is regarded with three possible values: required, possible and excluded. The values required and possible imply that at least a part of professional education is part time as otherwise the combination would not be possible. If the combination is excluded professional education can be completely integrated in full time university or higher education, which then can be followed by practical experience before the final examination, qualification or licensing.

Traditionally practical experience has a more important position in common law countries than in civil law countries, where education systems tend to be more directed towards a theoretical approach. The analysis shows that for the majority of the countries included in the research project, both with a common law and a civil law background, there is a tendency towards mandatory practical experience before qualification. This is not yet general but IFAC guidelines, EU Directives and actual developments taking place mostly point in the same direction. There are however major differences in the requirements to be fulfilled during practical experience. These are reflected in the employment sectors that are allowed, the required programmes, the assessment of practical experience and the systems that are in place for monitoring and supervision.

Education background is the final classification parameter. It is chosen in view of two distinctions, which together determine the knowledge, skills and competences that are available at the start of additional professional education (if available) and practical experience. The first one is the focus of full time education programmes: general or specific. Specific is defined as aimed at accounting, finance or business. The second is the level of the programmes: university or other forms of higher education. Actual participation is chosen above entry possibilities. The reason is quite simple. Many professional bodies give access to a wide range of candidates. Mostly however if specific programme requirements are in place they have to be met by everyone seeking admission. This usually means exemptions after specific programmes or additional requirements after general programmes.

Chapter 9   Recommendations

The recommendations are based on the results of the research project in relation to a review of international developments. Attention is given to the scope and influence of international guidelines on accountancy education, the promotion of the international development of accountancy education and to the influence of regional and local characteristics on accountancy education. The final paragraph contains recommendations for future research. The recommendations are presented here without the arguments in Chapter 9.

Scope and Influence of International Guidelines

Recognize the fact that no single accountant or auditor can satisfy all the requirements of the accountancy profession and make differentiation in qualifications possible. Older professions like law and medicine have preceded the accountancy profession in recognising the need for specialisation in an increasingly complex environment. Logical starting points could be the education and training requirements for auditors, management accountants and government accountants. Benchmarks should be formulated on an international level to facilitate comparability and recognition. Define the possible contributions of full time and part time education and of practical experience in relation to employment sector.

Evaluate programme content and level demanded in the guidelines in relation to employment sectors and functions. Differentiate between qualification requirements in general to be met at the final examination and actual requirements for certain functions, which have to be met at the final examination or can be fulfilled later during mandatory CPE as a necessary part of education.

Recognize the contributions of formal education and practical experience to the development of skills and professional values by including them both in a systematic way in programme requirements.

Define the minimum levels of professional education that have to be reached before practical experience can be effective. Stipulate that the final examination of professional competence can only be taken after fulfilment of the education and training requirements. This approach ensures a relevant professional qualification. The alternative approach is to set the examination at the end of the period of general and professional education without regard for the practical experience, which may follow later. This leads to an educational title that can be valuable in itself without however a complete coverage of the professional competence that is necessary for qualification or licensing.

Stimulate the further development of final examinations, which follow after professional education and practical experience have been concluded and credit their combined contribution to professional competence. Stimulate the further development of assessment procedures that strengthen the competence approach of accountancy education and training, and respect conditions of relevance and equal treatment. As the first would mean more use of individual result, the second would mean a move `from product to process control. It has to be recognized that this is mostly already the case in the assessment of practical experience.

Promotion of International Development

Focus General Knowledge on university exit level in each country and concentrate on programme content. Define clearly the subjects of Organisational & Business Knowledge that should be present in all accountancy education programmes and, when necessary, stimulate that universities implement them in their regular programmes.

For IT Knowledge and Accounting & Accounting Related Knowledge a two-step approach as recommended by the accountancy firms could be used. The draft International Education Standards, available at the IFAC website mid 2002, reflects the requirements for internationally operating accountants and auditors. These can be checked against the presently available programmes. As a first step the accountancy firms in the Forum of Firms have expressed their willingness to make additional programmes available to fill possible gaps with international expectations. As a second step this additional programmes can over a period of time be implemented in local professional and higher education programmes. In addition the advancement of competence approaches to education that has really started in the last ten years should be promoted with vigour. The possible contribution of different education methods to achieve competence should be recognized. The two major approaches discussed in the IFAC Education Committee are sequential, knowledge followed by competence, and integrated.

The main issues regarding Practical Experience are its formal requirement before qualification and its contribution to professional competence. Experience in the European Union has made it clear that a formal requirement can, sometimes against expectations, help in acquiring progressive levels of expertise and that it is possible to stimulate actual cooperation between professional body, employers and educators. It may be necessary to change legislation or professional regulation to get a firm basis for practical experience, but the effect can contribute to a harmonized system of accountancy education and training in which candidates can combine theoretical learning with hands-on experience. A Final Examination where the candidate can show his or hers competence is then the logical last step towards qualification.

Influence of Regional and Local Characteristics

Check local legislation, including guidelines and directives, to see whether they provide an adequate framework for accountancy qualification, education and training. If necessary, decide how to promote necessary change. Seek convergence in already existing international standards, directives and guidelines on accountancy education. In addition promote activities of the major accountancy firms aimed at the level of expertise necessary for trans-national audits with comparable audit methodologies and training systems.

Prepare systematic benchmarking of accountancy education based on the research results actively supported by the international professional organisations. The focus in this should be on 'good practice' in the meaning of 'standards to achieve' as it is highly unlikely that 'best practice' can be identified in ways that reflect local and regional circumstances. In particular for emerging and transition countries critical features must be identified in the context of their present and future position, including underlying qualifications. It is necessary to actively promote the authority and influence of benchmarks on accountancy education by giving attention to dissemination, applicability and the relation to local and regional legislation. Investment of appropriate resources is necessary to achieve lasting results.

Recommendations for Future Research

Promote an international research agenda covering the main topics of accountancy education. Future research can both be general and specific. Examples of general research can be found in further theory building, including the possible influence of capital markets on accountancy education. More specific research could be aimed at certain regions. Given the fact that Latin America and China were not able to be part of the full project and their importance for economic development these two areas would be logical choices to evaluate comparability and applicability of the general framework that has been developed.

CHAPTER 1   INTRODUCTION

This chapter gives an overview of the objective, scope and key issues of the project.

The research project has as its general objective to contribute to the understanding of the present position and the possible future development of accountancy education in various parts of the world. The results of the study include an overview of developments in the accountancy profession influencing accountancy education, an analysis of general trends and objectives in accountancy education and a conceptual model to describe systems of accountancy education. The information can be used for realistic and achievable guidelines on accountancy education, contribute to a structured implementation of global accounting and auditing standards, promote harmonisation and mutual recognition of professional qualifications of accountants and stimulate the development of accountancy education. Recommendations for the development of accountancy education in an international context are based on the results of the research project.

100   Mission Statement and Objective

Research into the impact of globalisation on accountancy education was conducted at a time when the debate on international accounting and auditing standards had become a prominent policy issue. The importance being attached to the subject is clearly shown by the role being played by the World Bank, the International Accounting Standards Board (IASB), the European Commission and in particular by the International Federation of Accountants (IFAC) and the accountancy profession, including the accountancy firms. The establishment of the International Forum on Accountancy Development (IFAD) (1999) is a distinct example of the importance attached to these matters.

The research project has as its *general objective* to contribute to the understanding of the present position and the possible future development of accountancy education in various parts of the world. To this end a conceptual model for the classification of the different accountancy education systems in various parts of the world has been developed that can be used to describe and compare accountancy education worldwide. Furthermore the model can be used to monitor and in part explain global changes in accountancy education as a result of international developments in the accountancy profession. IFAC International Education Guidelines in combination with regional (for instance European Union) Directives have been used as benchmarks. Comparative country studies were undertaken to describe accountancy education in the countries involved and to test the model.

The *subject area* of the project is the general and professional qualification, education and practical training of accountants and auditors in public practice as one of the important areas for the accountancy profession and the domain of international standards. The results of the study provide information that can be used for realistic and achievable guidelines on accountancy education, contribute to a structured implementation of global accounting and auditing standards, promote harmonisation and mutual recognition of professional qualifications of accountants and stimulate the development of accountancy education. Information from the project will help to find efficient and effective ways to secure the necessary professional education and training for accountants and auditors in various regions of the world. In a general sense the term *accountancy education* is used to indicate all the relevant elements mentioned above.

110   **Central Research Question**

All over the world major developments in accountancy education are taking place. These are a result of local, regional and global developments of the accountancy profession in an emerging global economy. IFAC in growing co-operation with global and regional bodies plays an important role in standard setting and the development of benchmarks. The General Agreement on Trade in Services (GATS) of the World Trade Organisation (WTO) encourages mutual recognition of qualifications as a means of promoting greater mobility of qualified accountants.

These developments take place in countries and regions, which show great differences in cultural background, legal and educational system and economic position. Accountancy education is influenced both from the accountancy profession and by the institutes of higher education in the countries involved. Governmental regulation and directives from regional bodies set standards for professional and higher education, which may differ from country to country.

International conferences and research make information available on accountancy education in various parts of the world. The specific contribution of this research project is a comparative analysis using a model developed for the classification of accountancy education systems which links accountancy education with the development of the accountancy profession and with relevant general characteristics of the countries included in the study. The design and use of the model contributes to the understanding of and the insight in accountancy education, the set of minimal conditions to be fulfilled in mature systems of accountancy education and effective approaches towards international harmonisation and recognition.

Central Research Question

Develop, test and evaluate a conceptual model for accountancy education in various parts of the world. Describe and compare accountancy education worldwide and use the results to contribute to the understanding of the present position and the possible future development of systems of professional qualification, education and training of accountants and auditors.

To achieve the goal set in the Central research Question the subject was divided in separate issues that are addressed throughout the research project with an integrated evaluation at the end.

120   **Research into Accountancy Education**

The 7th International Conference on Accounting Education, organised in 1992 by the International Association for Accounting Education and Research (IAAER) in Washington, focused on 'Accounting Education for the 21st Century: the Global Challenges'. Its objective was to provide an up-to-date view of the state of accounting education throughout the world and of the global challenges facing accounting education in the approach of the next century. The 8th International Conference on Accounting Education in 1997 (Paris) followed up the subject under the motto 'The Changing World of Accounting – Global and Regional Issues'. The 9th International Conference on Accounting Education on 'Accounting Education and Research Challenges in the New Millennium' took place in November 2002 in Hong Kong.

The subjects of the IAAER conferences reflect the increasing importance of developments in the professional qualification, education and training of professional accountants. 'Drivers of change'[1] effecting the accountancy profession include external factors like the impact of Information and Communication Technology (ICT), business imperatives like globalisation, individual demands and education. This makes it necessary to promote the development of professional accountancy education and training worldwide based on a clear understanding of the present position. The interest shown by international bodies in the objectives, the content and the results of the research study, in combination

---

[1] Institute of Chartered Accountants of Australia, Vision 2020 (1998).

with the cooperation with professional accountancy bodies and major accountancy firms, clearly illustrate this point.

The importance of accountancy education for the development of the accountancy profession is also demonstrated by the motto chosen for the XVI World Congress of Accountants, jointly organised by the Hong Kong Society of Accountants and IFAC in November 2002: 'Knowledge-based Economy and the Accountant'.

The importance of accountancy education for the profession and for society is nicely illustrated in the introduction to the IFAC International Education Guideline IEG 9[2]. We quote from the text.

'(1) Historically, accountancy has been looked upon as a profession that plays an important role in all societies. As the world moves toward market economies, and with investments and operations crossing borders to a greater extent, the professional accountant must have a broad-based global perspective to understand the context in which business and other organisations operate.
(2) Rapid change is the predominant characteristic of the environment in which professional accountants work. Businesses and other organisations are engaging in more complex arrangements and transactions. Information technology is advancing at a rapid pace. Trade and commerce have become more international. Privatisation has become an increasingly important goal in many countries. Many societies have become more litigious. Concern for the environment has grown. Because of these trends, the need for accountability and the resulting demand on the profession is high in all cultures and continues to increase.'

Over the years these statements have lost nothing of their value. On the contrary as recent developments in the USA show, where the accountancy profession is challenged for its role in procuring clear, transparent and trustworthy financial statements. The unquestioned importance of the accountancy profession may turn into a threat to its existence when in some cases it fails to deliver the financial information society holds it responsible for. It is clear the profession is working hard to meet these challenges. It is also clear that, again according to IFAC IEG 9. To meet the challenges brought about by change, the competence of individuals becoming professional accountants must be enhanced. Since the means by which individuals obtain competence is through education and experience, the profession must aspire to increasingly higher standards in both of these areas.'

All this is easier said than done. There are limits to what intelligent and hard working young people can learn in their educational period. There are also limits to what professional bodies, accountancy firms and institutes of higher education can contribute to accountancy education, training and assessment. It is our belief that only if cross-border partnerships can be developed between providers of education and training and if choices are made what to expect of an accountant at the beginning of his or her career real progress becomes possible. Important steps have already been set on that road by major institutes of the profession.

This Global Accountancy Education research project has been started in the hope and the expectation that research into accountancy education can contribute to comparability, cooperation and development.

130   Scope and Key Issues of the Project

Recognising the importance of general education, professional education, practical training and qualification a general and conceptual model was developed that can be used to present a comparison between accountancy education systems in various parts of the world and to judge the factors influencing the development of those systems. The main components of IFAC IEG 9 – Pre Qualification Education, Assessment of Professional Competence and Experience Requirements of

---

[2] IFAC Education Committee, International Education Guideline 9, *Prequalification Education, Assessment of Professional Competence and Experience Requirements of Professional Accountants*, Revised October 1996

Professional Accountants – are included as benchmarks. The respective roles of standard setting bodies, professional organisations and educational institutes have been analysed for their influence on accountancy education. In a general way the output of professional education and training is compared with the demands of the accountancy profession for qualified personnel.

A distinction is made between developed market economy countries, countries in transition from a planned economy to a market economy and emerging countries with developing economies. Major legal systems in the world as well as cultural background are considered for their influence on accounting and auditing and on accountancy education. The contribution and meaning of higher education, professional studies, practical experience and qualification for accountancy education are included in the model as possible distinguishing factors for classification purposes. The final selection of countries was based on a preliminary analysis of the differences in the main characteristics that can be expected to influence accountancy education.

Consideration of accountancy education was in general limited to the expertise needed by accountants and auditors in public practice as one of the important areas for the accountancy profession and the domain of international standards. Underlying general and professional qualifications were only included in view of their position in the system of accountancy education. Subjects that merit specific attention are the possible influence of international accounting and auditing standards on accountancy education, mutual recognition and reciprocity as a result of WTO and GATS, the demand for assurance services and the impact of information technology.

140   Project Plan and Resources

The research project was conducted at the European Institute for Advanced Studies in Management (EIASM) in Brussels with input from a network of international contacts. Experts from academe and the accountancy profession that were consulted during the preliminary preparation have given their full and voluntary support to the research project. On conclusion of the initial set-up of the project a liaison was established with the IFAC Education Committee and with the academic community as represented by the IAAER. A steering committee has been formed to overview both academic rigor and professional relevance.

Expert support was sought in the countries included in the research project and from relevant international organisations. International experts in accountancy education and related fields have been consulted on the project approach and eventual evaluation. Advice, support and sponsorship from professional accountancy bodies and major accountancy firms helped to ensure the relevance of the project and its execution.

The research project started in September 1999 with finalisation in 2002. Intermediate results became available after each separate part of the project. Education contacts worldwide were approached in the first half of April 2001. The data gathering in the selected countries was followed by analysis and publication of country results in December 2001 and March 2002. The final results were presented at the 9th World Congress of the IAAER in 2002 in Hong Kong preceding the 16th IFAC World Congress of Accountants. Intermediate and final reports have been made available to the participants in the research project.

150   Justification

General coverage of issues concerning accountancy education and training in an integrated way was given precedence over more focused research in restricted areas. The idea behind this choice is that at this moment in time there is a great need of comparability between countries and regions and between systems of accountancy qualification, education and training. In order to contribute to comparability a number of steps had to be taken.

First an analysis was made of the requirements given in existing guidelines and directives on accountancy education and of the demands the profession and society put on the plate of accountancy education. This in itself is not new. What may be new is the integration of the various elements.

Second a theoretical model for accountancy education was formulated. Two choices that normally are not made were deemed necessary. (1) The model starts at the qualification level, as this is the only road to comparability. The consequence was that all the information had to be rearranged from the usual way, which is bottom-up starting with secondary or higher education. (2) Normally the programmes are described, but not the system. In the belief that programme development depends on available expertise and room for renewal information about responsibilities and providers was included in the model.

Selected respondents were asked to share their expertise by filling in an extended questionnaire. The information they supplied was used to evaluate the model and to describe local and regional systems of accountancy education. Although the information was checked with all possible thoroughness mistakes may still have taken place. It is also possible that systems have changed between the date of publication and the collection of the information around a year ago.

The research project has resulted in a classification of accountancy education systems and in comparable country information. The research project has been conducted under conditions of academic rigor and professional relevance. A steering group, composed of academic and professional experts, was appointed to supervise the project. In the last chapter of this publication recommendations are given. They are the sole responsibility of the author and do not follow automatically out of the research results.

160   Research Progress and Results

According to the original objectives the research project was expected to result in the classification of accountancy education systems and to contribute to the understanding and further development of accountancy education. In general this target has been reached. The detailed results are presented in the following chapters. As a result of the project recommendations are given on the promotion of the international development of accountancy education, including the furtherance of mutual recognition and harmonisation.

Preliminary activities covered general activities and a study of literature on the areas distinguished in the research project, preparation of the research objectives and a first classification model, consultation with international experts and organisations, development of selection criteria for country studies and regions and the development of an organisational structure for the project. The original fact-finding in the Netherlands, the United Kingdom, the USA and France has been finished based on the preliminary model for accountancy education that was developed for that purpose.

As a result of the review of the original questions on scope and comparability of the answers major changes and additions were effected in the questionnaire which now covers country characteristics; background information about the profession; accountancy qualification, education and training; comparison with international guidelines and future developments. Subsequently the country information is the basis for the scientific analysis of systems for accountancy education and training around the world in relation to the country characteristics that are being distinguished as possible explaining factors and in view of international developments effecting the accountancy profession.

At the conclusion of the project considerably more countries (28) and professional bodies (34) were included in the research analysis than originally foreseen. In combination with the larger scope of the questionnaire the resulting analysis gives a more complete global coverage. At the same time less emphasis could be placed on developments in time and the explanation of global changes.

The *results of the study* include an overview of developments in the accountancy profession influencing accountancy education, an analysis of general trends and objectives in accountancy education and a conceptual model to describe systems of accountancy education. Based on a comparative analysis of accountancy education in selected countries and regions conclusions are formulated about the applicability of the model in different surroundings and about impact and applicability of international guidelines on accountancy education under different regional or local circumstances.

CHAPTER 2   DEVELOPMENT OF ACCOUNTANCY EDUCATION

The discussion of the development of accountancy education in this chapter is based on an analysis of the relevant elements of accountancy education, the possible function of international education guidelines and directives as benchmarks and the impact of external influences on accountancy education.

200	Subject Area
210	Elements of Accountancy Education
220	International Guidelines
230	Developments in Accountancy Education

A review for benchmarking purposes was undertaken of IFAC Education Guidelines, the relevant Directives of the European Union (EU) and the Guideline for a Global Accounting Curriculum by the United Nations Conference on Trade and Development (UNCTAD). International Accounting Standards (IAS) by the IASB and International Standards in Auditing (ISA) by IFAC directly influence accountancy education programmes. Their necessary coverage is included in the IFAC education guidelines. IFAC guidance on the recognition of professional accountancy qualifications follows the requirements of the General Agreement on Trade in Services on the mutual recognition of the qualifications of professional accountants. This issue is also covered by the European Union.

For the analysis of developments in accountancy education a distinction is made between the drivers of change effecting the business community, the influences on accountancy education and the expected changes in international guidelines and directives, which in itself are a result of change perceived by the regulators.

200   Subject Area

When discussing accountancy education the diversity of the accountancy profession must be considered. The WTO[3] in 1998 mentioned specific points that have a direct influence on the professional education and training of accountants and auditors: 'Accountancy is an important element in the production of both physical goods and other services. Perhaps even more important is accountancy's essential role in respect to the implementation and enforcement of prudential requirements and other financial regulatory measures. Another consideration is that the range of activities undertaken by accountancy firms is wide and expanding. Perhaps the most significant issue in respect to international trade in accountancy services is the widespread nature of local qualification and licensing requirements, both in regard to individual practitioners and as conditions for the ownership and management of firms. While accounting and auditing services constitute the core activities of accountancy firms, a wide range of additional services may also be offered, most notably merger audits, insolvency services, tax advice, investment services and management consulting'. It must be noted that the WTO remarks were made in 1998.

Rapid changes have occurred in the accountancy profession since the start of the research project in 1999. The IASB is working on global accounting standards. There is an increasing demand on the expertise of accountants and auditors. All of this directly effects their qualification, education and training. IFAC, international organisations, as well as the major firms work together in the setting of international education standards. Programme development has been promoted through cooperation between professional bodies and institutes of higher education. Clear results are necessary especially as the accountancy profession faces new challenges following recent major business and accounting problems in the USA. Possible consequences for accountancy education are discussed at the end of this chapter.

---

[3] WTO, Accountancy Services, Note by the Secretariat (1998).

210   **Elements of Accountancy Education**

Recognising the importance of general education, professional education, practical training and qualification a general and conceptual model was developed that can be used to present a comparison between accountancy education systems in various parts of the world and to judge the factors influencing the developments of those systems. The main components of IFAC IEG 9 – Pre Qualification Education, Assessment of Professional Competence and Experience Requirements of Professional Accountants – are included as benchmarks. The respective roles of standard setting bodies, professional organisations and educational institutes have been analysed for their influence on accountancy education. In a general way the output of professional education and training is compared with the demands of the accountancy profession for qualified personnel.

Consideration of accountancy education was in general limited to the expertise needed by accountants and auditors in public practice as one of the important areas for the accountancy profession and the domain of international standards.

A detailed description of the model with a justification of the elements included can be found in Chapter 3 of this publication. The analysis of developments is focused on the major components of accountancy education.

220   **International Guidelines**

International Guidelines and Directives can be used as benchmarks for the comparative analysis of national systems of accountancy education. As part of this research study a review was undertaken of existing International Guidelines and Directives on accountancy education. This review focused on the elements of the conceptual framework, namely content, structure and recognition of accountancy education. International benchmarks on accountancy education and training considered for this purpose include the IFAC Education Guidelines, the relevant Directives of the European Union (EU) and the Guideline for a Global Accounting Curriculum by the United Nations Conference on Trade and Development (UNCTAD). International Accounting Standards (IAS) by the IASB and International Standards in Auditing (ISA) by IFAC directly influence accountancy education programmes. Their necessary coverage is included in the IFAC IEG's.

Research Question 2.1

Analyse International Guidelines and Directives that are relevant for accountancy qualification, education and training in a format that makes it possible to use the results as benchmarks for the comparative analysis of national systems of accountancy education.

IFAC has developed guidance on the recognition of professional accountancy qualifications in its Statement of Policy (1995). This statement follows the requirements of the General Agreement on Trade in Services (GATS). The IFAC International Education Guideline IEG 9 addresses pre-qualification education, assessment of professional competence and experience requirements of professional accountants (1996) with additional guidance on ICT in IEG 11 on Information Technology in the Accounting Curriculum (1995). The UNCTAD Guideline on National Requirements for the Qualification of Professional Accountants (1998) is intended to provide a benchmark for programme comparison. Common standards for the education, training and qualification of statutory auditors are defined in the Eighth Directive of the European Union (1984). Consideration is also given to the EU Directive for the recognition of higher education diplomas awarded on completion of professional education of at least three years' duration (1988).

The development of international guidelines on accountancy education by the IFAC Education Committee is well under way. International and regional bodies pay increasing attention to issues like harmonisation and recognition. Moreover in August 2001 IFAC decided to move from Education Guidelines to a mandatory system of International Education Standards.

An overview of the analysis of international guidelines is added to this report in Annex 1. Below the results are shown in the summarised form of a comparative programme content matrix. This representation and part of its content were derived from an article by Charles Calhoun and Michael Walsh[4]. The GATS requirements are discussed in Chapter 7 under 'recognition of qualifications' in paragraph 740.

	IFAC IEG 9	UNCTAD	EU 8th Directive
	IFAC defines as the goal of accountancy education and experience to produce competent professional accountants with the necessary knowledge, skills and professional values and with an attitude of learning to learn.	UNCTAD follows IEG 9	The EU 8th Directive sets common standards for the education, training and qualification of statutory auditors; these are mandatory inside the European Union.
General knowledge	Arts, sciences, humanities for the development of general knowledge, intellectual skills and communication skills Two years of four year degree (or equivalent)	Not specified (but adopts IEG 9); course of appropriate studies from an accredited higher education institution prior to becoming certified	University entrance level qualification, completion of a course of theoretical instruction, a practical training phase and passing an examination of professional competence of university final examination level
Organisational & business knowledge	Economics Quantitative methods and statistics for business Organisational behaviour Operations management Marketing International business	Economics Statistics Management functions and practices, organisational behaviour Operations management and strategy Marketing Principles of international business, general business policy and basic organisational structures	General and financial economics Mathematics and statistics Business, basic principles of the financial management of undertakings.
IT knowledge	IT concepts for business systems; internal control in computer-based systems; management of IT adoption, implementation and use; development standards and practices for business systems	In addition to IFAC IEG 9: Managing the security of information; artificial intelligence, expert systems, fuzzy logic; electronic commerce	Information and computer systems

---

[4] Charles Calhoun and Michael Walsh, Comparative Accounting Curricula, Accounting & Business, September 2000.

	Evaluation of computer-based business systems User role, manager role, designer role, evaluator role IFAC IEG 11 gives details about ICT requirements		
Accounting & accounting related knowledge	Financial accounting and reporting, management accounting Taxation Business and commercial law Auditing Finance and financial management Professional ethics	Basic and advanced financial accounting and reporting, basic and advanced management accounting Taxation Business and commercial law Auditing, fundamentals and advanced Business finance and financial management Professional ethics included in other modules	General accounting, consolidated accounts, cost and management accounting, standards relating to the preparation of annual and consolidated accounts and to methods of valuing balance sheet items and of computing profits and losses Tax law Company law, the law of insolvency and similar procedures, civil and commercial law, social security law and law of employment Legal and professional standards relating to the statutory auditing of accounting documents and to those carrying out such audits Auditing, analysis and critical assessment of annual accounts, internal audit
Practical experience	Prior to recognition a minimum of two years (IFAC 1995), respectively three years (IEG 9) approved and properly supervised practical experience primarily in the function concerned and in a suitable professional environment.	Minimum of three years of relevant experience	Three years' practical training in the auditing of annual accounts, consolidated accounts or similar financial statements prior to taking the final qualification examination under persons providing adequate guarantees regarding training
Qualification	Final examination of professional competence assessing theoretical knowledge and the ability to apply that knowledge competently in a practical situation.	UNCTAD follows IEG 9	Examination of professional competence of university final examination level that guarantees theoretical knowledge relevant to statutory audit and the ability to apply that knowledge in practice

Table 220.1 Comparative Programme Content Matrix

For reasons of comparability a top-down approach has been chosen for the model of accountancy education that is discussed in the next chapters. The analysis of international guidelines and directives shows that the main elements of any system for the qualification of accountants and auditors should be a final examination of professional competence, supervised practical experience before certification and a programme of professional and general education.

230   Developments in Accountancy Education

The majority of the professional bodies that were consulted on their system of accountancy education and training foresaw major developments in the near future in regulation of the profession, qualification requirements, professional education and practical experience. Out of a total of 34 professional bodies 23 mentioned regulation of the profession, 24 qualification requirements, 28 professional education and 22 practical experience as areas of change. Two out of three professional bodies expected major changes in three or four of the areas that were indicated. A more detailed overview is included in Chapter 7. The answers were given in the year 2000 after the Asia crisis, but for the great majority of the respondents before the Enron case.

This short overview is a clear indication that accountancy education and training is confronted with extensive change in all areas. There is an abundance of general evidence, that supports this observation and which illustrates the ever-increasing speed of change. For the analysis of accountancy education to be relevant for even the near future the factors that make change necessary must be considered.

Research Question 2.2

Analyse the factors that make change of accountancy education necessary and that influence the requirements regarding the professional qualification, education and training of accountants and auditors.

For the analysis in this paragraph a distinction is made between the drivers of change effecting the business community, the influences on accountancy education and the expected changes in international guidelines and directives, which in itself are a result of change perceived by the regulators.

Drivers of change

Developments in the accountancy profession that merit specific attention when considering the development of accountancy education are the influence of international accounting and auditing standards on accountancy education, international recognition and reciprocity as a result of WTO and GATS, the demand for assurance services and other changes in the work environment, the impact of information technology.

In its 1998 study Vision 2020[5] the Institute of Chartered Accountants in Australia (ICA Australia) addressed a number of questions on the future of the accountancy profession that have worldwide relevance. Given that 'a number of overseas organisations had recently conducted extensive research projects into the future awaiting business and the accountancy profession, the Vision 2020 Taskforce determined not to conduct its own free-standing research. Instead, it used the documents published by those organisations as the starting point for the Australian review'. This approach contributes to the overall importance of the report. The main conclusions with, in our view, a major impact on the future of accountancy education are summarised below. They concern major changes that will impact on business, government and the community and the competencies – skills, knowledge, expertise and qualities – that will be required in the future.

---

[5] Institute of Chartered Accountants of Australia, Vision 2020 (1998).

The following seven major forces were identified that will drive significant change in the business environment in the next twenty years.

- Unrelenting competitive pressure
- The impact of information and communications technology
- The globalisation of business
- Changing business and organisation structures
- The focus on value
- Demand for new knowledge and skills
- Changing attitudes to work/family issues and changing work environment

ICA Australia considers the first two to be the 'primary drivers of change'. Specific effects of unrelenting competitive pressure include constant change, de-regulation and globalisation, a focus on the core business combined with out-sourcing, shorter time frames. The impact of IT and communications include greater access to telecommunications technology, greater systems reliability, greater access to information, real time flow of information, virtual organisations and new work practices.

The globalisation of business as the first of the three business imperatives shows according to ICA Australia global capital markets, global financial services, electronic commerce, elimination of trade barriers, the likely emergence of a universal currency and language and an increasing need of harmonized standards.

Considering the future of accountancy education in our view specific attention should be given to the demand for new knowledge, skills and professional values and to the changing attitudes to work/family issues and the changing work environment as individual issues.

Information management skills will become increasingly important, as according to Vision 2020 more easily interpreted information will be demanded with business seeking professionals who can source, authenticate, synthesise and interpret data obtained from multiple sources. Information will become a commodity; knowledge will be valued. Business success will depend on employing technology to convert information into knowledge value in a cost-effective manner. In addition to formal qualifications, workers of the future will undertake on-going training throughout their working lives. New skills and knowledge will be sought to assist business in managing change, appraising new markets and opportunities, implementing new systems, managing new structures and complying with an increasing number of new regulatory requirements.

Consideration of these factors is in our view of extreme importance for accountancy qualification, education and training to give adequate answers to future requirements and for the continuing appeal the accountancy profession must have to attract intelligent and dedicated young people. As stated at the centenary of Royal NIVRA (NIVRA) in the Netherlands: Accountancy is a business of 'People for People'. The challenges for accountancy education were illustrated at the conference on Global Business Development that was jointly organised in September 2000 by EIASM and the Institute of Chartered Accountants in England and Wales (ICAEW) at the start of the Global Accountancy Education research project. Speakers were invited from professional bodies, major accountancy firms, business schools and universities, commercial organisations and international institutes. Some of the main issues they covered are summarised below.

- A profession's only real capital is the human capital of its members, its principal asset the profession's reputation and, in particular, the value of its qualification. The accountancy profession needs to continue to attract intelligent and innovative thinkers, the business leaders of tomorrow. Professional bodies should be creators of learning and intelligence networks and must add value at every stage of an individual's career.

- Largely nationally based education systems must also fully reflect the global dimension. This should extent to understanding different cultures, legal and organisational systems and their impact on doing business in different jurisdictions. Education must be harmonized internationally and be relevant and customised for individuals and organisations.
- The modern professional needs to be able to deliver solutions in a complex and rapidly changing environment which requires general management skills and a broad understanding of business as well as specialist knowledge, emotional intelligence and intellectual ability. Functional expertise has to combine with transferable skills.
- Professionals must be equipped and motivated from the outset of their careers to continuously acquire new knowledge and skills and to see working and formal periods of study as part of integrated and ongoing opportunities for learning.
- Future accountants and auditors need demonstrable training in ethics and objectivity, a real appreciation of global markets and finance, understanding measures of business performance and appreciating the business process with both IT and people focus. Accountancy skills, managerial qualifications, soft skills and leadership are equally important. Anyone in a client serving business needs to understand his or her clients' business.

Influences on accountancy education

Developments in accountancy education that were considered in this study included the impact of international guidelines on accountancy education, the development of a competence based approach to accountancy education with work experience related to theoretical study, the possibilities of benchmarking as a tool towards strategic innovation and the interrelation between higher education and professional training.

The history of accounting education change gives important indicators for future approaches. For this purpose the following publications with a major impact on the development of accountancy education have been considered. They are given below in chronological order.

- American Accounting Association (AAA), Committee on the Future Structure, Content and Scope of Accounting Education (The Bedford Committee), (1986), *Future accounting education: Preparing for the expanding profession,* Issues in Accounting Education (Spring) (168-195).
- *Perspectives on Education: Capabilities for Success in the Accounting Profession* (The White Paper), (1989), Arthur Andersen & Co., Arthur Young, Coopers & Lybrand, Deloitte Haskins & Sells, Ernst & Whinney, Peat Marwick Main & Co., Price Waterhouse, and Touche Ross, New York, NY.
- Accounting Education Change Commission (AECC), (1990), *Objectives of education for accountants: Position statement number one.* Issues in Accounting Education (Fall) (307-312).
- Albrecht, W.S., & Sack, R.J., (2000), *Accounting Education: Charting the Course through a Perilous Future,* Accounting Education Series, Volume 16.

In considering these reports it must be recognized that although they are largely based on the situation in the USA their reflections, conclusions and recommendations have global relevance for the future of accountancy education. A selection of general remarks is quoted below.

Bedford Report: 'The accounting profession is expanding, entering a new era with new functions within organisations and within society and with new expectations of those who enter it. The current state of most professional accounting education programmes is inadequate to meet the needs of this expanded profession. The future scope, content and structure of accounting education, in all its phases, must undergo reassessment and redirection to meet the needs of the expended accounting profession and the future accounting professional'. The committee identified the following issues for accounting education as a result of trends in the accounting profession: 'expansion of services and products, changes in the nature and extent of competition, increased specialisation, proliferation of standards, litigation and legal liability, widespread computerisation and developments in continuing education'. As a result 'successful achievement of an effective education programme that will meet the demands of the 21st century will require (1) a revised, expanded curriculum, (2) a more effective education process and (3), a better articulated structure for the institutional units through which the programmes will be offered.

Big Eight White Paper: 'The current environment makes real curricular change essential and necessitates response from a dynamic partnership between practitioners and academics. First, the profession must specify capabilities necessary for practice and communicate these to the academic community. With this input faculty can develop a relevant and stimulating curriculum with state-of-the-art teaching methods. External factors, such as professional examinations and conditions of licensure, affect the educational process. In the future organisations responsible for such activities should recognize, in their policies and procedures, the broad skills and knowledge needed by the profession. Accreditation standards must be responsive to the desired outcomes of educational preparation. The accreditation process must also be sensitive to, and supportive of, the innovation and experimentation that are inherent in curricular change.'

AECC: Accounting education should prepare students to become professional accountants, not to be professional accountants at the time of entry to the profession. To attain and maintain the status of a professional accountant requires continual learning. Therefore, pre-entry education should lay the base on which life-long learning can be built. The base on which life-long learning is built has three components: skills, knowledge and professional orientation. Professional accounting education has three components following general education: (1) general business education, (2) general accounting education and (3) specialised accounting education.'

Quite a lot of both the general and more detailed recommendations have been included in the IFAC International Education Guideline IEG 9 that was revised in 1996. However, this does not automatically mean that actual implementation has taken place. In fact Albrecht and Sack are in their publication[6] negative about the results generally achieved in the USA and recommend immediate action. As basis for their recommendations they discuss 'changes in the business environment and how those changes are affecting accounting education, the problem of declining enrolments in accounting programmes, why practising accountants would not choose to major in accounting if pursuing their educational programmes again and why critics believe the accounting education models used by most schools provide less value than they used to.' Recognising differences between individual schools Albrecht and Sack conclude that six major categories of perceived problems should be addressed: (1) course content and curriculum, (2) pedagogy, (3) skill development, (4) use of technology, (5) faculty development and reward structures, (6) strategic planning and direction of accounting programmes and departments.'

The academic contribution to the development of accounting education has been addressed in the 'IAAER Report on Strategy of Implementation of IFAC International Education Guideline IEG 9: the Role of Academics.' In the report three principal issues associated with the implementation of the guideline are addressed: '(1) How to instil the characteristics of lifelong learning in future professional accountants through accounting education? (2) How to design and implement a programme of accounting education that achieves the objectives of the guideline? (3) How to develop awareness and encourage adaptation of the recommendations of the guideline by communicating and disseminating information through a series of projects within IFAC's constraints and policies?'

Issue 3 points back to the important role of IFAC both as a standard setter and a facilitator for the development of accountancy education of which accounting education is part.

---

[6] See page 2 and 3.

Expected changes in international developments

In the near future developments in the content of international guidelines and directives with an impact on accountancy qualification, education and training can be expected.

The influence of IAS and of ISA is rapidly increasing. The IASB in its new structure started – or rather continued - work in 2001. Some quotes from the Annual Report 2001 of the International Accounting Standards Committee Foundation (IASCF) are well worth remembering when discussing the future of accountancy education. 'For some years the forces of globalisation have made the need for effective, consistent and broadly accepted accounting standards increasingly apparent. Today, that conceptual need has been reinforced by evident practical problems of interpretation, enforcement and understanding of existing national standards. Hardly a day passes without problems of financial reporting appearing prominently in the international press. Clearly, the accounting profession and standard setters face difficult challenges. At the same time, the sense of confusion and uncertainty provides an opportunity for real reform and progress. A single set of high quality accounting standards that can command respect around the world will discipline auditing approaches, simplify listing in national markets and encourage effective enforcement by national and international authorities.'

The IASCF 'mentions support for IASB from two important sources. In the United States the Securities and Exchange Commission (SEC) voiced support for the proposed IASB as a global standard setter and this view was echoed by the Financial Accounting Standards Board (FASB). The European Commission proposed in June 2000 that the consolidated accounts of all listed companies in the European Union should be required to be prepared in accordance with the IASB's standards by 2005.'

Recognising the importance of the implementation of standards in accountancy education the IASCF launched in April 2002 an assessment and certification programme in International Accounting Standards (IASs) and International Financial Reporting Standards (IFRSs).

For IFAC the two major developments are the move from International Education Guidelines to mandatory International Education Standards and the competence approach of accountancy education. International Education Standards for Professional Accountants (IES) have been derived from the existing International Education Guidelines. Exposure Drafts of the proposed Standards were published on the IFAC website at the beginning of July 2002, with an exposure period of six months. The Standards are due to be implemented by the beginning of 2005. They cover the following subjects.

- Entry requirements
- Professional education
- Professional skills and general education
- Professional values and ethics
- Experience requirements
- Assessment of professional competence
- Continuing professional education and development.

The Compliance Committee of IFAC will need to monitor compliance with these Standards by the member bodies of IFAC. The Standards have adopted a "competence-based" approach following the publication of IFAC's revised Discussion Paper on Competence which defined competence as 'being able to perform a work role to a defined standard, with reference to real working environments'.

In the EU Committee on Auditing the overall objective of the EU strategy on statutory audit is the continuous improvement and harmonisation of audit quality throughout the European Union. Continuously improving and delivering audit quality is judged to be crucial for the maintenance of trust in the audit function and hence trust in the capital market. At present there exist at the European level provisions in the EU 8th Directive (1984) with regard to a detailed curriculum for the admission to the profession. There is no requirement for permanent education. In the EU Committee on Auditing questions have been raised regarding possible actions.

Education

- Is a modernisation of the curriculum laid down in the EU 8th Directive needed?
- Which subjects in education should be additionally addressed?
- Would it be better to introduce principles in the EU 8th Directive and build a flexible mechanism to permanently update and further harmonize the requirements?
- Should there be a reference to IFAC initiatives?
- How should the issue of mutual recognition be addressed?

Permanent education

- Should permanent education be addressed in the EU 8th Directive?
- What should be required as permanent education?
- If permanent education is required, should the specific requirements be laid down in detail or should there only be a principle in the EU 8th Directive with a flexible mechanism to permanently update and harmonize permanent education requirements?

Major initiatives are undertaken by both professional bodies and accountancy firms.

The developments at the IASB, IFAC and the EU as described in this paragraph are just some examples of the time that is invested in setting clearer standards, both for accounting and auditing and for the education and training of accountants and auditors. When the remarks on future developments made by the respondents to the questionnaire are reviewed in Chapter 7, this will show that there are multiple initiatives on a country level to enhance future accountancy qualification, education and training. Publications by the IAAER and UNCTAD can be of valuable assistance in the design and implementation of new programmes. An increasing number of professional bodies addresses the issue of mutual recognition. Mandatory Continuing Professional Education (CPE) for professional accountants and auditors is becoming the global standard as more and more professional bodies include it in their regulation.

Programme reform in an international or regional setting is undertaken in different places all over the world. The American Institute of Certified Public Accountants has taken the lead in focusing on assurance services as the future core of accountancy education with the objective of creating a global business credential. In the European Union seven professional bodies started a joint 'common content' project to explore how to bring their professional qualifications together within, approximately, five years. The participating institutes are the Institute of Chartered Accountants in England and Wales, the Ordre des Experts-Comptables in France, the Institut der Wirtschaftsprüfer in Germany, the Institute of Chartered Accountants in Ireland, the Consiglio Nazionale de Dottori Commercialisti in Italy, the Koninklijk Nederlands Instituut van Registeraccountants in the Netherlands and the Institute of Chartered Accountants of Scotland. Both initiatives will be open to other participants.

The major accountancy firms have shown their commitment to the furtherance of the qualification, education and training of accountants and auditors in IFAD and in the work now being done in the Forum of Firms and their Trans-national Audit Committee. Moreover all the major accountancy firms use international compatible audit methodologies and train their staff in the application of IASs and ISAs. Where necessary education and training is offered in addition to local qualifications. These programmes can also be made available to professional bodies and educational institutes.

Developments that at the moment are concentrated in the USA have shown the vulnerability of capital markets and as a result of the accountancy profession. What happened at ENRON set in motion a chain of events few would have thought possible. This is not the place to discuss the consequences for the accountancy profession. Attention however must be given to the possible impact on the qualification, education and training of professional accountants and auditors. One thing at least is very clear. The qualification requirements for accountants and auditors and the programmes for their education and training must make visible use of a competence based approach with a high priority for the integration of professional ethics.

CHAPTER 3   CLASSIFICATION OF ACCOUNTANCY EDUCATION

In this chapter a conceptual model for the classification of accountancy education is developed.

300	Classification Model and Methods
310	Distinguishing Factors
320	Country Selection
330	Conceptual Framework
340	Global Accountancy Education Questionnaire

Classification is chosen as an efficient way of describing and comparing the different systems for accountancy education. The selection of countries is based on an analysis of the differences in the main characteristics that can be expected to influence accountancy education.

A conceptual framework for accountancy education is used as the basis for a questionnaire that has been sent to respondents. In the Global Accountancy Education Questionnaire the following subjects are covered: respondent, country profile, profession, professional qualification, programme requirements and future developments.

300   Classification Model and Methods

The development of a conceptual model for the classification of accountancy education systems in various parts of the world is a key element of the research project. It will be shown that it is possible to develop one model that can be used to describe and compare accountancy education worldwide. Furthermore the model can be used to monitor and in part explain global changes in accountancy education as a result of international developments in the accountancy profession. Comparative country studies were undertaken to describe accountancy education in the countries involved and to test the model.

Research Question 3

Develop a conceptual model for the classification of accountancy education systems in various parts of the world that can be used for evaluation and comparison.

Ideas for the development of a model for the classification of accountancy education systems are based on earlier studies of Nobes and Parker[7] on the (changing) classification of financial reporting systems. The reasons they mentioned to illustrate the importance of classification of financial reporting systems in our views also apply to accountancy education, in particular as a result of the globalisation of the accountancy profession and the necessity to strengthen the comparability and to understand the development of accountancy education systems.

Classification can be chosen as an efficient way of describing and comparing different systems for accountancy education. Moreover classification can be used to help shape development, for instance by facilitating (a study of the logic of and the difficulties facing) harmonisation, by assisting in the training of accountants and auditors who operate internationally and by helping countries in transition and emerging countries in understanding the available types of accountancy education systems and choosing a direction for development that might be most appropriate. One important observation however has to be made. Traditional classification is permanent in time, which would make it difficult to cope with rapid developments in both the accountancy profession and in accountancy education.

---

[7] Christopher Nobes and Robert Parker; Comparative International Accounting, (1998).
Christopher Nobes, *Towards a General Model of the Reasons for International Differences in Financial Reporting*, ABACUS, Vol. 34, N° 2, (1998)

Major changes in legislation, regulation, world trade and in the accountancy profession during the last decade and results of globalisation to be expected in the next period make it essential to develop a flexible model with well defined parameters, which in themselves are constant in time, but allow systems of accountancy education to move from one state to another by changing the values of the parameters.

310 Distinguishing Factors

In developing a system for the classification of accountancy education it is important to isolate the features of a country's accountancy education system, which – in the words of Nobes[8] – 'may constitute long-run fundamental differences between countries'. As a starting point a selection of the possible distinguishing factors to be included was based on a study of the literature available. These factors, mentioned below, were tested on their relevance for accountancy education.

- The influence of differences in cultural background.
- The present economic position of the countries involved.
- The effect of the legal system on accountancy education.
- The contribution of higher education to the qualification of accountants.

The final selection of countries is based on a preliminary analysis of the differences in the main characteristics that can be expected to influence accountancy education. In this way a comparative study in a limited number of countries can lead to an effective way of comparing different systems.

Cultural Background

Important work on the cultural context of accounting has been done by Hofstede and others. Hofstede[9] distinguishes Power Distance and Uncertainty Avoidance as the most relevant dimensions for the functioning of organisations in a country. Power Distance[10] can be defined as 'the extent to which the less powerful members of institutions and organisations within a country expect and accept that power is distributed unequally'. Uncertainty Avoidance[11] can be defined as 'the extent to which the members of a culture feel threatened by uncertain or unknown situations'. The position of countries on the Power Distance and Uncertainty Avoidance scales gives a general indication of their differences in cultural background. Countries in this study were selected in such a way that the main groups of the classification given by Hofstede are covered. Existing literature on the influence of cultural background on accounting and auditing was studied as part of the project.

Economic Position

In view of its relevance for accountancy education the present economic position of the countries involved was considered with a preliminary distinction in three categories.

- Industrialised countries with a market economy as the overall system.
- Countries 'in transition' from a planned economy to a market economy.
- Developing countries with emerging economies.

As generally accepted definitions were not available the overall position of countries was compared with indicators[12] about country size (population, total labour force, female % of labour force) and economic position (Gross National Product, Gross National Product per capita, personal computers per

---

[8] Comparative International Accounting, page 59, (1998).
[9] G. Hofstede, Culture's Consequences, (2000).
[10] Culture's Consequences, page 98, (2000).
[11] Culture's Consequences, page 161, (2000).
[12] The World Development Indicators CD-ROM 2000, The International Bank for Reconstruction and Development/The World Bank.

1000 people). The results presented in chapter 5 show a marked correlation between the GNP per capita and the number of personal computers per 1000 people. This suggests a two-group system with (1) industrialised countries and (2) countries in transition and with emerging economies.

Legal Systems

Based on the work done by David and Brierley[13] the following major legal systems were considered at the start of the project for their possible relevance for the accountancy profession and as a result for accountancy education.

- Common Law as one group of systems.
- Codified Roman (or Civil) Law as another group of systems.
- Socialist Law as a system 'in transition'.
- Philosophical Religious as a factor of influence on market operations.

Consideration of recent literature[14] and discussions with accountancy education experts world-wide were instrumental in the decision to distinguish Common Law and Civil Law as the two major classes relevant for the accountancy profession. Civil law systems according to the publication by the University of Ottawa 'have drawn their inspiration largely from the Roman law heritage and, by giving precedence to written law, have opted for a systematic codification of their general law'. Common law systems are 'for the most part technically based on English common law concepts and legal organisational methods which assign a pre-eminent position to case-law, as opposed to legislation, as the ordinary means of expression of general law'. In the analysis former Socialist Law, Muslim Law and Customary Law are treated as sub-classes. Former Socialist Law, although not included in the classification used by the University of Ottawa, was added as a possible explanation of existing regulation in the accountancy sector. Muslim Law Systems 'are religious in nature and predominantly based on the Koran'. Customary Law Systems 'may be significant not only in matters of personal conduct but also in relation to the business environment'.

Higher Education

General education, professional education, practical training and qualification are the most important elements of systems for accountancy education. As a result divers influences on accountancy education have to be considered. This includes the contribution of higher education to the qualification of accountants and the respective roles of government, educational institutes and professional bodies in both offering education and in setting its standards. International and regional bodies develop international guidelines and directives as benchmarks.

Inside the systems approach a distinction was made between the contribution of higher education on one hand and of professional education and training on the other hand to the qualification of accountants as possible distinguishing factors for classification purposes. The major distinction for university education in regard to the contribution to professional accountancy education is general versus specific. The parallel distinction for professional education is integrated in university education versus post or outside university education. A more generally accepted system for the classification and comparison of higher education worldwide was not available.

---

[13] David, Brierley – Major Legal Systems in the World Today – 1985
[14] Alberto Chong and Luisa Zanforlin, Law Tradition and Institutional Quality: Some Empirical Evidence (2000)
Konrad Zweigert and Hein Kötz, Introduction to Comparative Law (1998)
World Legal Systems, University of Ottawa (web version 2002)

It is relevant to note that due to the Bologna Agreement the European Union decided to move towards a singular system of bachelors and masters degrees for the member states. This move will help comparability both inside and outside the EU. Standard reference sources used by the IFAC member bodies for the comparison of university and higher education qualifications are listed in the footnote[15].

320   Country Selection

The selection of countries for classification purposes started with the accounting system. GAAP 2000, A Survey of National Accounting Rules in 53 Countries[16] provides an overview of differences between national accounting rules and International Accounting Standards. Its general summary has been used in the country information. From the point of view described by Nobes and Parker[17] a distinction as shown below can be made between vital countries in view of economic and accounting significance and related countries.

Vital countries	Related countries
(Common Law)	
USA	Canada
UK	Ireland, Australia, New Zealand, Singapore, Hong Kong
(Codified Roman Law)	
Germany	(Sweden), Switzerland, Austria
France	Spain, Belgium, (Italy)
Netherlands	Denmark
Japan	South Korea

An important consideration when further developing the system to include countries 'in transition' and developing or emerging countries was the *hypothesis* that for countries which are strongly influenced by their background the best predictor of the accounting system might be found in their past position. This approach could also be valid for auditing and accountancy education. This concept of 'zones of influence' was first developed by the AAA[18].

The factors identified above were used as a starting point. Countries were grouped on the hypothesis that similarity of underlying characteristics can lead to comparable accountancy education systems. Countries chosen for actual research are selected in a manner to ensure coverage of all the relevant factors. This was done in a three-tier approach.

Initial development of the model

A preliminary model for accountancy education systems was developed based on the study of relevant literature to identify theoretical assumptions. Secondly this model was tested in a limited number of countries. Considering their influence on the development of the accountancy profession and of

---

[15] American Universities and Colleges, includes more than 1900 institutions of higher education in the USA
International Comparisons, National Academic Recognition Information Center (NARIC), UK, secondary and higher-level qualifications in 190 countries
International Handbook of Universities, Palgrave Macmillan, 6000 institutions in 174 countries with degrees and diploma's
The World of Learning, Europa Publications, higher education institutes worldwide, including universities and colleges
[16] GAAP 2000, A Survey of National Accounting Rules in 53 countries – Arthur Andersen, BDO, Deloitte Touche Thomatsu, Ernst & Young International, Grant Thornton, KPMG, PricewaterhouseCoopers – 2000.
[17] Comparative International Accounting, page 11, 13, (1998).
[18] American Accounting Association, Committee on International Accounting Operations and Education (1975-1976).

accountancy education and the different characteristics involved the following (vital) pilot countries were chosen.

- The Netherlands (commercially driven; business economics)
- UK, USA (commercially driven; business practice)
- France, Germany (government driven)

In view of underlying differences in the countries considered – for instance in legal systems and in higher education – it was expected that variations in the model would be necessary to achieve an adequate description of the accountancy education systems in place. This in itself would give a first indication of the applicability of the model and possible influence of international guidelines on accountancy education and as a result the practical possibilities and difficulties of harmonisation.

This part of the project resulted in a comparable analysis of accountancy education in the first group of countries and adaptation of the general model. Based on the results of the pilot and the positive results when using the preliminary model in a small scale OECD project in a number of South Eastern European countries it was decided to approach the selected countries worldwide simultaneously and not – as originally foreseen – in a step-by-step approach. Major changes that were made in the model before the questionnaire was distributed worldwide concerned background information about the professional bodies, international benchmarks and future developments.

Application of the model

The model was used in selected countries around the world to be able to reach conclusions about the applicability of the model with further variations to be expected and about applicability and influence of international guidelines. An overview of additional countries that were included in the selection is given below.

- European Union: Spain, Sweden
- North and Middle America: Canada, Mexico
- Central and Eastern Europe: Czech Republic, Hungary, Poland, Russian Federation
- Africa: Kenya, Senegal, South Africa
- Middle East: Lebanon, Turkey, Saudi Arabia
- Asia: Pakistan, India, Malaysia, China, Hong Kong
- Far East: Australia, New Zealand, Japan
- South America: Argentine, Brazil

Choosing from countries in the same region[19] or with the same background consideration has been given to existing contacts and expertise including (former) involvement in the IFAC Education Committee. With the exception of Senegal the characteristics of all countries mentioned above have been analysed. As the results of the global country studies in Chapter 5 show not all the professional bodies that were approached responded to the questionnaire. This had an effect on the regional coverage of the research project, as South America and China are not included.

---

[19] Major regional trade associations with countries in the research project denoted by *:
APEC (Asia Pacific Economic Cooperation): Australia*, Brunei, Canada*, Chile, China*, Hong Kong*, Indonesia, Japan*, Korea, Malaysia, Mexico*, New Zealand*, Papua New Guinea, Peru, Philippines, Russian Federation*, Singapore, Chinese Taipei, Thailand, United States*, Vietnam.
ASEAN: Brunei, Combonai, Indonesia, Malaysia*, Myanmar, Philippines, Singapore, Thailand, Vietnam.
European Union: Austria, Belgium, Denmark, Finland, France*, Germany*, Ireland, Italy, Luxemburg, Netherlands*, Portugal, Spain*, Sweden*, United Kingdom*.
NAFTA (North American Free Trade Organization): Canada*, Mexico*, United States*

International and regional membership of the professional bodies is included in the review. In this way a link is established with the following international and regional organisations of professional accountants.

IFAC	International Federation of Accountants
AFA	ASEAN Federation of Accountants
CAPA	Confederation of Asian and Pacific Accountants
ECSAFA	Eastern, Central and Southern African Federation of Accountants
EFA	Eurasian Federation of Accountants
EFAA	European Federation of Accountants and Auditors for SME's
FCM	Fédération des Experts-Comptables Méditerranéens
FEE	Fédération des Experts-Comptables Européens
FIDEF	Fédération Internationale des Experts-Comptables Francophones
ICAC	Institute of Chartered Accountants of the Caribbean
SAFA	South Asian Federation of Accountants

Finalisation of the model

After the initial development of the model and the subsequent testing the version of the model was designed that was used for worldwide data gathering. The overall characteristics are described in the next paragraphs. As expected a large variation in underlying characteristics was necessary to give an adequate description of accountancy education systems in various parts of the world. The results of the country studies are described in Chapter 5 and the resulting final model in Chapter 6 of this study.

330   Conceptual Framework

Classification of accountancy education systems must be based on comparable country information. To this end a conceptual framework was developed that is divided in three main components.

- The content of accountancy education.
- The structure of accountancy education.
- The recognition of accountancy education.

Benchmarks for the content of accountancy education can be found in the main components of the IFAC Guideline on Pre-Qualification Education, Assessment of Professional Competence and Experience Requirements of Professional Accountants (IEG 9, 1996) and in regional directives like the 8th Directive of the European Union (1984). General requirements are discussed by IFAC in its 1995 Statement of Policy on the Recognition of Professional Accountancy Qualifications.

The goal of accountancy education and experience as formulated by IFAC in IEG 9[20] is 'to produce competent professional accountants capable of making a positive contribution over their lifetimes to the profession and society in which they work. The maintenance of professional competence in the face of the increasing changes they encounter makes it imperative that accountants develop and maintain an attitude of learning to learn. The education and experience of professional accountants must provide a foundation of knowledge, skills and professional values that enables them to continue to learn and adapt to change throughout their professional lives.'

Knowledge prior to qualification can be divided in general and professional knowledge with a further distinction of the latter in organisational and business knowledge, information technology knowledge and accounting (related) knowledge. Competences and professional values have to be acquired through a combination of education and professional experience.

---

[20] IFAC IEG 9, paragraph 7

The structure of accountancy education is decisive for the ways accountancy education, including professional training is offered and assessed. In our view it includes legislation and standard setting, the respective roles of educational and professional institutes, available resources and know-how. Input, throughput and output of students in line with the demands of the labour market is a necessary condition for a strong accountancy profession that is able to meet the requirements of the business community.

The recognition of accountancy education can be approached both on a national and an international level. On a national level the recognition of professional accountants can be judged by their position on the labour market and by comparison with other professions. As the theme of this study is "globalisation" this issue is not included in the research project. Existing international recognition of university degrees and professional qualifications can be a measure for the effect of globalisation on accountancy education. As discussed before a general system for university recognition worldwide could not be found. As a result the analysis of existing international recognition had to be limited to accountancy qualifications.

Based on the importance of general education, professional education, practical training and qualification a conceptual framework was developed to present a comparison between accountancy education systems in various parts of the world and to judge the factors influencing the developments of those systems. International Education Guidelines and Directives were used as benchmarks.

In concordance with IFAC IEG 9 the following levels are distinguished as parts of the conceptual framework and the accountancy education model.

- Qualification requirements.
- Professional education requirements.
- Practical training requirements.
- General education requirements.
- Entry requirements.

In each level consideration is given to content, structure and recognition. A top-down approach – starting with qualification requirements – has been chosen, as the moment of qualification as an accountant or auditor represents the only fixed point in time for international comparison.

	Influence of the Accountancy Profession on Accountancy Education	
Country Characteristics	**Accountancy Education**	**International Developments**
Cultural background	Professional qualification objective	Standards
Legal system	Qualification standards, final examination of professional competence	Guidelines
Economic position	Professional education	Directives
Higher education	Practical experience	
	General education	

Table 330.1 Core Model of Accountancy Education

340   **Global Accountancy Education Questionnaire**

As part of the research project on the Impact of Globalisation on Accountancy Education a questionnaire was distributed to 38 selected respondents in the 28 countries that were included in the project. Answer sets were received from 34 respondents in 25 countries. Only partial or no information became available from Argentina, Brazil, China and Senegal. The consequences are discussed in Chapter 5.

The answers are used in the analysis and comparison of systems for accountancy qualification, education and training worldwide. In an overall meaning the term "Accountancy Education " is used to describe the whole set of subjects relevant for the qualification, education and training of professional accountants and auditors.

The questionnaire covers the subjects necessary to describe accountancy education. A distinction is made between professional qualification and licensing, professional education, practical training and general education. Information about the country and the profession is also considered. A separate questionnaire had to be answered for each professional body in combination with the professional title under consideration.

For comparative reasons respondents were asked to base their answers on the situation that existed on the first of January 2001. In questions were a period is considered this is normally the year 2000.

The questionnaire and technical support for the respondents were made available through the use of the Internet. In this way answers could be given directly and questions that are not relevant for the system under consideration did not have to be answered. The answers to the questionnaire are treated as confidential information to be used in the analysis and comparison mentioned above. The results were made available to the respondents for review before publication.

The questionnaire is divided in the following chapters.

Respondent: This short chapter identifies the respondent. The contribution of the respondents is acknowledged in the publication of the results.

Country Profile: General country information is collected from standard statistical sources and publications. Subjects covered are labour market, economic position, accounting and auditing, legal system and cultural background. General information on the comparison of systems of higher education was not available. In view of its relevance for accountancy education, the present economic position of the countries involved has been considered with a distinction being made between developed countries with market economies, countries 'in transition' from a planned economy to a market economy, and developing or emerging countries. GAAP 2000, A Survey of National Accounting Rules in 53 Countries provides an overview of differences between national accounting rules and International Accounting Standards. Its general summary is used in the country information. Major legal systems are considered for their relevance to the accountancy profession and for accountancy education. The cultural context of accounting has been included for classification purposes.

Profession: In this chapter of the questionnaire information about the accountancy profession is collected. This starts with general information about the professional body, followed by questions about the professional title and its regulation. Finally in the last paragraph attention is given to new entrants in the profession and their work and education background.

Subjects covered include regulation and recognition of the professional body, international membership, number and employment sector of members, growth of membership. Consideration is given to the professional title, mandatory membership, regulation of Continuing Professional Education (CPE) and to the number and employment sector of new members and their educational background.

The majority of the professional bodies focus on the national qualification in the country where they are registered. Organisations with the objective to train and qualify students in a variety of countries are the Association of Chartered Certified Accountants (ACCA), Certified General Accountants Canada (CGA-Canada) and CPA Australia.

Professional Qualification: In this chapter information is collected about the qualification of accountants and auditors and about the system of accountancy education and training. It is divided in the following paragraphs.

- Objective of professional qualification: qualification of competent accountants and/or auditors.
- Qualification standards: admission requirements, responsibility, international standards and recognition.
- Final examination of professional competence: objective and content, assessment methods, conditions and procedures, external review.
- Professional education: content, programme, duration and level; applications of Information Communication Technology (ICT); admission, exemptions and practical experience; providers, review and recognition.
- Practical experience: content and duration, admission and exemptions; providers, review and recognition.
- General education: admission requirements, entrance level and content.

If a paragraph is not relevant, for example because practical experience is not required, the questions on that subject are suppressed. This approach is used throughout the questionnaire.

Programme Requirements: In this chapter of the questionnaire the actual programme requirements for accountancy education as described in the preceding chapter are compared with international benchmarks as defined by IFAC, UNCTAD and regional organisations like the European Union. Respondents are asked to base their answers on the main entry routes that are used by the majority of the students. The review covers subjects, key skills, ICT applications and professional values.

Concluding Remarks: In this chapter future developments are described in the main areas of the questionnaire. This gives respondents an opportunity to highlight important developments that are foreseen for the near future. The following areas are distinguished.

- Regulation of the profession
- Professional qualification requirements
- Professional education
- Practical experience

The results of this chapter can help identify areas for future research and mutual interesting co-operation on accountancy education and training.

The structure of the questionnaire with a summary description of the questions is given in Annex 2.

CHAPTER 4   RESEARCH QUESTIONS AND METHOD

In this chapter the research objectives, questions and method are discussed.

400	Research Objectives and Questions
410	Research Method
420	Theoretical Assumptions
430	Classification Model
440	Research Data
450	Research Plan and Timetable
460	Data Collection, Analysis and Interpretation
470	Theoretical Conclusions

The Central Research Question is to develop, test and evaluate a conceptual model for accountancy education in various parts of the world and to use the results to contribute to the understanding of the present position and the possible future development of systems of professional qualification, education and training of accountants and auditors. For operational use partial research questions are distinguished.

The research method is inductive, from observation to generalisation, rather than deductive. Most of the data were gathered through the consultation of experts. A study of literature provided general and country information. International guidelines and directives on accountancy education were used as benchmarks. For comparative reasons a top-down structure was chosen for the classification model. Classification criteria as described in standard literature are used in the design of the model for accountancy education.

400   Research Objectives and Questions

The research project has as its general objective to contribute to the understanding of the present position and the possible future development of accountancy education in various parts of the world. The Central Research Question is introduced in Chapter 1. It sets as general objective of the research project to "develop, test and evaluate a conceptual model for accountancy education in various parts of the world and to use the results to contribute to the understanding of the present position and the possible future development of systems of professional qualification, education and training of accountants and auditors".

To reach this objective various stages must be distinguished, which in their turn can be formalised in partial research questions. These are discussed below. Chapter 2 identifies what is expected of accountancy education and what are the changes effecting accountancy education by answering two research questions.

Research Question 2.1: Analyse International Guidelines and Directives that are relevant for accountancy qualification, education and training in a format that makes it possible to use the results as benchmarks for the comparative analysis of national systems of accountancy education.

Research Question 2.2: Analyse the factors that make change of accountancy education necessary and that influence the requirements regarding the professional qualification, education and training of accountants and auditors.

The underlying assumption is that in international guidelines and directives on accountancy education general accepted recommendations and requirements are formulated which set at least the minimum standards to be achieved. An analysis of the recent past and of ongoing developments can help in setting a course for the future. Essential is a clear understanding of the necessary elements of accountancy education and their inter relations. This issue is addressed in Chapter 3 by answering the following research question.

Research Question 3: Develop a conceptual model for the classification of accountancy education systems in various parts of the world that can be used for evaluation and comparison.

The resulting model is at the basis of a questionnaire that has been used to collect information on the qualification, education and training of accountants and auditors and on related subjects. Chapter 4 discusses in particular the research questions and method. It brings together the theoretical model and the collected data by specifying the theoretical assumptions, the classification model and the research data.

Research Question 4: Analyse the data relevant for accountancy education as a basis for decisions on the final model of the professional qualification, education and training of accountants and auditors.

The available data can and have been used on three levels: (1) descriptive (2) analytical and (3) comparative.

Chapter 5 gives an overview of accountancy education in the countries that are included in the project and gives the descriptive basis for further analysis and comparison. The following research question is answered.

Research Question 5: Describe country characteristics and accountancy education as a basis for classification, comparison and analysis.

In Chapter 6 and Chapter 7 the material is used in two different ways. In Chapter 6 a classification is developed that leads to conclusions about the final model of accountancy education and its applicability in different surroundings. Chapter 7 analyses local and regional differences. The following research questions are addressed.

Research Question 6: Develop a classification of accountancy education based on a conceptual model and evaluation of distinguishing factors.

Research Question 7: Analyse regional and local differences of accountancy education in the selected countries.

Finally a conclusion must be reached on the question whether the Central Research Question has been answered. This is discussed in Chapter 8 followed by recommendations in Chapter 9.

410   Research Method

From the start of the project it was in a general way quite clear what was wanted as a result of Global Accountancy Education research project: a contribution to a better understanding of accountancy education. Setting up the project a combination was sought between professional relevance and academic rigor.

The formulation of the research questions is described in the preceding paragraph. The research method is discussed here. It is inductive, from observation to generalisation, rather than deductive. Most of the material had to be gathered through the consultation of experts, as international comparable information was hardly available.

International guidelines and directives on accountancy education were put in a model matrix to make them comparable. Their content covers the necessary programmes and gives some attention to methods for education, training and assessment. Hardly any attention is given to the structure of accountancy qualification, education and training with the allocation of responsibilities, the expertise that is needed and the roles of the various actors, like governments, professional bodies, institutes of higher education and accountancy firms.

This leads to the conclusion that for the GAE research project a model for accountancy qualification, education and training is needed that contains all relevant components, their relations and the outside actors that influence accountancy education. A pilot version of the model was tested in France, the Netherlands, the United Kingdom and the USA.

For comparative reasons a top-down structure was chosen for the model starting with the professional qualification. This is followed by information about the final examination, professional education, practical training and general education. A standard questionnaire was developed and tested for data gathering. In the pilot stage attention was paid to definitions to ensure comparability throughout the questionnaire on the various levels of accountancy education and training. The core information in the questionnaire is preceded by chapters, which cover general characteristics of the country and information about the professional body and its membership. In the final chapters attention is given to education content in relation to international guidelines and to foreseeable future developments.

Co-operation was sought with experts on accountancy education world-wide, who were willing to share their expertise. The collected data were summarised in overviews that are given in Annex 3 after a description of the Questionnaire in Annex 2.

The resulting analysis is mostly of a comparative nature. The use of statistical methods is limited by the relatively small number of observations. Still, whenever possible, statistics have been used to check on the results achieved by comparison.

420   Theoretical Assumptions

The model of accountancy education as described in paragraph 330 has been specifically designed for the project. At the core of the model is the system of accountancy education. Two assumptions are central in the approach that has been chosen.

(1) The definition of accountancy education does not only include the content of accountancy education and training – the usual approach – but also its structure and recognition. Although the content of education and training programmes is important to judge the present abilities of professional accountants and auditors, it does in itself not indicate the potential that is available for further development. This is largely decided by the structure of accountancy education, including the allocation of responsibilities and the available expertise in a national setting. On the other hand existing international recognition can be used as a measure for the relative positions of professional accountancy qualifications.

(2) Accountancy education cannot be considered as a closed system, but is influenced by outside actors. Based on a field study and existing literature a distinction is made between (1) international requirements and developments in the accountancy profession and in accountancy education, (2) influences from the accountancy profession on accountancy education and (3) the influence of country characteristics. The first and the second are analysed in Chapter 2, the third in Chapters 3 and 5.

In a setting of ongoing globalisation an important role is given to international standards, guidelines and directives. These reflect principles that have been agreed, but may not yet be a sufficient indication of future requirements. In order to get an overview of possible relevant future developments the issue is addressed in the accountancy education questionnaire and through a study of literature. The choice of country characteristics is based on existing literature.

The approach chosen for the research project as a whole can be characterised as an inductive (from observation to theory) classification of accountancy education, using a system of parallel processing (theory development and country studies combined in a step-by-step approach) with input from selected academics and professionals as database. The supporting literature review was both theory oriented and country oriented. In terms of research methodology[21] the study can be characterised as a combination of *empirical descriptive* (use of a questionnaire), *empirical statistical* (statistical analysis of data) and *modelling*.

Theory development addressed three central questions.

- Which factors should logically be considered?
- How are they related?
- What are the underlying dynamics that justify the selection of variables?

Based on a publication by Needles[22], referring to a research classification by Choi and Mueller, possible outcomes of the Global Accountancy Education research project were distinguished in the following categories.

- Description of phenomena observed
- Systematic classification
- Comparison and analysis
- Abstraction of general characteristics and principles
- Determination of relatively few underlying basic concepts
- Theory (model) building and testing

Chapter 5 gives an overall description of accountancy education. The results of the classification, comparison and analysis are described in Chapter 6. The overall results of the study in regard to the general characteristics and principles, the basic concepts and the theoretical model are discussed in Chapter 7.

430   Classification Model

The conceptual model as presented in the previous chapter in its final form is meant to provide the basis for an adequate classification of accountancy education systems around the world with a fair representation of the underlying characteristics. To this end the model was tested in selected countries around the world with a varied background in culture, legal and educational systems, state of development and accounting and auditing practices. The overall selection of countries should ensure that 'all features of accountancy education systems are considered that may constitute long-run fundamental differences between countries'[23]. Conclusions were sought about the applicability of the model and about the applicability and influence of international guidelines.

In general the target has been reached. The detailed results of the analyses are presented in the following chapters. As a result of the project recommendations are given on the promotion of the international development of accountancy education, including the furtherance of mutual recognition and harmonisation. Whereas the possible relevance of classification of accountancy education in view of the research objectives is discussed in Chapter 3, the prerequisites of classification and the extent to which these are met, must be addressed in this chapter.

As early as the seventies of the last century the American Accounting Association conducted a major effort for classification in comparative accounting studies[24]. Four fundaments of good classification are listed as follows.

---

[21] Belverd E. Needles, Jr., International Accounting Research: An Analysis of Thirty-Two Years from the International Journal of Accounting (1997).
[22] Belverd E. Needles, Jr., International Auditing Research: Current Assessment and Future Direction (1989).
[23] Comparative International Accounting, page 59, (1998).
[24] American Accounting Association, Accounting Review, Supplement to Vol. 52 (1977).

- The *characteristics* of a chosen classification should be adhered to consistently.
- The subsets of a given universe should be *exhaustive*, i.e., they should jointly cover the whole field.
- The subsets should be *pair-wise disjoint*, i.e., be mutually exclusive.
- There should be a preservation of *hierarchical integrity*, i.e., elements of one hierarchical rank should not be confused or mixed with elements of some other ranks.

The analysis, interpretations and theoretical conclusions in regard to the classification of accountancy education are discussed in paragraphs 460 and 470. These are compared with the general distinction of classifications in *cataloguing*, *grouping* (dichotomous, multiple), *dimensioning*, *ordering* (ordinal, interval, ratio) and *systemising* (decomposition, network, static reciprocity, dynamic).

440   Research Data

In order to be able to develop the conceptual model three sets of data were considered: country characteristics, accountancy education influenced by the accountancy profession and international development. The three sets of data were divided in clusters of presumed connected information, which were subjected to comparative and statistical analysis in order to decide on correlations inside and between clusters.

Country characteristics
Under the heading of 'country characteristics' general information was considered on cultural background, legal system and economic position that may – but not necessarily will – influence accountancy education in the countries studied. The choice of distinguishing characteristics is discussed in Chapter 3. Existing classifications were used and compared in view of possible relations between the country characteristics.

Accountancy education
The comparative analysis of 'accountancy education' on a country level was based on similar descriptions of relevant characteristics of accountancy education. The model that was developed in order to achieve comparability of information is described in Chapter 3. Local fact-finding was augmented by a study of literature with two objectives. First test and if necessary adapt the model. Second present country overviews in a comparable format.

International developments
The heading 'international development' focused on possible relevant developments in the accountancy profession and resulting requirements that can influence accountancy education. The scope and influence of international guidelines on accountancy education was included. The main source of information is a study of literature augmented by local fact finding.

Research Question 4

Analyse the data relevant for accountancy education as a basis for decisions on the final model of the professional qualification, education and training of accountants and auditors

450   Research Plan and Timetable

The research project was managed in an international context using synergy and existing international contacts. A steering committee had as its task to overview both academic rigor and professional relevance. Expert support was sought in the countries included in the research project and from relevant international organisations. International experts in accountancy education and related fields were consulted on the project approach and eventual evaluation.

Preliminary activities covered general activities and a study of literature on the areas distinguished in the research project, preparation of the research objectives and a first classification model, consultation with international experts and organisations, development of selection criteria for country studies and regions and the development of an organisational structure for the project. The original fact-finding in the Netherlands, the United Kingdom, the USA and France has been finished based on the preliminary model for accountancy education that was developed for that purpose.

As a result of the review of the original questions on scope and comparability of the answers major changes and additions were effected in the questionnaire which now covers country characteristics; background information about the profession; accountancy qualification, education and training; comparison with international guidelines and future developments. Subsequently the country information is the basis for the scientific analysis of systems for accountancy education and training around the world in relation to the country characteristics that are being distinguished as possible explaining factors and in view of international developments effecting the accountancy profession.

At the conclusion of the project considerably more countries (28) and professional bodies (34) were included in the research analysis than originally foreseen. In combination with the larger scope of the questionnaire the resulting analysis gives a more complete global coverage. At the same time less emphasis could be placed on developments in time and the explanation of global changes.

The results of the study include an overview of developments in the accountancy profession influencing accountancy education, an analysis of general trends and objectives in accountancy education, a conceptual model to describe systems of accountancy education with conclusions about the applicability of the model in different surroundings, a comparative analysis of accountancy education in selected countries and regions, conclusions about impact and applicability of international guidelines on accountancy education under different regional or local circumstances.

The research project took no more than three years – 1999, 2000 and 2001 – with finalisation in 2002. Intermediate results became available after each separate part of the project. The final results for the profession were presented at the 9th World Congress of the IAAER in Hong Kong, November 2002 preceding the 16th IFAC World Congress of Accountants.

460   Data Collection, Analysis and Interpretation

Data collection in view of country information was largely done by sending a questionnaire to selected respondents at 37 professional bodies in 28 countries. The questions were asked for the year 2000 if they concerned a period and for January 1, 2001 if they concerned a moment in time. In June 2002 answers had been received from 34 professional bodies in 25 countries. The selection of subjects and the preparation of the theoretical model of accountancy education are described in the previous chapter. Country information was completed with brochures, leaflets and web information.

The study of literature was divided in two parts. The first part concerned fact finding in view of the problem definition, the selection of research methods and the analysis of general developments. The second part concerned local and regional fact finding relevant for the country research. Standard literature was considered as well as articles in leading research and professional journals in the field of accounting and auditing. Journals covered included Accounting Education: An International Journal, the European Accounting Review, the International Journal of Accounting, Issues in Accounting Education and the Journal of Accounting Education. Articles were also selected from other journals. Emphasis was given to the last ten years but older articles were included if they had a specific relevance for the research project. Publications from international bodies were considered as far as they were considered important for the research project.

For the design and distribution of the questionnaire the KPMG Qubus Competence Center in the Netherlands made software available. The Qubus® Software, questionnaire-building system for windows and web is an intelligent questionnaire and reporting building software tool. Its use contributed towards a systematic design of the questionnaire. Decision rules make it possible that the respondents only have to answer questions that are relevant in their particular situation. In view of the global coverage of the research project use was made of WebQubus, which made it possible to run the application on the World Wide Web, working with Netscape Navigator and Microsoft Internet Explorer. The respondents had access to their own answer set. For the research project the results could be reviewed and compared. All questions and answers were stored in a database with technical support provided by the KPMG Qubus Competence Center. In addition to online access standard country reports and consolidated overviews were available as basis for the analysis.

The Economic and Social Institute of the Free University in the Netherlands provided academic support with modification of the pilot model for accountancy education, conversion of the questionnaire into a standardised one and statistical analysis of the data. In the questionnaire as much use as possible was made of closed questions – including option (single choice), check (multiple choice) and yes/no – augmented when necessary with open questions – field, text and numeric. The contribution of the statistical analysis to the research results was limited as a result of the relatively small number of separate data. Still the results proved to be a valuable addition to the content analysis.

470   Theoretical Conclusions

All the answers to the questionnaire were checked on (1) plausibility, (2) consistency and (3) if relevant summation. If necessary and possible this was followed by additional fact-finding. The results on a country level are discussed in Chapter 5, the test of the accountancy education model in Chapter 6 and the comparison of country characteristics in Chapter 7. This is the basis for the classification of accountancy education that is described in Chapter 8.

After control of the data supplied by the respondents frequency tables were prepared as a basis for the first comparison. For all relevant questions and answers this was completed by frequency distributions. The use of the frequency distributions was limited to the cases were (1) comparison was deemed relevant in view of content relevance and (2) there was statistical relevance. As measure for the later the standard deviation divided by the mean had to be smaller than 1.

The frequency distributions that were used in the analysis in the following chapters are included in Annex 4. In addition to the frequency distributions cross tables were prepared for all relevant combinations of variables. It was not possible to use the statistical results as usually the number of entries in each cell was too low for relevance.

A combination of content analysis and statistical analysis, as far as possible, led to the results described in the following chapters. It proved possible to design a classification of accountancy education in four hierarchical levels.

- Regulation Index (4 groups)
- Final Examination (2 groups)
- Professional Education and Practical Experience (3 groups)
- Education Background (6 groups)

For the classification use was made of grouping into dichotomous and multiple categories. Except for 'professional education and practical experience' the basis for the classification of each of the parameters is an ordinal relationship between the subsets composing the main categories. This is worked out in the Chapters 6 and 8.

CHAPTER 5   GLOBAL COUNTRY STUDIES

This chapter is dedicated to an analysis of the country profile, followed by a general comparison of the characteristics of the existing systems for the qualification, education and training of accountants and auditors.

500	Introduction to Country Studies
510	Country Profile
520	GAE Questionnaire
530	Overviews of Accountancy Education
540	International Standards and Recognition
550	Professional Bodies and Qualification
560	Professional Examination, Education and Training
570	Compliance with International Guidelines

The two main indicators for the country profile are the legal system and economic position. For general considerations legal systems are divided in common law and civil law. Based on an analysis of underlying factors for economic position a dichotomy has been found between on the one hand countries that can be classified as industrialised and on the other hand countries that can be classified as in transition/emerging.

A descriptive review of accountancy education follows the analysis of the country profile. This covers the accountancy profession and the professional qualification of accountants and auditors with its system of education and training. The accounting and auditing system in place is discussed under the accountancy profession. Programme requirements are compared with international guidelines. Country overviews summarised from the answers to the questionnaire are given in Annex 3.

500   Introduction to Country Studies

A preliminary model for accountancy education systems is based on the study of relevant literature to identify theoretical assumptions. Considering the position in the accountancy profession, the contribution to accountancy education and the different characteristics involved this first model was tested in France, the Netherlands, the United Kingdom and the USA. In view of underlying differences in these countries the expectation that variations in the model would be necessary to achieve an adequate description of the various systems in place turned out to be realistic.

This part of the project resulted in a comparative analysis of accountancy education in the pilot countries that were considered followed by adaptation and enlargement of the general model as described in paragraph 520. After this initial stage further research was conducted in selected countries in the following regions: European Union and North America, Central and Eastern Europe, Africa and the Middle East, Asia and the Far East, South and Middle America. Countries in each region were selected in a manner that ensures that all the possible relevant factors are covered as a necessary condition to achieve a balanced result with global relevance.

The distinguishing factors that were used for the country selection are described in paragraph 310. They relate to economic position, legal system and cultural background. In this chapter an overall description is given of accountancy education in the countries that are part of the project.

Research Question 5

Describe country characteristics and accountancy education as a basis for classification, comparison and analysis.

510   **Country Profile**

It was possible to collect country information for all selected countries with the exception of Senegal. The overview in this paragraph is – in that sequence – divided in cultural background, legal system and economic position. The summarised descriptions of legal systems are derived from the Central Intelligence Agency (CIA) fact book[25]. The regional position of the countries is included in the resulting analysis. Detailed information is given in Table 510.1 Country Profile.

Table 510.1 Country Profile

Pop	Country population in millions
TLF	Total labour force in millions
F%LF	Female percentage of the total labour force
GNP	Gross National Product in millions of US $
GNP pp	Gross National Product per capita in US $
PC/1000	Number of personal computers per 1000 people

Cultural Background and Legal Systems

The cultural background of countries can be represented by comparing power distance and uncertainty avoidance. Power Distance can be defined as 'the extend to which the less powerful members of institutions and organisations within a country expect and accept that power is distributed unequally'. Uncertainty Avoidance can be defined as 'the extend to which the members of a culture feel threatened by uncertain or unknown situations'. The results according to Hofstede[26] for the countries included in the research project are given in Table 510.2: Cultural Background.

Table 510.2 Cultural Background

A combination of cultural background with legal systems is shown below.

Small Power Distance and Weak Uncertainty Avoidance

Common Law	Australia, Canada, New Zealand, UK, USA
Civil Law	Netherlands, Sweden
Common Law with Civil Law	South Africa

The common law countries in this group have a legal system based on English common law with the exception of the province of Quebec in Canada, where civil law based on French law prevails. The Netherlands has a civil law system incorporating French penal theory. Sweden has a civil law system influenced by customary law. South African law is based on Roman-Dutch law and English common law. All countries in this group accept compulsory jurisdiction of the International Court of Justice (ICJ), with reservations.

Small Power Distance and Strong Uncertainty Avoidance

Common Law	Not included in the selection[27]
Civil Law	Argentina, Germany, Hungary

Argentina has a mixture of US and West European legal systems. Germany has a civil law system with indigenous concepts and judicial review of legislative acts in the Federal Constitutional Court. Argentina and Germany have not accepted compulsory ICJ jurisdiction. Hungary has moved from socialist law to a rule of law based on a western model.

---

[25] Central Intelligence Agency: www.cia.gov/cia/publications/factbook.
[26] Geert Hofstede, Culture's Consequences, Second edition, 2001.
[27] Common law countries in this segment of cultural background were not available.

Country	Pop	TLF	F% LF	GNP	GNP pp	PC/1000
Argentina	36	14	32	290261	11728	44
Australia	19	10	43	387006	21795	412
Brazil	166	76	35	767568	6460	30
Canada	30	16	45.4	580872	22814	330
China	1238	743	45	923560	3051	9
Czech Republic	10	6	47	53034	12197	97
France	59	26	44.8	1465399	21214	207.8
Germany	82	41	42	2179802	22026	305
Hong Kong	7	3	37	158238	20763	254
Hungary	10	5	45	45660	9832	59
India	980	431	32	427407	2060	2.7
Japan	126	68	41	4089140	23592	237
Kenya	29	15	46	10201	964	3
Lebanon	4	1.4	29	15976	3700	46
Malaysia	22	9	38	81311	7699	59
Mexico	96	38	33	368059	7450	47
Netherlands	16	7	40.2	389005	22325	317.6
New Zealand	4	2	44.6	55356	16084	282
Pakistan	132	49	28	61451	1652	4
Poland	39	20	46	151285	7543	44
Russia	147	78	49	331799	6180	41
Saudi Arabia	21	7	15	143361	10498	50
South Africa	41	16	38	136868	8296	47
Spain	40	30	40	555244	15960	350
Sweden	9	5	48	226454	19848	361
Turkey	63	30	37	200530	6594	23
UK	59	30	44	1264262	20314	263
USA	270	70	45.7	7902976	29240	458.6

Table 510.1 Country Profile

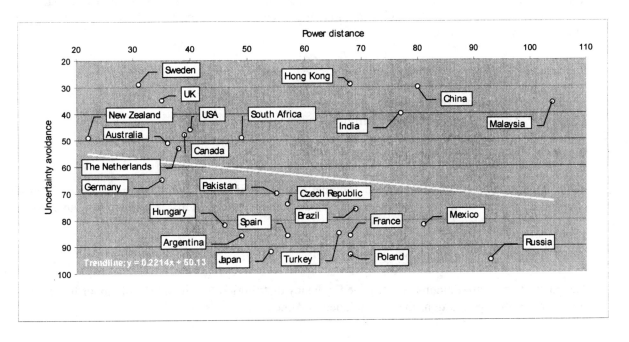

Table 510.2 Cultural Background

Large Power Distance and Weak Uncertainty Avoidance

Common Law	Hong Kong, India, Kenya, Malaysia
Civil Law	China

The common law countries in this group have a legal system based on English common law with Islamic and customary influences in India and Kenya. India and Kenya accept compulsory ICJ jurisdiction, Malaysia does not. China has a complex amalgam of custom and statute, largely criminal law with a rudimentary civil code in effect since 1987.

Large Power Distance and Strong Uncertainty Avoidance

Common Law	Pakistan, Saudi Arabia
Civil Law	Brazil, Czech Republic, France, Japan, Lebanon, Mexico, Poland, Russian Federation, Spain, Turkey

Pakistan and Saudi Arabia have a legal system based on English common law with Islamic influences. The civil law countries in this group have a mixed background: Brazil based on Roman codes; the Czech Republic has replaced former socialist law by civil law based on Austrian-Hungarian codes; France has a Civil law system with indigenous concepts; Mexico shows a mixture of US constitutional theory and civil law; Poland has a mixture of continental (Napoleonic) civil law and former socialist legal theory; the Russian Federation based on civil law, Spain a civil law system with regional applications and Turkey a legal system derived from various European continental legal systems. Lebanon has a mixture of Ottoman law, canon law, Napoleonic code and civil law. Japan has a legal system modelled after European civil law with English-American influence. Japan, Mexico, Pakistan and Turkey accept compulsory ICJ jurisdiction, with reservations; Brazil, the Czech Republic, Lebanon, Saudi Arabia and Spain do not.

Economic Position

At the start of the project a preliminary distinction was made between industrialised countries with a market economy as the overall system, countries 'in transition' from a planned economy to a market economy and developing countries with emerging economies. In addition – as mentioned in paragraph 310 – the following indicators[28] with a possible relevance for the comparison of the economic position of countries were considered.

- Country population in millions
- Total labour force in millions
- Female percentage of the total labour force
- Gross National Product in millions of US $
- Gross National Product per capita in US $
- Number of personal computers per 1000 people

High correlations were found between 'population and total labour force', 'population and female labour force' and 'total labour force and female labour force'. This is shown in Table 510.3: Population and Labour Force.

Table 510.3: Population and Labour Force

The correlation is also demonstrated by the frequency distributions of 'female % of labour force' and 'total labour force/population' that are included in Annex 4.

---

[28] The World Development Indicators CD-ROM 2000, The International Bank for Reconstruction and Development/The World Bank.

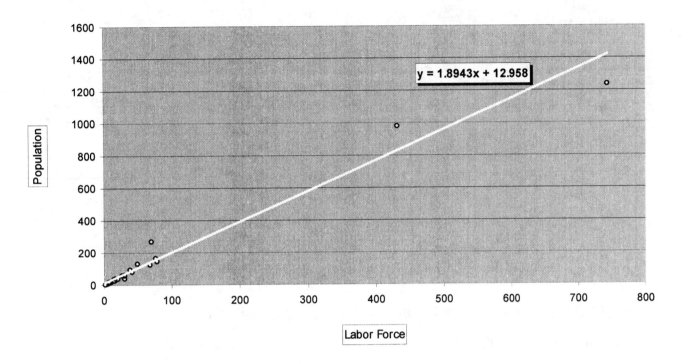

Population and Total Labour Force (corr. coeff. = 0,982999)

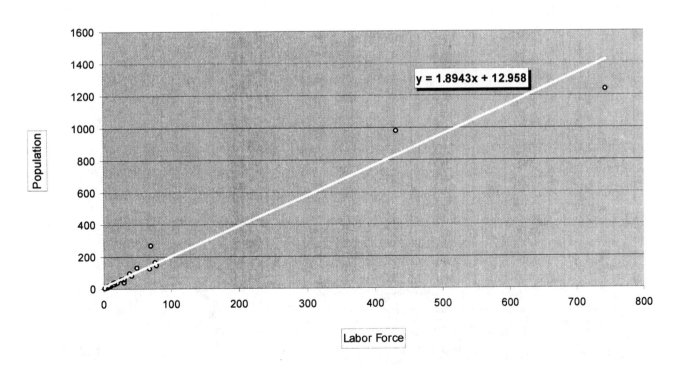

Population and Female Labour Force (corr. coeff. = 0,982115)

Table 510.3 Population and Labour Force

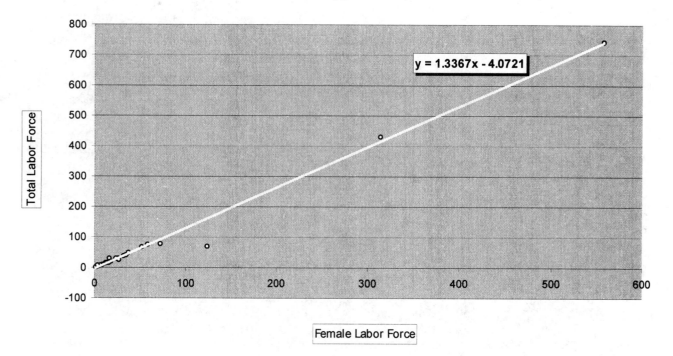

Total Labour Force and Female Labour Force (corr. coeff. = 0,994097)

Table 510.3 Population and Labour Force (continued)

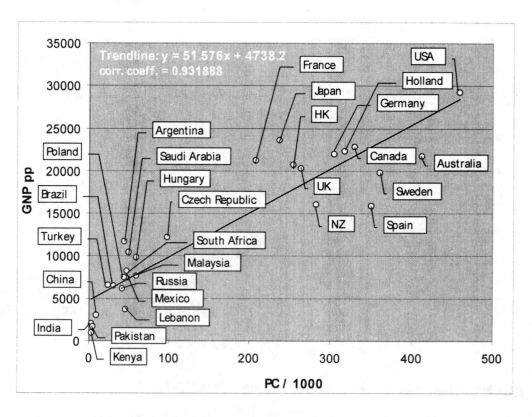

Table 510.4 Gross National Product and Personal Computers

The data show that, with the exception of country size, these variables do not discriminate between countries. As a result they are not included as possible distinguishing factors in the research analysis.

A high correlation was found between 'Gross National Product per capita' and 'number of personal computers per 1000 people'. This is shown in Table 510.4 Gross National Product and Personal Computers.

Table 510.4: Gross National Product and Personal Computers

Contrary to the first comparison these data discriminate highly between countries, showing a dichotomy between on the one hand countries that in general can be classified as 'industrialised' and on the other hand countries that in general can be classified as 'in transition/emerging'. Although we recognize that there are important differences, especially in the second group, the two-way classification is included as a possible distinguishing factor in the research analysis presented in Chapter 6.

520   GAE Questionnaire

The Global Accountancy Education questionnaire as used in the research pilot for France, the Netherlands, the United Kingdom and the United States of America was aimed almost completely at the existing systems of accountancy qualification, education and training. After review of the results it was decided to add specific chapters on country characteristics, professional bodies, International Education Guidelines and future developments.

After the test of the preliminary model in the pilot countries the Global Accountancy Education questionnaire as shown in Annex 2 was after updating sent to all selected professional bodies simultaneously. The results were used to test the applicability of the model and to decide on the existence of general characteristics in the regions considered.

The answers to each question of the questionnaire were tested for plausibility, consistency and statistical relevance. If necessary the respondents were approached for additional information and if possible answers were checked with existing literature and websites. The more general conclusions that were considered in the analysis are summarised below. The numbers between brackets refer to the numbering of the questions as given in Annex 2.

Legal System (1.9): allocation to common law and civil law as the main legal systems.
Economic Position (1.10): the original comparison in industrialised, in transition and emerging was replaced by a two-tier division.
Higher Education (1.13): worldwide comparison of Higher Education systems not available.
Admission Requirements (3.2.1): differences in the interpretations of final examination, professional education and practical training had to be accounted for.
Level Final Examination (3.3.3) and Professional Education (3.4.5): the use of the terms postgraduate, graduate and undergraduate depends on the existing Higher Education system.
Duration Professional Education (3.4.3): could include or follow Higher Education.
Practical Training (3.5.4): distinction between practical experience (unregulated) and practical training (regulated).
Duration General Education (3.6.3): differences in the interpretation had to be accounted for.

A descriptive review of accountancy education is given in the following paragraphs. This follows the chapters of the questionnaire and as a result covers the accountancy profession and the professional qualification of accountants and auditors with its system of education and training. The accounting and auditing system in place is discussed under the accountancy profession. Programme requirements are compared with international guidelines. Country overviews summarised from the answers to the questionnaire are given in Annex 3. The respondents were asked to review the texts of the overviews in order to check the correctness of the summarised information.

Classification and comparison of data is described in Chapter 6. In view of the comparative and statistical analysis the questions were allocated to the following clusters. One of the objectives of the analysis is to decide on correlations inside and between clusters.

- Cluster 1: Country Profile
- Cluster 2: Regulation and Recognition
- Cluster 3: Professional Qualification and Background
- Cluster 4: Professional Body
- Cluster 5: Examination, Education and Training
- Cluster 6: International Benchmarks
- Cluster 7: Future Developments

530   Overviews of Accountancy Education

As discussed in Chapter 3 professional bodies have been approached in the following regions and countries.

- European Union: France, the Netherlands, the United Kingdom, Germany, Spain, Sweden
- North and Middle America: Canada, Mexico and the USA
- Central and Eastern Europe: Czech Republic, Hungary, Poland, Russian Federation
- Africa: Kenya, Senegal, South Africa
- Middle East: Lebanon, Turkey, Saudi Arabia
- Asia: Pakistan, India, Malaysia, China, Hong Kong
- Far East: Australia, New Zealand, Japan
- South America: Argentine, Brazil.

The overviews in Annex 3 are given in alphabetical order and cover the institutes mentioned below. The professional bodies in Argentina, Brazil and China are not included as the necessary information on the qualification, education and training of accountants and auditors could not be completed.

Country	Professional Body	Abbreviation
Australia	Institute of Chartered Accountants in Australia	ICA Australia
Australia	CPA Australia	CPA Australia
Canada	Certified General Accountants Canada	CGA Canada
Canada	Society of Management Accountants of Canada	CMA Canada
Canada	Institute of Chartered Accountants of Alberta	ICA Alberta
Czech Republic	Chamber of Auditors of the Czech Republic	CACR
France	Ordre des Experts-Comptables	Ordre
Germany	Institut der Wirtschaftsprüfer in Deutschland	IDW
Hong Kong	Hong Kong Society of Accountants	HKSA
Hungary	Chamber of Hungarian Auditors	CHA
India	Institute of Chartered Accountants of India	ICA India
India	Institute of Cost and Works Accountants of India	ICWAI
Japan	Japanese Institute of Certified Public Accountants	JICPA
Kenya	Institute of Certified Public Accountants of Kenya	ICPAK
Lebanon	Lebanese Association of Certified Public Accountants	LACPA
Malaysia	Malaysian Association of Certified Public Accountants	MACPA
Malaysia	Malaysian Institute of Accountants	MIA
Mexico	Instituto Mexicano de Contadores Públicos, A.C.	IMCP
Netherlands	Royal NIVRA	NIVRA
New Zealand	Institute of Chartered Accountants of New Zealand	ICANZ
Pakistan	Institute of Chartered Accountants of Pakistan	ICAP
Pakistan	Institute of Cost and Management Accountants of Pakistan	ICMAP
Poland	Association of Accountants in Poland	SKwP

Poland	National Chamber of Statutory Auditors	KIBR
Russian Fed.	Institute of Professional Accountants	IPA Russia
Saudi Arabia	Saudi Organisation for Certified Public Accountants	SOCPA
South Africa	South African Institute of Chartered Accountants	SAICA
Spain	Instituto de Auditores-Censores Jurados de Cuentas de España	IACJCE
Sweden	Föreningen Auktoriserade Revisorer	FAR
Turkey	Union of Chambers of Certified Public Accountants	TURMOB
United Kingdom	Association of Chartered Certified Accountants	ACCA
United Kingdom	Institute of Chartered Accountants in England & Wales	ICAEW
United Kingdom	Institute of Chartered Accountants of Scotland	ICAS
USA	American Institute of Certified Public Accountants	AICPA

Table 530.1: Overviews of Accountancy Education

The overviews give an impression of the main characteristics of the systems of accountancy qualification, education and training that have been considered. Using frequency states and tables that were prepared for that purpose an overview of the results is given in this chapter.

540   International Standards and Recognition

The description of the accounting rules in each country is derived from GAAP 2000, A Survey of National Accounting Rules in 53 Countries with in some cases comments by the respondents to the questionnaire.

A detailed comparison of requirements on accounting and auditing rules falls outside this study. It is however interesting to compare the influence of International Accounting Standards with national regulations and to consider the respective positions of governments and professional bodies.

Country	Accounting Rules
Australia	Australian requirements on accounting rules are based mainly on the Corporations Law and the standards of the Australian Accounting Standards Board and Abstracts of the Urgent Issues Group
Canada	Canadian requirements on accounting rules are based on the standards issued by the Accounting Standards Board of the Canadian Institute of Chartered Accountants
Czech Republic	Czech requirements on accounting rules are based mainly on the Act on Accounting, the Chart of Accounts and the Accounting Procedures of the Ministry of Finance
France	French requirements on accounting rules are based on the Code de Commerce, company law and decrees, the Plan Comptable Général (General Accounting Plan) and interpretations of the Comité d'urgence (Urgent Issues Committee) as applying to consolidated financial statements
Germany	German accounting requirements are based mainly on the Commercial Code (HGB). In addition, the standards of the German Accounting Standards Committee published by the Ministry of Justice represent Principles of Proper Accounting for consolidated financial statements. Companies whose securities are listed on exchanges may apply IAS or US GAAP to the extent that these comply with the 4th and 7th EU Directives in place of German accounting requirements in their consolidated financial statements
Hong Kong	Hong Kong requirements on accounting rules are based on the Companies Ordnance, standards and interpretations issued by the Hong Kong Society of Accountants and the Listing Rules of the Stock Exchange

Hungary	Hungarian requirements on accounting rules are based on the Accounting Act of 1991
India	Indian requirements on accounting rules are mainly based on the Companies Act 1956, on regulations of the Company Law Board and on standards issued by the Institute of Chartered Accountants of India. In addition, listed companies must follow the rules, regulations and releases issued by the Securities and Exchange Board of India
Japan	Japanese requirements on accounting rules are based on the Commercial Code and accounting standards developed by the Business Accounting Council, Accounting Standards Board and the Japanese Institute of Certified Public Accountants
Kenya	Kenya requirements on accounting rules are based on International Accounting Standards and local Company Law
Lebanon	Lebanese requirements on accounting rules are based on local laws and International Accounting Standards. The General Accounting Plan follows the French accounting system
Malaysia	Malaysian requirements on accounting rules are based on the Companies Act 1965 and on the standards of the Malaysian Accounting Standards Board. The Malaysian Accounting Standards Board uses IASs as the basis for developing accounting standards
Mexico	Mexican requirements on accounting rules are based on the standards issued by the Mexican Institute of Public Accountants, Bulletin A-8 of which requires that IAS must be followed on a supplementary basis when Mexican requirements are silent. The IASC standards are considered in Mexico as supplementary standards in the absence of any accounting rule or principle issues by the Mexican Institute of Public Accountants
The Netherlands	Dutch accounting requirements can be found in the Civil Code as amended by EU Directives and in Guidelines of the Council for Annual Reporting. Although the guidelines are not mandatory, they should not be departed from without good reason. However, departure is required if application of the requirements does not provide a true and fair view of the state of affairs and results of the enterprise
New Zealand	New Zealand requirements on accounting rules are based on the Financial Reporting Act 1993 and accounting standards issued by the Institute of Chartered Accountants of New Zealand
Pakistan	Pakistan requirements on accounting rules are based on the Companies Ordinance 1984, regulations issued by the Securities and Exchange Commission of Pakistan (SECP) and those IASs adopted by the SECP for listed companies only
Poland	Polish requirements on accounting rules are based on the Commercial Code, the Law on Accounting and decree on consolidation rules. The format of the financial statements and disclosure for public companies are regulated by the Polish Securities and Exchange Commission
Russian Fed.	Russian requirements on accounting rules are based on the government program of reformation of the accounting system in accordance with IAS/ISA
Saudi Arabia	Saudi Arabian requirements on accounting rules are based on governmental Regulations for Companies and on accounting standards issued by the Saudi Organization of Certified Public Accountants (SOCPA). The accounting standards issued by SOCPA are a comprehensive basis for accounting. In situations where no Saudi standard is available, companies are requested to use the American accounting standards with some modification to suit the Saudi environment.
South Africa	South African reporting requirements are based on Statements of Generally Accepted Accounting Practice (GAAP) issued by the Accounting Practices

	Board of the South African Institute of Chartered Accountants, the disclosure requirements of Schedule 4 to the Companies Act and where applicable, the Johannesburg Stock Exchange Listing Requirements
Spain	Spanish requirements on accounting rules are mainly based on the Code of Commerce, the General Accounting Plan, the Companies Act and on standards issued by the Official Institute of Accounting and Audit (ICAC). The methodology for evaluation of post-retirements benefits is governed by the Insurance Regulatory Authority (DGS).
Sweden	Swedish requirements on accounting rules are based on the Annual Accounts Act incorporating EU Directives, and on the accounting standards of the Redovisningsrädet (RR). In rare circumstances, a RR standard can be departed from if the departure is disclosed and adequately justified. Full adherence to the RR standards is not required for unlisted companies, although the adoption of the standards is becoming increasingly common
Turkey	Turkish requirements on accounting rules are based on accounting standards issued by the Finance Ministry of Turkey and by the Capital Markets Board. Regulations for the finance sector are made by the Treasury Department. Finally there is also a standard setter body within the TURMOB, whose name is the TMUDESK, the Turkish Accounting and Auditing Standards Board
United Kingdom	UK statutory requirements on accounting rules are based on the Companies Act 1985, and comply with EU Directives. The Act states that disclosure should be made as to whether accounts have been prepared in accordance with applicable accounting standards. Accounting standards issued by the Accounting Standards Board and its Urgent Issues Task Force are applicable for the purposes of this Act
USA	The USA has a very detailed framework of generally accepted accounting principles (US GAAP), based on accounting standards and guidance of the Financial Accounting Standards Board, statements from the AICPA and consensus reached by the Emerging Issues Task Force. Listed companies must follow the rules, regulations and releases of the Securities and Exchange Commission SEC

Table 540.1: Accounting Rules

In most cases (27 out of 34) professional bodies indicate that the accountancy sector is regulated both by law and by professional self-regulation. Only five professional bodies are regulated exclusively by law, two by professional self-regulation. The majority of the professional bodies (26 out of 34) is recognized as a regulatory and a disciplinary body. Sole recognition as a regulatory body is limited to four cases, as a disciplinary body to four cases.

Standard setting for the qualification of accountants and auditors is the joint responsibility of government and professional body in 16 cases out of 34. The government is solely responsible in four cases, the professional body in 14.

Responsibility of the providers of professional education and especially of practical training tends to be centred at the professional bodies. Professional education is the joint responsibility of government and professional body in eight cases out of 32, sole government responsibility in eight cases and sole responsibility of the professional body in 13 cases. Other forms of regulation exist in three cases. Practical training is the joint responsibility of government and professional body in three cases out of 27, sole government responsibility in two cases and sole responsibility of the professional body in 22 cases.

On the international level the position of IFAC is well established: 33 out of 34 professional bodies are member. The majority of the professional bodies is also affiliated to one or more mostly regional organisations of accountants. The IFAC International Education Guidelines with emphasis on IEG 9 are followed on a voluntary basis by 26 of 34 professional bodies. Inside the European Union EU Directives are mandatory. The eight professional bodies inside the EU follow the directives and on a voluntary basis two professional bodies in Central and Eastern Europe. Other guidelines or directives were not mentioned in the answers to the questionnaire. Recognition of qualifications between countries has been achieved from the home country in other countries (24 out of 34) and from other countries in the home country (28 out of 34).

Mandatory membership of the professional body exists in 23 out of 34 cases and is required to use the designatory title. In almost all cases continuing professional education is mandatory for members in public practice (32 out of 34) and is almost always regulated by the professional body (29 out of 32). In most cases (exceeding 80 %) CPE is also mandatory for members in industry and commerce, in government and in other areas with regulation by the professional body (also exceeding 80 %).

The frequency distributions of the number of hours of mandatory CPE are given in Annex 4.

550 Professional Bodies and Qualification

One of the possible distinguishing factors between the professional bodies is the employment sector of their members. Contrary to expectation almost all of the professional bodies have members in each of the employment sectors that were considered. The results are presented in percentages.

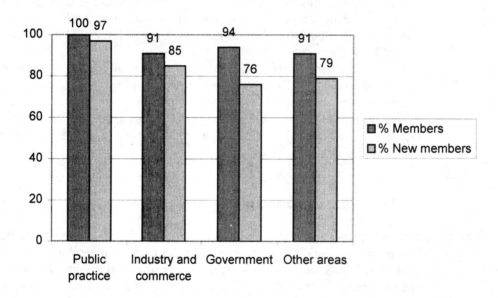

Table 550.1 Employment Sector

Membership Composition is discussed in the Chapters 6 and 7.

There is a marked difference between the average 30% of female members on 01/01/2001 and the average 38% of new female members in the year 2001. Moreover the number of new female members shows a marked increase with an average of 27% in 1995 and an expected 42% in 2005.

The allocation of members and of new members to employment sector differs. This can be considered to be a direct result of the regulation of practical training for the new members and of job development for the members.

Out of a total of 34 professional bodies three define 'to become a professional accountant' as the goal of accountancy education, three 'to become a professional auditor' and 28 combine the two objectives. In almost all cases the admission requirements to the profession include a formal final examination of professional competence (32 out of 34) with before the examination can be taken a prescribed programme of professional education (28 out of 34) and a prescribed programme of practical training or experience (22 out of 34).

The educational background of new members of 34 professional bodies in 2000 can be distinguished in university – non-university and in specific – non-specific.

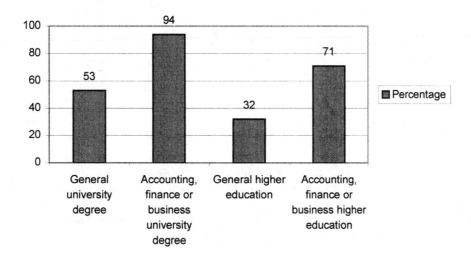

Table 550.2: Educational Background

The actual frequency distributions are compared in Chapter 6.

560   Professional Examination, Education and Training

This paragraph gives a general description of some of the major elements of the existing systems of the professional examination, education and training of accountants and auditors. Programme requirements are compared with international guidelines in the next paragraph. A further analysis and comparison is given in Chapter 6.

The objectives and methods of the final examination of professional competence as used by 32 professional bodies can be summarised as follows. Two professional bodies do not have a final examination. One, MIA in Malaysia, recognizes other qualifications, the other, SKwP in Poland is an association of accountants.

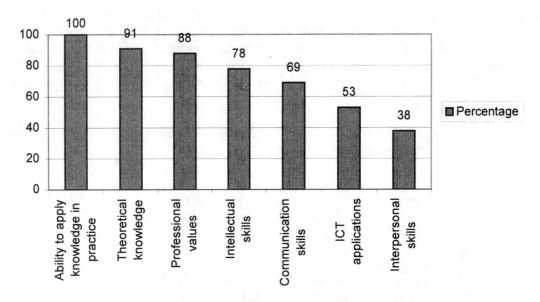

Table 560.1: Final Examination Objectives

Although interesting in itself this information, and the information about the examination methods given below must be handled with care in view of the different systems in use. For example with some professional bodies theoretical knowledge has been completely tested before the final examination, while with other professional bodies it is included in the final examination. Nevertheless it is relevant to compare the examination objectives with the examination methods.

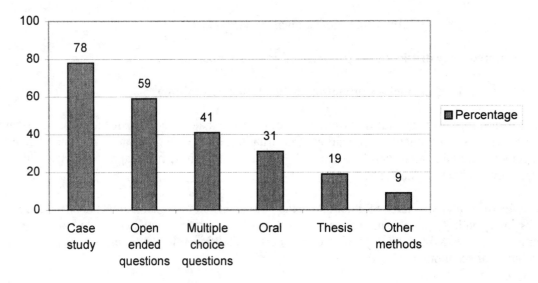

Table 560.2: Final Examination Methods

Professional bodies play a major role as providers of the final examination. Out of the total of 32 institutes 29 are providers of the final examination, of which in four cases together with the government, in one case together with the universities and in one case together with the government, universities and other providers. The government is the sole provider of the final examination in three cases. The majority of the respondents (29 out of 32) indicate that the necessary expertise and resources are available.

In 24 cases out of a total of 30 professional bodies offer professional education. Seven institutes are the sole provider of professional education. The others cooperate with universities (13) and/or commercial companies (9). In six cases universities provide professional education, in three of these commercial companies are also involved. The programme of professional education is completely full time (4), completely part time (15) or a combination (11). Combination of professional education with practical experience is mostly required (22 out of 30), sometimes possible (5) and seldom excluded (3). The majority of the respondents (29 out of 30) indicate that the necessary expertise and resources are available.

When practical training is mandatory it is mostly full time (27 out of 29). The normal amount of time is three years, with a minimum of one year and a maximum of five years. If part time practical training is allowed it is mostly on the condition that the corresponding number of days has to be met. The majority of the respondents (27 out of 29) indicate that the necessary expertise and resources are available.

The distribution of providers of practical training in relation to the employment sector is given below. This indicates possibilities, not the frequency distribution of the actual places of practical training. On average a majority of 70% of the trainees follow (part of) their practical training in public practice, 32% in industry and commerce, 15% in government and 16% in other areas.

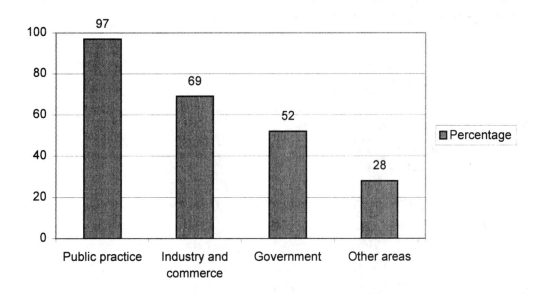

Table 560.3: Providers of Practical Training

570   Compliance with International Education Guidelines

Information has been gathered on the core programmes of professional education. Resulting summarised information is included in the overviews in Annex 3. In addition the subjects that are included in the required programmes of professional education were compared with a standardised list of subjects derived from the IFAC International Education Guidelines, the EU 8th Directive and the UNCTAD Guideline for a Global Accounting Curriculum. As probably could be expected the results show a high compliance in the matter of subjects, especially in the accounting and accounting related core programmes, combined with relatively less attention for skills.

Core subjects	Frequency	Percentage
Financial accounting and reporting	32 out of 32	100
Management accounting	32	100
Taxation	32	100
Auditing	32	100
Finance and financial management	32	100
Business and commercial law	31	97
Information and computer systems	31	97
Professional ethics	31	97
Economics	30	94
Quantitative methods and statistics for business	29	91
Organisational behaviour	29	91
Operations management	24	75
International business	23	72
Marketing	21	66

Table 570.1: Core subjects

In accordance with the definitions in IFAC IEG 9 skills were divided in intellectual skills, interpersonal skills and communication skills. The results are shown below.

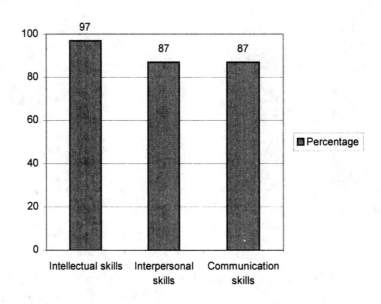

Table 570.2: Key Skills

ICT applications are either given directly or are included in subjects. The same applies to professional values. The table shows the results in relation to the core subjects in accounting and accounting related knowledge.

ICT Applications	Frequency	Professional Values	Frequency
Information & computer systems	26 out of 31	Auditing	30 out of 31
Financial accounting & reporting	23	Professional ethics	28
Auditing	22	Financial accounting & reporting	27
Management accounting	18		
Taxation	15	Taxation	26
Finance & financial management	15	Business & commercial law	23
Business & commercial law	11	Finance & financial management	23
Professional ethics	7		
		Management accounting	21
		Information. & computer systems	19

Table 570.3: ICT Applications

CHAPTER 6   CHARACTERISTICS OF ACCOUNTANCY EDUCATION

In this chapter the model for accountancy education is tested for relevance and interdependence of its variables. The resulting model is instrumental in the discussion of local and regional differences in accountancy education in Chapter 7.

600	Classification
610	Country Characteristics
620	Characteristics of the Accountancy Profession
630	Characteristics of Accountancy Education
640	Model of Accountancy Education

To facilitate the analysis the questions of the GAE questionnaire have been separated into clusters of possibly connected subjects.

- Cluster 1: Country Profile: see paragraph 610 and the previous analysis in Chapter 5
- Cluster 2: Regulation and Recognition: see paragraph 620
- Cluster 3: Professional Body: see paragraph 620
- Cluster 4: Professional Qualification and Background: see paragraph 620
- Cluster 5: Examination, Education and Training: see paragraph 630
- Cluster 6: Programme Requirements: see paragraph 630

Based on the discussion in the previous paragraphs the model parameters and their distinguishing values are summarised in paragraph 640.

600   Classification

This chapter is dedicated to the classification of accountancy education based on comparison and analysis of the country data that have been collected through the use of the global accountancy education questionnaire. Classification criteria, conceptual model of accountancy education and research methods have been discussed in the Chapters 3 and 4. Country results are summarised in Chapter 5 with overviews for each professional body in Annex 3. The comparative country studies are now used to test the model.

Research Question 6

Develop a classification of accountancy education based on a conceptual model and evaluation of distinguishing factors

The possible distinguishing factors that have been considered for their relevance can be divided in country characteristics, characteristics of the accountancy profession and characteristics of accountancy education. The country characteristics are discussed in paragraph 610. The characteristics of the accountancy profession are discussed in paragraph 620 and those of accountancy education in paragraph 630. The results of the analysis are the basis for the model of accountancy education that is described in paragraph 640.

To facilitate the analysis the questions of the GAE questionnaire have been separated into clusters of possibly connected subjects. The relation between paragraphs, clusters and questions is given in Table 600.1. Cluster Analysis Chapter 6

Table 600.1: Cluster Analysis Chapter 6

Table 600.1	Cluster Analysis Chapter 6	
	Cluster	**Question Numbers in the GAE Questionnaire**
Par. 610	**Country Characteristics**	
Cluster 1	**Country Profile**	
1.1	Country Size	1.1, 1.2, 1.3
1.2	Economic Position	1.4, 1.5, 1.6, 1.10
1.3	Country Background	1.9, 1.11, 1.12
Par. 620	**Accountancy Profession**	
Cluster 2	**Regulation and Recognition**	
2.1	Government and Recognition	2.1.2.1, 2.1.2.2, 3.2.2, 3.4.11, 3.5.15
2.2	International Position	2.1.2.3, 2.1.2.4, 2.1.2.5, 3.2.3, 3.2.4, 3.2.5, 3.2.6, 3.2.7, 3.2.8
2.3	Mandatory Membership	2.2.3
2.4	Mandatory CPE	2.2.4, 2.2.5, 2.2.6, 2.2.7, 2.2.8, 2.2.9, 2.2.10, 2.2.11, 2.2.12
2.5	Accounting System	1.7, 1.8
Cluster 3	**Professional Body**	
3.1	Number of Members	2.1.3.1, 2.1.3.2, 2.1.3.3, 2.1.3.9
3.2	Composition of Members	2.1.3.4, 2.1.3.5, 2.1.3.6, 2.1.3.7, 2.1.3.8
3.3	Number of New Members	2.3.1, 2.3.2, 2.3.3, 2.3.9, 2.3.10, 2.3.11, 2.3.12
3.4	Composition of New Members	2.3.4, 2.3.5, 2.3.6, 2.3.7, 2.3.8
Cluster 4	**Professional Qualification and Background**	
4.1	Education Background	2.3.13, 2.3.14, 2.3.15, 2.3.16, 2.3.17
4.2	Qualification Objective	3.1.1, 3.1.2
4.3	Qualification Standards	3.2.1, 3.3.10, 3.4.6, 3.5.1, 3.5.2, 3.6.4
4.4	Qualification Level	3.3.3, 3.4.5, 3.6.1, 3.6.2, 3.6.3
4.5	External Review	3.3.9, 3.4.12, 3.5.16
Par. 630	**Characteristics of Accountancy Education**	
Cluster 5	**Examination, Education and Training**	
5.1	Examination Objective	3.3.2, 3.3.1
5.2	Examination Methods	3.3.4, 3.3.5, 3.3.8
5.3	Examination Standards	3.3.6, 3.3.7
5.4	Providers, Expertise and Resources Exam. + Education	3.3.11, 3.3.12, 3.3.13, 3.4.9, 3.4.10, 3.4.11
5.5	Education Programme and Methods	3.4.2, 3.4.1, 3.4.3, 3.4.4
5.6	Education Standards	3.4.7, 3.5.7
5.7	Education and Training	3.4.8
5.8	Training Programme and Methods	3.5.4, 3.5.3, 3.5.5, 3.5.6, 3.5.17, 3.5.18
5.9	Providers, Expertise and Resources Training	3.5.8, 3.5.9, 3.5.10, 3.5.11, 3.5.12, 3.5.13, 3.5.14, 3.5.15
Cluster 6	**Programme Requirements**	
6.1	Subjects	4.1
6.2	Skills	4.2, 4.3, 4.4
6.3	ICT Applications	4.5
6.4	Professional Values	4.6

610   Country Characteristics

This paragraph covers the country profile (Cluster 1).

Cluster 1   Country Profile

The choice of country characteristics to be included in the model of accountancy education is based on an analysis of the country profile. This covers the country size, its economic position and background. Country Characteristics were already discussed in the Chapters 3, 4 and 5. The results are summarised below in relation to the questionnaire.

Country Size (Cluster 1.1)

Country Size: the population in millions (Q 1.1), the total labour force in millions (Q 1.2) and the female percentage of the labour force (Q 1.3).

The data discussed in paragraph 510 show that, with the exception of country size, these variables do not discriminate between countries. As a result they are not included as possible distinguishing factors in the research analysis and the model of accountancy education.

Economic Position (Cluster 1.2)

Economic Position: the Gross National Product in millions of USD (Q 1.4), the Gross National Product per capita (Q 1.5), the number of personal computers per 1000 people (Q 1.6) and the economic position (Q 1.10).

As is shown in paragraph 510 these data discriminate highly between countries, showing a dichotomy between on the one hand countries that in general can be classified as 'industrialised' and on the other hand countries that in general can be classified as 'in transition/emerging'. Although we recognize that there are important differences, especially in the second group, the two-way classification is included as a possible distinguishing factor in the research analysis and the model of accountancy education. This replaces the original distinction in 'industrialised', 'in transition' and 'emerging' used in Q 1.10.

Country Background (Cluster 1.3)

Country Background: the legal system (Q 1.9) and the cultural background, divided in power distance (Q 1.11) and uncertainty avoidance (Q 1.12). As mentioned before general information on higher education (Q 1.13) was not available.

The original distinction of legal systems used in the questionnaire included common law, codified roman or civil law, socialist law and philosophical religious as classes. As discussed in paragraph 310 consideration of recent literature and discussions with accountancy education experts worldwide were instrumental in the decision to distinguish common law and civil law as the two major classes relevant for the accountancy profession. The only country with major elements from both common and civil law is South Africa. Due to other characteristics that are discussed later in this chapter South Africa is classified as a common law country.

Statistical analysis shows that for the sample of countries included in the GAE project economic position and legal system can be considered to be independent variables. However there is association between power distance and uncertainty avoidance. Moreover both variables are associated with economic position. The cross tables are included in Annex 4.

As a result cultural background is not included in the model of accountancy education as a possible distinguishing factor. However differences in cultural background are considered in the discussion of regions in Chapter 7.

An overview of professional bodies, countries and regions with legal system and economic position is given in Table 610.1 Country Characteristics. The table contains the 28 countries out of an original sample of 29. For Senegal no country information was available. In the further analysis Argentina, Brazil and China are not included as there is too little information on accountancy qualification, education and training. With the exception of Turkey regions are given as in Chapter 3. Due to similarities in legal system, trade alliances and negotiations to achieve EU membership for economic reasons Turkey is considered in the group of Central and Eastern European countries.

Table 610.1: Country Characteristics

The two major parameters for the country profile are *economic position* and *legal system*.
Economic position is divided in (1) industrialised and (2) in transition/emerging.
Legal system is divided in (1) common law and (2) civil law.

620   Characteristics of the Accountancy Profession

This paragraph covers regulation and recognition (Cluster 2), professional body (Cluster 3) as well as professional qualification and background (Cluster 4). In total the position of 34 professional bodies is analysed in 25 countries, of which 11 in industrialised common law countries, 9 in common law countries with emerging or transition economies, 6 in industrialised civil law countries and 8 in civil law countries with emerging or transition economies. Lack of information made it necessary to exclude Argentina, Brazil and China. If in the analysis in this and the next chapter the number does not add up to 34 the reason is that for certain subjects information from individual professional bodies is not available.

Cluster 2   Regulation and Recognition

Regulation and Recognition is divided in government and recognition (Cluster 2.1), international position (Cluster 2.2), mandatory membership (Cluster 2.3), mandatory CPE (Cluster 2.4) and accounting system (Cluster 2.5).

Government and Recognition (Cluster 2.1)

Government and Recognition: regulation of the accountancy sector (Q 2.1.2.1), recognition of the accountancy sector (Q 2.1.2.2), responsibility for qualification standards (Q 3.2.2), recognition of the providers of professional education (Q 3.4.11) and recognition of the providers of practical training (Q 3.5.15).

To achieve comparability a measure has been sought to distinguish between government regulation and professional self-regulation. To achieve this goal relative values have been added to the answers to the questions in cluster 2.1. The relative values were chosen to give a total value of 0 with mixed government and professional responsibility. The weight of the first three subjects is 2, as is the combined weight of the last two.

Regulation accountancy sector:	by law –2; by professional self-regulation +2; by both 0.
Recognition accountancy profession:	as a regulatory and a disciplinary body +2; as a regulatory or a disciplinary body 0; as neither –2 (–2 does not exist).
Responsibility qualification standards:	government -2; professional body +2; both 0
Recognition professional education:	by government -1; by professional body +1; by both 0.
Recognition practical training:	by government -1; by professional body +1; by both 0.

For each professional body the values are given in Table 620.1 Government and Recognition.

Table 610.1		Country Characteristics			
Professional Body	Country	Region	Economic Position	Legal System	Remarks
CGA Canada	Canada	North and Middle America	industrialised	common law	
CMA Canada	Canada	North and Middle America	industrialised	common law	
ICAAlberta	Canada	North and Middle America	industrialised	common law	
AICPA	USA	North and Middle America	industrialised	common law	
ACCA	United Kingdom	European Union	industrialised	common law	
ICAEW	United Kingdom	European Union	industrialised	common law	
ICAS	United Kingdom	European Union	industrialised	common law	
CPA Australia	Australia	Far East	industrialised	common law	
ICA Australia	Australia	Far East	industrialised	common law	
HKSA	Hong Kong	Far East	industrialised	common law	
ICANZ	New Zealand	Far East	industrialised	common law	
ICPAK	Kenya	Africa	in trans./emerging	common law	islamic and customary law inf.
SAICA	South Africa	Africa	in trans./emerging	common law	strong civil law influences
ICA India	India	Asia	in trans./emerging	common law	islamic and customary law inf.
ICWAI	India	Asia	in trans./emerging	common law	islamic and customary law inf.
MACPA	Malaysia	Asia	in trans./emerging	common law	
MIA	Malaysia	Asia	in trans./emerging	common law	
ICAP	Pakistan	Asia	in trans./emerging	common law	islamic law influences
ICMAP	Pakistan	Asia	in trans./emerging	common law	islamic law influences
SOCPA	Saudi Arabia	Middle East	in trans./emerging	common law	islamic law influences
ORDRE	France	European Union	industrialised	civil law	
IDW	Germany	European Union	industrialised	civil law	
NIVRA	Netherlands	European Union	industrialised	civil law	
IACJCE	Spain	European Union	industrialised	civil law	
FAR	Sweden	European Union	industrialised	civil law	
JICPA	Japan	Far East	industrialised	civil law	
FACPCE	Argentina	South America	in trans./emerging	civil law	
IBRACON	Brazil	South America	in trans./emerging	civil law	
IMCP	Mexico	North and Middle America	in trans./emerging	civil law	
CICPA	China	Asia	in trans./emerging	civil law	customary law influences
CACR	Czech Republic	Central Eastern Europe	in trans./emerging	civil law	
CHA	Hungary	Central Eastern Europe	in trans./emerging	civil law	
SKwP	Poland	Central Eastern Europe	in trans./emerging	civil law	
KIBR	Poland	Central Eastern Europe	in trans./emerging	civil law	
IPA Russia	Russian Federation	Central Eastern Europe	in trans./emerging	civil law	
LACPA	Lebanon	Middle East	in trans./emerging	civil law	
TURMOB	Turkey	Central Eastern Europe	in trans./emerging	civil law	region on economic grounds

Table 620.1		Government and Recognition					
Professional Body	**Country**	**Regulation Acc. Sector**	**Recognition Prof. Body**	**Qualification Standards**	**Professional Education**	**Practical Training**	**Regulation Index**
							HPS (6,7,8)
		by law -2	regulatory 0	government -2	government -1	government -1	EPS (3,4,5)
		prof. selfr. +2	disciplinary 0	profession +2	profession +1	profession +1	EGR (0,1,2)
		both 0	both+2	both 0	both 0	both 0	HGR (-4,-3, ,-2,-1)
Industrialised, common law							
CGA Canada	Canada	both	both	both	profession	profession	emphasis PS
CMA Canada	Canada	prof. selfr.	both	profession	profession	profession	high PS
ICAAlberta	Canada	both	both	profession	profession	profession	high PS
AICPA	USA	both	disciplinary	both	government	government	high GR
ACCA	UK	both	both	both	both	profession	emphasis PS
ICAEW	UK	both	both	both	profession	profession	emphasis PS
ICAS	UK	both	both	both	both	profession	emphasis PS
CPAAustralia	Australia	both	both	profession	profession	profession	high PS
ICAA	Australia	prof. selfr.	both	profession	profession	profession	high PS
HKSA	Hong Kong	both	both	profession	both	not available	emphasis PS
ICANZ	NZealand	both	both	profession	both	profession	emphasis PS
In trans/emerg, common law							
ICPAK	Kenya	both	both	profession	both	not available	emphasis PS
SAICA	South Africa	both	both	profession	profession	profession	high PS
ICAIndia	India	both	both	profession	both	profession	emphasis PS
ICWAI	India	by law	both	both	profession	both	emphasis GR
MACPA	Malaysia	both	both	profession	both	profession	emphasis PS
MIA	Malaysia	both	both	both	profession	not appplicable	emphasis PS
ICAP	Pakistan	both	both	profession	government	profession	emphasis PS
ICMAP	Pakistan	both	regulatory	profession	profession	profession	emphasis PS
SOCPA	Saudi Arabia	both	regulatory	both	government	both	high GR
Industrialised, civil law							
ORDRE	France	both	both	both	government	profession	emphasis GR
IDW	Germany	both	both	government	not appplicable	profession	emphasis GR
NIVRA	Netherlands	both	both	both	government	profession	emphasis GR
IACJCE	Spain	by law	disciplinary	both	government	profession	high GR
FAR	Sweden	both	regulatory	government	government	government	high GR
JICPA	Japan	by law	disciplinary	government	not available	not available	high GR
In trans/emerg, civil law							
IMCP	Mexico	both	both	profession	both	not available	emphasis PS
CACR	Czech Rep.	both	both	both	not appplicable	both	emphasis GR
CHA	Hungary	by law	regulatory	profession	profession	profession	emphasis GR
SKwP	Poland	by law	both	government	not appplicable	not appplicable	high GR
KIBR	Poland	both	both	both	profession	profession	emphasis PS
IPARussia	Russian Fed	both	disciplinary	both	profession	not appplicable	emphasis GR
LACPA	Lebanon	both	both	both	not appplicable	profession	emphasis PS
TURMOB	Turkey	both	both	both	government	profession	emphasis GR

Table 620.1: Government and Recognition

Some general observations on the distinction between government regulation and professional self-regulation are given below for 34 professional bodies.

Government Regulation versus Professional Self-regulation	Mean
Overall for 34 professional bodies in 25 countries	2,68
Common law for 20 professional bodies in 12 countries	4
of which industrialised 11 professional bodies in 6 countries	4,45
and in transition/emerging 9 professional bodies in 6 countries	3,44
Civil law for 14 professional bodies in 13 countries	0,79
of which industrialised 6 professional bodies in 6 countries	-0,83
and in transition/emerging 8 professional bodies in 7 countries	2
	-

Table 620.2: Government and Professional Self-regulation

Overall there is a marked difference between common law countries and civil law countries in the relative importance of professional self-regulation compared with government regulation. Industrialised common law countries score higher in professional self-regulation than common law countries with economies that are in transition or emerging. For civil law countries the situation is reversed with high government regulation for industrialised countries. This may well be an effect of EU regulation as five out of the six industrialised, civil law countries are members of the European Union.

The total values range from –4 to +8. These can be divided in four groups to be distinguished in the *regulation index* (see Table 620.1)

High professional self-regulation (HPS):	values 6, 7 and 8 with 5 professional bodies
Emphasis on professional self-regulation (EPS):	values 3, 4 and 5 with 15 professional bodies
Emphasis on government regulation (EGR):	values 0, 1 and 2 with 9 professional bodies
High government regulation (HGR):	values -4, -3, -2 and –1 with 5 professional bodies

International Position (Cluster 2.2)

International position: IFAC membership (Q 2.1.2.3), membership of other organisations (Q 2.1.2.4 and 2.1.2.5), international standards on accountancy education (Q 3.2.3 and 3.2.4), international recognition of qualifications (Q 3.2.5, 3.2.6, 3.2.7 and 3.2.8).

As shown in paragraph 540 the position of IFAC is well established: 33 out of 34 professional bodies are member with for the moment IPA Russia as the only exception. This means that for the countries in the research project IFAC membership is not a distinguishing factor. However, in view of future use of the model, IFAC membership is included as one of the parameters in the model. Most of the professional bodies are also affiliated to one or more mostly regional organisations of accountants. Information about possible education activities of regional bodies is outside the project, so for the moment a decision whether membership of regional organisations of accountants should be included in the accountancy education model was postponed.

The IFAC International Education Guidelines with emphasis on IEG 9 are followed at least partly on a voluntary basis by 26 of 34 professional bodies with emphasis on IFAC IEG 9. With the exception of Saudi Arabia all professional bodies in common law countries follow IFAC Education Guidelines. Seven professional bodies in civil law countries do not follow the IFAC Education Guidelines. Three of those implement EU Directives on a mandatory basis, one on a voluntary basis. Three professional bodies in civil law countries do neither follow IFAC Education Guidelines nor EU Directives. These are JICPA in Japan, IPA Russia in the Russian Federation and LACPA in Lebanon.

IFAC is moving from Education Guidelines to Education Standards. These will be mandatory for IFAC members. Inside the European Union EU Directives are mandatory. In the near future they will also be mandatory for new member states from Central and Eastern Europe. As the analysis in Chapter 2 shows the IFAC Education Guidelines and the EU 8th Directive cover the same areas of expertise. Other guidelines or directives were not mentioned in the answers to the questionnaire.

The coincidence between the guidelines and directives is also illustrated by the fact that three EU professional bodies in a common law country and two in civil law countries implement both. As a result it seems logical to include one model parameter based on the voluntary or mandatory implementation of (1) IFAC International Education Guidelines or (2) EU Directives on the qualification of auditors. An overview is given in Table 620.3 International Position and Membership.

Table 620.3 International Position and Membership Regulation

Recognition of qualifications has been achieved from the home country in other countries (24 professional bodies out of 34) and from other countries in the home country (28 out of 34). This is mostly partial recognition on an individual basis with admittance to examinations and exemptions. Some form of mutual recognition is usual for common law countries, whether they are industrialised or in transition or emerging. The MACPA qualification is not recognized outside Malaysia but qualifications from outside Malaysia can be recognized. MIA has a specific position as a regulatory body for Malaysia. The situation is different for civil law countries. EU countries have a system of mandatory mutual recognition. Outside the EU for Japan no agreement is mentioned, neither is there for most of the civil law countries, which have emerging or transition economies. Chapter 7 gives a description on a country-by-country basis. The results at this moment in time do not yet warrant inclusion as a model parameter.

Mandatory membership and mandatory CPE (Clusters 2.3 and 2.4)

Mandatory membership and mandatory CPE: mandatory membership (Q 2.2.3); mandatory CPE (Q 2.2.4) in public practice (Q 2.2.5 and 2.2.6), in industry and commerce (Q 2.2.7 and 2.2.8), in government (Q 2.2.9 and 2.2.10) and in other areas (Q 2.2.11 and 2.2.12).

The overall situation is described in paragraph 540. Mandatory membership exists in 23 out of 34 cases and is generally required to use the professional title. Only three professional bodies, MACPA in Malaysia, SKwP in Poland and TURMOB in Turkey, do not have mandatory CPE. In all other cases continuing professional education is mandatory for members in public practice (32 out of 32) and is almost always regulated by the professional body (30 out of 32). The only exceptions are AICPA in the USA and SAICA in South Africa. In most cases (exceeding 80 %) CPE is also mandatory for members in industry and commerce, in government and in other areas with regulation by the professional body (also exceeding 80 %).

Mandatory membership and mandatory CPE have been compared on professional self-regulation by adding the relative values for mandatory membership and for mandatory CPE in relation to employment sector. The employment sectors considered are public practice, industry and commerce, government and other.

Table 620.3		International Position		Membership Regulation				
		Education Guidelines						
							Regulation	Membership
Professional Body	Country	IFAC IEG #9	EU 8th Directive	Mandatory Members.	Members. Categories	Mandatory CPE	CPE by the Prof. Body	Regulation Index
					a publ. pract.	c governm.		high
					b ind.& com.	d other		medium
								low
Industrialised, common law								
CGA Canada	Canada	IFAC		yes	abcd	abcd	abcd	high
CMA Canada	Canada	IFAC		yes	abcd	abcd	abcd	high
ICAAlberta	Canada	IFAC		yes	abcd	abcd	abcd	high
AICPA	USA	IFAC		no	abcd	abcd		medium
ACCA	UK	IFAC	EU	yes	abcd	a	a	medium
ICAEW	UK	IFAC	EU	yes	abcd	a	a	medium
ICAS	UK	IFAC	EU	yes	abcd	abcd	a	high
CPAAustralia	Australia	IFAC		no	abcd	abcd	abcd	high
ICAA	Australia	IFAC		yes	abcd	abcd	abcd	high
HKSA	Hong Kong	IFAC		yes	abcd	abcd	abcd	high
ICANZ	New Zealand	IFAC		yes	abcd	abcd	abcd	high
In trans/emerg, common law								
ICPAK	Kenya	IFAC		no	abcd	abcd	abcd	high
SAICA	South Africa	IFAC		yes	abcd	abcd		medium
ICAIndia	India	IFAC		yes	abcd	ab	ab	medium
ICWAI	India	IFAC		yes	abcd	abcd	abcd	high
MACPA	Malaysia	IFAC		yes	abcd			low
MIA	Malaysia	IFAC		yes	abcd	abcd	abcd	high
ICAP	Pakistan	IFAC		no	abcd	abcd	abcd	high
ICMAP	Pakistan	IFAC		yes	abcd	abcd	abcd	high
SOCPA	Saudi Arabia			yes	abcd	abcd	abcd	high
Industrialised, civil law								
ORDRE	France	IFAC	EU	yes	abcd	abcd	abcd	high
IDW	Germany		EU	no	a	a	a	high
NIVRA	Netherlands	IFAC	EU	yes	abcd	abcd	abcd	high
IACJCE	Spain		EU	no	abcd	a	a	high
FAR	Sweden		EU	no	ac	ac	ac	high
JICPA	Japan			yes	abcd	abd	a	medium
In trans/emerg, civil law								
IMCP	Mexico	IFAC		yes	abcd	abcd	abcd	high
CACR	Czech Rep.	IFAC	EU	yes	a	a	a	high
CHA	Hungary	IFAC		yes	abcd	abcd	abd	high
SKwP	Poland	IFAC		no	abcd			low
KIBR	Poland		EU	yes	abcd	abcd	abcd	high
IPARussia	Russian Fed			no	abcd	abcd	abcd	high
LACPA	Lebanon			yes	abcd	abcd	abcd	high
TURMOB	Turkey	IFAC		yes	abcd			low

Mandatory membership: value 2; no mandatory membership value 0.
Mandatory CPE for each relevant employment sector: values 0 to 4^{29}.
Regulation by the profession of mandatory CPE: values 0 to 4^{30}.

The total scores have been separated in three categories: High (8-10), Medium (4-6) and Low (0-3).
In most cases (24 out of 34) the score on the *membership regulation index* is High, in six cases it is Medium and in four it is Low (see Table 620.3 International Position and Membership Regulation). The country situation is discussed in Chapter 7. There is no general relation visible with country characteristics or with government regulation versus professional self-regulation.

Accounting System (Cluster 2.5)

Accounting system: accounting and auditing system (Q1.7), compliance with IAS/ISA (Q1.8).

A summary description of accounting rules in each country, derived from GAAP 2000, is given in paragraph 540. In general these descriptions correlate with the relative importance of government regulation and professional self-regulation as discussed in this chapter. For that reason it is not necessary to include regulation of the accounting system as a possible separate parameter in the model of accountancy education. This is even more the case for auditing as the ISA are not in general use and, for example, implementation by the EU is unlikely in view of the present developments in the USA.

Cluster 3   Professional Body

Professional Body is divided in number and composition of members and of new members (Cluster 3).

Number and Composition of Members (Clusters 3.1 and 3.2)

Number and Composition of Members: members on 01/01/2001 (Q 2.1.3.1), members on 01/01/1996 (Q 2.1.3.2), members on 01/01/2006 (Q 2.1.3.3), female members on 01/01/2001 (Q 2.1.3.9), employment sector (Q 2.1.3.4), percentage public practice (Q 2.1.3.5), percentage industry and commerce (Q 2.1.3.6), percentage government (Q 2.1.3.7), percentage other areas (Q 2.1.3.8).

Number and Composition of New Members (Clusters 3.3 and 3.4)

Number and Composition of New Members: new members in 2000 (Q 2.3.1), new members in 1995 (Q 2.3.2), new members in 2005 (Q 2.3.3), average age new members in 2000 (Q 2.3.9), new female members 2000 (Q 2.3.10), new female members 1995 (Q 2.3.11), new female members 2005 (Q 2.3.12), employment sector (Q 2.3.4), percentage public practice (Q 2.3.5), percentage industry and commerce (Q 2.3.6), percentage government (Q 2.3.7), percentage other areas (Q 2.3.8).

A selection of information on members and new members and of their employment sector is included in the Table Membership Composition.

Table 620.4: Membership Composition

For classification purposes membership in 2000 is considered. In view of qualification objectives and the existing or necessary systems of professional education and training a particular importance has to be attached to the employment sector of members and of new members. Most professional bodies have members in all four sectors: public practice, industry and commerce, government and other areas. As the primary focus of the research project is on accountants and auditors in public practice the following distinction has been made.

---

[29] The value is 4 if CPE is mandatory for all existing employment sectors
[30] The value is 4 if each employment sector with mandatory CPE is regulated by the profession.

Table 620.4		Membership Composition						
Professional Body	Country	Members. Categories	New Members	Members % Public Practice	NewMem % Public Practice	Position Public Practice	Female % Memb	Additional% NewFemale Members
		a publ. pract.	c governm.					
		b ind.& com.	d other	M members	N new memb.	1high 4low		
Industrialised, common law								
CGA Canada	Canada	abcd	abcd	0-25%	0-25%	MN 4	25-50%	17%
CMA Canada	Canada	abcd	abcd	0-25%	0-25%	MN 4	25-50%	6%
ICAAlberta	Canada	abcd	a	25-50%	.100%	M3 N1	25-50%	23%
AICPA	USA	abcd	abcd	25-50%	75-100%	M3 N1	25-50%	19%
ACCA	UK	abcd	abcd	25-50%	25-50%	MN 3	25-50%	17%
ICAEW	UK	abcd	abc	25-50%	75-100%	M3 N1	0-25%	19%
ICAS	UK	abcd	ab	25-50%	25-50%	MN 3	0-25%	21%
CPAAustralia	Australia	abcd	abcd	0-25%	0-25%	MN 4	25-50%	8%
ICAA	Australia	abcd	abcd	25-50%	50-75%	M3 N2	0-25%	17%
HKSA	Hong Kong	abcd	abcd	25-50%	25-50%	MN 3	25-50%	15%
ICANZ	New Zealand	abcd	abcd	25-50%	not avail	M3	25-50%	not available
In trans/emerg, common law								
ICPAK	Kenya	abcd	abcd	25-50%	25-50%	MN 3	0-25%	-7%
SAICA	South Africa	abcd	abcd	0-25%	25-50%	M4 N3	0-25%	18%
ICAIndia	India	abcd	abcd	50-75%	50-75%	MN 2	0-25%	11%
ICWAI	India	abcd	abcd	0-25%	0-25%	MN 4	0-25%	unchanged
MACPA	Malaysia	abcd	ab	50-75%	75-100%	M2 N1	25-50%	17%
MIA	Malaysia	abcd	abcd	25-50%	25-50%	MN 3	25-50%	-2%
ICAP	Pakistan	abcd	bd?	0-25%	0-25%	MN 4	25-50%	-3%
ICMAP	Pakistan	abcd	abcd	0-25%	0-25%	MN 4	0-25%	19%
SOCPA	Saudi Arabia	abcd	abc	25-50%	25-50%	MN 3	0-25%	unchanged
Industrialised, civil law								
ORDRE	France	abcd	not avail	not avail	not avail		not avail	not available
IDW	Germany	a	a	.100%	.100%	MN 1	75-100%	-58%
NIVRA	Netherlands	abcd	abcd	25-50%	25-50%	MN 3	0-25%	16%
IACJCE	Spain	abcd	abcd	25-50%	0-25%	M3 N4	0-25%	10%
FAR	Sweden	ac	a	.100%	.100%	MN 1	0-25%	22%
JICPA	Japan	abcd	a	.100%	.100%	MN 1	0-25%	11%
In trans/emerg, civil law								
IMCP	Mexico	abcd	abcd	75-100%	75-100%	MN 1	0-25%	10%
CACR	Czech Rep.	a	a	75-100%	.100%	MN 1	25-50%	16%
CHA	Hungary	abcd	abcd	75-100%	25-50%	M1 N3	50-75%	4%
SKwP	Poland	abcd	abcd	25-50%	25-50%	MN 3	50-75%	unchanged
KIBR	Poland	abcd	abcd	75-100%	75-100%	MN 1	50-75%	15%
IPARussia	Russian Fed	abcd	abcd	0-25%	0-25%	MN 4	50-75%	unchanged
LACPA	Lebanon	abcd	abcd	75-100%	75-100%	MN 1	0-25%	unchanged
TURMOB	Turkey	abcd	abcd	50-75%	50-75%	MN 2	0-25%	5%

Percentage of members and of new members in public practice:
(1) 75-100%, (2) 50-75%, (3) 25-50%, (4) 0-25%

For most professional bodies the percentage of members in public practice and the percentage of new members in public practice fall either in the same group or in adjacent categories. Effectively this leads to a four-way classification with some exemptions.

All professional bodies in common law countries with the exception of ICA India and MACPA in Malaysia fall in category (3) or (4). Institutes of cost and management accountants – CMA Canada, ICWAI in India and ICMAP in Pakistan – belong to category (4), but not exclusively as CGA Canada, CPA Australia and SAICA in South Africa belong to the same category. For some professional bodies the situation is quite different for new members. The clearest examples with all or almost all new members in public practice while membership is spread over all employment sectors are ICA Alberta in Canada, AICPA in the USA and ICAEW in the UK. For ICA Alberta and ICAEW the explanation can be sought in the requirements for practical training, which are explored later. For AICPA however practical training is not a requirement for qualification, although it may be for licensing.

Most professional bodies in civil law countries fall in category (1). Exemptions are in category (2) TURMOB in Turkey, in category (3) NIVRA in the Netherlands, IACJCE in Spain and SKwP in Poland, and in category (4) IPA Russia. In some cases the number of new members in public practice is lower than the number of members in public practice. This is the case for IACJCE in Spain and for CHA in Hungary.

For classification purposes the following distinction in employment sectors in effect covers all possibilities: (1) members and new members in all employment sectors; (2) members in all employment sectors; new members in public practice; (3) members and new members in public practice.

The results on a country-by-country basis are further discussed in Chapter 7.

In addition to membership categories in view of their potential importance for education and training some trends on the number of members can be given. If MIA in Malaysia as a regulatory body and SKwP in Poland as an association of accountants are disregarded 29 professional bodies in the survey for which the information is available at the end of the year 2000 had in total 1.080.000 members. At the moment the questionnaire was filled in a further growth to 1.150.000 members at the end of the year 2005 was expected. This of course was before 'ENRON' had a tremendous impact on the accountancy profession.

For 23 professional bodies out of 33 the percentage of new female members in 2000 is higher than that of female members. The increase is given in Table 620.4. If IDW with a very high percentage of female members and an increase in the percentage of new male members is disregarded the following picture emerges. Overall there is a 10% increase in new female members compared with female members in 2000. Most professional bodies (26 out of 31) expect a further growth of the percentage of new female members in 2005, but the average percentage is now 6%. This could mean that the trend towards an increasing percentage of female members is levelling out.

Cluster 4   Professional Qualification and Background

Professional Qualification and Background is divided in education background, qualification objective, standards and level of qualifications, external review.

Education Background (Cluster 4.1)

Education Background: new members with a general university degree (Q 2.3.13 and 2.3.14), with a accounting, finance or business university degree (Q 2.3.13 and 2.3.15), with general higher education (Q 2.3.13 and 2.3.16) and with accounting, finance or business higher education (Q 2.3.13 and 2.3.17).

Information on the professional qualification and background is included in Table 620.5 Professional Qualification.

Table 620.5: Professional Qualification

The education background of candidates can be divided in general university degree (GU in Table 620.5), accounting, finance or business university degree (AU), general higher education (GH) and accounting, finance or business higher education (AH). Considering education background the same distinction in degree percentages can be used as in membership percentages in public practice. Percentages of 10% and lower were neglected.

(1) 75-100% (H=High), (2) 50-75% (E=Emphasis), (3) 25-50%, (4) 10-25%

Looking at the actual figures in the table it was decided to focus for classification purposes on the first two categories (High and Emphasis). The results are given in Table 620.5. Based on the descriptions of the admission requirements it was possible to classify the professional bodies for which the actual percentages were not available. In the Table this is marked with *. The results show that 27 out of 34 professional bodies have either a high percentage of new members with an accountancy, finance or business university degree or emphasis in that sector. Another four professional bodies have either a high percentage of new members with a general university degree (HGU) or emphasis in that sector (EGU).

Three professional bodies do not fit in one of the above categories. ICAEW has a mixture of the categories EGU and EAU. ICPAK has a slight emphasis on general higher education (EGH). ICAP and IMCP attract members with accountancy, finance or business higher education (HAH).

Qualification Objective, Standards and Level (Clusters 4.2, 4.3 and 4.4)

Qualification Objective: accountant, auditor, specialisation (Q 3.1.1 and 3.1.2)
Qualification Standards: admission requirements to the profession (Q 3.2.1), to the final examination (Q 3.3.10), to professional education (Q 3.4.6), to practical training (Q 3.5.1 and 3.5.2), university entrance level (Q 3.6.4)
Qualification Level: level final examination (Q 3.3.3), level professional education (Q 3.4.5), degree and programme requirements (Q 3.6.1, 3.6.2 and 3.6.3)

The main qualification objectives mentioned in the questionnaire are accountant and auditor. Clear definitions for general use are not available. IFAC defines 'accountant' as a member of a professional body that is a member of IFAC. This of course includes external audit. For the majority of the professional bodies the qualification objective is accountant and auditor (28 out of 34). There is no clear classification distinction. Specialisation is disregarded as in most cases, if mentioned at all, there was no visible differentiation in programme requirements.

The admission requirements to the profession in general include a final examination of professional competence (32 out of 34). For MIA it is not directly relevant as it does not have its own qualification but recognizes qualifications for professionals who want to practice in Malaysia. SKwP in Poland as an association of accountants does not have its own final examination. Admission requirements for professional education and practical training are discussed as part of the education system. It was not possible to use the information on the qualification level in the categories postgraduate, graduate and undergraduate because of differences in the definitions that were used by the respondents. University

Table 620.5		Professional Qualification							
Professional Body	Country	Degree a gen univ b acc univ c gen high d acc high	General university degree	Accounting finance business university degree	General higher education	Accounting finance business higher education	Degree Cate-gory	Qualification Objective Accountant Auditor Both	Qualification Standards a final examin. b university entrance c ext. review
Industrialised, common law									
CGA Canada	Canada	abcd	25-50%	0-25%	25-50%		EGU	acc&auditor	ac
CMA Canada	Canada	ab	not avail.	not avail.			HAU*	acc&auditor	ab
ICAAlberta	Canada	b		75-100%			HAU	accountant	abc
AICPA	USA	b		75-100%			HAU	acc&auditor	abc
ACCA	UK	abcd	0-25%	25-50%		0-25%	EAU	acc&auditor	abc
ICAEW	UK	abcd	25-50%	25-50%			EGU/AU	acc&auditor	abc
ICAS	UK	abd	25-50%	50-75%			EAU	acc&auditor	abc
CPAAustralia	Australia	b		75-100%			HAU	accountant	abc
ICAA	Australia	ab		75-100%			HAU	acc&auditor	abc
HKSA	Hong Kong	abcd	0-25%	50-75%			EAU	acc&auditor	abc
ICANZ	N Zealand	abd	not avail.	not avail.		not avail.	HAU*	acc&auditor	abc
In trans/emerg, common law									
ICPAK	Kenya	abcd		25-50%	25-50%	not avail.	EGH	acc&auditor	ac
SAICA	South Africa	bd		75-100%			HAU	acc&auditor	abc
ICAIndia	India	abcd		75-100%			HAU	acc&auditor	ac
ICWAI	India	ab	25-50%	50-75%			EAU	acc&auditor	abc
MACPA	Malaysia	bcd		50-75%	25-50%	0-25%	EAU	acc&auditor	ab
MIA	Malaysia	bd		50-75%		30%	EAU	accountant	not applicable
ICAP	Pakistan	bd		not avail.		not avail.	HAH*	acc&auditor	ab
ICMAP	Pakistan	ab	75-100%	0-25%			HGU	acc&auditor	ab
SOCPA	S Arabia	bd		75-100%		0-25%	HAU	acc&auditor	abc
Industrialised, civil law									
ORDRE	France	bcd		not avail.	not avail.	not avail.	EAU*	acc&auditor	abc
IDW	Germany	bd		75-100%			HAU	auditor	ab
NIVRA	Netherlands	bd		75-100%		0-25%	HAU	acc&auditor	abc
IACJCE	Spain	abcd		75-100%			HAU	acc&auditor	abc
FAR	Sweden	b		75-100%			HAU	acc&auditor	abc
JICPA	Japan	a	75-100%				HGU	auditor	abc
In trans/emerg, civil law									
IMCP	Mexico	b		75-100%			HAU	acc&auditor	abc
CACR	Czech Rep.	abcd	not avail.	not avail.	not avail.	not avail.	EAU*	acc&auditor	abc
CHA	Hungary	bd		50-75%		25-50%	EAU	acc&auditor	abc
SKwP	Poland	abcd	25-50%	50-75%			EAU	acc&auditor	not applicable
KIBR	Poland	ab	25-50%	50-75%			EAU	auditor	ab
IPARussia	Russian Fed	bd		75-100%		0-25%	HAU	acc&auditor	abc
LACPA	Lebanon	abd	50-75%	25-50%			EGU	acc&auditor	ab
TURMOB	Turkey	bd		75-100%		0-25%	HAU	acc&auditor	ab

entrance level is usually requested. The only exemptions are CGA Canada, ICPAK in Kenya, ICA India and SKwP in Poland. CGA Canada requests a bachelor's degree before qualification.

External Review (Cluster 4.5)

External review: external review of the final examination (Q 3.3.9), periodic review of professional education (Q 3.4.12), of practical training (Q 3.5.16)

External review of the final examination is the usual situation with a limited number of exceptions, mainly in countries with emerging or transition economies. In the industrialised countries the only exceptions are CMA Canada and IDW in Germany. CMA Canada has full responsibility for the examination, so the review is internal. In Germany the government is directly responsible for the examination. The other professional bodies without external review of the final examination are MACPA in Malaysia, ICMAP in Pakistan, KIBR in Poland, LACPA in Lebanon and TURMOB in Turkey.

The actual allocation of professional bodies to categories of education background and qualification is described in Chapter 7.

630   Characteristics of Accountancy Education

The subjects on accountancy education are divided into examination, education and training (Cluster 5) and programme requirements (Cluster 6).

Cluster 5   Examination, Education and Training

Examination, Education and Training is divided in final examination objective, methods and standards; professional education programme, methods and standards; practical training programme, methods and standards; providers, expertise and resources final examination, professional education and practical training.

Final Examination Objective, Methods and Standards (Clusters 5.1, 5.2 and 5.3)

Examination Objective: examination objectives (Q 3.3.2), core programme (Q 3.3.1)
Examination Methods: methods (Q 3.3.4), length (Q 3.3.5), conditions and procedures (Q 3.3.8)
Examination Standards: pass mark (Q 3.3.6), pass rate (Q 3.3.7)

In order to distinguish between possible kinds of examinations the core programme, the objectives, the methods and the entrance requirements have been compared on a scale between 'theory oriented' (TH) and 'practice oriented' (PR). For each of the four parameters the total value is 2 to be allocated as follows: (2 to theory), (1 to theory and 1 to practice) or (2 to practice). The total for theory and for practice determines the relative position of the examination on the scale between 'theory oriented' and 'practice oriented'.

Core programme: based on an evaluation of the core programmes of the final examination the following distinction has been made.
- Emphasis on subjects (theory 2)
- Emphasis on application (practice 2)
- Mixed (theory 1, practice 1)

Objectives: the objectives of the final examination have been classified as follows.
- Emphasis on theoretical knowledge, ability to apply knowledge in practice, intellectual skills (theory 2)
- Emphasis on skills, ICT applications, professional values (practice 2)

- Mixed (theory 1, practice 1)

Methods: the methods of the final examination have been classified as follows.
- Emphasis on open ended and multiple choice questions (theory 2)
- Emphasis on case study, thesis, oral, other methods (practice 2)
- Mixed (theory 1, practice 1)

Entrance requirements: entrance requirements to the final examination have been classified as follows.
- Professional and/or general education (theory 2)
- Practical experience (practice 2)
- Mixed (theory 1, practice 1)

On a scale between 0 and 8 the following categories can be distinguished for the final examination.
- Theoretical orientation: value 6,7,8 for theory, corresponding with 2,1,0 for practice
- Mix theoretical and practical: value 3,4,5 for theory, corresponding with 5,4,3 for practice
- Practical orientation: value 0,1,2 for theory, corresponding with 8,7,6 for practice

The outcomes have been compared with pass mark and pass rate and with conditions and procedures. The answers are summarised in Table 630.1: Final Examination. The length of the final examination was not used, as the answers were not comparable through differences in the definitions in the various systems.

Table 630.1: Final Examination

Overall most professional bodies (20 out of 34) have a mixed approach in their final examination with comparable attention for theory and practice. A theoretical orientation exists at 9 bodies, a practical orientation at 3 bodies. Two of the professional bodies, MIA in Malaysia and SKwP in Poland do not have a final examination.

The overall mean for theoretical and practical orientation is exactly the same for all common law countries in the survey together and for all civil law countries. There is however a difference between industrialised countries and countries in transition or emerging. This is shown in Table 630.2.

Theoretical Orientation versus Practical Orientation	Mean Theory - Practice
Overall for 32 professional bodies in 25 countries	4,8 – 3,2
Common law for 19 professional bodies in 12 countries of which industrialised 11 professional bodies in 6 countries and in transition/emerging 8 professional bodies in 6 countries	4,8 – 3,2 4,4 – 3,6 5,4 – 2,6
Civil law for 13 professional bodies in 13 countries of which industrialised 6 professional bodies in 6 countries and in transition/emerging 7 professional bodies in 7 countries	4,8 – 3,2 4,0 – 4,0 5,6 – 2,4 -

Table 630.2 Theoretical Orientation versus Practical Orientation

85

Table 630.1		Final Examination							
Professional Body	**Country**	**Admission** a prof education b pract exper. c general educ.	**Theory** core programme exam objectives exam methods entrance requirem	**Practice**	**Orientation Final Exam** theoretical practical mixed	**Pass Mark**	**Pass Rate**	**Conditions** a uniform b simultan c security d qual staff	**Providers** a government b prof body c university
Industrialised, common law									
CGA Canada	Canada	ac	theory 6	practice 2	theoretical	.65	.62	abcd	b
CMA Canada	Canada	ac	theory 5	practice 3	mixed	.60	.61	acd	b
ICAAlberta	Canada	ac	theory 4	practice 4	mixed	.60	.63	abcd	b
AICPA	USA	ac	theory 7	practice 1	theoretical	.75	.30	abcd	ab
ACCA	UK	ac	theory 6	practice 2	theoretical	.50	.41	acd	b
ICAEW	UK	abc	theory 2	practice 6	practical	.50	.95	abcd	b
ICAS	UK	abc	theory 4	practice 4	mixed	.50	.72	abcd	b
CPAAustralia	Australia	abc	theory 4	practice 4	mixed	.60	.75	abcd	b
ICAA	Australia	abc	theory 4	practice 4	mixed	.50	.80	abcd	b
HKSA	Hong Kong	abc	theory 4	practice 4	mixed	.50	.53	abcd	b
ICANZ	NewZealand	abc	theory 2	practice 6	practical	.60	.92	abcd	b
In trans/emerg, common law									
ICPAK	Kenya	c	theory 7	practice 1	theoretical	.50	.35	abcd	b
SAICA	South Africa	ab	theory 4	practice 4	mixed	.50	.55	abcd	b
ICAIndia	India	abc	theory 5	practice 3	mixed	.50	.15	abcd	b
ICWAI	India	ab	theory 5	practice 3	mixed	.50	.05	abcd	b
MACPA	Malaysia	abc	theory 5	practice 3	mixed	.50	.26	abcd	b
MIA	Malaysia	not applicable	not appl	not appl	not appl	notappl	notappl	notappl	notappl
ICAP	Pakistan	ab	theory 6	practice 2	theoretical		.21	abcd	b
ICMAP	Pakistan	abc	theory 5	practice 3	mixed	.60	.17	abcd	b
SOCPA	Saudi Arabia	a	theory 6	practice 2	theoretical	.60	.10	ad	b
Industrialised, civil law									
ORDRE	France	abc	theory 4	practice 4	mixed	not avail	not avail	abcd	a
IDW	Germany	bc	theory 5	practice 3	mixed	not avail	.50	cd	a
NIVRA	Netherlands	abc	theory 2	practice 6	practical	.55	.65	abcd	abc
IACJCE	Spain	abc	theory 4	practice 4	mixed	.50	.70	acd	ab
FAR	Sweden	abc	theory 5	practice 3	mixed	.75	.63	bcd	ab
JICPA	Japan	ab	theory 4	practice 4	mixed		.57	b	a
In trans/emerg, civil law									
IMCP	Mexico	a	theory 8	practice 0	theoretical	.70	.39	abcd	b
CACR	Czech Rep.	c	theory 6	practice 2	theoretical	.50	.65	abcd	ab
CHA	Hungary	abc	theory 5	practice 3	mixed	.60	.60	abcd	c
SKwP	Poland	not applicable	not appl	not appl	not appl	not appl	notappl	notappl	notappl
KIBR	Poland	abc	theory 4	practice 4	mixed	not avail	.98	cd	b
IPARussia	Russian Fed	abc	theory 5	practice 3	mixed	.80	.73	ac	b
LACPA	Lebanon	a	theory 6	practice 2	theoretical	.50	.55	abcd	ab
TURMOB	Turkey	bc	theory 5	practice 3	mixed	.60	.35	abcd	b

First of all this illustrates the overall mixed orientation of the examination. Second the more theoretical approach in countries that are in transition or emerging can possibly be explained by the present contribution of higher education to professional education.

Of the 11 bodies with a pass rate of less than 50% 6 have a theoretical orientation, the others belong to the mixed category but on the theoretical side. Almost all professional bodies have written examinations that are uniform for all students, given simultaneously, developed and administered under adequate security conditions and objectively graded by qualified staff. Differences mostly are the result of the examination methods that are in use. The country results are discussed in Chapter 7.

Professional Education Programme and Methods, Education Standards, Education and Training (Clusters 5.5, 5.6 and 5.7)

Education programme, methods and standards: programme (Q 3.4.2), content (Q 3.4.1), duration (Q 3.4.3), position of ICT (Q 3.4.4), exemptions (Q 3.4.7), combination professional education with practical experience (Q 3.4.8)

Practical Training Programme, Methods and Standards (Cluster 5.8)

Training programme, methods and standards: programme (Q 3.5.4), content (Q 3.5.3), duration (Q 3.5.5 and 3.5.6), exemptions (Q 3.5.7), regulations (Q 3.5.17 and 3.5.18)

Providers, Expertise and Resources (Clusters 5.4 and 5.9)

Final examination: providers (Q 3.3.11), recognition (Q 3.3.12), expertise and resources (Q 3.3.13) Professional education: providers (Q 3.4.9), recognition (Q 3.4.11), expertise and resources (Q 3.4.10) Practical training: providers overall (Q 3.5.8) and divided in public practice (Q 3.5.9), industry and commerce (Q 3.5.10), government (Q 3.5.11) and other (Q 3.5.12), recognition (Q 3.5.15), expertise and resources (Q 3.5.13 and 3.5.14)

Information about the providers of the final examination is included in Table 630.1 Final Examination.

All professional bodies in common law countries are provider of their own examination, in the case of AICPA in the USA together with the State Boards of Accountancy, who are the official providers.
The situation in civil law countries is more mixed with often a dominant role of the government. Cooperation with the professional bodies takes two forms: (1) official as co-provider or (2) in the selection of experts. The Netherlands and Hungary are the only two countries with an official responsibility of the universities in the final examination. In all countries university experts participate in the examination.

The final examination can be recognized by the government (15) or by the professional body itself (15) or in a combination (2). Two observations can be made. First there is no principal difference between the two systems, as the professional bodies, who recognize their own examination normally do so under government charter. Second direct government responsibility is concentrated more in civil law countries (8 out of 13) than in common law countries (7 out of 19).

Information about professional education and practical experience is given in Table 630.3 Education and Training.

Table 630.3 Education and Training

Table 630.3		Education and Training						
Professional Body	**Country**	**Degree**	**Qualification**	**Profess. Education**		**Providers Pr Ed**	**Practical Experience**	
		a general univ	**Objective**	full time	Combination	a government	full time	Providers
		b acc univ	Accountant	parttime	practical	b prof body	parttime	public pr +75%
		c gen high ed	Auditor		experience	c university	years	industry/c +75%
		d acc high ed	Both			d comm companies		mixed
Industrialised, common law								
CGA Canada	Canada	abcd	acc&auditor	ft and pt	required	b	fulltime 3	mixed
CMA Canada	Canada	ab	acc&auditor	parttime	required	b	fulltime 2	industry, comm
ICAAlberta	Canada	b	accountant	parttime	required	bc	fulltime	mixed
AICPA	USA	b	acc&auditor	fulltime	excluded	c	fulltime 1	mixed
ACCA	UK	abcd	acc&auditor	ft and pt	possible	cd	fulltime 3	mixed
ICAEW	UK	abcd	acc&auditor	parttime	required	bd	fulltime 3	public practice
ICAS	UK	abd	acc&auditor	ft and pt	required	bc	fulltime 3	public practice
CPAAustralia	Australia	b	accountant	parttime	possible	b	fulltime 3	mixed
ICAA	Australia	ab	acc&auditor	parttime	required	bc	fulltime 3	mixed
HKSA	Hong Kong	abcd	acc&auditor	parttime	required	b	not availab	not available
ICANZ	NewZealand	abd	acc&auditor	parttime	required	bc	fulltime 3	mixed
In trans/emerg, common law								
ICPAK	Kenya	abcd	acc&auditor	ft and pt	possible	bd	not availab	not available
SAICA	South Africa	bd	acc&auditor	ft and pt	required	cd	fulltime 3	public practice
ICAIndia	India	abcd	acc&auditor	parttime	required	b	fulltime 3	mixed
ICWAI	India	ab	acc&auditor	not av	required	not available	parttime 3	mixed
MACPA	Malaysia	bcd	acc&auditor	ft and pt	required	bcd	fulltime 3	public practice
MIA	Malaysia	bd	accountant	not appl	not appl	not applicable	not appl	not applicable
ICAP	Pakistan	bd	acc&auditor	fulltime	required	bd	fulltime 4	public practice
ICMAP	Pakistan	ab	acc&auditor	parttime	required	b	fulltime 3	mixed
SOCPA	Saudi Arabia	bd	acc&auditor	ft and pt	excluded	c	not av	mixed
Industrialised, civil law								
ORDRE	France	bcd	acc&auditor	fulltime	excluded	cd	fulltime 3	public practice
IDW	Germany	bd	auditor	ft and pt	required	bd	fulltime 3	public practice
NIVRA	Netherlands	bd	acc&auditor	parttime	possible	bc	fulltime 3	public practice
IACJCE	Spain	abcd	acc&auditor	parttime	possible	bc	fulltime 3	public practice
FAR	Sweden	b	acc&auditor	fulltime	required	bcd	fulltime 3	public practice
JICPA	Japan	a	auditor	not av	not av	not available	not availab	not available
In trans/emerg, civil law								
IMCP	Mexico	b	acc&auditor	fulltime	required	c	fulltime 3	mixed
CACR	Czech Rep.	abcd	acc&auditor	parttime	required	b	fulltime 3	mixed
CHA	Hungary	bd	acc&auditor	ft and pt	required	bcd	fulltime 3	public practice
SKwP	Poland	abcd	acc&auditor	not appl	not appl	not applicable	not appl	not applicable
KIBR	Poland	ab	auditor	fulltime	required	bcd	fulltime 3	public practice
IPARussia	Russian Fed	bd	acc&auditor	fulltime	required	bcd	fulltime 5	not available
LACPA	Lebanon	abd	acc&auditor	not av	not available	not available	fulltime 3	public practice
TURMOB	Turkey	bd	acc&auditor	parttime	required	bc	fulltime 2	public practice

To avoid misunderstanding the data about professional education and practical training are discussed in their context in Chapter 7 as isolated information could give a completely wrong impression about the actual situation. For example some professional bodies include university education in professional education, while others do not. So in one case seven years, as 4 + 3, might mean the same as three years, following university.

Some general conclusions however are possible. In many cases practical experience must be combined with professional education (22 out of 34), sometimes it is possible but not required (5), while in three cases it is excluded. Two professional bodies do not have specific requirements on professional education and practical experience. In two cases the information is not available.

The majority of the professional bodies (23 out of 29) is involved in professional education, in many cases in cooperation with universities (12) and/or commercial companies (9). In the other six cases professional education is given at the universities, in three of these also by commercial companies. Recognition of professional education can be a (joint) responsibility of the professional body (19 out of 27; for 9 together with the government) or rests with the government (8). This information is not available for two bodies.

For most professional bodies practical experience is for more than 75% offered in public practice (14 out of 32) or in a combination of employment sectors (13). Only CMA Canada has a majority of more then 75% of its candidates in industry and commerce. In four cases the information is not available, in two cases practical experience is not applicable. The normal duration is three years or more fulltime (24 out of 34). In situations where part time practical experience is allowed the usual condition is that the total amount of time spent on practical experience stays the same.

Recognition of providers of practical experience almost always rests with the professional bodies (21 out of 34) or with the professional body in combination with the government (4). Sole government responsibility only occurs twice. For two professional bodies practical experience is not applicable and in five cases the information is not available.

Cluster 6   Programme Requirements

Programme requirements according to IFAC IEG 9 start with General Knowledge. This can be related to the Education Background discussed in paragraph 620. Specific programme requirements are divided in Subjects (Cluster 6.1), Skills (Cluster 6.2), ICT Applications (Cluster 6.3) and Professional Values (Cluster 6.4).

Subjects: organisational and business knowledge, information and computer systems, accounting and accounting related knowledge (Q 4.1)
Skills: intellectual skills (Q 4.2), interpersonal skills (Q 4.3), communication skills (Q 4.4)
ICT Applications: ICT applications in subjects (Q 4.5)
Professional Values: professional values in subjects (Q 4.6)

Information about programme requirements is given in Table 630.4 Programme Requirements.

Table 630.4 Programme Requirements

More detailed information available from the questionnaire is summarised in the following categories.

General Knowledge: Education Background and University Entrance Level
Categories Education Background divided in degree requirements for new members in the year 2000:

Table 630.4 — Programme Requirements

	A1	2	3	4	5	6	7	8	9	10	11	B1	2	3	4	5	6	7	8	9	C1	2	3	4	5	6	D1	2	3	4	5	6	7	8
Professional Body	A1	2	3	4	5	6	7	8	9	10	11	B1	2	3	4	5	6	7	8	9	C1	2	3	4	5	6	D1	2	3	4	5	6	7	8
General Knowledge																																		
education backgr.	d	a	a	a	a	bd	b	a	a	b	a	f	a	a	b	a	a	b	b	c	a	a	a	a	a	c	e	b	a	a	a	c	c	a
univ entrance level	0	1	1	1	1	1	1	1	1	1	1	0	1	0	1	1	1	1	1	1	1	1	1	1	1	1	1	1	1	1	1	1	1	1
Org.&Bus. Knowl.	b	a	a	a	a	a	a	a	b	b	a	b	a	a	a	a	a	a	a	a	a	R	a	a	b	b	b	b	b	R	R	b	R	a
economics	1	1	1	1	1	1	1	1	1	1	1	1	1	1	1	1R	1R	1	1	1	1	1	1	1	1	1	1	1R	1R	1R	1R	1R	1R	1
quant. methods	1	1	1	1	1	1	1	1	1	1	1	1	0	1	1	1R	1R	1	1	1	1	1	1	1	1	0	1	0R	0R	0R	0R	0R	0R	1
org. behaviour	1	1	1	1	1	1	1	1	0	0	1	0	1	1	1	1R	1R	1	1	1	1	1	1	1	1	1	1	0R	0R	1R	1R	1R	1R	1
operations man.	1	1	1	1	1	1	1	1	0	0	0	0	0	1	1	1R	1R	1	1	1	1	0	1	1	0	0	0	0	0	1R	1R	0R	0R	1
marketing	0	0	1	1	1	1	1	1	0	0	0	0	1	1	1	1R	1R	1	1	1	1	0	1	1	1	0	0	0	0	1R	0R	0R	0R	1
int. business	0	0	1	1	1	1	1	1	1	1	0	0	0	1	1	1R	1R	1	1	1	1	1	1	1	0	0	0	0	0	0R	1R	0R	1R	1
IT Knowledge	4	3	2	2	4	4	2	2	4	4	2	2	4	2	4	3R	4R	4	4	4	R	4	2	4	4	4N	2	4	4R	4R	4R	4R	4R	2
Acc.&Acc.Related Knowledge																																		
fin. acc.&rep.	4	4	4R	4	4	4	4	2	3	4	4	3	3	4	4	2R	2R	4	3	3	R	4	4	3	4	3	4	4R	4R	4R	4R	4R	2R	4
man. accounting	4	1	2R	4	3	4	2	2	3	3	4	3	3	4	4	1R	1R	4	3	2	R	4	2	3	1	1	4	4R	4R	4R	4R	4R	2R	3
taxation	4	3	3R	4	3	4	2	2	3	3	4	3	4	4	4	1R	1R	3	3	3	R	3	1	3	4	3	3	3R	3R	3R	4R	3R	3R	3
bus.&comm.law	4	1	2R	4	3	4	4	4	3	4	4	3	3	4	4	3R	3R	3	3	3	R	3	3	3	3	1N	1	3R	3R	3R	3R	3R	2R	3
auditing	4	3*	4	4	4	4	4	4	4	4	4	3	3	4	4	4R	4R	4	4	4	R	3	4	3	3	3	4	4R	4R	4R	4R	4R	4R	3
finance & fin. man.	4	1	3R	4	3	4	2	2	4	4	4	1	3	3	4	1R	1R	3	3	3	R	3	2	1	1	1	3	3R	3R	3R	4R	2R	2R	4
prof. ethics	4	3	3	3	3	4	3	4	3	3	3	0	3	3	3	3R	3R	3N	2	3	R	3	3	3	3	3	3	0R	0R	3R	4R	4R	4R	3
Skills in Education																																		
intellectual	3	3	3R	3	3	3	3	2	3	3	3	1	3	3	3	3R	3R	3	3	3	R	5	3	2R	2R	1R	4	3R	3R	3R	3R	3R	1	3	0
interpersonal	3	2	2R	3	3	4	2	2	3	2	3	1	3	3	2	3R	3R	3	2	2	R	0	2	0	2R	1R	N	N	2	2R	3	3	0	2
communication	3	2	3R	3	2	2	2	3	2	3	2	1	3	3	2	3R	3R	5	2	2	R	0	2	0	2R	1R	N	N	3	3R	3	3	0	0
Skills in Pract Exp																																		
intellectual	1	0	1R	0	0	1	0	0	1	0	0	0	1	1	1	1R	1R	1	0	1	R	1	1	1R	1R	0R	3	1R	1	0	1	0	1	1
interpersonal	1	0	1R	0	1	0	0	0	0	0	0	0	1	1	1	1R	1R	0	0	1	R	1	1	0	0R	0R	N	N	1	0R	0	0	0	1
communication	1	0	1R	0	1	1	1	1	0	0	2	0	0	1	1	1R	1R	1	1	1	R	0	1	0	0R	0R	N	N	1	0R	0	0	0	1

Accounting, finance or business university degree for 75-100%
  (a) Accounting, finance or business university degree for 50-75%
  (b) General university degree for 75-100%
  (c) General university degree for 50-75%
  (d) Accounting, finance or business higher education for 75-100%
  (e) Accounting, finance or business higher education for 50-75%

Worldwide a majority of new members has either an accounting, finance or business university degree or a general university degree.

University entrance level is almost always mandatory. Only three professional bodies, CGA Canada, ICPAK in Kenya and ICA India do not have that requirement. CGA Canada requires a bachelor's degree before certification. In 2000 ICPAK had 25% new members with an accounting, finance or business university degree and 45% new members with general higher education. For ICA India 84% had an accounting, finance or business university degree.

The question this raises is whether university entrance level should always be mandatory or could be replaced by approved university exit level.

Organisational and Business Knowledge: (a) included, (b) partially included, (c) not included
For separate subjects: (1) included, (0) not included, (N) information not available.
In general the symbol (R) notes a remark about a specific situation, that is explained in the text.

MIA in Malaysia is a regulatory body that recognizes, among others, professional qualifications.
For IDW in Germany programmes may differ for separate universities, but the uniform WP-examination covers all subjects except 'international business'.
SKwP in Poland is an association of accountants without a prescribed programme.
For LACPA an undergraduate degree in business or accounting is required but the subjects are not specified.

Economics, Quantitative Methods and Organisational Behaviour are covered in almost all programmes. For Operations Management, Marketing and International Business choices are made.

IT Knowledge and Accounting & Accounting Related Knowledge are covered in all programmes.
In Table 630.4 the inclusion of ICT Applications and Professional Values is for each subject indicated as follows: (1) subject included, (2) with ICT applications, (3) with professional values, (4) with both, (N) information not available. Remarks, noted by (R), are again given when appropriate.
In the programme of the Ordre all subjects are covered, but the information about skills is not available.

The results clearly show that ICT Applications and professional values are integrated in a wide range of subjects. Professional Ethics is almost generally included as a separate subject.

Apart from the integration of ICT applications in subjects, ICT is increasingly used in accountancy education for collecting information (17 out of 34), communication (teacher-student, between students, assignments) (17) and diagnostic tools (counselling, tests) (11).

The ways skills are approached in education can be described as (1) theoretical, (2) practical or (3) both. For the allocation of these two categories *theoretical* is defined as 'mastery of subjects, lectures, tutorials, reading material, classes, seminars, written examinations'. *Practical* is defined as 'oral and written assignments, workshops, projects, case studies, public speaking'. Skills can be also (1) included in practical experience or (0) not included as part of the education objectives. This of course leaves open the not systematic contribution of practical experience to the acquirement of skills. Remarks are made in the usual way and concern the following professional bodies.
AICPA : emphasis is shifting from knowledge of rules to skills; methods are not specified.
Ordre : no information is available on the methods that are used for the acquirement of skills.
FAR : increasing attention for intellectual skills; methods are not specified.

IMCP : skills are not addressed separately.

The results indicate that skills, with an emphasis on intellectual skills, are addressed in all education programmes. The systematic approach of skills, as part of monitored programmes, in practical experience is still in its beginning stages. It has to be remarked however that this does not mean that skills are not addressed during practical experience. This is clearly shown by the experience in the European Union before the introduction of the 8th Directive. In countries like the Netherlands where practical experience was not mandatory at that time it nevertheless played an important role in assuring study success, as was documented by student evaluations.

640   Model of Accountancy Education

Based on the discussion in the previous paragraphs the model parameters and their distinguishing values can be summarised as follows. This is the basis for the country review in the next chapter.

Country Characteristics
Economic Position
- Industrialised or In Transition/Emerging
Legal system
- Common Law or Civil Law

Accountancy Profession
Government and Recognition
- High Professional Self-regulation
- Emphasis on Professional Self-regulation
- Emphasis on Government Regulation
- High Government Regulation
International Position
- IFAC Membership; IFAC Education Guidelines; EU Directives
Mandatory Membership and Mandatory CPE
- Categories High, Medium, Low for Membership Regulation
Employment Sectors
- Values from High to Low for Membership in Public Practice
- Members and New Members in all Employment Sectors
- Members in all Employment Sectors, New Members in Public Practice
- Members and New Members in Public Practice
Education Background
- High Percentage of Accountancy, Finance or Business University Degrees
- Emphasis on Accountancy, Finance or Business University Degrees
- High Percentage of General University Degrees
- Emphasis on General University Degrees
- High Percentage of Accountancy, Finance or Business Higher Education
- Emphasis on General Higher Education
Qualification
- Accountant, Auditor or Both

Accountancy Education
Final Examination
- Theoretical Orientation, Mix of Theory and Practice or Practical Orientation

The results for the categories mentioned above are summarised in Table 640.1 Model Accountancy Education.

Table 640.1	Model Accountancy Education							
Professional Body	**Country Characteristics**	**Regulation Index**	**Education Guidelines**	**Membersh. Regulation**	**Members Public Practice**	**Degree Category**	**Accountant Auditor Both**	**Orientation Final Exam**
		PS prof self	IFAC IEG 9	Mandatory	**Practice**		**Both**	theoretical
		GR gov reg	EU 8th Dir	membership				practical
		regulation		and CPE				mixed
Industrialised, common law								
CGA Canada	Canada	emphasis PS	IFAC	high	0-25%	EGU	acc&auditor	theoretical
CMA Canada	Canada	high PS	IFAC	high	0-25%	HAU*	acc&auditor	mixed
ICAAlberta	Canada	high PS	IFAC	high	25-50%	HAU	accountant	mixed
AICPA	USA	high GR	IFAC	medium	25-50%	HAU	acc&auditor	theoretical
ACCA	United Kingdom	emphasis PS	IFAC/EU	medium	25-50%	EAU	acc&auditor	theoretical
ICAEW	United Kingdom	emphasis PS	IFAC/EU	medium	25-50%	EGU/AU	acc&auditor	practical
ICAS	United Kingdom	emphasis PS	IFAC/EU	high	25-50%	EAU	acc&auditor	mixed
CPA Australia	Australia	high PS	IFAC	high	0-25%	HAU	accountant	mixed
ICA Australia	Australia	high PS	IFAC	high	25-50%	HAU	acc&auditor	mixed
HKSA	Hong Kong	emphasis PS	IFAC	high	25-50%	EAU	acc&auditor	mixed
ICANZ	New Zealand	emphasis PS	IFAC	high	25-50%	HAU*	acc&auditor	practical
In trans/emerg, common law								
ICPAK	Kenya	emphasis PS	IFAC	high	25-50%	EGH	acc&auditor	theoretical
SAICA	South Africa	high PS	IFAC	medium	0-25%	HAU	acc&auditor	mixed
ICA India	India	emphasis PS	IFAC	medium	50-75%	HAU	acc&auditor	mixed
ICWAI	India	emphasis GR	IFAC	high	0-25%	EAU	acc&auditor	mixed
MACPA	Malaysia	emphasis PS	IFAC	low	50-75%	EAU	acc&auditor	mixed
MIA	Malaysia	emphasis PS	IFAC	high	25-50%	EAU	accountant	not appl
ICAP	Pakistan	emphasis PS	IFAC	high	0-25%	HAH*	acc&auditor	theoretical
ICMAP	Pakistan	emphasis PS	IFAC	high	0-25%	HGU	acc&auditor	mixed
SOCPA	Saudi Arabia	high GR		high	25-50%	HAU	acc&auditor	theoretical
Industrialised, civil law								
ORDRE	France	emphasis GR	IFAC/EU	high	not avail	EAU*	acc&auditor	mixed
IDW	Germany	emphasis GR	EU	high	.100%	HAU	auditor	mixed
NIVRA	Netherlands	emphasis GR	IFAC/EU	high	25-50%	HAU	acc&auditor	practical
IACJCE	Spain	high GR	EU	high	25-50%	HAU	acc&auditor	mixed
FAR	Sweden	high GR	EU	high	.100%	HAU	acc&auditor	mixed
JICPA	Japan	high GR		medium	.100%	HGU	auditor	mixed
In trans/emerg, civil law								
IMCP	Mexico	emphasis PS	IFAC	high	75-100%	HAU	acc&auditor	theoretical
CACR	Czech Republic	emphasis GR	IFAC/EU	high	75-100%	EAU*	acc&auditor	theoretical
CHA	Hungary	emphasis GR	IFAC	high	75-100%	EAU	acc&auditor	mixed
SKwP	Poland	high GR	IFAC	low	25-50%	EAU	acc&auditor	not appl
KIBR	Poland	emphasis PS	EU	high	75-100%	EAU	auditor	mixed
IPA Russia	Russian Fed.	emphasis GR		high	0-25%	HAU	acc&auditor	mixed
LACPA	Lebanon	emphasis PS		high	75-100%	EGU	acc&auditor	theoretical
TURMOB	Turkey	emphasis GR	IFAC	low	50-75%	HAU	acc&auditor	mixed

Table 640.1: Model Accountancy Education

Details of the education and training systems are discussed in Chapter 7 on a regional basis with a focus on the existence of the following elements starting from university entrance level.
- Full time education (university, higher education, professional education)
- Part time professional education
- Practical experience in relation to professional education
- Final examination requirements and orientation

CHAPTER 7   DIFFERENCES IN ACCOUNTANCY EDUCATION

Details of the qualification, education and training systems are discussed in this chapter on a regional basis.

700   Comparative Country Analysis
710   Regions and Regulation
720   Professional Qualification and Background
730   Accountancy Education
740   International Benchmarks
750   Development in Time
760   IFAC international Education Standards

Regions and regulation are compared with the country. Characteristics of the professional qualification and background and of accountancy education are discussed in the same regional setting. Subjects are considered according to the same clusters that have been defined in the previous chapter. International benchmarks concern the implementation of education guidelines and directives and the mutual recognition of qualifications between countries. Development in time reflects on changes that can be expected in the near future.

700   Comparative Country Analysis

The research project has resulted in the classification of accountancy education systems worldwide. Overviews of accountancy education are available for 34 professional bodies in 25 countries. Overviews for each professional body are given in Annex 3. Three countries, Argentina, Brazil and China, are included in the country analysis but for these countries there is no information on accountancy education available. This chapter is dedicated to an overall analysis of accountancy education worldwide.

Research Question 7

Analyse regional and local differences of accountancy education in the selected countries.

Based on an abstraction of general characteristics and principles a conceptual model has been developed and tested that can be used to describe systems of accountancy education. Conclusions about the applicability of the model in different surroundings have been given in Chapter 6. In this chapter the collected material is used for a comparative analysis of the regional and local differences of accountancy education in the selected countries that are included in the project. This is the basis for conclusions about impact and applicability of international guidelines on accountancy education under different regional or local circumstances. Indicators for necessary developments in time are found in the general analysis in Chapter 2 and in the answers regarding future developments in the global accountancy education questionnaire.

Regional and local differences are discussed in view of (1) regulation, (2) professional qualification and background, (3) accountancy education.

710   Regions and Regulation

Region in itself may be less relevant than other factors like historical background and international associations. In this paragraph attention is given to the region, the legal system, the regulation index for government regulation compared with professional self-regulation, membership of regional organisations of professional accountants and professional self-regulation of mandatory membership and mandatory CPE according to the membership regulation index. Starting with America and going from West to East the following picture emerges for the countries and professional bodies included in the research project.

America: Canada and USA have a common law background; Mexico has a civil law background. Canada, Mexico, USA are members of the North American Free Trade Association (NAFTA). High professional self-regulation: CMA Canada (Canada) and ICA Alberta (Canada). Emphasis on professional self-regulation: CGA Canada (Canada) and IMCP (Mexico). High government regulation: AICPA (USA). Membership: CGA Canada is a member of CAPA, ICAC and FIDEF.

For AICPA regulation is not consistent with the country characteristics. This can at least partly be explained by regulatory practices in the USA and by the separate responsibilities of the State Boards of Accounting for the licensing of practicing accountants. IMCP regulation is comparable to common law characteristics although Mexico is a civil law country. Regulation for the Canadian professional bodies is consistent with the country characteristics. The international objective of CGA Canada is reflected in its membership of regional organisations.

In Canada and Mexico professional self-regulation of mandatory membership and mandatory CPE is classified as high. For AICPA the score is medium because membership is not mandatory and CPE, although mandatory is not regulated by the professional body. Here again the responsibilities of the State Boards of Accounting must be kept in mind.

European Union: The United Kingdom has a common law background; France, Germany, the Netherlands, Spain and Sweden have a civil law background. Emphasis on professional self-regulation: ACCA (UK), ICAEW (UK), ICAS (UK). Emphasis on government regulation: Ordre (France), IDW (Germany) and NIVRA (The Netherlands). High government regulation: IACJCE (Spain) and FAR (Sweden). Membership: all professional bodies are members of FEE; ACCA is an associate member of AFA, CAPA and ECSAFA; the Ordre is a member of FIDEF.

For all the professional bodies regulation is consistent with the country characteristics. Compared with the other common law countries the relatively high government influence in the UK can be explained by EU regulation. In the Netherlands the influence of the government has grown as a result of the implementation of the EU 8th Directive.

With the exception of ACCA and ICAEW in the UK professional self-regulation of mandatory membership and mandatory CPE is classified as high. There is no difference in relation to a common law or civil law background. For ACCA and ICAEW the classification is medium because CPE outside public practice is not mandatory. It has to be noted that this is a direct result of the methodology that has been chosen. If instead of giving the same weight to all employment sectors priority had been given to public practice the classification for ACCA and ICAEW would also have been high. If the position of ICAS is also considered, with mandatory CPE for all employment sectors but regulation by ICAS only in public practice, two interesting questions can be asked. (1) Are there valid reasons to treat CPE in public practice different from CPE in other employment sectors as an accountant? (2) How does the answer to the first question influence possible regulation of CPE by the professional body? The relevance of the questions for the qualification, education and training of accountants and auditors is discussed in Chapter 9.

Central and Eastern Europe: The Czech Republic, Hungary, Poland, the Russian Federation and Turkey have a civil law background. Emphasis on professional self-regulation: KIBR (Poland). Emphasis on government regulation: CACR (Czech Republic), CHA (Hungary), SKwP (Poland), IPA Russia (Russian Federation) and TURMOB (Turkey). Membership: CACR is a member of FEE, SKwP is a member of EFAA, IPA Russia is a member of EFA.

Similarities in legal system, major trade alliances and, except for the Russian Federation, negotiations that have been started or are foreseen to achieve EU membership are the reasons to consider these countries together. Except for KIBR in Poland regulation is consistent with the country characteristics. It is interesting that KIBR as an organisation of auditors shows an emphasis on professional self-regulation, which is quite consistent through all the elements that are considered in the regulation index.

With the exception of TURMOB in Turkey professional self-regulation of mandatory membership and mandatory CPE is classified as high. For TURMOB the classification is low because, although membership is mandatory, CPE is not. This will change due to a General Assembly decision in 1999 that mandatory CPE will start for all members in public practice and industry beginning June 2002.

Africa: Kenya and South Africa have a common law background. In South Africa this is combined with a strong civil law influence.
High professional self-regulation: SAICA (South Africa).
Emphasis on professional self-regulation: ICPAK (Kenya).
Membership: ICPAK and SAICA are members of ECSAFA.

Regulation is consistent with the country characteristics. The differences between SAICA and ICPAK originate in the regulation of professional education and practical training.

Professional self-regulation of mandatory membership and mandatory CPE is classified as high for ICPAK in Kenya and medium for SAICA in South Africa. The latter is the result of the fact that membership is not mandatory and CPE, although mandatory is not regulated by the profession.

Middle East: Lebanon has a civil law background and Saudi Arabia has a common law background.
Emphasis on professional self-regulation: LACPA (Lebanon)
High government regulation: SOCPA (Saudi Arabia)
Membership: LACPA is a member of FIDEF.

Regulation is not consistent with the country characteristics. In the case of LACPA it is interesting that in a civil law country with important European, in particular French, connections the emphasis is on professional self-regulation. For SOCPA the explanation for the high government regulation could be found in the Muslim background, although this is not apparent in other Muslim countries.

Professional self-regulation of mandatory membership and mandatory CPE is classified as high.
Membership is mandatory for both professional bodies, as is CPE for all employment sectors, which is regulated by the professional bodies.

Asia: India, Malaysia, Pakistan and Hong Kong have a common law background; China and Japan have a civil law background.
Emphasis on professional self-regulation: ICA India (India), MACPA (Malaysia), MIA (Malaysia), ICAP (Pakistan), ICMAP (Pakistan) and HKSA (Hong Kong).
Emphasis on government regulation: ICWAI (India)
High government regulation: JICPA (Japan)
Membership: with the exception of ICA India all professional bodies are member of CAPA; ICA India, ICAP and ICMAP are member of SAFA; MIA is member of AFA.
With the possible exception of ICWAI, regulation is consistent with the country characteristics.
For ICWAI this is mainly a result of the government influence on regulation of the profession. This is interesting as the two other bodies with their main objective outside public practice, CMA Canada and ICMAP in Pakistan, have a different profile.

Professional self-regulation of mandatory membership and mandatory CPE is classified as high with the exception of medium for ICA India (India) and JICPA (Japan) and low for MACPA (Malaysia). In the case of MACPA CPE is not mandatory. However it is regulated by law that members of MACPA and other professional bodies, who want to work as an accountant in Malaysia, must also be members of MIA. In MIA regulation CPE is mandatory. If this is considered the classification of MACPA on membership regulation would be medium.

Australia and New Zealand: both countries have a common law background.
High professional self-regulation: CPA Australia, ICA Australia
Emphasis on professional self-regulation: ICANZ (New Zealand)
Membership: all three professional bodies are members of CAPA; CPA Australia is member of AFA.

Regulation is consistent with the country characteristics.
Professional self-regulation of mandatory membership and mandatory CPE is classified as high.

720 Professional Qualification and Background

In this paragraph attention is given to membership categories, education background and qualification objective. Qualification standards are discussed in the next paragraph on accountancy education. The qualification objective, accountant and/or auditor, could be expected to be significant for the education and training system. The same applies to the education background as this decides the starting level for additional professional education not included in the system of higher education. Membership categories, especially for new members, possibly reflect practical training requirements. The relations with accountancy education and training are discussed in the next section.

Professional bodies in America: CGA Canada, CMA Canada and ICA Alberta in Canada, AICPA in the USA and IMCP in Mexico.

Except for ICA Alberta the common qualification objective is 'accountant' and 'auditor'. For ICA Alberta only 'accountant' is mentioned. This may be a less important distinction for education and training than it seems at first sight when membership categories are considered. CGA Canada and CMA Canada have less than 25% of members and new members in public practice. ICA Alberta and AICPA have between 25% and 50% of members in public practice, but the number of new members in public practice exceeds 75%. IMCP has more than 75% of members and new members in public practice.

ICA Alberta and AICPA require that new members have an accountancy, finance or business university degree. In fact the same applies to CMA Canada as 'entrance to the profession requires a four year 120 hours accounting or comparable business degree'. CGA Canada has an emphasis on candidates with a general university degree with in addition considerable input of candidates with an accountancy, finance or business university degree and with general higher education. This could be a result of the international position of its programme. IMCP requires 'a degree course in public accountancy studies with an average of 4-5 years at universities.

Professional bodies in the European Union: ACCA, ICAEW and ICAS in the UK, the Ordre in France, IDW in Germany, NIVRA in the Netherlands, IACJCE in Spain and FAR in Sweden.

Except for IDW the common qualification objective is 'accountant' and 'auditor'. For IDW it is 'auditor'. Almost all members and new members of IDW work in public practice. This is also the situation for FAR. The other professional bodies have between 25% and 50% of members in public practice. The same is true for the number of new members in public practice except for ICAEW with almost all new members in public practice.

FAR requires that new members have an accountancy, finance or business university degree. For IDW, NIVRA and IACJCE more than 75% of new members have an accountancy, finance or business university degree. In addition NIVRA has a considerable input of candidates with accountancy, finance or business higher education. ACCA, ICAEW and ICAS have an emphasis on candidates with an accountancy, finance or business university degree. In addition there is a considerable input of candidates with a general university degree. ACCA also has a fairly large proportion of candidates with accountancy, finance or business higher education. This could be a result of the international position of its programme. Members of the Ordre come from universities (management education), business schools and colleges.

Professional bodies in Central and Eastern Europe: CACR in the Czech Republic, CHA in Hungary, SKwP and KIBR in Poland, IPA Russia in the Russian Federation and TURMOB in Turkey.

Except for KIBR the common qualification objective is 'accountant' and 'auditor'. For KIBR it is 'auditor'. It is interesting that CACR as an institute of auditors includes the qualification objective of 'accountant'. This resembles the situation in the EU where regulation concerns auditors and most professional bodies include accountants. CACR, CHA and KIBR have more than 75% of members in public practice. Almost all new members of CACR and more than 75% for KIBR also work in public practice. For CHA this number is less than 50%. Members and new members of TURMOB work for 50% to 75% in public practice, For SKwP and IPA Russia the percentage is 25% or less.

For IPA Russia and TURMOB more than 75% of new members have an accountancy, finance or business university degree. CACR, CHA, SKwP and KIBR have an emphasis on candidates with an accountancy, finance or business university degree. In addition for SKwP and KIBR there is a considerable input of candidates with a general university degree and for CHA and IPA Russia with accountancy, finance or business higher education. In fact for CHA that percentage is almost 50%.

Professional bodies in Africa: ICPAK in Kenya, SAICA in South Africa.

The common qualification objective is 'accountant' and 'auditor'. ICPAK has between 25% and 50% of members in public practice. For SAICA that number is slightly below 25%. Between 25% and 50% of new members of ICPAK and SAICA work in public practice.

All new members of SAICA have an accountancy, finance or business university degree. Almost halve of the new members of ICPAK have general higher education, with in addition considerable input of candidates with an accountancy, finance or business university degree. This reflects the situation that existed in for example the Netherlands and the UK in the near past.

Professional bodies in the Middle East: LACPA in Lebanon, SOCPA in Saudi Arabia.

The common qualification objective is 'accountant' and 'auditor'. More than 75% of members of LACPA work in public practice. SOCPA has between 25% and 50% of members and new members in public practice.

All new members of SOCPA have an accountancy, finance or business university degree. For LACPA emphasis is on a general university degree with considerable input of candidates with an accounting, finance or business university degree.

Professional bodies in Asia: ICA India and ICWAI in India, MACPA and MIA in Malaysia, ICAP and ICMAP in Pakistan, HKSA in Hong Kong and JICPA in Japan.

The qualification objective for ICA India, ICWAI, MACPA, ICAP, ICMAP and HKSA is 'accountant' and 'auditor'. It is of interest to note that ICWAI as an institute of cost and work accountants and ICMAP as an institute of cost and management accountants include 'auditor' as a qualification objective. MIA mentions 'accountant' and JICPA 'auditor'. This for JICPA is consistent with employment sector as almost all its members and new members work in public practice. The number of members in public practice falls within 50% and 75% for ICA India and MACPA, between 25% and 50% for HKSA and MIA, and is less than 25% for ICAP, ICWAI and ICMAP.

ICA India has more than 75% of new members with an accountancy, finance or business university degree. HKSA, ICWAI, MACPA and MIA have an emphasis on candidates with an accountancy, finance or business university degree. In addition for HKSA and ICWAI there is a considerable input of candidates with a general university degree, for MACPA and MIA with both accountancy, finance or business higher education and general higher education. More than 75% of the new members of ICMAP and JICPA have a general university degree with for ICMAP additional input of candidates with an accountancy, finance or business university degree.

Professional bodies in Australia and New Zealand: CPA Australia and ICAA in Australia, ICANZ in New Zealand.

The qualification objective for ICAA and ICANZ is 'accountant' and 'auditor', for CPA Australia it is 'accountant'. The number of members and new members in public practice is less than 25% for CPA Australia and between 25% and 50% for ICAA and ICANZ.

Almost all members of CPA Australia and ICAA have an accountancy, finance or business university degree. ICANZ admits candidates after a recognized four-year academic programme.

730 Accountancy Education

The discussion of the country results on accountancy education is divided in comments on (1) the final examination and (2) on professional education and practical experience. The same regional approach is followed as in the preceding section on 'regions and regulation'.

Final Examination

An overview of the final examination programmes is given in Table 730.1 Final Examination Core Programmes.

Table 730.1 Final Examination Core Programmes (see end of the chapter)

The main categories for the final examination are (1) high orientation on theory, (2) mix of theory and practice, (3) high orientation on practice.

In general for common law countries a higher emphasis on practice can be expected then in civil law countries. On the other hand the actual situation may very well depend on the actual contribution of higher education to accountancy education, both in content and in number of students. In industrialised countries with a high participation in higher education, prospective accountants will in general start their professional education and training after they have already reached a certain expertise. This can be recognized by the professional body or regulatory agency. As a result it becomes possible to concentrate additional professional education and the final examination more on the practical aspects of the accountancy profession. In emerging countries and countries in transition it may presently be necessary to concentrate more on knowledge. This approach could be reflected in the final examination. Last the effects of regulation have to be considered as is shown in the European Union where practical experience before qualification is now mandatory.

America: Canada, Mexico and the USA
Theoretical orientation: CGA Canada, AICPA (USA), IMCP (Mexico)
Mix of theoretical and practical: CGA Canada, CMA Canada, ICA Alberta (Canada)

For CMA Canada and ICA Alberta the final examination is consistent with the country characteristics. There is however a certain tendency towards an orientation on theory because practical experience before the final examination is not mandatory. This is also true for CGA Canada, which in addition has a more theoretical objective for the examination. The specific position of AICPA as discussed before explains the orientation on theory. IMCP is the only professional body in the whole project with all indicators on the theoretical side.

European Union: France, Germany, the Netherlands, Spain, Sweden and the United Kingdom
Theoretical orientation: ACCA (UK)
Mix of theoretical and practical: Ordre (France), IDW (Germany), IACJCE (Spain), FAR (Sweden), ICAS (UK)
Practical orientation: NIVRA (The Netherlands), ICAEW (UK)

If the effect of EU regulation is taken into account the final examination is consistent with the country characteristics for the Ordre, IDW, IACJCE, FAR and ICAS. IDW and FAR show a tendency towards theory, the Ordre towards practice. In comparison with the other professional bodies NIVRA and ICAEW have moved relatively far towards a practical approach but theoretical elements remain. The main reason for the orientation of ACCA towards theory, close however to a mixed approach, is that practical experience before the membership examination is not mandatory. Qualification as an auditor is a post-membership qualification as the final examination for Registered Auditors comes after an additional two years of training in an Approved Training Practice. It consists of a three-day course which includes a test and is very practical. Combined with the final pre-qualification examination for membership entry this gives a combined theoretical/practical test.

Central and Eastern Europe: Czech Republic, Hungary, Poland, Russian Federation and Turkey
Theoretical orientation: CACR (Czech Republic),
Mix of theoretical and practical: CHA (Hungary), KIBR (Poland), IPA Russia (Russian Federation), TURMOB (Turkey)

In general the final examination is consistent with the country characteristics. CACR has an orientation on theory because practical experience before the final examination is not requested. It is close to a mixed approach. The other professional bodies have a mixed approach that is close to an orientation on theory.

Africa: Kenya and South Africa
Theoretical orientation: ICPAK (Kenya)
Mix of theoretical and practical: SAICA (South Africa)

ICPAK has a relatively high theoretical orientation, which might be explained by its economic position. For SIACA the final examination is consistent with the country characteristics.

Middle East: Lebanon and Saudi Arabia
High orientation on theory: LACPA (Lebanon), SOCPA (Saudi Arabia)

For LACPA the final examination is consistent with the country characteristics. Both LACPA and SOCPA do not have a practical experience requirement before the final examination, which explains their relative positions.

Asia: China, Hong Kong, India, Japan, Malaysia and Pakistan
Theoretical orientation: ICAP (Pakistan)
Mix of theoretical and practical: HKSA (Hong Kong), ICA India, ICWAI (India), JICPA (Japan), MACPA (Malaysia), ICMAP (Pakistan)

For most professional bodies in this group the final examination is consistent with the country characteristics. Although the ICAP final examination is oriented on theory it is close to a mixed approach. The mixed approach at JICPA is not entirely consistent with the country characteristics.

Australia and New Zealand
Mix of theoretical and practical: CPA Australia, ICAA (Australia)

Practical orientation: ICANZ (New Zealand)

For the professional bodies in this group the final examination is consistent with the country characteristics. The relatively high concentration on practice at ICANZ can be explained by the concentration of the examination on skills.

Professional Education and Practical Experience

As announced in paragraph 630 professional education and practical experience are discussed together with degree requirements and the final examination in order to get a clear picture of the whole system and the relations between the elements.

An overview of the professional education programmes is given in Table 730.2 Professional Education Core Programmes. An overview of the practical training programmes is given in Table 730.3 Practical Training Core Programmes.

Table 730.2 Professional Education Core Programmes (see end of the chapter)
Table 730.3 Practical Training Core Programmes (see end of the chapter)

Professional bodies in America: CGA Canada, CMA Canada and ICA Alberta in Canada, AICPA in the USA and IMCP in Mexico.

CGA Canada

Final Examination: theoretical; following professional education; provider professional body.
Professional Education: ten years full time and part time; provider professional body; combination with practical experience required.
Practical Experience: three years full time; providers in public practice, industry and commerce, government, other areas.
General Education: a bachelor's degree is required prior to receiving the CGA designation.

CMA Canada

Final Examination: theoretical and practical; following professional education; provider professional body.
Professional Education: two years part time; provider professional body; combination with practical experience required.
Practical Experience: two years full time; providers in industry and commerce, government.
General Education: prior to professional education and practical experience a four year 120 hours accounting or comparable university degree with 17 pre-requisite courses in accounting and business.

ICA Alberta

Final Examination: theoretical and practical; following professional education; provider professional body.
Professional Education: three years part time; providers professional body and universities; combination with practical experience required.
Practical Experience: three years full time; providers in public practice.
General Education: prior to professional education and practical experience an undergraduate university degree in any discipline with specific requirements in core subjects.

AICPA

Final Examination: theoretical; following university education; providers government and professional body.

Professional Education: in university education; combination with practical experience excluded.

Practical Experience: not required for qualification; can be required for licensing after qualification.

General Education: prior to the final examination a four year bachelors degree with an additional 30 semester hours in total to include 36 hours of 'upper level' accountancy and 39 hours of business.

IMCP

Final Examination: theoretical; following higher education; provider professional body.

Professional Education: four to five years full time; providers universities.

Practical Experience: three years full time; providers in public practice, industry and commerce, government, other areas; required for admission to the profession.

General Education: prior to the final examination a degree course in public accountancy at universities registered with the Ministry of Education.

Professional bodies in the European Union: ACCA, ICAEW and ICAS in the UK, the Ordre in France, IDW in Germany, NIVRA in The Netherlands, IACJCE in Spain and FAR in Sweden.

ACCA

Final Examination: theoretical; following professional education; provider professional body

Professional Education: three years part time; providers universities and commercial companies; combination with practical experience possible

Practical Experience: three years full time; providers in public practice, industry and commerce, government

General Education: minimum qualification for entry to a UK degree programme

ICAEW

Final Examination: practical; following professional education and practical experience; provider professional body

Professional Education: three years part time; providers professional body and commercial companies; combination with practical experience required

Practical Experience: three years full time; providers in public practice, industry and commerce, government

General Education: minimum qualification for entry to a UK degree programme

ICAS

Final Examination: theoretical and practical; following professional education and practical experience; provider professional body

Professional Education: three years full time and part time; providers professional body and universities; combination with practical experience required

Practical Experience: three years full time; providers in public practice, industry and commerce

General Education: qualifying degree holders

Ordre

Final Examination: theoretical and practical; following professional education and practical experience; provider government

Professional Education: four years full time; providers universities and commercial companies; combination with practical experience excluded

Practical Experience: three years full time after professional education; providers in public practice

General Education: baccalauréat level (university entrance) prior to professional education

IDW

Final Examination: theoretical and practical; following university education* and practical experience; provider government (*professional education is not mandatory)
Professional Education: one year full time and part time; providers professional body and commercial companies; combination with practical experience required
Practical Experience: three years full time; providers in public practice
General Education: university degree in business administration or law

NIVRA

Final Examination: practical; following professional education and practical experience; providers government, professional body and universities
Professional Education: three years part time; providers professional body and universities; combination with practical experience possible
Practical Experience: three years full time; providers in public practice, industry and commerce, government
General Education: university or higher education degree in accounting or economics

IACJCE

Final Examination: theoretical and practical; following professional education and practical experience; providers government and professional body
Professional Education: three years part time; providers professional body and universities; combination with practical experience possible
Practical Experience: three years full time; providers in public practice
General Education: finance and business degree or graduation

FAR

Final Examination: theoretical and practical; following professional education and practical experience; providers government and professional body
Professional Education: three years part time; providers professional body, universities and commercial companies; combination with practical experience required
Practical Experience: three years full time; providers in public practice
General Education: bachelor's degree in finance or accounting or advanced qualification

Professional bodies in Central and Eastern Europe: CACR in the Czech Republic, CHA in Hungary, SKwP and KIBR in Poland, IPA Russia in the Russian Federation and TURMOB in Turkey.

CACR

Final Examination: theoretical; following university education* and practical experience; providers government and professional body (*professional education is not mandatory)
Professional Education: three years part time; provider professional body; combination with practical experience required
Practical Experience: three years full time; providers in public practice
General Education: possession of a five-year university degree

CHA

Final Examination: theoretical and practical; following professional education and practical experience; providers universities
Professional Education: two years part time; providers professional body, universities and commercial companies; combination with practical experience required

Practical Experience: three years full time; providers in public practice
General Education: university or college degree of business, accounting, finance

SKwP (not applicable)

KIBR

Final Examination: theoretical and practical; following professional education and practical experience; provider professional body
Professional Education: four years part time; providers professional body, universities and commercial companies; combination with practical experience required
Practical Experience: three years part time; providers in public practice
General Education: university degree with approved curriculum

IPA Russia

Final Examination: theoretical and practical; following professional education and practical experience; provider professional body
Professional Education: in university and higher education; providers professional body, universities, and commercial companies; combination with practical experience required
Practical Experience: five years full time after higher education; providers in public practice, industry and commerce, government
General Education: diploma of higher education in economic specialities

TURMOB

Final Examination: theoretical and practical; following university education and practical experience; provider professional body
Professional Education: two years part time; providers professional body and universities; combination with practical experience required
Practical Experience: two years full time; providers in public practice, industry and commerce
General Education: a four-year university degree

Professional bodies in Africa: ICPAK in Kenya, SAICA in South Africa.

ICPAK

Final Examination: theoretical; following general education; provider professional body
Professional Education: four years full time and part time; providers professional body and commercial companies; combination with practical experience possible
Practical Experience: required to obtain license for public practice
General Education: high school and academic course of instruction

SAICA

Final Examination: theoretical and practical; following professional education and practical experience; provider professional body
Professional Education: four years full time and part time; providers universities and commercial companies; combination with practical experience required
Practical Experience: three years full time; providers in public practice, industry and commerce
General Education: university and higher education qualifications accredited by the professional body

Professional bodies in the Middle East: LACPA in Lebanon, SOCPA in Saudi Arabia.

LACPA

Final Examination: theoretical; following professional education; provider professional body
Professional Education: not mandatory; providers universities and commercial companies
Practical Experience: three years full time; providers in public practice
General Education: degree in business or accounting at a recognized university

SOCPA

Final Examination: theoretical; following professional education; provider professional body
Professional Education: four years full time and part time; providers universities; combination with practical experience excluded
Practical Experience: required for license; providers in public practice, industry and commerce, government
General Education: university level with 30 credit hours accounting, auditing and tax

Professional bodies in Asia: ICA India and ICWAI in India, MACPA and MIA in Malaysia, ICAP and ICMAP in Pakistan, HKSA in Hong Kong and JICPA in Japan.

ICA India

Final Examination: theoretical and practical; following professional education and practical experience; provider professional body
Professional Education: three years part time; provider professional body; combination with practical experience required
Practical Experience: three years full time; providers in public practice, industry and commerce
General Education: senior secondary examination or equivalent recognized examination

ICWAI

Final Examination: theoretical and practical; following professional education and practical experience; provider professional body
Professional Education: two years part time; provider professional body; combination with practical experience possible
Practical Experience: three years full time; providers in public practice, industry and commerce, government
General Education: graduation at any recognized university of India

MACPA

Final Examination: theoretical and practical; following professional education and practical experience; provider professional body
Professional Education: two years full time and part time; providers professional body, universities and commercial companies; combination with practical experience required
Practical Experience: three years full time; providers in public practice, industry and commerce, government
General Education: approved degree or diploma at the tertiary level

MIA (not applicable)

ICAP

Final Examination: theoretical; following professional education and practical experience; provider professional body

Professional Education: three years part time; provider professional body; combination with practical experience required

Practical Experience: four years full time; providers in public practice, industry and commerce

General Education: minimum higher secondary education

ICMAP

Final Examination: theoretical and practical; following professional education and practical experience; provider professional body

Professional Education: three years part time; provider professional body; combination with practical experience required;

Practical Experience: three years full time; providers in public practice, industry and commerce, government

General Education: basic qualification is graduate university degree

HKSA

Final Examination: theoretical and practical; following professional education and practical experience; provider professional body

Professional Education: one year part time at least; provider professional body; combination with practical experience required

Practical Experience: three years full time; providers not specified

General Education: recognized accountancy degree

JICPA

Final Examination: theoretical and practical; following professional education and practical experience; provider government

Professional Education: two years part time after second stage CPA examination; provider professional body; combination with practical experience possible

Practical Experience: two years full time; providers in public practice

General Education: university entrance level

Professional bodies in Australia and New Zealand: CPA Australia and ICAA in Australia, ICANZ in New Zealand.

CPA Australia

Final Examination: theoretical and practical; following professional education and practical experience; provider professional body

Professional Education: two and a half years part time; provider professional body; combination with practical experience possible

Practical Experience: three years full time; providers in public practice, industry and commerce, government

General Education: accepted bachelors degrees

ICAA

Final Examination: theoretical and practical; following professional education and practical experience; provider professional body

Professional Education: two years part time; providers professional body and universities; combination with practical experience required

Practical Experience: three years full time; providers in public practice, industry and commerce, government

General Education: qualifications at degree level and if necessary conversion course

ICANZ

Final Examination: practical; following professional education and practical experience; provider professional body
Professional Education: - years part time; providers professional body and universities; combination with practical experience required
Practical Experience: three years full time; providers in public practice, industry and commerce, government
General Education: recognized four-year academic programme

740   International Benchmarks

International Guidelines and Directives

According to the analysis in Chapter 2 IFAC IEG 9 defines as 'the goal of accountancy education and experience to produce competent professional accountants with the necessary knowledge, skills and professional values and with an attitude of learning to learn.' A programme for qualification should consist of the following elements.

- General Knowledge
- Organisational & Business Knowledge
- IT Knowledge
- Accounting & Accounting Related Knowledge
- Practical Experience
- Qualification

General knowledge is described as 'Arts, sciences, humanities for the development of general knowledge, intellectual skills and communication skills. Two years of a four-year degree (or equivalent).' If this is compared with the actual situation two conclusions are apparent.

(1) Worldwide the majority of new accountants and auditors has either an accountancy, finance or business university degree or a general university degree. Higher education has a relatively higher importance in countries that are in transition or emerging. This is discussed in the paragraphs 620 and 720. In general it can be concluded that the education of accountants and auditors is at the same level as the education of other professionals in their country. This of course is a reasonable and achievable goal and the maximum that can be expected in this area about the implementation of a guideline on accountancy education. Without further information about the international comparability of, for example, university degrees this does not help in identifying the qualification levels. If a more transparent system of international recognition of university degrees was available it would be of great help in the mutual recognition of accountancy qualifications.

(2) It may well be that the content of university and higher education programmes does not fit the general knowledge as described in IFAC IEG 9. In fact it can be expected that only in countries like the USA with a very high participation in university education two years of a four year degree will be devoted to arts, sciences and humanities in general. This is not necessarily a problem. It is quite logical that general knowledge of accountants is developed on the highest country level. Furthermore in countries where a high participation in university education has not yet been achieved intelligent, young people should find opportunities to become accountant in a work-study combination. This is not only to their advantage but also to the benefit of the accountancy profession, which has to attract the best candidates in competition with other employers. The positive effects of such a dual system have been clearly shown in the education of teachers and accountants in the Netherlands during the last century.

The conclusions about the subjects in the various programmes of accountancy education can only be general. If subjects are included this is only a first step towards, for example, mutual recognition of qualifications. Separate content analysis is outside the scope of this research project. Conclusions however have been reached about subjects in the programme and the relation between knowledge, skills and professional values.

In Organisational & Business Knowledge economics, quantitative methods and organisational behaviour are covered in almost all programmes. This is not the case for operations management, marketing and international business. Probably specific attention is needed for the inclusion of the last subject. IT Knowledge and all subjects in Accounting & Accounting Related Knowledge are at least covered. IT knowledge and applications in other subjects are becoming to get more attention but from discussions in the IFAC Education Committee it is known that much is still to be desired about the implementation of IFAC IEG 11[31]. In respect to ICT it makes a vast difference whether candidates follow full time education or have the opportunity to combine professional education with hands-on experience during practical experience. In respect to the first situation AICPA has made an important contribution to the implementation of IFAC IEG 11[32]. In respect to the second situation it is necessary for qualification purposes to ensure that all candidates receive the appropriate practical experience.

Skills get increasingly attention in professional education, for the moment with emphasis on intellectual skills. The systematic integration of skills in practical experience is at the beginning.

Practical experience is described as 'prior to recognition a minimum of three years approved and properly supervised practical experience primarily in the function concerned and in a suitable professional environment'. The definition leaves open the question whether practical experience should take place before or after the final examination.

Practical experience before the final examination is not always requested. The exemptions are in America: CGA Canada, CMA Canada, AICPA in the USA, IMCP in Mexico; in the European Union: ACCA in the UK; in Central and Eastern Europe: CACR in the Czech Republic; in Africa: ICPAK in Kenya; in the Middle East: SOCPA in Saudi Arabia. Variations in content, length, requirements and employment sector are analysed in the previous paragraph.

Qualification depends on a final examination of 'professional competence assessing theoretical knowledge and the ability to apply that knowledge competently in a practical situation'. Here there is an important difference between IFAC IEG 9 and the EU 8th Directive. The 8th Directive requires 'the ability to apply that knowledge in practice'. In the review here the position is taken that for a professional qualification experience in the work place is a necessary element.

For 32 out of 34 professional bodies a final examination is requested before qualification. In all common law countries and in most civil law countries the professional body provides the examination, or is one of the providers. In civil law countries where the government provides the examination, there is usually a close cooperation with the profession. Normally there is a system of mandatory or voluntary professional education before the final examination. In most cases the professional body is one of the providers, frequently in cooperation with the universities.

Recognition of Qualifications

For the comparison of mutual recognition agreements professional bodies are represented in Table 740.1 Mutual Recognition on the regional basis given in the preceding paragraph.

---

[31] IFAC Education Committee, IFAC International Education Guideline 11, Information Technology in the Accounting Curriculum, 1995

[32] IFAC Education Committee, Implementing International Education Guideline 11 Information Technology in the Accounting Curriculum, Strategies of the American Institute of Certified Public Accountants, 1996

Table 740.1 Mutual Recognition (see end of the chapter)

Mutual recognition is ruled by the GATS, by IFAC and regional directives and by agreements between countries. The GATS as a general agreement does not relate to content, but to the procedures that should be followed. The GATS requires that all countries have procedures to verify qualifications of professionals from other countries. Though GATS is multinational in scope it does provide for bilateral implementation. Rules set out by GATS are meant to ensure the same privileges for foreign providers and domestic counterparts, to remove discriminatory obstacles and to provide transparency.

Responsibility of the professional body is addressed by IFAC. Member bodies of IFAC should not only satisfy themselves that the assessment(s) undergone by applicants indeed test the body of knowledge and the ability to apply it, but that the policies and procedures for its construction, security and marking are adequate to ensure the integrity of the assessment process. Agreement should also be reached on the need for a periodic review of the education and assessment process so as to ensure that conditions for recognition continue to apply. The only regional directive is the EU Directive on Mutual Recognition[33]. In combination with the EU 8th Directive the effect is that auditor qualifications are recognized throughout the European Union and the European Free Trade Association (EFTA) with the exception of an examination in local law and regulation.

Comparison of the material in Table 740.1 shows that we are only at the beginning of mutual recognition agreements between professional bodies and countries. Interest in cross border recognition is certainly increasing and results are being achieved, but at the moment these are still limited and on an individual basis. Limited in the sense that (1) most agreements only give access to examinations, sometimes with exemptions, (2) there is no systematic coverage of relations between countries. A specific problem is that mutual recognition may not yet be possible because a system is further developed than its counterpart. Sometimes also objectives are incompatible as is shown by the following example. The UK government blocked mutual recognition between CPA's in the USA and Chartered Accountants in the United Kingdom because the agreement did not include other qualifications of professional accountants in the UK.

750   Development in Time

The development in time can be measured by the changing demands on the qualification, education and training of accountants and auditors, the changing approaches in and content of standards, guidelines and directives and, last but by no means least, major local initiatives to keep accountancy education up to par.

It is well to realise that accountancy education has gone through various stages of development. The oldest system in place, ICAS in the United Kingdom, has a history of almost 150 years. Others may have started their present development as part of an increasingly global market economy in the last twenty years. Looking back over the last half century it seems clear that in the industrialised countries much attention was given to the development of theoretical programmes and to the implementation of those programmes in regular university and general higher education. In the same period participation in university education in those countries increased enormously. As a result the number of degree holders increased also, which effectively gave accountancy education an opportunity to concentrate on higher levels of knowledge, skills and competences.

If in this paragraph we concentrate on relatively new developments it is with the clear understanding that in each country priorities have to be set and that these may well have to concentrate on establishing the profession and the basic programmes that are necessary. In the recent past the accountancy profession has contributed to the emancipation of higher education to the benefit of

---

[33] Council Directive of 21 December 1988 on a General System for the Recognition of Higher-education Diplomas awarded on completion of professional education and training of at least three years' duration.

economic development and personal development. This role should not be neglected in view of new challenges.

Drivers of chance identified by the ICA Australia and discussed in Chapter 2 will have a tremendous effect on accountancy education. Just one quote from Chapter 2 can illustrate the kind of developments accountancy educators and trainers are facing. 'Largely nationally based education systems must also fully reflect the global dimension. This should extent to understanding different cultures, legal and organisational systems and their impact on doing business in different jurisdictions. Education must be harmonized internationally and be relevant and customised for individuals and organisations.' Without co-operation on all levels the necessary changes will or rather cannot be realised.

As far back as 1986 systematic chance in a global setting was addressed in the Bedford Committee report. It translated the demands on the profession in demands on accountancy education. Even then the total was far too much for any individual. Therefore it was of paramount importance that the Accounting Education Change Commission in 1990 concluded that 'accounting education should prepare students to <u>become</u> professional accountants, not to <u>be</u> professional accountants at the time of entry to the profession. To attain and maintain the status of a professional accountant requires continual learning.' Since then CPE has become mandatory for a large number of professional bodies. It now has become high time to recognize in education guidelines that a qualification as an accountant or auditor is a starting point in a professional career and that it does not reflect the final level of professional competence. Without that realisation accountancy education may well face an impossible task in trying to cope with a too ambitious wish list.

In the Global Accountancy Education questionnaire respondents were asked to indicate in which of the following areas future developments were expected. For each of the four areas the three most frequent answers are summarised below.

- Regulation of the Profession: (1) more self-regulation; (2) more independent regulation; (3) development of CPE.
- Professional Qualification Requirements: (1) examination requirements; (2 and 3) expansion of accountancy qualifications; (2 and 3) programme development.
- Professional Education: (1) programme development; (2) education system; (3 and 4) quality assurance, (3 and 4) international harmonisation.
- Practical Training: (1) practical experience requirements; (2) programme development; (3) international harmonisation.

It seems logical to conclude that, notwithstanding the importance of clear and achievable guidelines, the real issue for accountancy education could very well be how to set an agenda for implementation and compliance that respects local circumstances and possibilities.

760   **IFAC International Education Standards**

Recently the IFAC Education Committee has published draft International Education Standards for Professional Accountants. These reflect new developments and are partly based on previous statements[34].

- Guiding Principles for International Education Statements (May 2002)
- Entry Requirements (June 2002)
- Content of Professional Education Programmes (June 2002)
- Professional Skills and General Education (June 2002)
- Experience Requirements (June 2002)
- Assessment of Professional Competence (June 2002)
- Continuing Professional Education and Development (June 2002)

The 'Guiding Principles' provide information on objectives and terms of reference, international education standards and guidelines, mission and strategic objectives of the IFAC Education Committee and about the nature, scope and authority of statements. A 'Glossary of Terms' is included.

The IFAC Education Committee has provided definitions of standards, guidelines and papers.
International Education Standards for Professional Accountants prescribe standards of generally accepted "good practice" in education and development for professional accountants.
International Education Guidelines for Professional Accountants assist in the implementation of generally accepted "good practice" in the education of professional accountants by providing advice or guidance on how to achieve "good practice" or current "best practice".
International Education Papers for Professional Accountants promote discussion or debate on education issues affecting the accounting profession, present findings, or describe situations of interest relating to education issues affecting the accounting profession.

---

[34] IFAC Education Committee statements quoted in this paragraph.

- Guiding Principles for International Education Statements (May 2002)
- Entry Requirements, Proposed International Education Standard for Professional Accountants (June 2002)
- IEG 9, Prequalification Education, Assessment of Professional Competence and Experience Requirements of Professional Accountants, International Education Guideline 9 (First Issued 1991, Revised 1996)
- Content of Professional Education Programmes, Proposed International Education Standard for Professional Accountants (June 2002)
- IEG 11, Information Technology for Professional Accountants,, International Education Guideline 11 (First Issued 1995, Revised 1998 and 2002)
- Professional Skills and General Education, Proposed International Education Standard for Professional Accountants (June 2002)
- Competence-based Approaches to the Preparation and Work of Professional Accountants, Discussion paper (First Issued 1998, Revised 2001)
- Experience Requirements, Proposed International Education Standard for Professional Accountants (June 2002)
- Practical Experience, Discussion Paper (Issued 1998)
- Specialization in the Accounting Profession, Discussion Paper (Issued 1992)
- Assessment of Professional Competence, Proposed International Education Standard for Professional Accountants (June 2002)
- Advisory on Examination Administration, Study (Issued 1998)
- Continuing Professional Education and Development, Proposed International Education Standard for Professional Accountants (June 2002)
- IEG 2, Continuing Professional Education, International Education Guideline 2 (First Issued 1982, Revised 1998)

The 'Glossary of Terms' that is given in the 'Guiding Principles' comprises 'a collection of defined terms, many of which have been specifically defined within existing Education Committee Statements. The Committee acknowledges that terms may be understood to have different nuances of meaning, and may have different applications, among the various countries in which member bodies operate. The glossary does not prescribe the use of terms by member bodies. Rather, the glossary is a list of defined terms *as they are used within the Standards, Guidelines and Papers* produced by the Education Committee.'

In the view of the author great importance must be attached to the use of standard definitions for the field of accountancy education. A better understanding and comparability of statements, publications and research results can be achieved and will advance international development. For this reason the IFAC Glossary of Terms is included in this report as Annex 7. However, as the definitions became available towards the end of the Global Accountancy Education research project, terms may have been used in a different meaning.

The Standard on 'Entry Requirements' prescribes 'the entry requirements for candidates beginning the qualifying process for becoming professional accountants'. The standard is based on IEG 9 and requires that 'the entry requirement for an individual seeking to begin a programme of study leading to membership as a professional accountant should be at least equivalent to one that would entitle the individual to admission into a recognized university degree programme or its equivalent'. Standard reference sources are provided for the comparison of the level of general qualifications.

The Standard on the 'Content of Professional Education Programmes' prescribes the 'primary content of professional education programs under three major headings: organizational and business knowledge, IT knowledge and accounting, finance and related knowledge.' In general the recommendations in IEG 9 and IEG 11 are followed. Comparison shows the following differences with IEG 9 as analysed in Chapter 2.

Under 'organisational and business knowledge' new subjects are mentioned: 'business environment, international business, corporate governance and business ethics'. These subjects are not covered as separate topics in the analysis in Chapter 6. In comparison with IEG 9 the draft Standard gives more attention to IT requirements and the environment in which these can be acquired. Specific reference is made to work experience. Compared with IEG 9 there are some important changes in the subject headings for 'accounting and accounting related knowledge': 'management accounting and control' in stead of 'management accounting', 'audit and assurance' in stead of 'auditing', 'professional values and ethics' in stead of 'professional ethics'. Moreover 'strategic decision making' is added as a separate subject. In the draft standard some differentiation is allowed 'to meet the needs of particular environments'.

The Standard on 'Professional Skills and General Education' prescribes 'the skills, both personal and professional, that candidates must have to qualify as professional accountants. Part of this purpose is to show how the acquisition of a broad general education, that may be gained in a variety of ways and within different contexts, can contribute to the development of these skills. This Standard prescribes the skills professional accountants require grouped under five main headings: intellectual skills, technical and functional skills, personal skills, interpersonal and communication skills, organizational and business management skills.' The Standard is based on IEG 9 and previous discussion papers on Competence-based Approaches. The previous description of skills in IEG 9 is restricted to 'intellectual skills, interpersonal skills and communication skills'.

The Standard on 'Experience Requirements' prescribes 'the practical experience and training member bodies should require their members to obtain to qualify as professional accountants. Further training may be required after qualification to bring a candidate up to the level of a statutory auditor or some other form of specialization. Life-long learning will be required to renew professional competence and keep it up to date'. The monitoring, control and assessment of practical experience by the IFAC member body or the regulatory authority are included in the Standard. The Standard is based on IEG 9 and previous discussion papers on Competence-based Approaches, Practical Experience and Specialisation.

The Standard on 'Assessment of Professional Competence' prescribes 'the requirement for a process of assessment of a candidate's professional competence before admission to the profession'. In comparison with IEG 9 a competence approach of assessment has been chosen, in which competence is defined as 'being able to perform a work role to a defined standard with reference to real working environments. The critical consideration is whether the evidence collected is a valid, reliable and credible means of establishing whether a particular aspect of competence has been achieved'. The Standard is based on IEG 9 and previous discussion papers on Competence-based Approaches, Examination Administration and Specialisation.

The Standard on 'Continuing Professional Education and Development' requires 'member bodies to implement a mandatory continuing professional education and development (hereafter referred to as continuing professional development or CPD) programme'. It is based on IEG 2 and introduces a minimum level of mandatory CPD. These levels may be input based (e.g., prescribed number of hours per year) or output based (e.g. demonstrable competences at an appropriate level).

In general the new draft International Education Standards, IES for short, give additional guidance elaborating on the already existing system of approved International Education Guidelines.

Table 730.1   **Final Examination Core Programmes**

Country Prof. Body	Final Examination Core Programmes
Canada CGA Canada	The certification level of the Program of Professional Studies requires a candidate to pass four (4 hour) final examinations for a total of 16 hours. These consist of Financial Accounting 4, Professional Applications 1 and 2 other PACE level courses from a course selection offered from one of four career options. The career options include: corporate / small-medium enterprises, information technology, government, not-for-profit and public practice. The course selection offered in these career options include: Finance 2, Management Auditing 1 or Auditing 2, Taxation 2, Management Information Systems 2, and Public Sector Financial Management. The objective of the professional examinations is to assess whether a candidate has met the established standards of knowledge, skills, and professional values required for certification as a professional accountant, is competent to provide reliable service to a professional level to the public.
Canada CMA Canada	Syllabus includes: Financial Management, Corporate Finance, Operations Management, Information Technology, Strategic Management, International Business, Human Resources, Marketing, Taxation, Internal Control. Objectives: to indicate the cognitive skills and learning objectives to be tested for each topic and subtopic in the syllabus. The cognitive skill level expectations are based on Bloom's Taxonomy of Educational Objectives. Cognitive skills tested are: Knowledge, Comprehension and Application.
Canada ICA Alberta	Core skills-apply the knowledge specified in the subject areas-identify, define and rank problems and issues-analyse information-address problems in an integrative manner-evaluate alternatives and propose practical solutions that respond to user needs-communicate clearly and effectively. Syllabus: Profession as a practice, assurance and related services: 25-35%. Risk management, control and IT 5-10%. Financial accounting and reporting 25-35%. Managerial accounting 5-10%. Taxation 10-20%.
Mexico IMCP	Since 1999 the IMCP implemented a 12 hours uniform accounting examination, in order to certify those accountants that already have an accounting certificate issued by the university and also the professional licence issued by the Ministry of Education. The examination includes Financial Accounting, Taxation, Business Law, Finance, Auditing, Ethics and Managerial Accounting.
USA AICPA	The CPA examination consists of four parts. See AICPA Information to Candidates brochure: Examination Content Specifications. Subjects: Business Law, Auditing, Financial Reporting, Accountancy & Reporting
France Ordre	The final examination includes 3 tests with no possible exemptions: 1. A thesis on a subject related to the professional domain 2. A written test on the statutory and contractual auditing of financial statements 3. An oral test related to the traineeship and covering professional knowledge in general.
Germany IDW	Accounting, Financial Statement Audit, Other Audits, Business Administration, Economics, Business Law, Tax Law.
The Netherlands NIVRA	The final examination consists of a theoretical and a practical part. For both parts a separate thesis must be written and defended.

Spain IACJCE	Exam about audit matters, to confirm: - practical experience - profitability of professional training.
Sweden FAR	Approved Public Accountant: Passing the examination of professional competence as approved public accountant (revisorsexamen) to ensure the necessary level of theoretical knowledge (to the extent that this does not follow from the academic degree) and the ability to apply the knowledge in practice. Authorised Public Accountant: passing the examination of professional competence as authorised public accountant (högre revisorsexamen).
United Kingdom ACCA	ACCA's membership qualification includes 14 written examinations divided into three parts. The final part consists of three core papers plus two papers chosen from four options.
United Kingdom ICAEW	Integrated business case study and associated technical subjects.
United Kingdom ICAS	50% technical and 50% communicative in a case study format.
Czech Republic CACR	The final exam consists of 7 written and a final oral exam. Written exams: 1. Macro- and Microeconomics 2. Accounting 3. Business Combinations and Consolidated Accounts 4. Business, Civic and Financial Law including Taxation 5. Corporate Finance 6. Statistics and Information Technology 7. Auditing
Hungary CHA	The final examination consists of six topics: Law (the learning course consists of 60 class hours); Organisation and Management (the learning course consists of 45 class hours); Finance (the learning course consists of 75 class hours); Accountancy and Analysis (the learning course consists of 140 class hours); Organisation of Accountancy (Similar to Information Technology) (The learning course consists of 80 class hours); Auditing and Internal Control (The learning course consists of 120 class hours). Auditing and Internal Control is the last important examination, because it consists of all the components of the formal education.
Poland SKwP	No final examination
Poland KIBR	The final exam is an oral exam and tests the experience gained during practice as well as theoretical knowledge in the areas of financial accounting, economics and management, civil law, labour law, economic law, tax law, finance, cost accounting and management accounting, financial statements and analysis of financial statements, auditing and other services rendered by auditors.
Russian Fed. IPA Russia	The certification of professional accountants confirms the conformity of the specialist to the requirements of professional competence (level of special training, skills, experience in the corresponding type of business). Auditor certification is possible for persons with economic or legal (higher or intermediate special) education who have worked for not less than three years out of the last five years as either an auditor, specialist of an auditing organisation (auditing firm), accountant, economist, inspector, manager of an enterprise, member of staff of a scientific body, or teacher in an economics field. Requirements for financial directors are very close to the requirements for chief accountants but for the big enterprises.

Turkey TURMOB	Financial Accounting, Cost and Management Accounting, Financial Statement Analysis, Business Law, Taxation, Auditing, Accounting Law
Kenya ICPAK	Financial Accounting, Business Finance, Management, Auditing, Information Technology & Systems.
South Africa SAICA	Auditing, Financial Accounting, Taxation, Managerial Accounting & Financial Management, Information Technology. Other supportive courses, including company law, communication skills, human resource management, marketing, etc.
Lebanon LACPA	General Accounting (including management and analytical accounting), (2) Advanced Accounting (including international accounting standards), (3) Auditing, (4) Taxation & Business Law Plus final interview.
Saudi Arabia SOCPA	The exam consist of five subjects: 1- Accounting (all areas); 2- Auditing; 3- Tax and Zakah (islamic due); 4- Commercial laws; 5- Figh almamalat (how to conduct operation in Islam). SOCPA fellowship examination rules include professional, practical and scientific aspects of the audit profession and applicable regulations.
Hong Kong HKSA	Main objective of the final examination is to provide formal verification that candidates can demonstrate a competent practitioner level of performance.
India ICA India	Group-1: Advanced Accounting, Management Accounting and Financial Analysis, Advanced Auditing, Corporate Laws and Secretarial Practice; Group-2: Cost Management, Management Information and Control Systems, Direct Taxes, Indirect Taxes
India ICWAI	Advanced Financial Accounting, Information Technology and Computer Applications, Operation Management and Control, Project Management and Control, Advanced Management Accounting-Technique and Applications, Advanced Financial Management, Advanced Management Accounting-Strategic Management, Cost Audit. In addition the students are required to undergo training in different fields by way of Group Discussion, Business Communication, Project preparation, hands-on on computer.
Japan JICPA	The first stage assesses whether the candidate has the basic knowledge required to apply for the second stage examination. The test covers the Japanese language, mathematics, English and an essay. At the second stage the applicants are assessed for professional knowledge required for an accountant. The examination consists of multiple-choice test and written test. Multiple-choice: Accounting and commercial code. Written: Required: accounting (bookkeeping, financial statements, cost accounting and auditing) and commercial code. Choose two out of three: business management, economics and civil code. At the third stage the applicants are assessed for technical competence in professional judgment required for a CPA. The four subjects for the final examination are auditing, accounting, financial analysis and taxation.
Malaysia MACPA	(1) Financial Accounting and Reporting II - (2) Advanced Taxation - (3) Audit Practice - (4) Business Finance and Strategy.
Malaysia MIA	No final examination
Pakistan ICAP	Objective of the examination is tot test the knowledge and skills of candidates which they have gained through studies and during with registered CA firms. The syllabus covers subjects that will enable the candidates to be proficient in

	the current trends and developments in the profession and to assume leadership roles. Subjects examined are : 1- Advanced Auditing 2- Advanced Accounting & Financial Reporting 3- Corporate Laws 4- Business Management 5- Management Accounting 6- Business Finance Decisions 7- Advanced Taxation 8- Information Technology Management, Audit and Control
Pakistan ICMAP	Institute examinations and courses cover Foundation I and II; Professional I, II, III, IV and V. Levels of competency are defined for all course outlines with a distinction between general education, conceptual and theoretical knowledge, specialized knowledge and skills, professional knowledge and skills
Australia ICA Australia	Our test of professional competence includes examination and non-examination components. The broad range of knowledge skills and values developed needs to be assessed using a variety of different tools such that the maximum examination component for any one module is 50%. The program consists of 5 modules.
Australia CPA Australia	Reporting and Professional Practice and Corporate Governance and Accountability plus 3 electives
New Zealand ICANZ	The Professional Competence Programme is required to develop within candidates a range of relevant attributes covering knowledge; technical skills; organisational skills; personal skills; interpersonal skills; analytical and constructive cognitive skills; synthetical, appreciative, and judgemental cognitive skills; and professional values.

Table 730.2   **Professional Education Core Programmes**

Country Prof. Body	Professional Education Core Programmes
Canada CGA Canada	Foundation Studies LEVEL 1 Financial Accounting 1, Economics1, Law 1; LEVEL 2: Financial Accounting 2, Practice Set 1, Quantitative Methods1, Quantitative Methods Bridging, Management Accounting 1, Communications1; LEVEL 3: Financial Accounting 3, Practice Set 2, Finance 1, Management Information Systems 1; Advanced Studies LEVEL 4: Management Accounting 2, Accounting Theory 1, Auditing 1, Practice Set 3, Taxation 1; Professional Certification PACE LEVEL: Financial Accounting 4, Finance 2, Auditing 2, Management Auditing 1, Management Information Systems, Public Sector Financial Management
Canada CMA Canada	Core Program: Strategy, Management, Management Accounting, Operations Management, Marketing, Information Technology. Objectives: To shape CMAs as financial and strategic management professionals to lead successful enterprises. Content, structure and delivery designed to hone strategic leadership capabilities and ensure they bring integrating perspective to organizational decision making. Two-year program of distance education plus interactive sessions taken on a part time basis.
Canada ICA Alberta	Will vary from province to province but all include financial accounting, auditing and taxation. Main objective is to prepare the candidates to be professional accountants and to understand their professional responsibilities. Professional program emphasizes accounting, auditing and tax.
Mexico IMCP	Accounting, Managerial Accounting, Taxation, Business Law, Auditing, Finance, Economics, Information Technology, Quantitative Methods and Statistics, Organisational Behaviour and Operations Management. A typical accounting university programme is 4 to 5 years, 200 hours and 40 to 50 courses. In order to get the university accounting certificate the students must write a dissertation or take a national accounting examination developed by Ceneval (note that this examination is different from IMCP's Uniform Accounting Examination) or take additional postgraduate courses.
USA AICPA	Principles of Financial & Managerial Accountancy, Intermediate Financial Accountancy, Cost, Tax, Auditing, Accountancy Systems. AACSB requires that general education makes up 50% of an undergraduate accounting degree programme. Foundation knowledge also has to include basic financial and managerial accounting, behavioural science, economics, mathematics and statistics plus operations and technology management. The standards include coverage of written and oral communication. Specialised skills cover concepts of financial reporting, managerial accounting, information systems, auditing and taxation. Topics on not-for-profit/governmental accounting should also be covered.
France Ordre	To succeed to a complete syllabus divided into 16 parts corresponding to 3 diplomas: - Diplôme préparatoire aux études comptables et financières, DPECF (preliminary accounting diploma); - Diplôme d'études comptables et financières, DECF (intermediate accounting diploma); - Diplôme d'études supérieures comptables et financières, DESCF (higher accounting diploma). The whole curriculum requires a learning period of 8 years, including the three-year training period.

	Core programme of professional education: DPECF (5 written tests): 1/ introduction to business law 2/ economics 3/ quantitative methods, mathematics and statistics 4/ accounting 5/ French and foreign languages. DECF (7 written tests): 1/ business law and tax law 2/ credit law, labour law and contentious law 3/ organisation and management 4/ financial management 5/ mathematics, statistics and information technology 6/ financial accounting and auditing 7/ management accounting and management control DESCF (2 written tests and 2 oral tests) : 1/ accounting and law 2/ accounting and management 3/ economics (oral) 4/ discussion on a report of 6 - week practical training period (oral) DEC (3 examinations): 1/ written test in audit to insure that the candidates have the ability to make a decision (to certify or not the financial statements) and to discuss a complex situation; 2/ oral test, experience assessment 3/ discussion of a thesis which test the ability to perform research, autonomy in thinking, and the ability to carry out self education.
Germany IDW	A university degree in business administration or law recognized in Germany (eg. Diplom-Kaufmann, etc.) and the final Examination are required. There are no additional professional educational programs required. The legally required minimum duration for the university is 8 semesters (four years), but the majority takes ten to twelve semesters (five to six years). The additional examination tutoring usually requires an additional one to two years of part-time study during the period of practical work experience.
The Netherlands NIVRA	Main areas of accountancy: Financial Accounting and Management Accounting, Accounting Information Systems, Auditing. The majority of the students start after a four year degree education at a university (masters degree in accounting or economics) or an institute of higher economic education. There is also a seven year part time programme that starts directly after secondary education
Spain IACJCE	Accounting, Taxation, Legal, Audit. Lecture: 5 days per week/15 hours. Self: 10 hours per week. More or less three years for graduates.
Sweden FAR	The basic qualification level consists of 3 years academic studies and 3 years of practical training. For the higher qualification the answer is 4 + 5 years. The theoretical studies up to graduation are full time. During practical training 350 hours of classes is recommended for the first three years and another 100 for the last two years to the higher qualification. Basic qualification: Bachelor degree in finance and accounting (3 years). Advanced qualification: Master degree (4 years) or bachelor with 1 additional year of free subjects. Immediately after primary and secondary education or later in life under an adult education programme.
United Kingdom ACCA	The examinations papers cover the following: 1.1 Preparing financial statements; 1.2 Financial information for management; 1.3 Managing people; 2.1 Information systems; 2.2 Corporate and business law; 2.3 Business taxation; 2.4 Financial management and control; 2.5 Financial reporting; 2.6 Audit and internal Review; 3.1 Audit and assurance services; 3.2 Advanced taxation; 3.3 Performance measurement; 3.4 Business information management; 3.5 Strategic business planning and development; 3.6 Advanced corporate reporting; 3.7 Strategic information management.
United Kingdom ICAEW	Professional (First) Stage aims to provide knowledge and understanding of concepts and principles. Examinations are: Accounting, Financial Reporting, Auditing and Assurance, Taxation, Business Finance, Business Management, Business and Company Law. Advanced (Second) Stage provides an integrated

	approach to the giving of business and financial advice. There are two Tests of Technical Competence plus an Advanced Case Study that include Audit and Assurance, Financial Reporting, and Taxation.
United Kingdom ICAS	Attendance at compulsory ICAS classes and completion of education programme. This requires a three/four-year university degree plus a three-year training contract during which students follow up to 26 weeks of full time ICAS classes.
Czech Republic CACR	Macroeconomics and Microeconomics, Accounting, Business Combination and Consolidated Accounts Business, Civic and Financial Law (Including Taxation, Social and Health Insurance), Corporate Finance, Quantitative Methods and Information Technology, Auditing, Final Oral Exam.
Hungary CHA	Subjects Law, Organisation and Management, Finance, Financial and Management Accounting, IT, Auditing and Internal Control. Full time and part time; total minimal class hours 520 in 2 years.
Poland SKwP	Not applicable
Poland KIBR	The core programme of professional education includes 10 subjects: financial accounting - part 1; economics and management; civil law, labour law, economic law; tax law - part 1; finance; tax law - part 2; financial accounting – part 2; cost accounting and management accounting; financial statements and analysis of financial statements; auditing and other services rendered by auditors.
Russian Fed. IPA Russia	The accountancy curriculum at the universities follows four educational cycles: 1) Humanities and social Disciplines 2) Mathematical and general naturally-scientific disciplines 3) General professional disciplines 4) Special disciplines. The 'special discipline cycle' is the professional training of a student, which reflects the specifics of a particular branch and its advanced training. It assumes professional activity of the specialist in different areas of the economy. Only institutions authorised by the State can give a special graduation diploma to their graduates. These diplomas are: Diploma of higher education, given after graduation from any institute if higher education (university, academy, institute); Diploma of professional secondary education in bookkeeping, given after graduation from a college; having earned this diploma a graduate has the right to take the entrance exam to the third year of a university program; Diploma of professional secondary education given after graduation from a vocational training school; this diploma is ranked lower because it gives the right to take the entrance exam to the first year of a university program.
Turkey TURMOB	Accounting fields, Finance Fields, Law, Tax, Business Administration
Kenya ICPAK	Financial Accounting, Business, Management & Finance, Auditing, Information Technology & Systems
South Africa SAICA	Financial Accounting, Auditing, Managerial Accounting & Financial Management, Taxation, Information Technology.
Lebanon LACPA	Students in preparation for the final examination usually rely on their own learning at the university or accounting professional technical centres. The LACPA does not oversee any formal professional education program for exam purposes.

Saudi Arabia SOCPA	SOCPA offers courses covering SOCPA fellowship examination. The aim of these courses is to enable the trainee to be acquainted with the theoretical and practical aspects of accounting and auditing and to apply it skilfully. Each course consists of a number of training materials and each training material covers one or more topics of SOCPA fellowship exam subjects, which include accounting, auditing, zakat and tax, jurisprudence and business law. Each training material includes a discussion of the objectives and elements of the topic, a sufficient explanation of each element, and the same is connected to the relevant professional standards. It also includes problems and application cases
Hong Kong HKSA	The objective of the Professional Programme is to provide candidates with the opportunity, through the different modules of the programme and under the guidance of workshop facilitators, to develop the necessary application skills and competencies, which are essential for a professional accountant. The Professional Programme comprises 4 modules: Financial Reporting, Financial Management, Auditing and Information Management, Taxation. Each of the 4 modules requires 15 weeks' self-study and attendance in 4 three-hour workshops. The modules may be taken in any order and up to 2 modules can be taken at any one time, therefore the shortest duration of professional education is 1 year.
India ICA India	Professional Education Course-1 (PE-1): Fundamentals of Accounting, Mathematics and Statistics, Economics, Business Communication and Organisation and Management. Professional Education Course-2 (PE-2): Accounting, Auditing, Business and Corporate Laws, Cost Accounting and Financial Management, Income Tax and Central Sales Tax, Information Technology. Final CA Course: Advanced Accounting, Management Accounting and Financial Analysis, Advanced Auditing, Corporate Laws and Secretarial Practice, Cost Management, Management Information and Control Systems, Direct Taxes, Indirect Taxes.
India ICWAI	Cost and Management Accountancy, General Accounting, Auditing, Management Audit, Taxation, Financial Management etc (see examination programme). Our course is designed to accommodate working people in Trade/Commerce and Industry also and hence the training provision is part time only. Minimum duration of Intermediate Course is 18 months. After passing Intermediate Examination, one is eligible for admission to Final Exam. After Graduation, one has to be registered (admitted) in the Institute.
Japan JICPA	Two-year education courses offered by the JICPA in auditing, accounting, ethics, and taxation.
Malaysia MACPA	Professional Examination I Module A: Audit Fundamentals, Financial Accounting & Reporting I, Information Systems; Module B: Company Law & Practice, Managerial Planning & Control, Organisational Management. Professional Examination II Module C: Financial Accounting & Reporting II, Advanced Taxation. Module D: Audit Practice, Business Finance & Strategy. The programme is offered full-time and part-time. The minimum amount of time required to adequately prepare for the CPA examination is 2 years.
Malaysia MIA	Not applicable
Pakistan ICAP	Auditing, Accounting and Reporting, Business & Commercial Laws, Taxation, IT. Objectives are given in the syllabus of each paper which can be found at the ICAP website.

Pakistan ICMAP	Foundation-1: Principles of Accounting, Computer Systems & Applications, Business English, Economics & Business Environment. Foundation-II: Financial Accounting, Information Technology, Industrial & Commercial Laws. Professional-I: Management Science Applications, Cost Accounting, Business Communication & Report Writing, Quantitative Methods. Professional-II: Advanced Financial Accounting, Operational Cost Accounting, Business Taxation, Corporate Laws & Secretarial Practices. Professional-III: Financial Reporting, Strategic Management Accounting, Organisational Behaviour Strategic Management, Auditing. Professional-IV: Strategic Financial Management, Corporate Performance Audit & Evaluation, Marketing Management, Information Management. The completion of each stage shall require a period of six months, which shall include 120 days for coaching and 60 days for self-study and examination. The candidate has to clear Foundation as well as two parts of Prof 1 and 2 before sitting in the final exam. Education takes place by attending regular classes provided by ICMAP or fulfilling correspondence requirements and on the job training and biannual exam. About three years is required in total.
Australia ICA Australia	The CA Program consists of five modules:- CA Foundations- Financial Reporting & Assurance- Taxation & Financial Reporting- Strategic Business Management- CA Integrative. The CA Program is a minimum of 2 years part time. Candidates are required to be in employment whilst undertaking the CA program. The amount of time provided depends upon the employer, however, candidates are advised that a minimum commitment of 190 hours is required per module.
Australia CPA Australia	The core subjects in the CPA Program are 'Reporting and Professional Practice', 'Corporate Governance and Accountability' plus three electives
New Zealand ICANZ	Academic study covers financial accounting, management accounting, auditing, taxation, business finance/treasury, information technology/accounting information systems, economics, organisational management, commercial law and statistics. At least 20% of the required four years of bachelor's degree level study must be in (non-specified) general studies. The professional programme deals with the structure and authority of the profession, professional ethics, current non-technical topics relevant to the profession, professional skills, business environment, compliance (i.e. external reporting, audit, taxation), financial management and business strategy.

Table 730.3   **Practical Training Core Programmes**

Country Prof. Body	Practical Training Core Programmes
Canada CGA Canada	Students on the CGA Program must attain a minimum of two years of acceptable practical experience before receiving certification as a CGA. This experience may be attained in any sector of the economy; industry, government, public practice, commerce, not-for-profit, basically anywhere that accounting and financial work is done. This enables students of the CGA to begin directing their careers into the areas of their choice before they have even completed their studies. Practical experience can start immediately but is reviewed for relevance. Requirement is 36 months of competency based practical training based on the (IFAC) requirement and standard but may be met with minimum 24 months if competencies are achieved
Canada CMA Canada	Two years of experience in operational and management roles which are pre-defined. At least six months of the two-years must be at a managerial level. Practical training is on the job training. Candidates must be working full time. There is a more than sufficient number of jobs available for candidates. Admission requirements before the start of practical training: pass entrance examination. Practical training takes place in industry and commerce and in government The professional body assesses practical training for each candidate based on reports provided by employers.
Canada ICA Alberta	Admission after completion of an undergraduate degree (bachelors, 4 year university). Candidates must complete 30 months (exclusive of study time) in an approved public accounting firm; must complete a total of 2500 chargeable hours of which 1250 hrs must be assurance (audit or review) experience of which 200 (625 in most other provinces) must be audit; 100 hrs of tax experience is also required. Providers must meet standards set by ICAA. Supervision by a CA with 2 years immediate full time public accounting experience; suitable premises; diversity of clients; progressive experience over the required period; participate in client, tax, bank and other meetings; access to hardware and software orientation; procedures training sessions; written evaluation of student performance.
Mexico IMCP	In order to take the uniform accounting examination, the candidates are required to have at least 3 years of practical experience under the supervision of a Certified Public Accountant. The professional experience period starts when the candidates get the accounting certificate from the university and the professional licence from the Ministry of Education.
USA AICPA	In States where practical training is required the minimum for employment is usually a degree in accounting or equivalent. In most states 1-2 years after degree. Licenses to audit can also require experience. Practical experience is gained on the job, provided by employers; no courses or examinations. Public accounting largely, some government, education allowed in most states. Degree of monitoring varies from state to state.
France Ordre	Candidates must obtain the higher accounting studies diploma, DESCF, (4 years at least after the Baccalauréat) before registration as trainee. This includes the six-week practical training period necessary for the DESCF. Full – time three year traineeship (part time in a few circumstances). Two years at least in a professional accountancy or audit firm located in France or in EU. Monitoring by a qualified professional (mentor). Trainees typically work on a variety of accounting, auditing and taxation assignments. - 8 specific one-day

	seminars/year. Half of these seminars focus on technical matters, the other half deal with ethical rules and professional standards. Delivery of 4 written reports on the practical activity.
Germany IDW	A candidate with a university degree must complete at least three years of practical experience (two of which in a Wirtschaftsprüfungsgesellschaft in the area of financial statement audit before being admitted to the final examination. The Wirtschaftsprüfungsgesellschaften have the expertise and resources to provide the practical training required. The WPK recognizes the Wirtschaftsprüfungsgesellschaften.
The Netherlands NIVRA	Candidates for membership require a minimum of 3 year's practical experience. Experience can be obtained after possession of a university or higher education degree in accounting or economics or a diploma of the first four years NIVRA-Nyenrode part time professional education. Practical training is almost full time, four days a week with one day available for classes. The objective of practical training is the application of theoretical knowledge. The areas of practical training are specified in relation to statutory audit. Practical training can be followed in public practice or related fields on the condition that the actual work is comparable to and relevant for statutory audit. Practicing registeraccountants (in the areas distinguished) are responsible as mentor for at least two out of three years practical training. Under government statute providers are recognized by the Board for Practical Training appointed by Royal NIVRA.
Spain IACJCE	Three years full time or part time (200 days per year) in accordance with the possibilities and needs of the student and auditor or firm. No requirements on practical training content. No admission requirements before the start of practical training. Providers of practical training are recognized by the professional body by professional certificate of auditor, firm or company if appropriate.
Sweden FAR	Law requires individual training programmes, containing at least 1500 hours of audit experience. Qualified investigations and experience of solving ethical problems must be included. FAR has issued supplementary guidance. Duration is three years for the basic level of qualification. For advanced qualification another 2 years are required. Part time work is possible, but then the time requirements must be converted pro rata, whereby full time is to be considered as at least 1600 hours per year.
United Kingdom ACCA	Candidates require a minimum of 3 year's practical experience. This can be obtained before, during or after the examinations and in any (combination of) employment sector - industry, commerce, public practice or the public sector. ACCA lays down standards of competence for membership in a Students Training Record. Assessments by supervisors are subject to a sample check by ACCA. For Registered Auditors: 3 years experience in a company audit environment including 2 years after membership in an approved training office under a qualified principal (other national legislation may apply outside the UK). ACCA's latest competency framework covers: Financial information, Business analysis and measurement, Taxation, Statutory audit, Internal review and consultancy, Asset management, Business growth and development, Manage information systems, Manage people. A separate training record for Registered Auditors covers: Audit, Accountancy, Taxation and Business Advice.

United Kingdom ICAEW	3 years under a training contract which includes 450 days technical work experience of which accounting and auditing must occupy a minimum of 100 days. Firms of Chartered Accountants and approved employers offer practical training. Providers are authorised by ICAEW following an approval process carried out by ICAEW training advisors. Regulations include authorised employer, supervision by ICAEW member, training contract, breadth and length of experience, training in professional ethics.
United Kingdom ICAS	At least 450 days experience excluding study holiday and administration. Minimum 43 days in three subject areas. Achievement of competency standards in communication and technical areas per the Achievement Log. The minimum period of Approved Service shall be three years for holders of "fully accredited" degrees, holders of "qualifying" degrees, members of the Association of Chartered Certified Accountants and of the Chartered Institute of Management Accountants and for student members of the two with all the relevant examinations of their own body while working in a training office authorised by ICAS. Four years for others.
Czech Republic CACR	According to the Act on Auditors any new member must work as Assistant Auditor for three years. This practical experience is concretised by the Auditor Guideline of the Chamber, that specifies the content of this "Managed Practice". There are no admission requirements before the start of practical training. Practical training takes place in public practice. Necessary expertise and resources are available with auditing firms and auditors that are looking for future employees, partners or collaborators. The Chamber manages the List of Auditors.
Hungary CHA	Three years full time according to monitoring system regulation; part time is also possible. Admission requirements before the start of practical training: University or college degree of business, accounting, finance. Practical training takes place in public practice. Providers of practical training are recognized by the professional body. One of the CHA membership requirements is professional practice under CHA control. The continuously controlled form of practice is called monitoring system regulation. This on-the-job-training can provide valuable practical exposure to formal education. The monitoring system regulation will be obligatory from September 2002. At present monitoring is the duty of the Admission Committee of CHA. The Admission Committee examines the practical training when it judges applications for membership admission.
Poland SKwP	Not Applicable
Poland KIBR	Candidates must have three years of practice in Poland, including at least a two-year practice under an auditor's supervision. They can start the first year of practical experience straight away; practice under supervision of an auditor can be started only after a candidate has finished the first year of practical experience and after he/ she has passed 7 out of 10 professional exams. The first year of practical training includes independent bookkeeping, computerised system of bookkeeping in accordance with the Accounting Law regulations, knowledge of internal regulations. The two-year practice includes reviewing audit documentation with regard to the documentation's completeness, correctness and consistency; technical work and selected audit work together with audit documentation and preparing lists of documents; participating in auditor's activities connected especially with audit planning, choice of methods and sampling, analysis of company's equity, company's financial and income

	position and checking whether the company acts in compliance with law regulations; participating in auditing of at least two annual financial statements and independent documenting of all activities assigned to the candidate by auditor, preparing proposals of audit report and of auditor's opinion; full audit of an annual financial statement under supervision of an auditor, preparing complete audit documentation, preparing proposals of auditor's opinion, audit report and letter to management of the company audited.
Russian Fed. IPA Russia	Certification of the professional accountant: not less than 5 years of practical experience in economic functions (not less than 3 years for the candidate (doctor) of economic sciences). Auditor certification: not less than three years out of the last five years as either an auditor, specialist of an auditing organisation (auditing firm), accountant, economist, inspector, manager of an enterprise, member of staff of a scientific body, or teacher in an economics field.
Turkey TURMOB	2 year practical experience (on the job training) is required under the supervision of a member. There is an exam to start for practical experience. First, a 4-year university degree is required. Then an entrance exam is needed for the practical experience. After completing practical experience, the final exam is taken.
Kenya ICPAK	Practical training is required for those intending to obtain license for public practice.
South Africa SAICA	The same core areas as for education must be covered in the training period, which could be either 36, 48 or 60 months, depending on the level of education of the trainee. There are no admission requirements before the start of practical training. Regulations for practical training cover training contract with core experience hours, core work attendance hours, core experience topics and supervision. From 2002, SAICA will conduct regular training office reviews. This accreditation will be conducted for training in public practice and outside public practice.
Lebanon LACPA	Training in a recognized office on tasks related primarily to accounting or auditing. University degree or professional accounting technical degree plus formal application before the start of practical training. Experience only counts when the accounting board is informed beforehand. Practical training takes place in public practice. Duration 3 years for holders of baccalaureate degree in business or accounting; 5 years for holders of professional TS degree in accounting (Technicien Supérieur). Providers of practical training are recognized by the professional body.
Saudi Arabia SOCPA	To be a Certified Public Accountant one has to have an experience in CPA firms or commercial or governmental sectors with a job related to accounting or auditing. There is no requirement for the content of practical training but experience. Practical training takes place in public practice, industry and commerce and in government. Each sector has its own expertise. Providers of practical training are recognized by the government and the professional body as each practical training provider has to have a license.
Hong Kong HKSA	Specified practical experience of 3 years for approved degree holders, 4 years for approved accountancy diploma holders and 5 years for holders of other academic qualifications.
India ICA India	Three years of full time practical training is mandatory. Conditions for admission to articleship: not less than 18 years of age, having passed the PE-2 examination, having successfully completed the computer training programme

	specified by the Council. Practical training takes place in public practice and in industry and commerce. The candidate has an option to go for Industrial Training during the third year of his Practical Training, under a member of the Institute serving in Industry, for a period which may range from 9 – 12 months. Regulations for practical training include training contract and reports on Practical Training as required in Chartered Accountants Regulations, 1988 and in recent amendments.
India ICWAI	As per the CWA Act and Regulation, three years training is mandatory for admission to the Associate membership of the Institute. Training is always on-job. The students are guided by senior staff of organisations where they are deployed. There are no admission requirements before the start of practical training. Training is recognized only when the fields are within our ambit of specialization and the organization is registered one to conduct their business activity
Japan JICPA	Two-year audit field work on-the-job training at accounting firms.
Malaysia MACPA	Practical training is normally 3 years full-time employment under the supervision of a member of MACPA in an approved training organization in public practice, commerce, industry or the public sector. Practical experience must include accounting/auditing and at least two of the following categories: Taxation, Financial Management, Insolvency, Information Technology. Admission requirements before the start of practical training are the same as for admission to professional education. Practical training is constantly monitored by the principal or training supervisor. Details of the training are to be submitted with the application for admission to membership for MACPA's evaluation.
Malaysia MIA	Not applicable
Pakistan ICAP	Practical Training in Auditing, Taxation, IT and Corporate/Secretarial Work with a duration of four to five years depending on the scheme of entry. Candidates who pass all ICAP's modular examinations (for Modules A, B, C and D), or obtained exemptions from Modular Foundation and Intermediate examinations or their equivalent, will register training arrangements with Principals at CA Firms. University graduates with First Division (or equivalent grades) and Post Graduates with 2nd Division (or equivalent grades) from recognized Universities will register training arrangements with Principals and CA Firms, upon obtaining exemption from Pre-entry Proficiency Test (PPT). Graduates with 2nd Division (or equivalent grades) from recognized Universities will register training arrangements with Principals at CA firms upon passing PPT, for a five year training period.
Pakistan ICMAP	Three years working experience in public practice/industry/commerce/ government job relevant for accountants under supervision of a qualified professional accountant as a condition for membership. Exemptions based on previous experience outside Pakistan are possible under the supervision of the professional body. There are no exemptions possible based on previous experience inside Pakistan. Members of the professional institutes are working in all fields and are available for training.

129

Australia ICA Australia	3 years relevant experience, mentored by an ICAA member (or member of another recognized professional body) either in public practice or an accredited organisation in commerce, industry, government or academia. A major review of practical experience is currently being undertaken. It is anticipated that this review will be completed and report delivered to the board in June 2002. The majority of the candidates are in full time employment, however, they are permitted to work part time provided it is at least 17.5 hours per week and full time equivalence is used to calculate the 3 years. Previous experience can be used in the calculation of the 3-year requirement. All candidates must have at least 52 weeks work experience prior to commencing their first technical module in the CA Program. The profession in Australia is self-regulating and therefore the ICAA has full discretion in the recognition of providers.
Australia CPA Australia	Three years supervised or mentored experience. Phasing out unsupervised 5-year option. Degree entry to Associate the Professional Education Program plus experience for CPA status.
New Zealand ICANZ	The first year of experience is not specified and can begin at any time. The (minimum) two years of specified experience cannot begin until the Institute's academic requirements have been satisfied. Candidates must cover three areas of accounting out of six (external reporting, management accounting, audit (internal or external), taxation, finance/treasury, and insolvency/reconstruction). The practical experience and training programmes are provided by Institute-approved employers.

Table 740.1   Mutual Recognition

Country Prof. Body	Mutual Recognition
Canada CGA Canada	The CGA-Canada qualification is recognized in the following countries outside Canada: Barbados, Trinidad, Bahamas, Bermuda, Belize (CA), Chile (SA), Belgium (EU), Hong Kong, China. The conditions, Examinations, Practical Experience, are exactly the same as for the CGA-Canada Canadian Program. Foreign students on a student or work visa may enrol in the CGA program. Admission to membership as a CGA requires Canadian citizenship or landed immigrant status. Other qualified Canadian accountants or qualified foreign accountants for example US CPAs or UK ACCAs and CIMAs, may enter the CGA program with advanced standing and complete a special program of studies.
Canada CMA Canada	CMA Canada is establishing agreements with other accounting organisations for mutual recognition of, and member eligibility for, professional designations.
Canada ICA Alberta	Recognition ICA Alberta through US-special international exam; UK, Australia, NZ, SA (and others)-special international exam. Recognition qualifications from UK, US, South Africa, Australia, Japan, France, Netherlands special exam, experience in public accounting can be required.
Mexico IMCP	There are no automatic recognition agreements. The Mexican Committee of International Accounting Practice (COMPIC), in the framework of the NAFTA, is working, with its counterparts in the United States and Canada on mutually acceptable standards and criteria for recognising their respective licenses (education, ethics, examination, professional experience). Negotiations with other countries, particularly those with which Mexico has signed free trade agreements, are also under way. Foreigners are subject to compliance with the requirements set out in Mexican law, including revalidation of studies, completion of community service and possession of the qualification, together with reciprocal treatment for Mexicans at the applicant's place of residence. Foreign educational qualifications are recognized by the process of the revalidation of studies (Article 15 of the LRA5).
USA AICPA	NASBA uses the standard of substantial equivalency to facilitate interstate practice and free movement of practitioners between states. This standard is also used for foreign applicants on the additional condition of reciprocity. IQAB (International Quality Assurance Board) has international reciprocity agreements with Australia (CA and CPA) and Canada (CA).
France Ordre	Recognition through EU mutual recognition directive and with the French speaking countries. In general a special examination is required.
Germany IDW	Recognition of the professional qualification from Germany under the 8. EU Directive in other EU member states by means of a mutual recognition examination. The recognition of the corresponding qualification from all other EU member states is also achieved by a mutual recognition examination.
The Netherlands NIVRA	Recognition inside the EU according to EU Directives and for other countries on an individual bases. USA – Dutch RA's with a university degree have a masters degree and followed more than 150 hours of education, so they can sit for the CPA Examination. Accountants from EU countries (and non EU

	countries that have signed the Treaty of Oporto on the European Economic Area - Norway, Iceland and Liechtenstein) must submit evidence that they are authorized to carry out audits in their own country in accordance with the requirements of the Eighth EU Directive. Accountants from countries outside the EU must possess an accountancy qualification that is equivalent to the Dutch Registeraccountant qualification. The foreign accountant who fulfils the first condition can take a Special Examination (in Dutch!). This examination tests the knowledge of the candidate in Dutch civil law with special regard to accountancy. i.e. company law; Dutch fiscal law; Dutch accounting rules as laid down in the law; Dutch professional rules and rules of conduct
Spain IACJCE	Recognition of the IA-CJCE qualification in EU countries and recognition of qualifications from EU countries according to EU regulation.
Sweden FAR	Recognition of the FAR qualification in other countries has been achieved; statistics are not available. Recognition of qualifications from other countries includes the UK, France, the Netherlands with an EU-style aptitude test for admission.
United Kingdom ACCA	ACCA is recognized under the European Union's Mutual Recognition Directive. The ACCA qualification is also fully recognized in the legislation of many other countries around the world e.g. in Hong Kong, Malaysia, Singapore, the Caribbean, and many countries in Africa. ACCA is also recognized for the purpose of registration as an auditor or liquidator under Australia's Corporation Act and enjoys reciprocal membership arrangements with the Institute of Chartered Accountants of New Zealand. Recognition of qualifications from other countries: EU Member States plus Iceland, Norway and Switzerland. Also Australia, Canada, Hong Kong, New Zealand, South Africa, Zimbabwe, and certain States in the US. Various conditions apply.
United Kingdom ICAEW	All EU States recognize the ICAEW qualification under EU 8th Directive. Australia, Canada, New Zealand, South Africa, Zimbabwe through reciprocal arrangements. Most other countries with developed accountancy professions recognize the ICAEW qualification through custom and practice. All EU States, Australia, Canada, New Zealand, South Africa, Zimbabwe are recognized by ICAEW through reciprocal arrangements.
United Kingdom ICAS	Recognition through reciprocal agreements with England, Ireland, New Zealand, Australia, Canada, South Africa and through EU mutual recognition directive.
Czech Republic CACR	The second stage of the Certification and Education System of the Union of Accountants (Bilanèní úèetní) is compatible with the "Bilance Buchhalter" in Germany, Austria and Switzerland. The qualification of "Accounting Expert" is recognized by 8 exams of the ACCA Professional Qualification in Great Britain. Auditors from other countries and applicants for the qualification of Accounting Expert who have passed all the requirements of ACCA professional qualification must pass the so called "Differential Exam" that is concentrated on the national environment of accounting, law and taxes.
Hungary CHA	No international recognition of the CHA qualification in other countries; no recognition in Hungary of qualifications from other countries.

Poland SKwP	International recognition of SKwP qualifications has not been achieved.
Poland KIBR	No recognition has been achieved of the KIBR qualification in other countries. Qualifications gained in the UK (ICAEW, ICAS, ACCA), in Denmark (Beskikkelse Som Statsutoriseret Revisor), in Australia (Australian Institute of Certified Public Accountants), in the US (Massachusetts Society of Certified Public Accountants, Oregon Board of Accountancy) have been recognized in Poland. Candidates had to pass the Polish Economic Law exam (in the Polish language).
Russian Fed. IPA Russia	International recognition of the IPA Russia qualification in other countries and recognition of qualifications from other countries in the Russia Federation has not been achieved.
Turkey TURMOB	Recognition of the qualification from Turkey in other countries and of qualifications from other countries in Turkey has not been achieved, but it is possible on the basis of mutual recognition.
Kenya ICPAK	Recognition of the ICPAK qualification in other countries has been achieved especially within Eastern and Southern Africa. Exemptions have been granted by CGA-Ontario in Canada and also by the ACCA in the UK. Recognition of qualifications from other countries by ICPAK is granted on a selective basis but foreign accountants are required to sit papers in local law and taxation.
South Africa SAICA	Recognition of the SAICA qualification in other countries: New Zealand, Australia, Canada, England and Wales, Scotland, Ireland. Recognition of the qualification from other countries by SAICA: New Zealand, Australia, Canada, England and Wales, Scotland, Ireland. All have to write conversion examination. SAICA is working closely with the neighbouring countries in the Southern African region, and a number of reciprocity agreements have been put in place. Regional accreditation of education and training programmes continues to play an important role in the economic development of the region and to uplift and ensure the implementation of international standards.
Lebanon LACPA	Some Middle Eastern countries recognize the LACPA qualification with some restrictions and subject to reciprocal treatment. US CPA, Canada Chartered, UK Chartered, French expert-comptable are recognized in Lebanon subject to examination in local tax and laws. Other countries recognition depends on reciprocal treatment.
Saudi Arabia SOCPA	International recognition of the SOCPA qualification in other countries has not been achieved. Qualifications from other countries (USA, UK, Canada) are considered for those who want to apply for the SOCPA fellowship examination.
Hong Kong HKSA	HKSA's examination programme is recognized by CPA Australia and the Association of Chartered Certified Accountants in Britain. HKSA recognizes professional examination programmes offered by the accountancy bodies in: the United Kingdom, the United States, Canada, Australia, New Zealand, South Africa and Zimbabwe.
India ICA India	MOUs have been entered into with ICA Pakistan, ICA Sri Lanka, AICPA USA, ICAEW, London ICAI Bangladesh for dialogues for professional collaboration and reciprocal recognition of qualifications. Initiatives are under way for recognition of qualification with ICA New Zealand and CICA Canada.

India ICWAI	CIMA (UK), CIA (USA), CMA (USA), CPA (Australia), CMA (Pakistan), CMA (Bangladesh), CMA (Sri Lanka), CPA (New Zealand), CGA (Canada), CII (London) etc. by way of reciprocal recognition. The countries, which have recognized the ICWAI qualification consider the Institute Members competent enough to take up jobs in the relevant fields in their countries.
Japan JICPA	There is no recognition of qualifications from other countries in Japan.
Malaysia MACPA	MACPA has not entered into official reciprocal recognition arrangement with professional bodies in other countries. However, the CPA qualification is well recognized in the Asian countries for employment. Recognition of the qualification from other countries by MACPA: (i) Australia (ii) Canada (iii) India (iv) New Zealand (v) United Kingdom (vi) USA. Requirements for admission to MACPA: (a) A recognized degree; (b) Having passed the professional examinations of the major accountancy body in the country in which the degree qualification originates; (c) Having passed the MACPA examination in Malaysian company law and revenue law; (d) Having obtained not less than 3 years of relevant work experience.
Malaysia MIA	No recognition of the MIA membership qualification in other countries This is mainly because MIA is a regulatory body and thus its membership qualification is recognized currently in Malaysia only. Qualifications from other countries are recognized in Malaysia, for example Australia - achieve the CPA exam and become a full member of CPA Australia; UK - achieve the ACCA / CIMA / ICAS / ICAI/ ICAEW exams and become a full member of the respective bodies; other countries like India, Pakistan, NZ
Pakistan ICAP	Mutual recognition on qualification and training exists with Bangladesh. Exemptions are given from examination papers by some accountancy bodies such as ACCA, CIMA. Recognition of qualifications from other countries by ICAP : Australia, Canada and the United Kingdom.
Pakistan ICMAP	The ICMAP qualification is recognized by CIMA, ACCA, SMA & others ICMAP recognizes – CIMA, ACCA, ICAP, SMA & others.
Australia ICA Australia	Reciprocal recognition agreements with Institutes of Chartered Accountants in England & Wales, Scotland, Ireland, Canada, South Africa, New Zealand and CPA USA. These require company and tax law only. Many other countries also recognize our qualification but no formal agreements are in place.
Australia CPA Australia	Recognition of the CPA Australia qualification in other countries: USA 4 year degree plus CPA Program including Auditing and 3 years relevant practical experience; HK, Malaysia and Singapore 3 year degree plus CPA Program and 3 years relevant practical experience; NZ and some UK bodies as above. CPA Australia recognizes members of AICPA (US), ICAEW, ICAS, ICAI (UK, Ireland), ICANZ (NZ), HKSA (HK new QP grads only) if they hold a relevant degree, have passed the professional exams and have permanent residence in Australia
New Zealand ICANZ	The Institute currently has reciprocity arrangements with Institutes in Scotland, Ireland, and England & Wales. Mutual recognition agreements with the Institutes in Australia, Canada, and South Africa are currently being reviewed. Institutes in other countries may recognize the Institute by offering exemptions

	from their own qualifying requirements. In addition, the New Zealand Government permits certain persons from overseas to act as an auditor of NZ companies. Specific professional bodies recognized for this purpose by the NZ government include the Institutes of Chartered Accountants in Australia, England & Wales, Scotland, and Canada. Also recognized for this purpose are CPA Australia, ACCA, and AICPA.

CHAPTER 8   CONCLUSIONS

In this chapter the results of the research project are evaluated resulting in the final classification model.

800	Research Questions
810	Research Evaluation
820	Classification of Accountancy Education
830	Overall Results

The objectives of the research evaluation are to conclude whether the objectives of the research project have been reached and to see what lessons can be learned from the results. Effectively a classification of accountancy education, with its elements of regulation, qualification, education and experience, can be described in four steps. The four steps identify the hierarchical levels of the classification model: regulation index, final examination, professional education and practical experience, education background. This provides the structure to evaluate the overall results of the research project in relation to its original objectives.

800   Research Questions

The *Central Research Question* of the Global Accountancy Education research project is to develop, test and evaluate a conceptual model for accountancy education in various parts of the world and to use the results to contribute to the understanding of the present position and the possible future development of systems of professional qualification, education and training of accountants and auditors.

The following *partial research questions* were formulated.

Research Question 2.1: Analyse International Guidelines and Directives that are relevant for accountancy qualification, education and training in a format that makes it possible to use the results as benchmarks for the comparative analysis of national systems of accountancy education.
Research Question 2.2: Analyse the factors that make change of accountancy education necessary and that influence the requirements regarding the professional qualification, education and training of accountants and auditors.

Research Question 3: Develop a conceptual model for the classification of accountancy education systems in various parts of the world that can be used for evaluation and comparison.
Research Question 4: Analyse the data relevant for accountancy education as a basis for decisions on the final model of the professional qualification, education and training of accountants and auditors.
Research Question 5: Describe country characteristics and accountancy education as a basis for classification, comparison and analysis.

Research Question 6: Develop a classification of accountancy education based on a conceptual model and evaluation of distinguishing factors.
Research Question 7: Analyse regional and local differences of accountancy education in the selected countries.

The results are evaluated below.

810   Research Evaluation

The objectives of the research evaluation are (1) to conclude whether the objectives of the research project have been reached and (2) to see what lessons can be learned from the results. For both subjects we start with the partial research questions and conclude with the central research question. Recommendations follow in Chapter 9.

Research Questions 2.1 and 2.2: In Chapter 2 a comparative programme content matrix is described that was used in the development of the accountancy education model in Chapter 3. In the following chapters it was shown that the result can be used at least as a partial benchmark to analyse and describe accountancy education worldwide. Other factors, mainly concerning the structure of accountancy education, had however to be included to achieve a more complete representation of systems of accountancy education.

Existing guidelines and directives focus on content with an emphasis on the theoretical side. Attention for skills and competences is increasing with much work still to be done on instructional and assessment methods. There are major differences between professional bodies in the realised and systematic contribution of practical experience to professional expertise. In guidelines and directives relatively little attention is given to requirements for providers and recognition. This is easily understood as a result of the wide range of approaches that exist worldwide. On the other hand it must be realised that possibilities for future development depend largely, not on existing programmes, but on a structure that is open for necessary change, is flexible in time and has access to expertise.

This is clearly shown by the demands on the accountancy profession and on accountancy education analysed in Chapter 2 and the developments in time described in Chapter 7. It will be well to bear in mind that choices have to be made and that accountancy education can not be expected to achieve for its students understanding of all the complexities related to modern corporate activities. For accountancy education to be able to concentrate on skills and competences it is necessary to differentiate between core knowledge that must be included in the mandatory programme and knowledge that can be acquired when needed after qualification. The most important issue is not 'how to become an accountant' but 'how to be an accountant during the whole career'.

Research Questions 3, 4 and 5: The conceptual model for accountancy education that was described in Chapter 3 was used as the basis for the questionnaire that was sent to selected respondents. This made it possible to collect information in a comparable way as the basis for country overviews and data analysis in view of classification purposes.

Research Questions 5 and 6: In fact the material for the Chapters 5 and 6 was developed simultaneously. It shows that model parameters can be distinguished with distinctive values that help to understand accountancy education in its country environment. This in itself is not sufficient to conclude that classification of accountancy education based on a conceptual model and evaluation of distinguishing factors is possible. This depends on the requirements for classification as listed in Chapter 4.

- The *characteristics* of a chosen classification should be adhered to consistently.
- The subsets of a given universe should be *exhaustive*, i.e., they should jointly cover the whole field.
- The subsets should be *pair-wise disjoint*, i.e., be mutually exclusive.
- There should be a preservation of *hierarchical integrity*, i.e., elements of one hierarchical rank should not be confused or mixed with elements of some other ranks.

The individual characteristics obey the first three requirements. This in itself does not mean that hierarchical integrity is observed. This issue is discussed in the next paragraph.

Central Research Question: The conceptual model has been used to contribute to the understanding of the present position of systems of professional qualification, education and training of accountants and auditors. Recommendations for the promotion of international developments and future research based on a personal evaluation of the research results are given in Chapter 9.

820   **Classification of Accountancy Education**

Effectively a classification of accountancy education, with its elements of regulation, qualification, education and experience, can be described in four steps. The four steps identify the hierarchical levels of the classification model. The results combine the model parameters with the distinguishing values that are given in Chapter 6.

- Regulation Index
- Final Examination
- Professional Education and Practical Experience
- Education Background

Regulation Index

In the analysis leading to the *regulation index* the following factors were included: (1) regulation of the accountancy sector, (2) recognition of the accountancy sector, (3) responsibility for qualification standards, (4) recognition of the providers of professional education and (5) recognition of the providers of practical training. Professional bodies on the regulation index are given below.

High professional self-regulation: CMA Canada, ICA Alberta, CPA Australia, ICAA and SAICA (5).
Emphasis on professional self-regulation: CGA Canada, ACCA, ICAEW, ICAS, HKSA, ICANZ, ICPAK, ICA India, MACPA, MIA, ICAP, ICMAP, IMCP, KIBR and LACPA (15).
Emphasis on government regulation: ICWAI, Ordre, IDW, NIVRA, CACR, CHA, IPA Russia and TURMOB (8).
High government regulation: AICPA, IACJCE, FAR, JICPA, SKwP and SOCPA (6).

As can be expected almost all professional bodies in common law countries have either high professional self-regulation or emphasis in that sector. The only exception is ICWAI with emphasis on government regulation; AICPA and SOCPA with high government regulation. On the other hand almost all professional bodies in civil law countries have either high government regulation or emphasis in that sector. The only exemptions here are IMCP, KIBR and LACPA with emphasis on professional self-regulation.

With the exception of SAICA and SOCPA both high professional self-regulation and high government regulation only occur in industrialised countries. There is no clear general distinction on cultural background and its main indicators power distance and uncertainty avoidance. However, all professional bodies with high professional self-regulation originate in countries with small power distance and weak uncertainty avoidance.

Membership regulation and *membership composition* are not included as parameters for the classification model as no direct relevance is visible for accountancy qualification, education and training. Membership regulation with the values high, medium and low includes indicators for mandatory membership, mandatory CPE and regulation of mandatory CPE by the professional body. In general professional bodies score higher on membership regulation than could be expected as a result of the regulation index. At least partly this may be the result of the standing of the professional bodies and the relatively small interest of governments, at least in the past, in mandatory membership and CPE. The only exception the other way around is MACPA with emphasis on professional self-regulation and low membership regulation. This can be directly attributed to the complementary position of MIA in Malaysia as a regulatory body.

Final Examination

In the survey both the *qualification standards* and the *final examination* were analysed. Qualification standards were defined as admission requirements to the profession. They can include: (1) a formal final examination of professional competence, (2) a prescribed programme of professional education and (3) a prescribed programme of practical experience. The results show that all three elements are almost always included. A final examination is always part of the qualification requirements. Professional education is always available in one form or another, mandatory or voluntary, post higher education or included in higher education. Practical experience is generally included in qualification or licensing requirements. Exceptions are AICPA, where practical experience for licensing is not mandatory in all jurisdictions and ICPAK, where practical experience is only mandatory for public practice. There is however a clear distinction between professional bodies in the requirement to have practical experience before the final examination. This is the main reason that the final examination was selected as a classification parameter in stead of qualification standards.

In the analysis of the *final examination* the following factors were included: (1) admission requirements, (2) core programme, (3) examination objectives and (4) examination methods. This resulted in three possible values for the orientation of the examination: theoretical, practical or mixed.

Professional Education and Practical Experience

Professional education and practical experience are part of almost all qualification programmes. The interesting distinction for the classification of accountancy education is their respective position. To this end the combination of professional education and practical experience is regarded with three possible values: required, possible and excluded.

The values required and possible imply that at least a part of professional education is part time as otherwise the combination would not be possible. If the combination is excluded professional education can be completely integrated in full time university or higher education, which then can be followed by practical experience before the final examination, qualification or licensing.

Education Background

Education background is the final classification parameter. It is chosen in view of two distinctions, which together determine the knowledge, skills and competences that are available at the start of additional professional education (if available) and practical experience. The first one is the focus of full time education programmes: general or specific. Specific is defined as aimed at accounting, finance or business. The second is the level of the programmes: university or other forms of higher education.

Actual participation is chosen above entry possibilities. The reason is quite simple. Many professional bodies give access to a wide range of candidates. Mostly however if specific programme requirements are in place they have to be met by everyone seeking admission. This usually means exemptions after specific programmes or additional requirements after general programmes. For education purposes the logical distinguishing factor is found in the most frequented full time programmes.

The possible values are: high percentage of accountancy, finance or business university degrees, emphasis on accountancy, finance or business university degrees, high percentage of general university degrees, emphasis on general university degrees, high percentage of accountancy, finance or business higher education and emphasis on general higher education.

Classification Results

The classification results are summarised below in four logical steps: (1) regulation, (2) final examination, (3) professional education and practical experience, (4) education background. Empty cells are not mentioned. In total the classification is given for 32 professional bodies out of a total of 34. MIA in Malaysia is not included as it is a regulatory body. SKwP in Poland is not included as it is an association of accountants with varying backgrounds.

In considering the results it would be well to keep the following considerations in mind. The classification is a summary of main characteristics. To get a more complete picture of the situation in a certain country it is useful to consult the more detailed information in Chapter 7 and Annex 3. Moreover the information may have changed since it has been collected. Developments go fast in all sectors so the characteristics can change accordingly. As a result this classification is not expected to be constant in time. New regulation and new programmes, as well as new approaches to professional education and practical experience will have their effect on the classification of professional bodies. The model parameters and the possible distinguishing values will remain constant in time, but the allocation of values to professional bodies will not. It may even prove possible to predict overall change as a result of globalisation.

The classification results are summarised in Table 820.1 Classification of Accountancy Education.

Table 820.1 Classification of Accountancy Education.

830   Overall Results

The overall results of the research project have to be checked with the objectives as they are formulated at the beginning of this chapter. First this means that in the model accountancy education should be linked with the development of the accountancy profession and with relevant country characteristics. Second the results should contribute to the understanding of and the insight in accountancy education, the set of minimal conditions to be fulfilled in mature systems of accountancy education and effective approaches towards international harmonisation and recognition.

Country Characteristics

The relevant country characteristics are included in the model. They are legal system and economic position. The results show that there is a connection between the elements of accountancy education[35] and the country characteristics, although important differences occur.

In general professional bodies in common law countries show a tendency towards professional self-regulation compared with a tendency towards government regulation in civil law countries. This is particularly true for common law countries with a historical UK background. The USA on the other hand shows a rule-based approach and a tendency towards government regulation. It is also clear that regional regulation can alter regulation patterns, as is shown in the European Union where EU Directives have to be implemented in the legislation of the member states. There is no overall distinction in regulation as a result of economic position.

Traditionally practical experience has a more important position in common law countries than in civil law countries, where education systems tend to be more directed towards a theoretical approach. The analysis shows that for the majority of the countries included in the research project, both with a common law and a civil law background, there is a tendency towards mandatory practical experience before qualification. This is not yet general but IFAC guidelines, EU Directives and actual developments taking place mostly point in the same direction. There are however major differences in the requirements to be fulfilled during practical experience and its organisational structure. These are reflected in the employment sectors that are allowed, the required programmes, the assessment of practical experience and the systems that are in place for monitoring and supervision. In general it can be said that practical experience ranges from 'practical experience', defined as holding a relevant position over a certain period of time, to 'practical training', defined as doing specified work in a controlled environment over a certain period of time. Probably the best approach, if that can be defined, is somewhere in the middle recognising that: (1) doing a relevant job is a necessary element of professional qualification that is different for every candidate; (2) there should be standards to

---

[35] Accountancy education here is used in the general sense and includes qualification, final examination, professional education, practical experience and general education.

Table 820.1	Classification Accountancy Education				
Professional Body	**Country Characteristics**	**Regulation Index**	**Orientation Final Exam**	**Combination Prof Educ-Pract Exp**	**Degree Category**
		PS professional self	theoretical	required	AU acc, fin, bus university
		GS government	practical	possible	GU general university
		regulation	mixed	excluded	AH acc, fin, bus higher ed
					GH general higher education
Industrialised, common law					
CMA Canada	Canada	high PS	mixed	required	high percentage AU*
ICAAlberta	Canada	high PS	mixed	required	high percentage AU
CPA Australia	Australia	high PS	mixed	possible	high percentage AU
ICA Australia	Australia	high PS	mixed	required	high percentage AU
CGA Canada	Canada	emphasis PS	theoretical	required	emphasis GU
ACCA	United Kingdom	emphasis PS	theoretical	possible	emphasis AU
ICAEW	United Kingdom	emphasis PS	practical	required	emphasis GU/AU
ICAS	United Kingdom	emphasis PS	mixed	required	emphasis AU
HKSA	Hong Kong	emphasis PS	mixed	required	emphasis AU
ICANZ	New Zealand	emphasis PS	practical	required	high percentage AU*
AICPA	USA	high GR	theoretical	excluded	high percentage AU
In trans/emerg, common law					
SAICA	South Africa	high PS	mixed	required	high percentage AU
ICPAK	Kenya	emphasis PS	theoretical	possible	emphasis GH
ICA India	India	emphasis PS	mixed	required	high percentage AU
MACPA	Malaysia	emphasis PS	mixed	required	emphasis AU
MIA	Malaysia	emphasis PS	not applicable	not applicable	emphasis AU
ICAP	Pakistan	emphasis PS	theoretical	required	high percentage AH*
ICMAP	Pakistan	emphasis PS	mixed	required	high percentage GU
ICWAI	India	emphasis GR	mixed	required	emphasis AU
SOCPA	Saudi Arabia	high GR	theoretical	excluded	high percentage AU
Industrialised, civil law					
ORDRE	France	emphasis GR	mixed	excluded	emphasis AU*
IDW	Germany	emphasis GR	mixed	required	high percentage AU
NIVRA	Netherlands	emphasis GR	practical	possible	high percentage AU
IACJCE	Spain	high GR	mixed	possible	high percentage AU
FAR	Sweden	high GR	mixed	required	high percentage AU
JICPA	Japan	high GR	mixed	required	high percentage GU
In trans/emerg, civil law					
IMCP	Mexico	emphasis PS	theoretical	required	high percentage AU
KIBR	Poland	emphasis PS	mixed	required	emphasis AU
LACPA	Lebanon	emphasis PS	theoretical	possble	emphasis GU
CACR	Czech Republic	emphasis GR	theoretical	required	emphasis AU*
CHA	Hungary	emphasis GR	mixed	required	emphasis AU
IPA Russia	Russian Fed.	emphasis GR	mixed	required	high percentage AU
TURMOB	Turkey	emphasis GR	mixed	required	high percentage AU
SKwP	Poland	high GR	not applicable	not applicable	emphasis AU

ensure professional relevance, but avoiding bureaucratic regulation. The past in countries, which nowadays have regulated practical experience, has shown that practical experience even if not mandatory can contribute in an important way towards the professional relevance of a qualification.

Education of accountants and auditors in both common law countries and in civil law countries can be either more theoretical oriented or more practical oriented. The legal system does not differentiate between the two approaches. There is however a tendency towards a theoretical approach in developing and transition countries. This is possibly a result of the differences in the realised contribution of full time higher education to the professional qualifications. Most systems contain an element of part time professional education, with combination with practical experience as a requirement or a possibility. The existing approaches are also reflected in the orientations of the final examinations.

Accountancy Profession

In the classification model for accountancy education two parameters are included, which in general describe the position of the accountancy profession as a co-standard setter for accountancy education. These are the *regulation index* and the *membership regulation index*. In the regulation index the respective positions of the governments and the professional bodies in the standard setting for qualification and the recognition of providers of professional education and practical experience are included.

In common law countries the qualification standards are either set by the professional body (12) or by the government and the professional body (8). In civil law countries the government is responsible (4), the professional body (2) or they set the standards together (8). There is a shift towards government responsibility in the recognition of providers of professional education and a shift towards responsibility of the professional bodies in the recognition of providers of practical experience. In the membership regulation index the responsibility for mandatory CPE is included in a comparable way. Overall, if CPE for an employment sector is mandatory, it is almost always regulated by the professional body.

Some interesting conclusions can come to mind. First, the importance of the actual contribution of the accountancy profession to the qualification, education and training of its members and their lifelong expertise is confirmed. To maintain this situation under changing circumstances a constant review is necessary of objectives, responsibilities and resources. The accountancy profession has a public responsibility, which is at the core of its existence. Governments have a responsibility to safeguard the public interest in setting achievable standards, which can be met by a viable profession. Universities and other educational institutes must offer their students programmes, which give access to rewarding occupations – both as a means of living and for personal development. Modern education is time consuming, costly and in need of expertise. These requirements can only be met in a public – private partnership with respect for the various contributions.

Changing needs and the demands placed on the accountancy profession have been discussed. The information collected during the research project may already be dated as events like ENRON and WORLDCOM happened after the period of data gathering. It could be of prime importance to come to new understandings of the contribution of accountancy education to the future expertise of the accountancy profession. The necessity of lifelong expertise in a situation of constant professional change makes it necessary to include CPE as one of the elements of accountancy education. In doing so the moment of qualification becomes the mark for entry into the profession without promising expertise in all areas. On one hand this gives room for differentiation in qualification programmes within achievable objectives. On the other hand requirements for CPE will become more strict both in the sense of education and of practical experience. In that respect a relevant example can be found in the UK where recognition as a registered auditor requires two years additional, relevant practical experience after qualification as a chartered accountant.

Accountancy Education

The elements of accountancy education have been analysed in respect to programmes, expertise and recognition. The main components are qualification, professional education and practical experience based on general education that is increasingly of university level. The minimal conditions that have to be fulfilled can be met in a number of ways as is shown by the country analysis in the preceding chapters.

University programmes have two major objectives in the acquirement of (1) general knowledge and skills and (2) basic professional knowledge and skills. IFAC IEG 9 recommends to dedicate two years of a four-year programme to the first objective. This is not the overall approach. There is a tendency to focus more and more on specific objectives, which could lead to a certain neglect of more general academic and personal development. This choice can hardly be influenced by the accountancy profession but has to be kept in mind when negotiating the content of university programmes, that give access to professional education or qualifying examinations.

Professional education has to bridge the gap between general education and qualification standards. It can be offered either full time or part time. One of the hallmarks of every profession is the responsibility for its expertise. This means that the accountancy profession should stay involved in professional education. The consequence is not automatic final responsibility but in the very least active partnership in the education and training network is necessary. In that respect the contribution of the accountancy profession to the availability of practical experience is essential as there are no alternatives for this function elsewhere.

Mutual recognition of accountancy qualifications is becoming increasingly important, but is still at the beginning of its development. An effective approach could be stimulated by using a detailed checklist, that covers all the necessary components: (1) general education and degree requirements, (2) professional education, (3) practical experience and (4) final examination. If complete mutual recognition is not (yet) possible it would be efficient to accept partial and if necessary not even mutual recognition on one or more of the identified areas. Mutual recognition can not be the final goal. Somewhere in the near future it has to be replaced be international recognition of a general nature. Comparability and exchange of information is a necessary requirement to be realised.

CHAPTER 9   RECOMMENDATIONS

In this chapter recommendations are based on a review of the outcomes of the research project

900   Overview of Recommendations
910   Scope and Influence of International Guidelines
920   Promotion of International Development
930   Influence of Regional and Local Characteristics
940   Recommendations for Future Research

The recommendations are based on the results of the research project in relation to a review of international developments. They contain the views of the author on necessary or advisable activities for change and development of accountancy education.

900   Overview of Recommendations

The recommendations are based on the results of the research project in relation to a review of international developments. Attention is given to the scope and influence of international guidelines on accountancy education, the promotion of the international development of accountancy education including the furtherance of mutual recognition and harmonisation and to the influence of regional and local characteristics on accountancy education. The final paragraph contains recommendations for future research.

910   Scope and Influence of International Guidelines

Goal of Accountancy Qualification, Education and Training

A logical starting point for the consideration of the scope and influence of international guidelines on accountancy education is the objective of the qualification of professional accountants and auditors followed by the required education and training. The content of the guidelines on accountancy education was analysed in Chapter 2 as a basis for the accountancy education model in Chapter 3, the overall description of accountancy education in Chapter 5, the test of model variables in Chapter 6 and the analysis of local and regional differences in Chapter 7. Attention was given to the IFAC International Education Guidelines, in particular IEG 9, the EU 8th Directive and the UNCTAD Guideline for a Global Accounting Curriculum. General requirements for the recognition of professional accountancy qualifications were formulated by IFAC in its 1995 Statement of Policy of Council. WTO and GATS have addressed international reciprocity of qualifications.

The recommendations of IFAC IEG 9 are directed towards establishing (1) 'the goal of accounting education and experience; its components of knowledge, skills and professional values; and the elements on which education and experience of all professional accountants should be founded'; (2) 'the minimum benchmarks of professional education and experience that professional accountants should meet in order to obtain membership in their professional body and to exercise their profession'; (3) 'the criteria for the assessment of professional competence'.

In the guideline the term 'professional accountants' refers to 'those individuals – whether they be in public practice, industry, commerce, the public sector or education – who are members of an IFAC member body'. A general definition of the core activities of professional accountants is not given, neither do the IFAC Statement of Policy nor the UNCTAD Guideline give any further indication. The EU 8th Directive is more specific as it is directed at 'the qualifications of persons entitled to carry out the statutory audits of accounting documents'.

The goal of accounting education and experience, again according to IFAC IEG 9, must be 'to produce competent professional accountants capable of making a positive contribution over their lifetimes to the profession and the society in which they work'. The guideline goes on to state that 'increasingly today's professional accountants, in addition to acquiring accounting skills, must have skills to enable them to be entrepreneurs, financial analysts, excellent sales persons, good communicators, capable negotiators and public relations specialists, as well as good managers'. The professional accountant also 'must have a broad-based global perspective to understand the context in which business and other organisations operate'.

These requirements reflect demands made on the accountancy profession in the last decade. However, they do not focus on the core activities of professional accountants, which can be used to set recognisable education standards. It seems unavoidable to differentiate between the core activities of the accountancy profession and the requirements for newly qualified accountants and auditors.

In the long run it may prove to be a positive development that discussions about the role of the accountancy profession in providing for the public interest 'reliable, transparent and comparable financial information for trade, investment and financial stability' (UNCTAD) can contribute to necessary choices in accountancy education and training, which are vital to its future development.

- There is a maximum to the time and effort that can be spent on accountancy education and training. Considering qualifications outside the accountancy profession, for instance for law, medicine and architecture, there is a natural limit in general not to exceed four or five years of university education followed by three years of practical training, possibly combined with additional professional education.
- The accountancy profession in order to survive needs a continuous inflow of intelligent, responsible and ambitious young people. Apart from the general setting – the amount of time, money and effort to become an accountant or auditor – there are more principal considerations. They include the possibility to find both in education and in the professional career room for personal development and satisfaction.
- In the present situation objectives for education and training used by professional bodies hardly differentiate between employment sectors which to say the least does not stimulate international recognition of qualifications. In addition the issue must be addressed what constitutes a suitable professional environment for practical experience and training.
- Expertise for accountancy education and training comes from a variety of sources. These include universities and other institutes of higher education, professional bodies, accountancy firms and accounting departments in commerce, industry and government. Their combined efforts should lead to integrated programmes based on common objectives.

Recommendation: Recognize the fact that no single accountant or auditor can satisfy all the requirements of the accountancy profession and make differentiation in qualifications possible. Older professions like law and medicine have preceded the accountancy profession in recognising the need for specialisation in an increasingly complex environment. Logical starting points could be the education and training requirements for auditors, management accountants and government accountants. Benchmarks should be formulated on an international level to facilitate comparability and recognition. Define the possible contributions of full time and part time education and of practical experience in relation to employment sector.

Benchmarks of Professional Education and Experience

At the moment benchmarks of professional education and experience do not differentiate between employment sectors. The main focus of the GAE research project is the professional qualification, education and training of accountants and auditors in public practice. The benchmarks will be considered in that light. This is defendable as the majority of the professional bodies, even those outside public practice, include accountant and auditor in their qualification objectives.

IFAC IEG 9 defines the knowledge, skills and professional values that are essential to professional competence. Knowledge is divided in general knowledge, organisational and business knowledge, information technology knowledge and accounting and accounting related knowledge. Teaching methods should be used 'that provide students with the tools for self-directed learning after qualification'. Intellectual, interpersonal and communication skills are not usually acquired from specific courses but from the total effect of education and professional experience.

The use of teaching methods that stimulate student participation is encouraged. This implies using measurement and evaluation methods that reflect the changing knowledge, skills and professional values of professional accountants, integration of knowledge and skills across topics and disciplines with emphasis on problem solving.

General knowledge as defined in IFAC IEG 9 has two purposes. A broad-based general education is '(1) critical to lifelong learning and (2) provides the foundation to build professional and accounting studies'. It can be argued however that its intended scope is too profound to be achieved in education alone. In reality both personal and professional development depend largely on areas outside higher education. In this project general knowledge is therefore solely treated as the basis for the professional and accounting studies.

According to IFAC IEG 9 'organisational and business knowledge provides the context in which professional accountants work. A broad knowledge of business, government and non-profit organisations, how they are organised, financed and managed, and the global environment in which they operate is essential for the functioning professional accountant'. The objectives mentioned include a broad range of knowledge, application, understanding and integration.

The Information Technology knowledge core as requested in IFAC IEG 9 is described more in detail in IFAC IEG 11, Information Technology in the Accounting Curriculum. It is based on the role of the professional accountant in the use and evaluation of information systems and in their design and management.

Accounting and accounting related knowledge provide 'the strong technical background essential to a successful career as a professional accountant'. As an exercise in programme development and evaluation it is interesting to consider what, according to IFAC IEG 9, it should ideally include.

- History of the accounting profession and accounting thought.
- Content, concepts, structure and meaning of reporting for organisational operations, both for internal and external use, including the information needs of financial decision makers and a critical assessment of the role of accounting information in satisfying those needs.
- National and international accounting and auditing standards.
- Financial management including managing resources, planning and budgeting, cost management, quality control and benchmarking.
- Environmental factors and the regulation of accounting.
- Ethical and professional responsibilities of an accountant.
- The concepts, methods and processes of control that provide for the accuracy and integrity of financial data and safeguarding of business assets.
- Taxation and its impact on financial and managerial decisions.
- Knowledge of the business legal environment including securities and companies law, appropriate for the role of the profession in the particular country.
- The nature of auditing and other attest services and the conceptual and procedural bases for performing them in manual and electronic environments.
- Knowledge of finance, including financial statement analysis, financial instruments and capital markets, both domestic and international.

There is little doubt that apart from the level that can be achieved all of this is relevant knowledge for accountants. Reporting, financial management, control and auditing are at the basis of what is traditionally seen as the accountancy profession. However, in every education programme choices have to be made on content and level at the moment of qualification in relation to employment sectors and functions.

Recommendation: Evaluate programme content and level demanded in the guidelines in relation to employment sectors and functions. Differentiate between qualification requirements in general to be met at the final examination and actual requirements for certain functions, which have to be met at the final examination or can be fulfilled later during mandatory CPE as a necessary part of education.

Skills are not usually acquired from specific courses but from the total effect of education and experience. They can be divided in intellectual skills, interpersonal skills and communication skills. Intellectual skills – like solving problems, making decisions and exercising good judgment in complex situations – are the most closely linked with traditional education. On the other hand the contribution of education to interpersonal skills – the ability to work and interact with others – and to communication skills – through the use of language – to a great extent depends on the methods that are chosen and the time that is taken for student participation. Learning in real life situations, the logical definition of practical experience is indispensable to reach the necessary skill level before qualification and, probably even more important, to continuous learning afterward.

This two-way approach is probably even more necessary for the professional values that potential accountants must acquire during their education and training. Education can provide the theoretical background, but experience in practical, real-life situations is necessary to develop a set of personal standards.

Recommendation: Recognize the contributions of formal education and practical experience to the development of skills and professional values by including them both in a systematic way in programme requirements.

The term 'relevant experience', as used in IFAC IEG 9, refers to 'participation in work activities in an environment appropriate to the application of professional knowledge, skills and values' with the objective to 'obtain the specialised accountancy training needed to ensure professional competence'. The consequences of this approach are partly formulated in the guideline, but partly they are not.

The guideline stipulates among others that: '(1) accounting positions for practical experience should be approved by the professional body, (2) experience must be conducted under the direction and supervision of experienced members and (3) that a monitoring system has to be established'. Close cooperation between the professional body, the candidate and the employer is seen as a necessary requirement for an effective programme of practical experience. Little attention however is given to the relation between professional education and practical experience.

Recommendation: Define the minimum levels of professional education that have to be reached before practical experience can be effective. Stipulate that the final examination of professional competence can only be taken after fulfilment of the education and training requirements. This approach ensures a relevant professional qualification. The alternative approach is to set the examination at the end of the period of general and professional education without regard for the practical experience, which may follow later. This leads to an educational title that can be valuable in itself without however a complete coverage of the professional competence that is necessary for qualification or licensing.

Criteria for Assessment of Professional Competence

According to IFAC IEG 9 'an appropriate process of assessment of professional competence must exist or be established. A required component of the assessment process for individuals seeking to become qualified is a final examination, administered by or with substantive input from the professional body or regulatory authority. The examination must be comprehensive, require a significant portion of responses to be in writing and be administered near the end of the educational, and where appropriate, experience requirement'.

An examination of professional competence is required because (1) professional bodies must ensure the competence of their members, (2) individuals have to demonstrate their competence and (3) it enhances the external credibility of the profession. The assessment process 'should be appropriate to the knowledge, skills and professional values being evaluated'. This overall approach leads to a number of comments.

- Assessment should be an integrated part of the education and training process in all its stages. This approach makes it possible to concentrate the final examination on the required professional competence, which according to IFAC IEG 9 can only be acquired after the appropriate education and experience.
- To encourage student participation in education makes it also necessary to use assessment methods, which give due credit to their contribution. This could lead to a relative shift from written answers to open or multiple-choice questions to defending a thesis or giving a presentation on a specified subject.
- The hallmark of a professional is sound technical knowledge and the ability to apply that knowledge in practice using the necessary skills and professional values. This means that the final examination of professional competence, or at the least licensing as an accountant or auditor, can only take place after both the education and experience requirements have been met.

Recommendation: Stimulate the further development of final examinations, which follow after professional education and practical experience have been concluded and credit their combined contribution to professional competence.

In 1998 the IFAC Education Committee made available an Advisory on Examination Administration[36] based on the practices of selected IFAC member bodies. The commonly used types of question were true/false, multiple choice, cases and essays. At that moment few of the consulted organisations included an oral component as part of their examination process.

Recommendation: Stimulate the further development of assessment procedures that (1) strengthen the competence approach of accountancy education and training, (2) respect conditions of relevance and equal treatment. As the first would mean more use of individual result, the second would mean a move from product to process control. It has to be recognized that this is mostly already the case in the assessment of practical experience.

920   Promotion of International Development

International guidelines and directives on the qualification, education and training of accountants and auditors can be considered to be the codification of general and accepted principles. The consideration of the actual implementation of the guidelines and directives in various parts of the world can help to answer two relevant questions. (1) Which parts of the guidelines are in place, which parts are not and what could be the possible explanation? (2) Are general trends becoming visible, that could merit inclusion in the guidelines and directives? The actual implementation can depend very much on local and regional differences.

---

[36] IFAC Education Committee, Advisory on Examination Administration, 1998

- General Knowledge is mostly included in line with country characteristics.
- Organisational & Business Knowledge is generally included as far as it is directly relevant for Accounting & Accounting Related Knowledge. There is much less coverage of subjects outside this area.

Recommendation: Focus General Knowledge on university exit level in each country and concentrate on programme content. Define clearly the subjects of Organisational & Business Knowledge that should be present in all accountancy education programmes and, when necessary, stimulate that universities implement them in their regular programmes.

- IT Knowledge and Accounting & Accounting Related Knowledge are included. Looking at available time for professional education there are substantial differences in the levels of expertise that can be achieved. The same is true for the actual integration of IT applications, professional values and skills in the programmes. Implementation of competence based approaches is at its beginning both in educational methods and assessment.

Recommendation: For IT Knowledge and Accounting & Accounting Related Knowledge a two-step approach as recommended by the accountancy firms could be used. The draft International Education Standards, available at the IFAC website mid 2002, reflect the requirements for internationally operating accountants and auditors. These can be checked against the presently available programmes. As a first step the accountancy firms in the Forum of Firms have expressed their willingness to make additional programmes available to fill possible gaps with international expectations. As a second step this additional programmes can over a period of time be implemented in local professional and higher education programmes. In addition the advancement of competence approaches to education that has really started in the last ten years should be promoted with vigour. The possible contribution of different education methods to achieve competence should be recognized. The two major approaches discussed in the IFAC Education Committee are sequential, knowledge followed by competence, and integrated.

- Practical Experience is increasingly present as a monitored system of practical training, it may also be required as practical experience without clear regulation on content and supervision or it is not mandatory.
- Final Examination as the final test for qualification mostly comes after professional education and practical experience. Sometimes it is open for candidates who have finished professional education. In that case practical experience can be, but not always is, an additional requirement for qualification and/or licensing.

Recommendation: The main issues regarding Practical Experience are its formal requirement before qualification and its contribution to professional competence. Experience in the European Union has made it clear that a formal requirement can, sometimes against expectations, help in acquiring progressive levels of expertise and that it is possible to stimulate actual cooperation between professional body, employers and educators. It may be necessary to change legislation or professional regulation to get a firm basis for practical experience, but the effect can contribute to a harmonized system of accountancy education and training in which candidates can combine theoretical learning with hands-on experience. A Final Examination where the candidate can show his or hers competence is then the logical last step towards qualification.

930 Influence of Regional and Local Characteristics

The regional and local circumstances determine to which possible areas of development precedence must be given. One of the first questions to consider is whether the legal framework is stimulating to encourage the development of the qualification, education and training of professional accountants and auditors. In many cases this will already be the case, but it has to be realised that it is not uncommon for legal obligations to be too fixed in view of changing circumstances. It is also important to realise that more regulation probably is not the answer to increasing demands for verifiable, transparent and trustworthy financial information. In the end the expertise, competence and professional values of the accountant or auditor, and the ways these are imbedded in their organisations, are decisive for the added value of the accountancy profession.

Recommendation: Check local legislation, including guidelines and directives, to see whether they provide an adequate framework for accountancy qualification, education and training. If necessary, decide how to promote necessary change. Seek convergence in already existing international standards, directives and guidelines on accountancy education. In addition promote activities of the major accountancy firms aimed at the level of expertise necessary for trans-national audits with comparable audit methodologies and training systems.

A second consideration is how the results of the research project can stimulate regional and local development. Some suggestions on that issue are given below.

The classification of accountancy education was studied with its elements of qualification, professional and general education and practical experience. These can be used to check the existing situation with international benchmarks to decide on priorities for future development in the following sectors.

- Qualification: accountant, auditor, specialisation
- Qualification Standards: final examination including content and method, professional education and practical experience requirements, general university and higher education
- Professional Education: subjects, content, assessment and place in the programme
- Practical Experience: programme requirements, duration, employment sector, supervision and mentoring
- General Education: degree requirements, contribution to professional education

If necessary support can be made available through advice from international bodies and consulting with professional organisations in other countries, who have chosen similar ways of programme development. Major accountancy firms have shown their willingness to share expertise in coping with international requirements.

Mutual recognition can be advanced if benchmarking is approached in comparable ways and the results are made available to interested parties. This could also be a useful tool to keep track of the implementation of international standards, guidelines and directives in view of compliance.

Recommendation: Prepare systematic benchmarking of accountancy education based on the research results actively supported by the international professional organisations. The focus in this should be on 'good practice' in the meaning of 'standards to achieve' as it is highly unlikely that 'best practice' can be identified in ways that reflect local and regional circumstances. In particular for emerging and transition countries critical features must be identified in the context of their present and future position, including underlying qualifications. It is necessary to actively promote the authority and influence of benchmarks on accountancy education by giving attention to dissemination, applicability and the relation to local and regional legislation. Investment of appropriate resources is necessary to achieve lasting results.

940   Recommendations for Future Research

Research will be most beneficial to the development of accountancy education if it can be fitted into a clear research agenda that is used to interest universities in contributing to the necessary common body of knowledge and helps to disseminate the results in view of implementation.

In relation to the sectors mentioned in the last paragraph suggestions could include topics like the following.

- Regional research in qualification objectives and their influence on actual programmes
- Research into competence based approaches to accountancy education, training and assessment
- Development of recognized cross country international programmes
- Stimulation of ICT applications in accountancy education including practical experience

It is well understood that a lot of relevant research is already taking place. The suggestion is to look into the possibility of creating an overall structure in which results can be brought to the attention of interested academics and professionals. The IAAER would be excellently positioned to set up such a systematic approach.

Recommendation: Promote an international research agenda covering the main topics of accountancy education. Future research can both be general and specific. Examples of general research can be found in further theory building, including the possible influence of capital markets on accountancy education. More specific research could be aimed at certain regions. Given the fact that Latin America and China were not able to be part of the full project and their importance for economic development these two areas would be logical choices to evaluate comparability and applicability of the general framework that has been developed.

ANNEXES

ANNEX 1   INTERNATIONAL GUIDELINES

Professional Qualification and Licensing

In the questionnaire that is used for the global analysis of accountancy education and training the following elements of accountancy qualification, education and training are considered.

- Professional qualification and licensing
- Professional education
- Practical training (work experience)
- General education

This is preceded by general characteristics of the country and information about the professional body and its membership.
The main standards of the International Guidelines and Directives that are under consideration are summarised in this Annex.

International Benchmarks

International Guidelines and Directives can be used as benchmarks for the comparative analysis of national systems of accountancy education. International benchmarks on accountancy education and training to be considered for this purpose will include the Education Guidelines given by the International Federation of Accountants (IFAC), the relevant Directives of the European Union (EU) and the Guideline for a global accounting curriculum given by the United Nations Conference on Trade and Development (UNCTAD). The following International Directives and Guidelines will be considered.

The International Federation of Accountants has developed guidance on the recognition of professional accountancy qualifications in its Statement of Policy (1995). This statement follows the requirements of the General Agreement on Trade in Services (GATS).

The IFAC International Education Guideline 9 (IEG 9) addresses pre-qualification education, assessment of professional competence and experience requirements of professional accountants (1996) with additional guidance on ICT in IEG 11 on Information Technology in the Accounting Curriculum (1995). The UNCTAD Guideline on National Requirements for the Qualification of Professional Accountants (1998) is intended to provide a benchmark for programme comparison.

Common standards for the education, training and qualification of statutory auditors are defined in the Eighth Directive of the European Union (1984). Consideration is also be given to the EU Directive for the recognition of higher education diplomas awarded on completion of professional education of at least three years' duration (1988).

Members of the profession

Employment sector
IFAC guidance does not consider employment sector. Neither do EU Directives although they apply to statutory audit.

Professional Qualification

Objective

Goal accountancy education
What is the goal of accountancy education and training?

- To become a professional accountant
- To become a professional auditor
- Specialisation

IFAC defines as the goal of accountancy education and experience to produce competent professional accountants with an attitude of learning to learn. The EU 8th Directive sets common standards for the education, training and qualification of statutory auditors; these are mandatory inside the European Union.

Standards

Admission requirements
What are the admission requirements to the profession?

This question addresses the admission requirements to the profession as far as they are directly related to previous accountancy education and training.

- A formal final examination of professional competence
- A prescribed programme of professional education
- A prescribed programme of practical training

The recognition of professional accountancy qualifications is addressed by IFAC in its Statement of Policy of Council (June 1995). This statement follows the requirements of the General Agreement on Trade in Services (GATS).

According to IFAC candidates for recognition of professional qualifications should demonstrate that they have passed an examination of professional competence. This examination must assess not only the necessary level of theoretical knowledge but also the ability to apply that knowledge competently in a practical situation. IFAC IEG 9 specifically requires that as a result of the educational programme and the professional experience candidates should acquire intellectual, interpersonal and communication skills. It is crucial for any professional not only to have a sound theoretical knowledge but also to be able to apply that knowledge competently. IFAC suggests that, prior to recognition for the purposes of performing a reserved function, an individual should have completed a minimum of two years approved and properly supervised practical experience primarily in the function concerned and in a suitable professional environment.

IFAC IEG 9 states that a required component of the assessment process for individuals seeking to become qualified is a final examination administered by or with substantial input from the professional body or regulatory authority. The examination must be comprehensive, require a significant portion of responses to be in writing and be administered near the end of the educational and, where appropriate, experience requirement. The assessment process, which may take a variety of forms, should be appropriate to the knowledge, skills and professional values being evaluated.

Responsibility
Who is responsible for the standard setting for qualification?
Responsibility of the government is addressed by the European Union.

The EU 8th Directive has laid down common standards for the education, training and qualification of statutory auditors. Basic provisions for education purposes are ruled by the articles 4 to 8.

Article 4 of the 8th Directive requires, for natural persons seeking approval to carry out statutory audits, the holding of a university entrance level qualification, completion of a course of theoretical instruction, a practical training phase and passing an examination of professional competence of university final examination level organized or recognized by the State.

Article 5 requires that the examination should guarantee acquisition of theoretical knowledge of subjects relevant to statutory auditing, ability to apply such knowledge in practice and that the examination should at least be partly written.

Article 6 refers to the theoretical subjects to be covered.

Article 7 grants eventual possibilities of exemptions from the test of theoretical knowledge and from the test of the ability to apply that knowledge in practice.

Article 8 requires three years' practical training in the auditing of annual accounts, consolidated accounts or similar financial statements prior to taking the final qualification examination and that member states shall ensure that all training is carried out under persons providing adequate guarantees regarding training.

Responsibility of the professional body is addressed by IFAC.

Member bodies of IFAC should not only satisfy themselves that the assessment(s) undergone by applicants indeed test the body of knowledge and the ability to apply it, but that the policies and procedures for its construction, security and marking are adequate to ensure the integrity of the assessment process. Agreement should also be reached on the need for a periodic review of the education and assessment process so as to ensure that conditions for recognition continue to apply.

Comparability between countries has been addressed in the General agreement on Trade in Services (GATS).

The GATS requires that all countries have procedures to verify qualifications of professionals from other countries. Though GATS is multinational in scope it does provide for bilateral implementation. Rules set out by GATS are meant to ensure the same privileges for foreign providers and domestic counterparts, to remove discriminatory obstacles and to provide transparency.

The EU 8th Directive in Article 11 sets out provisions for recognition of qualifications in other member states if two conditions are fulfilled: the qualification must be considered equivalent to that of the Member State and the possession of the legal knowledge required in that Member State must be proved.

Final Examination

Formal final examination
Describe the core programme of the final examination (main subjects and objectives).

In IFAC IEG 9 a distinction is made between accounting and accounting related knowledge, information technology knowledge, organizational and business knowledge, general knowledge. The EU 8th Directive is less specific in distinguishing between subjects directly necessary for statutory audit and related subjects.

According to IFAC IEG 9 assessment of professional competence should measure more than just theoretical knowledge. For example candidates should be able to demonstrate that they:

- have a sound technical knowledge of the specific subjects of the curriculum;
- have an ability to apply technical knowledge in an analytical and practical manner;
- are able to extract from various subjects the knowledge required to solve multiple topic problems;

- can identify information relevant for a particular problem by distinguishing the relevant from the irrelevant in a given body of data;
- are able, in multi-problem situations, to identify the problems and rank them in the order in which they need to be addressed;
- appreciate that there can be alternative solutions and understand the role of judgment in dealing with these;
- have an ability to integrate diverse areas of knowledge and skills;
- can communicate effectively to the user by formulating realistic recommendations in a concise and logical fashion;
- have knowledge of the ethical requirements of the profession.

Professional education

Specify education content
Specify the core programme of professional education (main subjects and objectives).

IFAC IEG 9 states that professional accountants need to acquire knowledge, skills and professional values through the educational program and professional experience.
Knowledge as part of professional education is divided in organizational and business knowledge, information technology knowledge and accounting and accounting related knowledge.
Skills enable the professional accountant to make successful use of the knowledge gained through education. They are not usually acquired from specific courses but from the total effect of the educational program and professional experience. The skills the individual must acquire are intellectual skills, interpersonal skills and communication skills.
A framework of professional values must be developed by the potential professional accountants for exercising good judgement and for acting in an ethical manner.

According to IFAC accounting and accounting related knowledge should cover the following subjects: financial accounting and reporting, management accounting, taxation, business and commercial law, auditing, finance and financial management, professional ethics.
For the requirements on information technology knowledge reference is made to IFAC IEG 11.
Organisational and business knowledge covers the following subjects: economics, quantitative methods and statistics for business, organisational behaviour, operations management, marketing, international business.

The EU 8th Directive defines the theoretical subjects to be covered in Article 6: auditing, analysis and critical assessment of annual accounts, general accounting, consolidated accounts, cost and management accounting, internal audit, standards relating to the preparation of annual and consolidated accounts and to methods of valuing balance sheet items and of computing profits and losses, legal and professional standards relating to the statutory auditing of accounting documents and to those carrying out such audits.
In so far as they are relevant to auditing: company law, the law of insolvency and similar procedures, tax law, civil and commercial law, social security law and law of employment, information and computer systems, business, general and financial economics, mathematics and statistics, basic principles of the financial management of undertakings.

UNCTAD in general supports IFAC guidance on pre-qualification education, assessment of professional competence and experience requirements of professional accountants. Furthermore UNCTAD has made available a guideline for a global accounting curriculum in order to promote global harmonisation of professional qualification requirements. The curriculum consists of 16 modules divided in organisational and business knowledge (5 modules), information technology (1 module) and accounting & accounting related knowledge (10 modules).

Duration professional education
What is the duration of professional education in years?

According to IFAC the professional education component must consist of at least two years of full-time study (or the equivalent) and must build on and develop further the intellectual, interpersonal and communication skills provided in general education.

Practical experience

Training content
Please describe the requirements of practical training if applicable (main areas and regulations).

According to IFAC IEG 9 an appropriate period of relevant experience in performing the work of professional accountants must be a component of a pre-qualification programme. The period of experience should be long enough to permit prospective accountants to demonstrate they have gained the knowledge, skills and professional values sufficient for performing with professional competence. This objective cannot normally be met in a period of less than three years.

The EU 8th Directive requires in Article 8 three years' practical training in the auditing of annual accounts, consolidated accounts or similar financial statements prior to taking the final qualification examination and that member states shall ensure that all training is carried out under persons providing adequate guarantees regarding training.
The term 'relevant experience' as used in IEG 9 refers to participation in work activities in a work environment appropriate to the application of professional knowledge, skills and values. Relevant experience provides a professional environment in which the accountant:

- enhances his or her understanding of the organization and functioning of business;
- is able to relate accounting work to other business functions and activities;
- becomes aware of the environment in which services will be provided;
- develops the appropriate professional ethics and values in practical, real-life situations;
- has an opportunity to work at progressive levels of responsibility;
- obtains the specialized accountancy training needed to ensure professional competence.

According to IFAC prospective professional accountants should gain their relevant experience in accounting positions deemed appropriate by the professional body. Experience leading to qualification should be conducted under the direction and supervision of experienced members of the professional body as identified by the body or regulatory agency. The professional body or regulatory agency should ensure that the experience gained is acceptable. Among the steps it might take are the following.

- Establish a monitoring system that provides for the monitoring and reporting of the experience actually gained by the student.
- Provide detailed written guidance in the form of manuals for employers and students.
- Establish a mechanism for approving employers as suitable for providing the appropriate experience for the students.
- Assess and approve the work experience environment before the commencement of employment.
- Assess the experience gained on the basis of a written and/or oral submission by the student, supported by employers at the point of application for membership.
- Review employers previously approved.

General education

Admission to the final examination
What are the requirements for general education to enter the final examination?
Please distinguish between degree requirements and programme requirements

The EU 8th Directive contains no requirements on general education. IEG 9 is more specific. It states that, although general education requirements vary greatly from programme to programme and from country to country, a portion of the education must focus on the development of general knowledge, intellectual skills and communication skills through a broad range of subjects that provide students with a grounding in arts, sciences and humanities.

Entrance level
Are candidates required to have a university entrance level?

Entry requirements are approached in a comparable way in the EU 8th Directive and in IEG 9. The 8th directive of the European Union requires a university entrance level qualification. In IEG 9 an education level equivalent to that for admission into a recognized university degree programme or its equivalent is set as the minimum standard.

The main requirements on the core programme of general education, professional education, practical experience and qualification are summarised in a separate comparative programme content matrix that is included in Chapter 2.

ANNEX 2   QUBUS QUESTIONNAIRE TREE

In this appendix the questionnaire that was used to gather information for the research project is presented as a questionnaire tree in order to show in a general way the scope of and the relations between the variables considered as part of the research project.

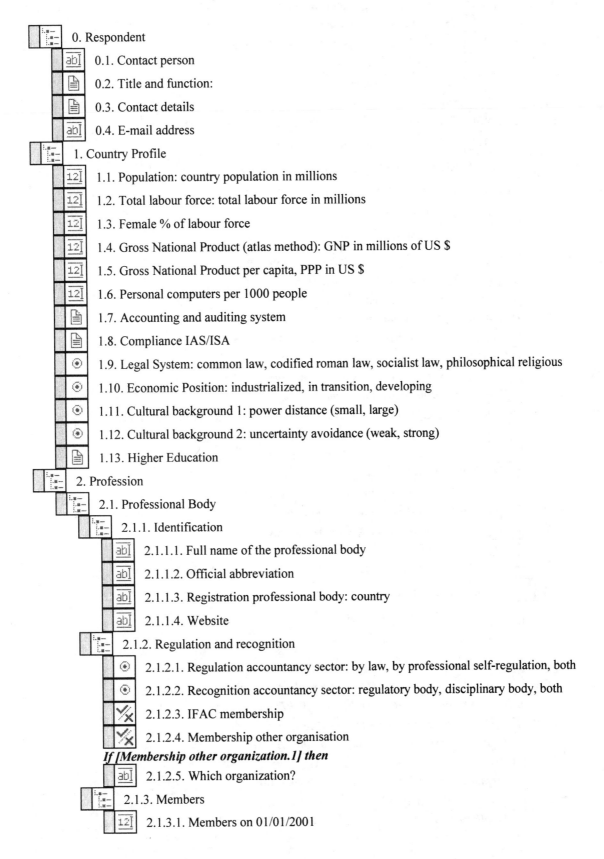

0. Respondent

   0.1. Contact person

   0.2. Title and function:

   0.3. Contact details

   0.4. E-mail address

1. Country Profile

   1.1. Population: country population in millions

   1.2. Total labour force: total labour force in millions

   1.3. Female % of labour force

   1.4. Gross National Product (atlas method): GNP in millions of US $

   1.5. Gross National Product per capita, PPP in US $

   1.6. Personal computers per 1000 people

   1.7. Accounting and auditing system

   1.8. Compliance IAS/ISA

   1.9. Legal System: common law, codified roman law, socialist law, philosophical religious

   1.10. Economic Position: industrialized, in transition, developing

   1.11. Cultural background 1: power distance (small, large)

   1.12. Cultural background 2: uncertainty avoidance (weak, strong)

   1.13. Higher Education

2. Profession

   2.1. Professional Body

      2.1.1. Identification

         2.1.1.1. Full name of the professional body

         2.1.1.2. Official abbreviation

         2.1.1.3. Registration professional body: country

         2.1.1.4. Website

      2.1.2. Regulation and recognition

         2.1.2.1. Regulation accountancy sector: by law, by professional self-regulation, both

         2.1.2.2. Recognition accountancy sector: regulatory body, disciplinary body, both

         2.1.2.3. IFAC membership

         2.1.2.4. Membership other organisation

         If [Membership other organization.1] then

         2.1.2.5. Which organization?

      2.1.3. Members

         2.1.3.1. Members on 01/01/2001

- [12] 2.1.3.2. Members on 01/01/1996
- [12] 2.1.3.3. Members on 01/01/2006
- [☑] 2.1.3.4. Employment sector

If [Employment sector (2).1] then

- [12] 2.1.3.5. Percentage public practice

If [Employment sector (2).2] then

- [12] 2.1.3.6. Percentage industry and commerce

If [Employment sector (2).3] then

- [12] 2.1.3.7. Percentage government

If [Employment sector (2).4] then

- [12] 2.1.3.8. Percentage other areas
- [12] 2.1.3.9. Female members (%) on 01/01/2001

- 2.2. Professional Title
  - [abl] 2.2.1. Official title
  - [abl] 2.2.2. Abbreviation of title
  - [✗] 2.2.3. Mandatory membership
  - [☑] 2.2.4. Continuing professional education

If [Continuing professional education.1] then

- [12] 2.2.5. Number of hours CPE in public practice

If [Continuing professional education.1] then

- [✗] 2.2.6. Regulation CPE public practice by the professional body

If [Continuing professional education.2] then

- [12] 2.2.7. Number of hours CPE in industry and commerce

If [Continuing professional education.2] then

- [✗] 2.2.8. Regulation CPE industry and commerce by the professional body

If [Continuing professional education.3] then

- [12] 2.2.9. Number of hours CPE in government

If [Continuing professional education.3] then

- [✗] 2.2.10. Regulation CPE government by the professional body

If [Continuing professional education.4] then

- [12] 2.2.11. Number of hours CPE in other areas

If [Continuing professional education.4] then

- [✗] 2.2.12. Regulation CPE other areas by the professional body

- 2.3. Entrance in the profession
  - [12] 2.3.1. New members in 2000
  - [12] 2.3.2. New members in 1995
  - [12] 2.3.3. New members in 2005
  - [☑] 2.3.4. Employment sector new members in 2000

If [Employment sector new members in 2000.1] then

- [12] 2.3.5. Percentage in public practice

If [Employment sector new members in 2000.2] then

- [12] 2.3.6. Percentage in industry and commerce

If [Employment sector new members in 2000.3] then

- [12] 2.3.7. Percentage in government

If [Employment sector new members in 2000.4] then

`12` 2.3.8. Percentage in other areas

`12` 2.3.9. Average age new members in 2000

`12` 2.3.10. New female members (%) in 2000

`12` 2.3.11. New female members (%) in 1995

`12` 2.3.12. New female members (%) in 2005

☑ 2.3.13. Educational background new members in 2000

If [Educational background new members in 2000.1] then

`12` 2.3.14. % with general university degree

If [Educational background new members in 2000.2] then

`12` 2.3.15. % with accounting, finance and business university degree

If [Educational background new members in 2000.3] then

`12` 2.3.16. % with general higher education

If [Educational background new members in 2000.4] then

`12` 2.3.17. % with accounting, finance and business higher education

3. Professional Qualification

3.1. Objective

☑ 3.1.1. Goal accountancy education: professional accountant, professional auditor, specialisation

If [Goal accountancy education.3] then

📄 3.1.2. Specify specialisation

3.2. Standards

☑ 3.2.1. Admission requirements: formal final examination of professional competence, prescribed programme of professional education, prescribed programme of practical training

☑ 3.2.2. Responsibility: government, professional body, other

☒ 3.2.3. International standards on accountancy education: mandatory, voluntary

If [International standards.1] then

📄 3.2.4. Specify international standards

☒ 3.2.5. Recognition standards I: recognition of the qualification in other countries

If [Recognition standards I.1] then

📄 3.2.6. Specify recognition standards I: conditions (examinations, practical experience)

☒ 3.2.7. Recognition standards II: recognition of qualifications from other countries

If [Recognition standards II.1] then

📄 3.2.8. Specify recognition standards II: conditions (examinations, practical experience)

If [Admission requirements.1] then

3.3. Final Examination

📄 3.3.1. Formal final examination: core programme (main subjects and objectives)

☑ 3.3.2. Objective final examination: theoretical knowledge, ability to apply knowledge in practice, intellectual skills, interpersonal skills, communication skills, ICT applications, professional values

◉ 3.3.3. Level final examination: postgraduate, graduate, undergraduate

☑ 3.3.4. Methods final examination: open ended questions, multiple choice questions, case study, thesis, oral

12 3.3.5. Length of final examination: total average duration in hours

12 3.3.6. Pass mark: points out of 100

12 3.3.7. Pass rate: average pass rate over the last 5 years

☑ 3.3.8. Conditions and procedures: uniform for all students, simultaneously, security conditions, objectively graded by qualified staff

✓✗ 3.3.9. External review

☑ 3.3.10. Admission requirements for final examination: professional education, practical training, general education

☑ 3.3.11. Providers: government, professional body, university, other

📄 3.3.12. External recognition

✓✗ 3.3.13. Expertise and resource

If [Admission requirements.2] then

3.4. Professional education

📄 3.4.1. Specify education content: core programme (main subjects and objectives)

☑ 3.4.2. Program professional education: full time, part time

12 3.4.3. Duration professional education in years

☑ 3.4.4. Position of ICT: ICT applications in subjects, use of ICT in collecting information, use of ICT for communication, diagnostic use of ICT

◉ 3.4.5. Level professional education: postgraduate, graduate, undergraduate

✓✗ 3.4.6. Admission requirements

✓✗ 3.4.7. Exemptions based on general education

◉ 3.4.8. Combination with practical experience

☑ 3.4.9. Providers: professional body, universities, commercial companies

✓✗ 3.4.10. Expertise and resources

☑ 3.4.11. Recognition of providers: by government, by professional body, other

✓✗ 3.4.12. Periodic review

☑ 3.4.13. Costs: who pays for professional education (employer, student, government, other)

If [Admission requirements.3] then

3.5. Practical experience

✓✗ 3.5.1. Admission requirements before practical training can be started

If [Admission requirements (4).1] then

📄 3.5.2. Specify admission requirements practical experience

📄 3.5.3. Training content: main areas and regulation

☑ 3.5.4. Practical training: full time or part time

12 3.5.5. Number of years

12 3.5.6. Days per year

✓✗ 3.5.7. Exemptions based on previous experience

☑ 3.5.8. Providers: public practice, industry and commerce, government, other

If [Providers (3).1] then

[12] 3.5.9. Percentage public practice

If [Providers (3).2] then

[12] 3.5.10. Percentage industry and commerce

If [Providers (3).3] then

[12] 3.5.11. Percentage government

If [Providers (3).4] then

[12] 3.5.12. Percentage other

☒ 3.5.13. Expertise and resources

If [Expertise and resources (2).1] then

▤ 3.5.14. Specify expertise and resources

☑ 3.5.15. Recognition: by government, by professional body, other

☒ 3.5.16. Periodic review

☒ 3.5.17. Regulations: training contract, supervision

If [Regulations.1] then

▤ 3.5.18. Specify regulations

3.6. General education

▤ 3.6.1. Admission to the final examination: degree requirements and programme requirements

▤ 3.6.2. General education system

[12] 3.6.3. Duration of general education in years

☒ 3.6.4. Entrance level: university entrance level requirement

4. Programme Requirements

☑ 4.1. Subjects compared with international guidelines

▤ 4.2. Intellectual skills: part of the programme, how addressed

▤ 4.3. Interpersonal skills: part of the programme, how addressed

▤ 4.4. Communication skills: part of the programme, how addressed

☑ 4.5. ICT applications included in subjects

☑ 4.6. Professional values included in subjects

5. Concluding Remarks

☑ 5.1. Future developments: regulation of the profession, professional qualification requirements, professional education, practical experience

If [Future developments.1] then

▤ 5.2. Short summary regulation

If [Future developments.2] then

▤ 5.3. Short summary professional qualification requirements

If [Future developments.3] then

▤ 5.4. Short summary professional education

If [Future developments.4] then

▤ 5.5. Short summary practical experience

ANNEX 3   INDIVIDUAL COUNTRY STUDIES

For each professional body under consideration an overview is given in the next pages.

Country	Professional Body	Abbreviation
Australia	Institute of Chartered Accountants in Australia	ICA Australia
Australia	CPA Australia	CPA Australia
Canada	Certified General Accountants Canada	CGA Canada
Canada	Society of Management Accountants of Canada	CMA Canada
Canada	Institute of Chartered Accountants of Alberta	ICA Alberta
Czech Republic	Chamber of Auditors of the Czech Republic	CACR
France	Ordre des Experts-Comptables	Ordre
Germany	Institut der Wirtschaftsprüfer in Deutschland	IDW
Hong Kong	Hong Kong Society of Accountants	HKSA
Hungary	Chamber of Hungarian Auditors	CHA
India	Institute of Chartered Accountants of India	ICA India
India	Institute of Cost and Works Accountants of India	ICWAI
Japan	Japanese Institute of Certified Public Accountants	JICPA
Kenya	Institute of Certified Public Accountants of Kenya	ICPAK
Lebanon	Lebanese Association of Certified Accountants	LACPA
Malaysia	Malaysian Association of Certified Public Accountants	MACPA
Malaysia	Malaysian Institute of Accountants	MIA
Mexico	Instituto Mexicano de Contadores Públicos, A.C.	IMCP
The Netherlands	Royal NIVRA	NIVRA
New Zealand	Institute of Chartered Accountants of New Zealand	ICANZ
Pakistan	Institute of Chartered Accountants of Pakistan	ICAP
Pakistan	Institute of Cost and Management Accountants of Pakistan	ICMAP
Poland	Association of Accountants in Poland	SKwP
Poland	National Chamber of Statutory Auditors	KIBR
Russian Fed.	Institute of Professional Accountants	IPA Russia
Saudi Arabia	Saudi Organisation for Certified Public Accountants	SOCPA
South Africa	South African Institute of Chartered Accountants	SAICA
Spain	Instituto de Auditores-Censores Jurados de Cuentas de España	IACJCE
Sweden	Föreningen Auktoriserade Revisorer	FAR
Turkey	Union of Chambers of Certified Public Accountants	TURMOB
United Kingdom	Association of Chartered Certified Accountants	ACCA
United Kingdom	Institute of Chartered Accountants in England & Wales	ICAEW
United Kingdom	Institute of Chartered Accountants of Scotland	ICAS
USA	American Institute of Certified Public Accountants	AICPA

Overview ICA Australia

Professional Body	**Institute of Chartered Accountants in Australia (ICAA)**
Professional Title	**Chartered Accountant (CA)**
Respondent	**Gillian Cappelletto, Divisional General Manager, Professional Education, ICAA**
Country	**Australia**

For additional information refer to www.icaa.org.au or Gillian Cappelletto at alisonc@icaa.org.au.

Australian requirements on accounting rules are based mainly on the Corporations Law and the standards of the Australian Accounting Standards Board and Abstracts of the Urgent Issues Group

The accountancy sector in Australia is regulated by professional self-regulation. The Institute of Chartered Accountants in Australia (ICAA) is recognized as a regulatory body and a disciplinary body. ICAA is a member of IFAC and CAPA.

Members of ICAA work in public practice, industry and commerce including government and in other areas. ICAA membership is mandatory to use the CA title. Continuing professional education is mandatory for members and is regulated by ICAA.

> There is no legislative requirement that restricts use of the title "accountant", however, membership of ICAA is required to use the designation "Chartered Accountant".

Admission requirements as member of ICAA include a formal assessment of professional competence, prescribed programmes of professional education and practical training.

> The professional body has sole responsibility for the standard setting for the qualification, however, government has control over the regulation and registration of auditors and tax agents.

International standards: ICAA follows IFAC IEG 9

> IFAC IEG9 is one standard referred to in developing our education program.

International recognition of qualifications

> Reciprocal recognition agreements with Institutes of Chartered Accountants in England & Wales, Scotland, Ireland, Canada, South Africa, New Zealand and CPA USA. These require company and tax law only. Many other countries also recognize our qualification but no formal agreements are in place.

Final assessment core programme

> Our test of professional competence includes examination and non-examination components. The broad range of knowledge skills and values developed needs to be assessed using a variety of different tools such that the maximum examination component for any one module is 50%. The program consists of 5 modules.

Objective final assessment: to test theoretical knowledge; the ability to apply knowledge in practice; intellectual, interpersonal and communication skills; ICT applications; professional values

> The program is designed to develop new members who are: - informed about the latest international, disciplinary and business knowledge; - innovative problem solvers; - forward-thinking change managers; - technology-literate; - collaborative team workers; - effective communicators; - service-oriented; - ethical; - professional; - reflective about their own knowledge, skills and values. These 10 attributes are developed and assessed in a comprehensive structure across the five modules. Candidates are assessed continuously throughout the module using criteria which link to the 10 attributes being

developed. There is no "final exam" as such. All candidates complete the program with the CA Integrative module which has a 3 hour exam.

The professional body is the provider of the final examination. ICAA examinations are subject to external review.

ICAA has full control over the education and assessment process. Examinations are developed by panels of experts, who are tightly guided by Institute staff. Panel members remain anonymous.

Admission requirements cover professional education, practical training and general education

Graduates with a general university degree are required to complete a conversion course prior to entering our post graduate education program. Qualifications lower than degree level are not accepted.

Professional education core programme

The CA Program consists of five modules:- CA Foundations- Financial Reporting & Assurance- Taxation & Financial Reporting- Strategic Business Management- CA Integrative. The CA Program is a minimum of 2 years part time. Candidates are required to be in employment whilst undertaking the CA program. The amount of time provided depends upon the employer, however, candidates are advised that a minimum commitment of 190 hours is required per module.

Admission requirements for professional education

To be eligible to enter the CA Program, applicants must have completed a relevant degree including coverage of required accounting and business related areas. Non-relevant degree holders can undertake a conversion course to satisfy requirements. The under graduate program is a minimum of 3 years.

ICAA is the provider of the professional education. Necessary expertise and resources are available.

Universities provide the undergraduate education. The professional body accredits universities as suitable to provide the undergraduate education. The professional body provides the CA Program. Our Institute places a very high priority on the education of new members as a result expertise and resources are dedicated to the process. In member satisfaction surveys members rate the maintenance of high entry standards as the most important activity of our Institute. Universities provide information on an annual basis and are subject to a full review every 5 years. Our CA Program is reviewed regularly.

Practical training content

3 years relevant experience, mentored by an ICAA member (or member of another recognized professional body) either in public practice or an accredited organisation in commerce, industry, government or academia. A major review of practical experience is currently being undertaken. It is anticipated that this review will be completed and report delivered to the board in June 2002. The majority of the candidates are in full time employment, however, they are permitted to work part time provided it is at least 17.5 hours per week and full time equivalence is used to calculate the 3 years. Previous experience can be used in the calculation of the 3 year requirement.
All candidates must have at least 52 weeks work experience prior to commencing their first technical module in the CA Program. The profession in Australia is self regulating and therefore the ICAA has full discretion in the recognition of providers.

ICAA expects for the near future major developments in practical training.

Overview CPA Australia

Professional Body	**CPA Australia**
Professional Title	**CPA**
Respondent	**Ann Johns, Director Education and Membership**
Country	**Australia**

For additional information refer to CPA Australia at www.cpaonline.com.au or Ann Johns at johnsa@natoff.cpaonline.com.au .

Australian requirements on accounting rules are based mainly on the Corporations Law and the standards of the Australian Accounting Standards Board and Abstracts of the Urgent Issues Group

The accountancy sector in Australia is regulated by law and by professional self-regulation. CPA Australia is recognized as a regulatory body and a disciplinary body. CPA Australia is a member of IFAC, CAPA and AFA.

Members of CPA Australia work in public practice, industry and commerce, government and in other areas. CPA Australia membership is not mandatory. Continuing professional education is mandatory for all members (Associates, CPAs and FCPAs) and is regulated by CPA Australia.

Admission requirements include a formal final examination of professional competence, prescribed programmes of professional education and practical training

> CPA Australia conducts its own CPA Program education course and examinations for CPA status. The admission requirement to Associate membership is an accredited undergraduate degree. Associates must then complete the CPA Program (5 subjects i.e. 15 hours of examination) plus three years supervised or mentored experience prior to being advanced to CPA status.

International standards: CPA Australia follows IFAC International Education Guidelines
International recognition of qualifications

> Recognition of the CPA Australia qualification in other countries: USA 4 year degree plus CPA Program including Auditing and 3 years relevant practical experience; HK, Malaysia and Singapore 3 year degree plus CPA Program and 3 years relevant practical experience; NZ and some UK bodies as above

> CPA Australia recognizes members of AICPA (US), ICAEW, ICAS, ICAI (UK, Ireland), ICANZ (NZ), HKSA (HK new QP grads only) if they hold a relevant degree, have passed the professional exams and have permanent residence in Australia

Final examination core programme

> Reporting and Professional Practice and Corporate Governance and Accountability plus 3 electives

Objective final examination: to test theoretical knowledge; the ability to apply knowledge in practice; intellectual and communication skills; ICT applications; professional values

The professional body is the provider of the final examination. CPA Australia examinations are subject to external review

> CPA Australia sets the examina..ons and they are moderated by academics. Questions are written by expert members. Necessary expertise and resources are available from CPA Australia membership and university academics.

Admission requirements cover professional education, practical training and general education

Professional education core programme

The core subjects in the CPA Program are 'Reporting and Professional Practice' and 'Corporate Governance and Accountability' plus three electives

Admission requirements for professional education

The acceptable bachelors degrees are those Australian University degrees which meet the joint CPA Australia and ICAA accreditation guidelines. The professional bodies expect to see a balanced curriculum, which covers more than technical content.

An accredited course leading to an undergraduate degree must:
a) include an accounting major or stream/sequence
b) include at least 60% of studies within the accounting and business-related curriculum areas
c) be sufficiently flexible to provide the opportunity for students to complete a minimum of 25% of studies within the general education curriculum area in disciplines other than accounting and business-related curriculum areas
d) integrate the generic skills within the course

CPA Australia is the provider of the professional education. Necessary expertise and resources are available.

The CPA Program is a distance education course with on-line support and voluntary workshops. Candidates are expected to spend 120 hours of study on each of the 5 subjects. Candidates are expected to study one subject each semester for 5 semesters. Some take less and others take longer. Minimum 1 year Max. 5 years allowed. Every 3 years there is a major program review. All courses are updated every semester as necessary.

Practical training content

Three years supervised or mentored experience. Phasing out unsupervised 5 year option. Degree entry to Associate the Professional Education Program plus experience for CPA status.

CPA Australia expects for the near future major developments in regulation of the profession, professional qualification requirements, professional education and practical training

Regulation of the profession: more self regulation
Professional qualification requirements: broader base and deeper knowledge
Professional education: increased use of technology
Practical training: increase mentoring program. From 2002 all CPA Program candidates will be asked to keep a Learning Journal

Overview CGA-Canada

Professional Body	**Certified General Accountants Association of Canada (CGA-Canada)**
Professional Title	**Certified General Accountant (CGA)**
Respondent	**Lynda Carson, Vice-President Education, CGA-Canada**
Country	**Canada**

For additional information refer to CGA-Canada at www.cga-canada.org or Lynda Carson at lcarson@cga-canada.org .

Canadian requirements on accounting rules are based on the standards issued by the Accounting Standards Board of the Canadian Institute of Chartered Accountants.

The accountancy sector in Canada is regulated by law and by professional self-regulation. The Certified General Accountants Association of Canada (CGA-Canada) is recognized as a regulatory body and a disciplinary body. CGA-Canada is a member of IFAC, CAPA, ICAC, FIDEF.

Members of CGA-Canada work in public practice, industry and commerce, government and in other areas. CGA-Canada membership is mandatory for all members. Continuing professional education is mandatory and is regulated by CGA-Canada.

Admission requirements as member of CGA-Canada include a formal final examination of professional competence, prescribed programmes of professional education and practical training.

Admission requirements and responsibility differ for each province. Quebec government regulation; other provinces professional body

International standards: IFAC IEG 9 and IEG 11
International recognition of qualifications

The CGA-Canada qualification is recognized in the following countries outside Canada: Barbados, Trinidad, Bahamas, Bermuda, Belize (CA), Chile (SA), Belgium (EU), Hong Kong, China. The conditions, Examinations, Practical Experience, are exactly the same as for the CGA-Canada Canadian Program.

Foreign students on a student or work visa may enrol in the CGA program. Admission to membership as a CGA requires Canadian citizenship or landed immigrant status. Other qualified Canadian accountants or qualified foreign accountants for example US CPAs or UK ACCAs and CIMAs, may enter the CGA program with advanced standing and complete a special program of studies.

Final examination core programme

The certification level of the Program of Professional Studies requires a candidate to pass four (4 hour) final examinations for a total of 16 hours. These consist of Financial Accounting 4, Professional Applications 1 and 2 other PACE level courses from a course selection offered from one of four career options. The career options include: corporate / small-medium enterprises, information technology, government, not-for-profit and public practice. The course selection offered in these career options include: Finance 2, Management Auditing 1 or Auditing 2, Taxation 2, Management Information Systems 2, and Public Sector Financial Management. The objective of the professional examinations is to assess whether a candidate has met the established standards of knowledge, skills, and professional values required for certification as a professional accountant, is competent to provide reliable service to a professional level to the public.

Objectives final examinations: to test theoretical knowledge; the ability to apply knowledge in practice; intellectual skills; professional values

The four certification examinations are designed to assess the knowledge, skills, and abilities at the advanced levels of the major subjects in the Program of professional studies; Financial Accounting, Finance, Auditing, Taxation, Management Auditing and Management Information Systems. The examinations test the ability to integrate and apply information across subject areas.

The professional body is the provider of the final examination. CGA-Canada examinations are subject to external review

The CGA-Canada Education committee is responsible to set and maintain the certification examinations. These are reviewed by primary review and supplementary review committee's which include: academics, professionals, practitioners and recently certified members. On occasion, there will also be an academic review. CGA-Canada contracts with University or College professors and public practitioners for the position of Examiner. In-house staff provide content expertise in editing to Examiners. CGA-Canada contracts the services of consultants to provide advise on test and measurement issues.

Admission requirements cover general education

Each certification examination has prerequisite courses that are required from the Education level of CGA's Program of Professional Studies.

Professional education core programme

Foundation Studies LEVEL 1 Financial Accounting 1, Economics1, Law 1; LEVEL 2: Financial Accounting 2, Practice Set 1, Quantitative Methods1, Quantitative Methods Bridging, Management Accounting 1, Communications1; LEVEL 3: Financial Accounting 3, Practice Set 2, Finance 1, Management Information Systems 1; Advanced Studies LEVEL 4: Management Accounting 2, Accounting Theory 1, Auditing 1, Practice Set 3, Taxation 1; Professional Certification PACE LEVEL: Financial Accounting 4, Finance 2, Auditing 2, Management Auditing 1, Management Information Systems, Public Sector Financial Management

Admission requirements for professional education: Foundation studies and advanced studies (or equivalent) are required for admission to Professional Admission Comprehensive Examinations (PACE)

A bachelors degree is required prior to receiving the CGA designation

Professional body provides professional education. Necessary expertise and resources are available

Practical training content

Students on the CGA Program must attain a minimum of two years of acceptable practical experience before receiving certification as a CGA. This experience may be attained in any sector of the economy ; industry, government, public practice, commerce, not-for-profit, basically anywhere that accounting and financial work is done. This enables students of the CGA to begin directing their careers into the areas of their choice before they have even completed their studies. Practical experience can start immediately but is reviewed for relevance. Requirement is 36 months of competency based practical training based on the (IFAC) requirement and standard but may be met with minimum 24 months if competencies are achieved

CGA-Canada expects for the near future major developments in regulation of the profession, professional qualification requirements, professional education and practical training

CGA monitors developments like IEG 9, IEG 11 and the exposure draft on Competence-Based Approaches to the Preparation and Work of Professional Accountants and is incorporating them where applicable.

Overview CMA-Canada

Professional Body	**Society of Management Accountants of Canada (CMA-Canada)**
Professional Title	**Certified Management Accountant (CMA)**
Respondent	**Richard Benn, Senior Vice President, CMA-Canada**
Country	**Canada**

For additional information refer to CMA-Canada at www.cma-canada.org. or Richard Benn at rbenn@cma-canada.org.

Canadian requirements on accounting rules are based on the standards issued by the Accounting Standards Board of the Canadian Institute of Chartered Accountants.

The accountancy sector in Canada is regulated by professional self-regulation. The Society of Management Accountants (CMA Canada) is recognized as a regulatory body and a disciplinary body. CMA Canada is a member of IFAC.

Members of CMA Canada work in public practice, industry and commerce, government and in other areas. Membership of CMA Canada is mandatory. Continuing professional education is mandatory in 3 out of 10 provinces; ultimately it will be mandatory around the country. CPE is regulated by the provincial bodies.

Admission requirements include a formal final examination of professional competence, prescribed programmes of professional education and practical training under the responsibility of the professional body

> CMA Canada is self regulatory and sets the standards for professional qualifications which is approved by a national Board of Directors.

International standards on accountancy education are followed. The programme covers IFAC IEG 9 with the exception of audit. Key skills are part of the programme.
International recognition of the CMA qualification in other countries

> CMA Canada is establishing agreements with other accounting organisations for mutual recognition of, and member eligibility for, professional designations.

Final examination core programme

> Syllabus includes: Financial Management, Corporate Finance, Operations Management, Information Technology, Strategic Management, International Business, Human Resources, Marketing, Taxation, Internal Control. Objectives: to indicate the cognitive skills and learning objectives to be tested for each topic and subtopic in the syllabus. The cognitive skill level expectations are based on Bloom's Taxonomy of Educational Objectives. Cognitive skills tested are: Knowledge, Comprehension and Application.

Objective final examination: to test theoretical knowledge; the ability to apply knowledge in practice; intellectual and communication skills; professional values

> Interpersonal skills are tested by means other than the examination.

CMA Canada is the provider of the final examination. CMA Canada examinations are not subject to external review. Necessary expertise and resources are available

> Graduates and professional educators are used in the process. Staff involved are all trained to administer and evaluate exam results.

Admission requirements as a CMA cover professional education, practical experience and general education

> Entrance to the profession requires a 4 year 120 hours accounting or comparable degree. University degree required with minimum of 17 pre-requisite courses in accounting and business. Many business degrees qualify. General degrees must be supplemented with additional courses to meet pre-requisite course requirements. Candidates must attend university programs and graduate prior to applying to CMA Canada.

Professional education core programme

> Core Program: Strategy, Management, Management Accounting, Operations Management, Marketing, Information Technology. Objectives: To shape CMAs as financial and strategic management professionals to lead successful enterprises. Content, structure and delivery designed to hone strategic leadership capabilities and ensure they bring integrating perspective to organizational decision making. Two-year program of distance education plus interactive sessions taken on a part time basis.

Admission requirements for professional education

> Entrance to the profession requires a 4 year 120 hours accounting or comparable university degree and passing of the Entrance Examination. It verifies that candidates have gained a sound technical knowledge through university studies and measures their integrative, judgemental, analytical, strategic thinking and written communication skills. The following topics are covered: Management Accounting, Corporate Finance, Operations Management, International Business, Human Resources, Marketing, Financial Accounting, Taxation and Internal Control.

CMA Canada provides professional education. Necessary expertise and resources are available

> Education staff plus outside consultants are used and are readily available. Recognition by CMA-Canada. Regularly review by National Certification Board of CMA Canada. For the Entrance Examination CMA-Canada accredits university programmes.

Practical training content

> Two years of experience in operational and management roles which are pre-defined. At least six months of the two-years must be at a managerial level. Practical training is on the job training. Candidates must be working full time. There is a more than sufficient number of jobs available for candidates Admission requirements before the start of practical training: pass entrance examination. Practical training takes place in industry and commerce and in government The professional body assesses practical training for each candidate based on reports provided by employers.

CMA Canada expects for the near future major developments in professional qualification requirements

> CMA Canada expects that mutual recognition of professional qualifications internationally will become a priority.

Overview ICA Alberta

Professional Body   **Institute of Chartered Accountants of Alberta (ICAA)**
Professional Title   **Chartered Accountant (CA)**
Respondent   **Steven Glover, Executive Director, ICAA**
Country   **Canada**

For additional information refer to www.icaa.ab.ca, or Steven Glover at s.glover@icaa.ab.ca .

Canadian requirements on accounting rules are based on the standards issued by the Accounting Standards Board of the Canadian Institute of Chartered Accountants.

The accountancy sector in Canada is regulated by law and by professional self-regulation. The Institute of Chartered Accountants of Alberta (ICAA) is recognized as a regulatory body and a disciplinary body. The Canadian Institute of Chartered Accountants (CICA) is a member of IFAC and ICAA is one of the ten provincial bodies comprising CICA.

Members of ICAA work in public practice, industry and commerce, government and in other areas. ICAA membership is mandatory. Continuing professional education is mandatory and is regulated by ICAA

Admission requirements as member of ICAA include a formal final examination of professional competence, prescribed programmes of professional education and practical training.

> The professional body sets the standards but certain matters also require government approval.

International standards: ICAA follows IFAC IEG 9
International recognition of qualifications

> Recognition ICAA through US-special international exam; UK, Australia, NZ, SA (and others)-special international exam. Recognition qualifications from UK, US, South Africa, Australia, Japan, France, Netherlands special exam, experience in public accounting can be required.

Final examination core programme

> Core skills-apply the knowledge specified in the subject areas-identify, define and rank problems and issues-analyse information-address problems in an integrative manner-evaluate alternatives and propose practical solutions that respond to user needs-communicate clearly and effectively. Syllabus: Profession as a practice, assurance and related services: 25-35%. Risk management, control and IT 5-10%. Financial accounting and reporting 25-35%. Managerial accounting 5-10%. Taxation 10-20%.

Objective final examination: to test the ability to apply knowledge in practice; intellectual, interpersonal and communication skills; professional values.

> Core skills-apply the knowledge specified in the subject areas-identify, define and rank problems and issues-analyse information-address problems in an integrative manner-evaluate alternatives and propose practical solutions that respond to user needs-communicate clearly and effectively. Syllabus: Profession as a practice, assurance and related services: 25-35%. Risk management, control and IT 5-10%. Financial accounting and reporting 25-35%. Managerial accounting 5-10%. Taxation 10-20%.

The professional body is the provider of the final examination. ICAA examinations are subject to external review

> The final examination is developed by the national body and reviewed by a team from the provincial bodies.
> Other requirements are set by each province.

Admission requirements cover professional education and general education.

Professional education core programme

Will vary from province to province but all include financial accounting, auditing and taxation. Main objective is to prepare the candidates to be professional accountants and to understand their professional responsibilities. Professional program emphasizes accounting, auditing and tax.

Admission requirements for professional education

Undergraduate degree required in any discipline; specific prerequisites in core subject areas required – delivered by universities.

Professional body and universities provide professional education. Necessary expertise and resources are available

Professional education program delivered by ICAA (to be replaced by CA School of Business in 2001). Government accredits the universities, which deliver the prerequisites and general education. Resources are available but there is a growing shortage of accounting profs.

Practical training content

Admission after completion of an undergraduate degree (bachelors, 4 year university). Candidates must complete 30 months (exclusive of study time) in an approved public accounting firm; must complete a total of 2500 chargeable hours of which 1250 hrs must be assurance (audit or review) experience of which 200 (625 in most other provinces) must be audit; 100 hrs of tax experience is also required.

Providers must meet standards set by ICAA. Supervision by a CA with 2 years immediate full time public accounting experience; suitable premises; diversity of clients; progressive experience over the required period; participate in client, tax, bank and other meetings; access to hardware and software orientation; procedures training sessions; written evaluation of student performance.

ICAA expects for the near future major developments in professional qualification requirements, professional education and practical training

New delivery of the professional (pre-certification) education (ie post university) by the CA School of Business set up by the four provincial CA Institutes in Western Canada. The CASB will use a competency referenced approach, with more internet delivery. There will be more flexibility on practical experience – a 36 month requirement, primarily based in public accounting but with an option for a portion to be in industry or government as a secondment. All employers have to meet training standards. Starting in 2002 new approaches will be used on the national final exam so that it is competency based, utilizes technology and allows access to prescribed reference material.

Overview CACR

Professional Body   **Chamber of Auditors of the Czech Republic (CACR)**
Professional Title   **Auditor, accountant**
Respondent   **Professor Bohumil Král, Chairman Education and Exam Ct, CACR**
Country   **Czech Republic**

For additional information refer to CACR at www.kacr.cz, or Bohumil Král at kral@vse.cz .

Czech requirements on accounting rules are based mainly on the Act on Accounting, the Chart of Accounts and the Accounting Procedures of the Ministry of Finance.

The accountancy sector in the Czech Republic is regulated by law and by professional self regulation. The Chamber of Auditors of the Czech Republic (CACR) is recognized as a regulatory body and a disciplinary body. CACR is a member of IFAC and a corresponding member of FEE.

> The Chamber of Auditors is founded and a substantial part of its activity is regulated by the Act on Auditors. The parts that are not regulated by law are regulated by internal professional directives of CACR. The activities of the Union of Accountants, the second professional body in the Czech Republic is regulated by professional self regulation. Both the Chamber and the Union are members of IFAC.

Members of CACR work in public practice. CACR membership is mandatory. Continuing professional education is mandatory according to internal professional regulations and is regulated by the profession

> The professional title 'auditor' is protected by law. The professional title 'accountant' is not protected by law; membership of the Union of Accountants is important to show quality. Due to an Act passed four years ago auditors have to work in public practice. The only exemption concerns university teachers.

Admission requirements include a formal final examination of professional competence, a programme of professional education and a prescribed programme of practical training

> The pre-requisite of the entrance to the profession of auditor (general university degree - 5 year Master degree) is required by Act on Auditors. The pre-requisite of the entrance into the Certification and Education System of Czech Union of Accountants is general higher education - it is required by internal professional requirements. The general standards and the Exam Order are stated by Act on Auditors. The Chamber of Auditors concretises the structure, content and other requirements of the exams. Union of Accountants: Standard setting is in the full authority and responsibility of the professional body.

International standards: CACR follows EU 8th Directive, IEG 9 and 11, UNCTAD Guideline
International recognition of qualifications

> The second stage of the Certification and Education System of the Union of Accountants (Bilanèní úèetní) is compatible with the "Bilance Buchhalter" in Germany, Austria and Switzerland. The qualification of "Accounting Expert" is recognized by 8 exams of the ACCA Professional Qualification in Great Britain.

> Auditors from other countries and applicants for the qualification of Accounting Expert who have passed all the requirements of ACCA professional qualification must pass the so called "Differential Exam" that is concentrated on the national environment of accounting, law and taxes.

Final examination core programme

The final exam consists of 7 written and a final oral exam. Written exams: 1. Macro- and Microeconomics 2. Accounting 3. Business Combinations and Consolidated Accounts 4. Business, Civic and Financial Law including Taxation 5. Corporate Finance 6. Statistics and Information Technology 7. Auditing

Objective final examination: to test theoretical knowledge; the ability to apply knowledge in practice; ICT applications; professional values

Theoretical knowledge in all areas of exams. Ability to apply the knowledge in practice mainly in the exams from Auditing, Corporate Finance, Accounting and Business Combinations and Consolidated Accounts. ICT Applications mainly in the sixth written exam mainly. Knowledge and practical experience are incorporated into all above stated areas.

Government, professional body and university co-operate in the final examination. CACR examinations are subject to external review.

The written exams are prepared by teams from Academia and practice The oral exam runs in front of the Exam Committee in which participate two members from the Ministry of Finance and two members either from Academia or auditors from practice. The Ministry of Finance officers are the chairmen and members of the Oral Exam Committees. The written exams are reviewed only on request by an applicant.

Admission requirements for the final examination cover general education

Professional education is offered but is not mandatory. Practical experience is mandatory for practice but it does not have to be finished before the final examination.

Professional education core programme

Macroeconomics and Microeconomics, Accounting, Business Combination and Consolidated Accounts Business, Civic and Financial Law (Including Taxation, Social and Health Insurance), Corporate Finance, Quantitative Methods and Information Technology, Auditing, Final Oral Exam.

Admission requirements for professional education are possession of a 5-year university degree CACR provides professional education

CACR operates the Institute of Education, in collaboration especially with the University of Economics, Prague. All guarants of the exams and also most of the lecturers work as the professors of the University.

Practical training content

According to the Act on Auditors any new member must work as Assistant Auditor for three years. This practical experience is concretised by the Auditor Guideline of the Chamber that specifies the content of this "Managed Practice". There are no admission requirements before the start of practical training. Practical training takes place in public practice. Necessary expertise and resources are available with auditing firms and auditors that are looking for future employees, partners or collaborators. The Chamber manages the List of Auditors.

CACR expects for the near future major developments in professional education and practical training

The Education Committee of CA CR would like to prepare conditions to extend the education of the auditors by interpersonal and communication problems, and by auditing techniques in the ICT environment. New Act on Auditors specified the new pre-condition for the entrance of the profession – to realise three-year practical experience as an assistant auditor. The main target connected with the pre-condition is to prepare detailed list of practical skills and experience that would create the basis of managed traineeship in the auditing companies and that would be also verified by CA CR on more concrete basis.

Overview ORDRE

Professional Body	**Ordre des experts-comptables (Ordre)**
Professional Title	**Expert-comptable**
Respondent	**Hélène Michelin**
Country	**France**

For additional information refer to www.experts-comptables.fr, or Hélène Michelin at hmichelin@cs.experts-comptables.org.

French requirements on accounting rules are based on the Code de Commerce, company law and decrees, the Plan Comptable Général (General Accounting Plan) and interpretations of the Comité d'urgence (Urgent Issues Committee) as applying to consolidated financial statements.

The accountancy sector in France is regulated by law and by professional self-regulation. The Ordre is recognized as a regulatory body and a disciplinary body. The Ordre is a member of IFAC and FEE.

Members of the Ordre work in public practice, industry and commerce, government and in other areas. Membership of the Ordre is mandatory to use the title. Continuing professional education is mandatory and is regulated by the Ordre.

Admission requirements as member of the Ordre include a formal final examination of professional competence, prescribed programmes of professional education and practical training.

> Admission requirements: To obtain the diploma of expertise comptable and take the professional oath. The different accounting diplomas (preliminary, intermediate and higher levels) needed to access to the three-year training period and, in the end, to the final diploma of expertise comptable, are organised and delivered by the Ministry of Education. The professional body is involved in standard setting for the different stages of the curriculum and for the final examination.

International standards : EU 8th Directive, IEG 9

> The French curriculum complies with the Eighth European Directive and with the IFAC IEG 9.The whole syllabus of the DPECF, DECF and DESCF is in accordance with the 8th European Directive concerning statutory auditors. The level of practical training is comparable to the standards of IFAC and EU.

International recognition of qualifications

> Recognition through EU mutual recognition directive and with the French speaking countries. In general a special examination is required.

Final examination core programme

> The final examination includes 3 tests with no possible exemptions: 1. A thesis on a subject related to the professional domain 2. A written test on the statutory and contractual auditing of financial statements 3. An oral test related to the traineeship and covering professional knowledge in general.

Objective final examination: to test theoretical knowledge and the ability to apply knowledge in practice. The government is the provider of the final examination. Examinations are subject to external review.

> Ministry of Education provides the final examination. The professional body co-manages with the Ministry of Education the examination syllabus for the whole curriculum. Professionals sit on the examination boards. External review is supervised by the Ministry of Education.

Admission requirements cover professional education and practical training

To access to the final examination, candidates must obtain the higher accounting studies diploma, «Diplôme d'études supérieures comptables et financières », DESCF, and complete there theoretical education with the three-year training period. The full studies focus on accounting, auditing, law, tax, economics, business administration, information technology.

Professional education core programme

To succeed to a complete syllabus divided into 16 parts corresponding to 3 diplomas: - Diplôme préparatoire aux études comptables et financières, DPECF (preliminary accounting diploma); - Diplôme d'études comptables et financières, DECF (intermediate accounting diploma); - Diplôme d'études supérieures comptables et financières, DESCF (higher accounting diploma). The whole curriculum requires a learning period of 8 years, including the three-year training period.

Core programme of professional education: DPECF (5 written tests): 1/ introduction to business law 2/ economics 3/ quantitative methods, mathematics and statistics 4/ accounting 5/ French and foreign languages. DECF (7 written tests): 1/ business law and tax law 2/ credit law, labour law and contentious law 3/ organisation and management 4/ financial management 5/ mathematics, statistics and information technology 6/ financial accounting and auditing 7/ management accounting and management control DESCF (2 written tests and 2 oral tests) : 1/ accounting and law 2/ accounting and management 3/ economics (oral) 4/ discussion on a report of 6 - week practical training period (oral) DEC (3 examinations): 1/ written test in audit to insure that the candidates have the ability to make a decision (to certify or not the financial statements) and to discuss a complex situation; 2/ oral test, experience assessment 3/ discussion of a thesis which test the ability to perform research, autonomy in thinking, and the ability to carry out self education.

Admission requirements for professional education

Baccalauréat level (final exam of the high school normally taken at the age of 18). Students don't need any specialised education and training background to be admitted in a professional education institute.

Universities and commercial companies provide professional education. Necessary expertise and resources are available

The leading professional education institute for the professional accounting examinations is the «Institut National des Techniques Economiques et Comptables », INTEC. The main centres are located in Paris, regional centres provide courses throughout the country and abroad. High schools and various private centres offer also courses. Many accountants and auditors specialists in subject matter teach at the INTEC, high schools or private centres. The Ordre is represented at the board of INTEC. The professional body does not provide professional education. The professional body is in charge of the three-year training period.

Practical training content

Candidates must obtain the higher accounting studies diploma, DESCF, (4 years at least after the Baccalauréat) before registration as trainee. This includes the six-week practical training period necessary for the DESCF. Full – time three-year traineeship (part time in a few circumstances). Two years at least in a professional accountancy or audit firm located in France or in EU. Monitoring by a qualified professional (mentor). Trainees typically work on a variety of accounting, auditing and taxation assignments. - 8 specific one-day seminars/year. Half of these seminars focus on technical matters, the other half deal with ethical rules and professional standards.- Delivery of 4 written reports on the practical activity.

The Ordre expects for the near future major developments in professional education.

Overview IDW

Professional Body	**Institut der Wirtschaftsprüfer in Deutschland e.V. (IDW)**
Professional Title	**Wirtschaftsprüfer (WP)**
Respondent	**Wolfgang P. Böhm, Referatsleiter, Accounting and Auditing, IDW**
Country	**Germany**

For additional information refer to IDW at www.idw.de, or Wolfgang Böhm at boehm@idw.de.

German accounting requirements are based mainly on the Commercial Code (HGB). In addition, the standards of the German Accounting Standards Committee published by the Ministry of Justice represent Principles of Proper Accounting for consolidated financial statements. Companies whose securities are listed on exchanges may apply IAS or US GAAP to the extent that these comply with the 4th and 7th EU Directives in place of German accounting requirements in their consolidated financial statements.

The accountancy sector in Germany is regulated by law and by professional self-regulation. In the Wirtschaftsprüferordnung (Law Pertaining to the Profession of Wirtschaftsprüfer), the government has established the Wirtschaftsprüferkammer (WPK) to meet needs of the profession (both Wirtschafts-prüfer and vereidigte Buchprüfer) as a whole and to monitor the fulfilment of professional obligations; the Institut der Wirtschaftsprüfer (IDW), as a private organization, does not have official government sanction, but the IDW does issue professional standards that are considered to be generally accepted by the profession. Both the IDW and the WPK are members of IFAC; the IDW (but not the WPK) also of FEE.

> The accountancy profession is divided into a number of separate professions from a legal point of view. Wirtschaftsprüfer (WP) are allowed to perform statutory audits of all kinds of entities of all sizes and also to provide public tax advice, accounting services and limited legal advice. Vereidigte Buchprüfer (vBP) are allowed to perform statutory audits of only mid-sized GmbH's and also to provide public tax advice, accounting services and limited legal advice. Steuerberater (StB) are allowed to provide public tax advice and accounting services. Rechtsanwälte (RA) may also provide public tax advice and accounting services in addition to all kinds of legal advice. Professional accountants in industry are not organized into a profession, but accounting technicians in industry (Bilanzbuchhalter) are. WP's, vBP's, StB and RA may not engage in a commercial business, nor be an employee of a commercial business or a government. Government accountants are a separate profession under government regulation. The same applies to auditors in the Rechnungshöfe (Auditors General) of the federal and state governments.

Full membership in the IDW is limited to Wirtschaftsprüfer, hence all full members of the IDW work in public practice. IDW membership is not mandatory; however the membership of WPK is mandatory. Continuing professional education is mandatory for all members, who are all in public practice.

Admission requirements include a formal final examination of professional competence, a programme of professional education (not mandatory) and practical training.

> The entrance requirements for the qualification are fixed by law in the Wirtschaftsprüferordnung.

International standards: the education and training requirements set by law meet the requirements of the EU 8th Directive; in future, it is intended that compliance with the IFAC Education Guidelines will also become an objective.

> The 8. EU Directive is mandatory. The IFAC Education Guidelines have not been officially implemented yet, but the profession intends to develop a process to ensure that they are incorporated into national requirements in future. This does not mean that the requirements in Germany do not

comply with the IFAC Education Guidelines – only that no formal process to determine compliance has been established yet.

International recognition of qualifications

Recognition of the professional qualification from Germany under the 8. EU Directive in other EU member states by means of a mutual recognition examination. The recognition of the corresponding qualification from all other EU member states is also achieved by a mutual recognition examination.

Final examination core programme

Accounting, Financial Statement Audit, Other Audits, Business Administration, Economics, Business Law, Tax Law.

Objective final examination: to test theoretical knowledge; the ability to apply knowledge in practice; intellectual and communication skills; professional values

Communication skills are tested as part of the oral examination.

The government is the provider of the final examination. Examinations are not subject to external review.

The state governments have established examination commissions comprising Wirtschaftsprüfer, university professors, civil servants, and a representative from industry.

Admission requirements cover practical training and general education.
Professional education core programme

A university degree in business administration or law recognized in Germany (e.g. Diplom-Kaufmann, etc.) and the final Examination are required. There are no additional professional educational programs required. The legally required minimum duration for the university is 8 semesters (four years), but the majority take ten to twelve semesters (five to six years). The additional examination tutoring usually requires an additional one to two years of part-time study during the period of practical work experience.

The IDW and commercial companies provide professional education (tutoring). Necessary expertise and resources are available.

Private organizations offer professional education in preparation for the WP-Exams in addition to the IDW. In addition, many accounting firms offer examination preparation courses to their employees, with varying time commitments. The period of time varies according to the nature of the programme. Professional bodies and most of the commercial organizations have the necessary expertise and resources available.

Practical training content

A candidate with a university degree must complete at least three years of practical experience (two of which in a Wirtschaftsprüfungsgesellschaft in the area of financial statement audit before being admitted to the final examination. The Wirtschaftsprüfungsgesellschaften have the expertise and resources to provide the practical training required. The WPK recognizes the Wirtschaftsprüfungs-gesellschaften.

IDW expects for the near future major developments in regulation of the profession, professional qualification requirements and professional education

IDW expects the regulation of the profession, professional qualification requirements and professional education to become increasingly harmonized at an international level.

Overview HKSA

Professional Body	**Hong Kong Society of Accountants (HKSA)**
Professional Title	**Professional Accountant and CPA**
Respondent	**Georgina Chan, Director of Education & Training, HKSA**
Country	**Hong Kong Special Administrative Region**

For additional information refer to HKSA at www.hksa.org.hk, or Georgina Chan at gchan@hksa.org.hk.

Hong Kong requirements on accounting rules are based on the Companies Ordnance, standards and interpretations issued by the Hong Kong Society of Accountants and the Listing Rules of the Stock Exchange.

The accountancy sector in Hong Kong is regulated by law and by professional self-regulation. The Hong Kong Society of Accountants (HKSA) is recognized as a regulatory body and a disciplinary body. HKSA is a member of IFAC .

Members of HKSA work in public practice, industry and commerce, government and in other areas. HKSA membership is mandatory. Continuing professional education is mandatory and is regulated by HKSA.

A member of the HKSA is designated as a Professional Accountant (AHKSA). A Certified Public Accountant (CPA) is a person holding a Practising Certificate eligible to practise public accountancy (sign statutory audit) in Hong Kong.

Admission requirements as member of HKSA include a formal final examination of professional Competence, a prescribed programme of professional education and specified practical experience.

HKSA is the only statutory licensing body of accountants in Hong Kong responsible for the regulation of the accountancy profession. The HKSA Qualification Programme is the only official professional qualifying programme for the accountancy profession in Hong Kong.

International standards: HKSA follows IFAC International Education Guidelines
International recognition of qualifications

HKSA's examination programme is recognized by CPA Australia and the Association of Chartered Certified Accountants in Britain. HKSA recognizes professional examination programmes offered by the accountancy bodies in: the United Kingdom, the United States, Canada, Australia, New Zealand, South Africa and Zimbabwe.

Final examination core programme

Main objective of the final examination is to provide formal verification that candidates can demonstrate a competent practitioner level of performance.

Objective final examination: to test theoretical knowledge; the ability to apply knowledge in practice; intellectual and communication skills; ICT applications; professional values

The final examination tests the ability of candidates to deal competently with professional-type situations, involving the drawing together and application of knowledge and skills from any part of the HKSA Professional Programme module syllabus, across all fields of competency. The final examination comprises of practical case questions and essay type questions.

The professional body is the provider of the final examination. HKSA examinations are subject to external review. Necessary expertise and resources are available.

> HKSA assumes full responsibility to ensure the standard and quality of its professional examinations are comparable to those of other reputable accountancy bodies around the world, and place itself in a better position to negotiate with other professional accountancy bodies for mutual recognition of membership. Our Examinations Board oversees the policies and operation of the HKSA's professional examinations. The Board is made up of professionals with expertise in different areas of accounting from both academic and industry

Admission requirements cover professional education

Professional education core programme

> The objective of the Professional Programme is to provide candidates with the opportunity, through the different modules of the programme and under the guidance of workshop facilitators, to develop the necessary application skills and competencies, which are essential for a professional accountant. The Professional Programme comprises 4 modules: Financial Reporting, Financial Management, Auditing and Information Management, Taxation. Each of the 4 modules requires 15 weeks' self-study and attendance in 4 three-hour workshops. The modules may be taken in any order and up to 2 modules can be taken at any one time, therefore the shortest duration of professional education is 1 year.

Admission requirements for professional education

> Recognized accountancy degree holders. A recognized accountancy degree from any Hong Kong tertiary institution or an overseas degree or academic qualification accepted by the HKSA as being of comparable standard. Programme requirements include generic skills, contextual skills and understandings and accounting skills and understandings in the areas of auditing, ethics, external reporting, financial management, management accounting, taxation and tax planning. No exemptions based on general education. Combination of professional experience with practical experience is required.

HKSA provides professional education. Necessary expertise and resources are available

> Our Examinations Board oversees the policies and operation of the HKSA's professional programme. The Board is made up of professionals with expertise in different areas of accounting from both academic and industry. The programme is reviewed periodically with the assistance of scholars and experts in different areas of accounting.

Practical training content

> Specified practical experience of 3 years for approved degree holders, 4 years for approved accountancy diploma holders and 5 years for holders of other academic qualifications.

HKSA expects for the near future major developments in regulation of the profession, professional qualification requirements, professional education and practical experience

> Implementing changes to the self-regulatory system to put in place a much more open and transparent system of dealing with disciplinary hearings. Develop course materials and assess aspects of the professional examinations. Define new Practical Experience requirements in competency-based standards. Finalise a new framework on Practical Experience.

Overview CHA

Professional Body	**Chamber of Hungarian Auditors (CHA)**
Professional Title	**Registered Auditor (HRA)**
Respondent	**Dr József Roóz**
Country	**Hungary**

For additional information refer to CHA at www.mkvk.hu, or József Roóz at rooz@matavnet.hu .

Hungarian requirements on accounting rules are based on the Accounting Act of 1991.

The accountancy sector in Hungary is regulated by law. The Chamber of Hungarian Auditors (CHA) is recognized as a regulatory body. CHA is a member of IFAC.

> The Law on the Chamber of Hungarian Auditors and the Activity of the Auditors endowed the following functions to the Chamber: licensing of performing auditing activities, registering the auditors, publishing information on member statutory auditors and recorded professional firms, education and qualification of auditors. The regularity of the Chamber's activities is examined by the Supervisory Board. Legal supervision over the Chamber is exercised by the Minister of Finance.

Members of CHA work in public practice, industry and commerce, government and in other areas. CHA membership is mandatory. Continuing professional education is mandatory for all members and is regulated by CHA.

> In Hungary only Registered Auditors are working in the field of regulated statutory audit. Other accountants who have the same qualification are not members of the Chamber. Duties of the Educational Committee include organising, controlling and managing activities connected with auditors' continuing professional education.

Admission requirements include a formal final examination of professional competence, prescribed programmes of professional education and practical training under the responsibility of the professional body (by law).

> Membership requirements include three years of professional practice, started after obtaining the chartered accountants qualification, and performed within five years prior to presenting application for membership, spent on the basis of employment or partner contract concluded with a member of Chamber or with an audit firm registered in the Chamber. The Educational Committee is in charge of elaborating the requirements of the qualifications of chartered accountants, including the approval of teaching materials and the supervision of training and examining. It also supervises the practical issues of professional training and keeps the records of the students.

International standards: CHA follows IFAC IEG 9 and 11.

No international recognition of the CHA qualification in other countries; no recognition in Hungary of qualifications from other countries.

Final examination core programme

> The final examination consists of six topics: Law (the learning course consists of 60 class hours); Organisation and Management (the learning course consists of 45 class hours); Finance (the learning course consists of 75 class hours); Accountancy and Analysis (the learning course consists of 140 class hours); Organisation of Accountancy (Similar to Information Technology) (The learning course consists of 80 class hours); Auditing and Internal Control (The learning course consists of 120 class hours). Auditing and Internal Control is the last important examination, because it consists of all the components of the formal education.

Objective final examination: to test theoretical knowledge and the ability to apply knowledge in practice.

The professional body is the provider of the final examination. CHA examinations are subject to external review. Necessary expertise and resources are available.

> The examining body is the provider of the final examination. The examiners are appointed by the Minister of Finance for five years. CHA delegates one member of the body.

Admission requirements cover professional education, practical training and general education.

Professional education core programme

> Subjects Law, Organisation and Management, Finance, Financial and Management Accounting, IT, Auditing and Internal Control. Full time and part time; total minimal class hours 520 in 2 years.

Admission requirements for professional education

> University or college degree of business, accounting, finance.

Professional body, universities and commercial companies provide professional education. Necessary expertise and resources are available and supervised by the professional body. Providers of professional education are recognized by the professional body (on application for permission) with periodic review(duration of permission three years).

> CHA invites tenders for providers. Universities and commercial companies won at the competition could provide professional education (in all 13). The duties of the Educational Committee of CHA consist in controlling activities connected with auditors' education. The by-law of CHA on regulations for conduct of examinations declares in par. 1 that the Examination Organisational Sub-department of CHA runs the tasks of the organisation of the examinations.

Practical training content

> Three years full time according to monitoring system regulation; part time is also possible. Admission requirements before the start of practical training: University or college degree of business, accounting, finance. Practical training takes place in public practice. Providers of practical training are recognized by the professional body. One of the CHA membership requirements is professional practice under CHA control. The continuously controlled form of practice is called monitoring system regulation. This on-the-job-training can provide valuable practical exposure to formal education. The monitoring system regulation will be obligatory from September 2002. At present monitoring is the duty of the Admission Committee of CHA. The Admission Committee examines the practical training when it judges applications for membership admission.

CHA expects for the near future major developments in professional education and practical training

> Law will be modified in the field of introduction of quality assurance. Three years of practical experience will be mandatory.

Overview ICA India

Professional Body	**The Institute of Chartered Accountants of India (ICA India)**
Professional Title	**Chartered Accountant**
Respondent	**C.R.T. Varma, Director of Studies**
Country	**India**

For additional information refer to ICA India at www.icai.org, or C.R.T. Varma at icainoda@del2.vsnl.net.

Indian requirements on accounting rules are mainly based on the Companies Act 1956, on regulations of the Company Law Board and on standards issued by the Institute of Chartered Accountants of India. In addition, listed companies must follow the rules, regulations and releases issued by the Securities and Exchange Board of India.

The accountancy sector in India is regulated by law and by professional self-regulation. The Institute of Chartered Accountants of India (ICA India) is recognized as a regulatory body and a disciplinary body. ICA India is a member of IFAC, CAPA and SAFA.

Members of ICA India work in public practice, industry and commerce, government and in other areas. ICA India membership is mandatory to use the designatory title. Continuing professional education will be mandatory from 2003 and is regulated for public practice, industry and commerce by ICA India.

Admission requirements as member of ICA India include a formal final examination of professional competence, professional education and practical training

> A candidate can apply for membership of ICA India as a Chartered Accountant after practical training has been completed, the Final Examination has been passed and a programme on general management and communication skills has been followed.

> Specialisation comes in the form of CPE only after attainment of the basic Professional Qualification. There are different post qualification courses like – Management Accountancy, Tax Management, Corporate Management, Information Systems Audit, Insurance and Risk Management, Trade Laws and WTO.

International standards: ICA India follows IFAC International Education Guidelines.
International recognition of qualifications

> MOUs have been entered into with ICA Pakistan, ICA Sri Lanka, AICPA USA, ICAEW, London ICAI Bangladesh for dialogues for professional collaboration and reciprocal recognition of qualifications. Initiatives are under way for recognition of qualification with ICA New Zealand and CICA Canada.

Final examination core programme

> Group-1: Advanced Accounting, Management Accounting and Financial Analysis, Advanced Auditing, Corporate Laws and Secretarial Practice; Group-2: Cost Management, Management Information and Control Systems, Direct Taxes, Indirect Taxes

Objective final examination: to test theoretical knowledge; the ability to apply knowledge in practice; intellectual, interpersonal and communication skills; ICT applications; professional values.

ICA India is the provider of the final examination. The examinations are subject to external review.

> All the examiners who examine the answer papers are outside examiners who are drawn from the members of the profession as well as other sister professions and academic community.

Admission requirements to the final examination cover professional education and practical training.

Professional education core programme

Professional Education Course-1 (PE-1): Fundamentals of Accounting, Mathematics and Statistics, Economics, Business Communication and Organisation and Management. Professional Education Course-2 (PE-2): Accounting, Auditing, Business and Corporate Laws, Cost Accounting and Financial Management, Income Tax and Central Sales Tax, Information Technology. Final CA Course: Advanced Accounting, Management Accounting and Financial Analysis, Advanced Auditing, Corporate Laws and Secretarial Practice, Cost Management, Management Information and Control Systems, Direct Taxes, Indirect Taxes.

ICA India and accredited institutions provide professional education. Necessary expertise and resources are available

The Board of Studies recognizes suitable institutions and grants accreditation for organising classes. From time to time the Institute reviews the scheme of education and training and brings about necessary reforms.

Practical training content

Three years of full time practical training is mandatory. Conditions for admission to articleship: not less than 18 years of age, having passed the PE-2 examination, having successfully completed the computer training programme specified by the Council. Practical training takes place in public practice and in industry and commerce. The candidate has an option to go for Industrial Training during the third year of his Practical Training, under a member of the Institute serving in Industry, for a period which may range from 9 – 12 months. Regulations for practical training include training contract and reports on practical Training as required in Chartered Accountants Regulations, 1988 and in recent amendments.

ICA India expects for the near future major developments in regulation of the profession, professional qualification requirements and professional education

A revised Code of Ethics for members of the Profession and a Code of Conduct for articled clerks undergoing practical training is likely to be finalised shortly.

Professional Education Examinations under the new syllabi are scheduled to start from November 2002. The requirement of compulsory attendance in the course on General Management and Communication Skills before applying for membership is expected to commence. A scheme for compulsory computer training for students before joining practical training and a compulsory course on general management and communication skills are under finalisation.

The new curriculum for the Professional Education Course as well as the Final Examination, with its emphasis on Information Technology, Communication Skills and coverage of contemporary developments within the scope of the syllabi for various papers is bound to produce more technology knowledge and better informed professional accountants. Introduction of new post-qualification courses such as Information Systems, Audit, WTO and Trade Laws will improve the technical competence of members and their ability to cope up with the changing environment both in public practice and industry.

The Training Guide governing practical training is expected to be revised shortly. Practical Training will be more concentrated and the quality of the entrants joining for practical training will also be superior and more matured. There will be more focussed emphasis on qualitative aspects of Practical Training.

Overview ICWAI

Professional Body	**The Institute of Cost and Works Accountants of India (ICWAI)**
Professional Title	**Cost and Work Accountant (CWA)**
Respondent	**Swapan Dey, Director of Studies, ICWAI**
Country	**India**

For additional information refer to ICWAI at www.icwai.org, or Swapan Dey at sdicwai@vsnl.net.

Indian requirements on accounting rules are mainly based on the Companies Act 1956, on regulations of the Company Law Board and on standards issued by the Institute of Chartered Accountants of India. In addition, listed companies must follow the rules, regulations and releases issued by the Securities and Exchange Board of India.

The accountancy sector in India is regulated by law. The Institute of Cost and Work Accountants in India (ICWAI) is recognized as a regulatory body and a disciplinary body. ICWAI is a member of IFAC, CAPA and SAFA.

> ICWAI is recognized as a regulatory body and the statutory educational Institute and examining authority in respect of the Cost Accountancy profession

Members of ICWAI work in public practice, industry and commerce, government and in other areas. ICWAI membership is mandatory to use the designatory title. Continuing professional education is not mandatory.

> CPE is not mandatory, but the members update themselves with current developments in the profession.

Admission requirements as member of ICWAI include a formal final examination of professional Competence, professional education and practical training

> Cost and Management Accountants are required to facilitate strategic management decisions in respect of diverse economic activities of an organisation where they are deployed as employee/ consultant. Strategic Cost Management and Cost Audit are their focus areas. The syllabus of the Institute is finally evaluated and approved by the Government. As the Institute is a member of IFAC,CAPA,SAFA etc. the syllabus and the standard is maintained with mutual exchange of ideas , industrial requirement and international standard.

International standards: ICWAI follows IFAC IEG 9
International recognition of qualifications

> CIMA (UK), CIA (USA), CMA (USA), CPA (Australia), CMA (Pakistan), CMA (Bangladesh), CMA (Sri Lanka),CPA (New Zealand), CGA (Canada), CII (London) etc. by way of reciprocal recognition. The countries, which have recognized the ICWAI qualification consider the Institute Members competent enough to take up jobs in the relevant fields in their countries.

Final examination core programme

> Advanced Financial Accounting, Information Technology and Computer Applications, Operation Management and Control, Project Management and Control, Advanced Management Accounting-Technique and Applications, Advanced Financial Management, Advanced Management Accounting-Strategic Management, Cost Audit. In addition the students are required to undergo training in different fields by way of Group Discussion, Business Communication, Project preparation, hands-on on computer.

Objective final examination: to test theoretical knowledge; the ability to apply knowledge in practice; intellectual, interpersonal and communication skills; ICT applications; professional values

The syllabus of the course is designed to equip the students with modern tools management so that they can to facilitate strategic management decisions in respect of diverse economic activities of an organisation.

ICWAI is the provider of the final examination. The examinations are subject to external review.

ICWAI is a unique Institute in India recognized by the Government of India to conduct coaching, training and examination etc in relation to the profession of Cost and Management Accountancy. The Institute has ninety examination centres in India and abroad. The Institute conducts the examination according to the provisions of ACT passed by Indian Parliament. The examiners are members of different professional Institutes in India and Professors of Universities.

Admission requirements cover professional education and practical training

For admission to Final Examination, Passing Intermediate Examination of the Institute is a must. For admission to Intermediate Examination, one has to pass graduation under any recognized university of India.

Professional education core programme

Cost and Management Accountancy, General Accounting, Auditing, Management Audit, Taxation, Financial Management etc (see examination programme). Our course is designed to accommodate working people in Trade/Commerce and Industry also and hence the training provision is part time only. Minimum duration of Intermediate Course is 18 months. After passing Intermediate Examination, one is eligible for admission to Final Exam. After Graduation, one has to be registered (admitted) in the Institute.

ICWAI provides professional education. Necessary expertise and resources are available

Education by way of oral coaching by Coaching Centres or by Postal Coaching. ICWAI has a network of 102 Coaching Centres spread all over the country and abroad with support of competent faculty.

Practical training content

As per the CWA Act and Regulation, three years training is mandatory for admission to the Associate membership of the Institute. Training is always on-job. The students are guided by senior staff of organisations where they are deployed. There are no admission requirements before the start of practical training. Training is recognized only when the fields are within our ambit of specialisation and the organization is registered one to conduct their business activity

ICWAI expects for the near future major developments in regulation of the profession, professional qualification requirements and professional education

Regulation of the profession is expected to develop so as to make it broad based and widely acceptable by all industries, trade and commerce. This is the obvious and natural course to use Management Accounting profession in a globally competitive economy.
The Professional requirement has undergone revolutionary change due to wide application of Information Technology and opening up of the Indian Economy. The syllabus of the Institute has been already revised and awaiting Government's Approval for implementation. The following subjects are taken care of - Economic Valuation and Measurement - Marketing Paradigm of Management - Human Resources and Behavioural Accounting - Case Analysis and Case Presentation as a distinct skill-service Sector Operations and Management – Banking, Insurance etc.
Professional education will be in the line of the changed requirements of profession to serve the Indian Economy more efficiently.

Overview JICPA

Professional Body	**Japanese Institute of Certified Public Accountants (JICPA)**
Professional Title	**Certified Public Accountant (CPA)**
Respondent	**Nobutake Ipposhi, Executive Director CPE, JICPA**
Country	**Japan**

For additional information about JICPA refer to www.jicpa.or.jp, or Nobutake Ipposhi at international@jicpa.or.jp.

Japanese requirements on accounting rules are based on the Commercial Code and accounting standards developed by the Business Accounting Council, Accounting Standards Board and the Japanese Institute of Certified Public Accountants.

The accountancy sector in Japan is regulated by the CPA law. The Japanese Institute of Certified Public Accountants (JICPA) is recognized as a disciplinary body. JICPA is a member of IFAC and CAPA.

Members of JICPA work in public practice. JICPA membership is mandatory to use the designatory title. Only JICPA members can provide audit services. Continuing professional education is mandatory for members in public practice beginning from April 1 2002 and is regulated by the JICPA.

In Japan almost all members are expected to be in public practice.

Admission requirements include a national CPA examination of professional competence

To be qualified as a CPA a candidate must pass the CPA examinations provided by the Certified Public Accountants Board in the Financial Services Agency . Although the CPA examinations consist of three stages, university graduated candidates can start from the second stage. Each examination is conducted once a year.

International standards on accountancy education are not followed
International recognition of qualifications

There is no recognition of qualifications from other countries in Japan.

Final examination core programme

The first stage assesses whether the candidate has the basic knowledge required to apply for the second stage examination. The test covers the Japanese language, mathematics, English and an essay. At the second stage the applicants are assessed for professional knowledge required for an accountant. The examination consists of multiple-choice test and written test. Multiple-choice: Accounting and commercial code. Written: Required: accounting (bookkeeping, financial statements, cost accounting and auditing) and commercial code. Choose two out of three: business management, economics and civil code. At the third stage the applicants are assessed for technical competence in professional judgment required for a CPA. The four subjects for the final examination are auditing , accounting, financial analysis and taxation.

Objective final examination: to test the ability to apply knowledge in practice

Qualification as CPA requires three examinations in Japan. The persons passing the second examination which tests theoretical knowledge are granted the title of junior CPA. The final examination tests practical abilities three years after the second examination. The final examination consists of paper and oral examinations.

The government is the provider of the CPA examination.

The CPA Board in the Financial Service Agency (FSA) is the provider of the examination. The FSA appoints the Board members from academics and experienced CPAs.

Admission requirements cover professional education and practical training

There are no education requirements to sit for the first stage of the examination. The first stage examination is waived for college/university graduates or those who have completed at least two years of their college or university education. Junior CPAs who passed the second examination, in order to become eligible to sit for the third stage examination, must have completed at least two-year training courses offered by the JICPA and two-year audit training at an accounting firm . However, most applicants would complete both trainings within three years as one year overlapping is permitted.

Professional education core programme

Two-year education courses offered by the JICPA in auditing , accounting, ethics, and taxation.

Admission requirements for professional education

Junior CPAs who passed second stage of CPA examination.

Providers of professional education. Necessary expertise and resources

JICPA provides courses. Education curriculum is developed by Education Committees in JICPA. Most of instructors are experienced CPAs and member of the Committees.

Practical training content

Two-year audit field work on-the-job training at accounting firms.

JICPA expects for the near future major developments in professional education

At present , we intend to develop more intensified education program for junior CPAs. We are now making efforts to develop an infrastructure for more substantial professional education.

Overview ICPAK

Professional Body	**Institute of Certified Public Accountants of Kenya**
Professional Title	**Certified Public Accountant CPA(K)**
Respondent	**John K. Njiraini, Chief Executive Officer**
Country	**Kenya**

For additional information refer to www.icpak.com, or John Njiraini at icpak@icpak.com.

Kenya requirements on accounting rules are based on International Accounting Standards and local Company Law.

The accountancy sector in Kenya is regulated by law and by professional self-regulation. The Institute of Certified Public Accountants of Kenya (ICPAK) is recognized as a regulatory body and a disciplinary body. ICPAK is a member of IFAC and ECSAFA.

> The accountancy profession in Kenya is regulated through the Accountants Act, Chapter 531 of the Laws of Kenya. The Act was enacted in 1977 and brought into being three bodies, namely: Institute of Certified Public Accountants of Kenya (ICPAK); Kenya Accountants and Secretaries National Examinations Board (KASNEB); Registration of Accountants Board (RAB). The three bodies operate autonomously, are governed by separate Boards, and perform different functions. The Certified Public Accountants certificate (CPA) is the ultimate qualification that entitles one not only to use the CPA(K) designation but also to practice accountancy (but only after due licensing by the RAB).

Members of ICPAK work in public practice, industry and commerce, government and in other areas. ICPAK membership is not mandatory. Continuing professional education is mandatory for all members and is regulated by ICPAK.

> ICPAK provides for the maintenance of competence by updating members' knowledge through publications and the conduct of Continuous Professional Education programmes.

Admission requirements include a formal final examination of professional competence and a prescribed programme of professional education. Those wishing to engage in independent accountancy practice are required to have acquired the prescribed practical training.

> ICPAK is responsible for the standard setting for the qualification but examinations are the responsibility of KASNEB. The Registration of Accountants Board (RAB) deals with registration and licensing of persons who have qualified to become CPAs after completion of the examinations of KASNEB. Qualified CPAs are initially registered only as such without conferment of any special privileges. Those who desire to practice are required to obtain a special license issued by the Board. ICPAK nominates three members to the Board of RAB although its Chairman is normally a CPA. ICPAK also nominates two members to the Board of KASNEB.

International standards on accountancy education are followed

> Education requirements are aligned to international benchmarks and in line with IFAC pronouncements.

International recognition of qualifications

> Recognition of the ICPAK qualification in other countries has been achieved especially within Eastern and Southern Africa. Exemptions have been granted by CGA-Ontario in Canada and also by the ACCA in the UK. Recognition of qualifications from other countries by ICPAK is granted on a selective basis but foreign accountants are required to sit papers in local law and taxation.

Final examination core programme

Financial Accounting, Business Finance, Management, Auditing, Information Technology & Systems.

Objective final examination: to test theoretical knowledge; the ability to apply knowledge in practice; intellectual, interpersonal and communication skills; ICT applications; professional values.

KASNEB provides the final examination, which is subject to external review.

> The Kenya Accountants and Secretaries National Examinations Board (KASNEB) administers qualifying examinations for both Accountants and Company Secretaries. KASNEB operates through its own Board in which ICPAK nominates two members.

Admission requirements cover general education

> Minimum High School at C+ grade, followed by academic course of instruction.

Professional education core programme

> Financial Accounting, Business, Management & Finance, Auditing, Information Technology & Systems.

Professional body and commercial companies provide professional education. Necessary expertise and resources are available. Providers of professional education are recognized by the government and the professional body.

> ICPAK has established the Kenya College of Accountancy (KCA), in 1999 as a means of providing a benchmark for excellence in accountancy training. KCA is now a leading trainer for the CPA qualification in addition to providing other education relevant to business management.

Practical training

> Practical training is required for those intending to obtain license for public practice.

ICPAK expects for the near future major developments in regulation of the profession, professional qualification requirements, professional education and practical training

> There are moves in progress to amend the statute that governs accountancy in Kenya that will give ICPAK greater control over licensing requirements and thereby help in enforcing professional and education requirements. There are also plans to implement a Practice Review programme within the next year.

> An ongoing review of the CPA examination syllabus proposes to introduce practical experience requirements as a pre-condition for qualification and to introduce requirements for providers of training services as means of ensuring quality delivery. Practical experience is already a requirement of those intending to engage in public practice.

Overview LACPA

Professional Body	**Lebanese Association of Certified Public Accountants (LACPA)**
Professional Title	**Lebanese Certified Public Accountant**
Respondent	**Munir D. Sidani, Senior Partner, Sidani & Co**
Country	**Lebanon**

For additional information refer to Munir Sidani at sidanico@cyberia.net.lb.

Lebanese requirements on accounting rules are based on local laws and international accounting standards. The General Accounting Plan follows the French accounting system.

The accountancy sector in Lebanon is regulated by law and by professional self-regulation. The Lebanese Association of Certified Public Accountants (LACPA) is recognized as a regulatory body and a disciplinary body. LACPA is a member of IFAC and FIDEF.

Members of LACPA work in public practice, industry and commerce, government and in other areas. LACPA membership is mandatory. Continuing professional education is mandatory and is regulated by LACPA.

Admission requirements as member of LACPA include a formal final examination of professional competence, required university degree or higher professional accounting degree and practical training under the responsibility of the government and the professional body

> The LACPA carefully guards the quality of its potential and existing members through extensive exams and requirements of a university or higher professional accounting degree. It also requires its existing members to conform to continuing professional education requirements.

International standards on accountancy education are not followed.
International recognition of qualifications

> Some Middle Eastern countries recognize the LACPA qualification with some restrictions and subject to reciprocal treatment. US CPA, Canada Chartered, UK Chartered, French expert-comptable are recognized in Lebanon subject to examination in local tax and laws. Other countries recognition depends on reciprocal treatment.

Final examination core programme

> General Accounting (including management and analytical accounting), (2) Advanced Accounting (including international accounting standards), (3) Auditing, (4) Taxation & Business Law Plus final interview.

Objective final examination: to test theoretical knowledge; the ability to apply knowledge in practice; intellectual, interpersonal and communication skills; professional values

> The exam uses a variety of methods and is given in three languages: Arabic, English & French. Many questions follow the CPA (USA) exam and French professional exams.

The government is the provider of the final examination. Examinations are not subject to external review.
The examination committee includes members from outside the profession (judge, university professors, and practitioners)

> The examination committee is formed by the ministry of finance and includes professionals, university professors, government employees, and a judge. Members enjoy a wide experience either as holders of

local and foreign professional qualifications (CPA, FCCA) or as being professors of accounting and auditing and related fields.

Admission requirements cover general education

Undergraduate degree in business or accounting at any recognized university (three years of general and technical education).

Professional education core programme

Students in preparation for the final examination usually rely on their own learning at the university or accounting professional technical centres. The LACPA does not oversee any formal professional education program for exam purposes.

Practical training content

Training in a recognized office on tasks related primarily to accounting or auditing. University degree or professional accounting technical degree plus formal application before the start of practical training. Experience only counts when the accounting board is informed beforehand. Practical training takes place in public practice. Duration 3 years for holders of baccalaureate degree in business or accounting; 5 years for holders of professional TS degree in accounting (Technicien Supérieur). Providers of practical training are recognized by the professional body.

LACPA expects for the near future major developments in regulation of the profession and professional qualification requirements

Regulation of the profession: More clarification will be brought forward about members of the LACPA who are not in public practice, their role, rights and responsibilities.
Professional qualification requirements: More clarifications of what foreign qualifications to recognize.

Overview MACPA

Professional Body	**The Malaysian Association of Certified Public Accountants (MACPA)**
Professional Title	**Certified Public Accountants (CPA)**
Respondent	**Tan Shook Kheng, Executive Director, MACPA**
Country	**Malaysia**

For additional information refer to MACPA at www.macpa.com.my, or Tan Shook Kheng at macpa@po.jaring.my.

Malaysian requirements on accounting rules are based on the Companies Act 1965 and on the standards of the Malaysian Accounting Standards Board. The Malaysian Accounting Standards Board uses IASs as the basis for developing accounting standards.

The accountancy sector in Malaysia is regulated by law and by professional self regulation. The Malaysian Association of Certified Public Accountants (MACPA) is recognized as a regulatory body and a disciplinary body. MACPA is a member of IFAC and CAPA.

Members of MACPA work in public practice, industry and commerce, government and in other areas. MACPA membership is mandatory. Continuing professional education is not mandatory.

Admission requirements include a formal final examination of professional competence, prescribed programmes of professional education and practical training under the responsibility of MACPA

> Admission requirements: (a) A recognized degree or diploma at the tertiary level; (b) Pass the MACPA professional examinations within the prescribed period; (c) Undergo 3 years of supervised practical training in an approved training organization in public practice, commerce, industry or the public sector.

International standards: CPA education, examination and training are consistent with IFAC guidelines International recognition of qualifications

> MACPA has not entered into official reciprocal recognition arrangement with professional bodies in other countries. However, the CPA qualification is well recognized in the Asian countries for employment.

> Recognition of the qualification from other countries by MACPA: (i) Australia (ii) Canada (iii) India (iv) New Zealand (v) United Kingdom (vi) USA. Requirements for admission to MACPA: (a) A recognized degree; (b) Having passed the professional examinations of the major accountancy body in the country in which the degree qualification originates; (c) Having passed the MACPA examination in Malaysian company law and revenue law; (d) Having obtained not less than 3 years of relevant work experience.

Final examination core programme

> (1) Financial Accounting and Reporting II - (2) Advanced Taxation - (3) Audit Practice - (4) Business Finance and Strategy.

Objective final examination: to test theoretical knowledge; the ability to apply knowledge in practice; intellectual and communication skills; ICT applications; professional values

> The final examination aims to equip students with the necessary technical knowledge and business skills to become effective CPAs and business advisors with a good understanding of the core subjects of financial accounting, auditing, taxation and business management, the professional skills of analysis of information, evaluation and action planning, as well as the professional values of objectivity and integrity. The examination aim to test candidates' ability to apply knowledge in a situation provided.

The professional body is the provider of the final examination. MACPA examinations are not subject to external review. Necessary expertise and resources are available.

Admission requirements cover professional education, practical training and general education.

Professional education core programme

Professional Examination I Module A: Audit Fundamentals, Financial Accounting & Reporting I, Information Systems; Module B: Company Law & Practice, Managerial Planning & Control, Organisational Management. Professional Examination II Module C: Financial Accounting & Reporting II, Advanced Taxation. Module D: Audit Practice, Business Finance & Strategy. The programme is offered full-time and part-time. The minimum amount of time required to adequately prepare for the CPA examination is 2 years.

Admission requirements for professional education

The minimum entry qualification is an approved degree (3 - 4 years of full-time study) or a diploma at the tertiary level (2 - 3 years of full-time study after high school education). Candidates with general education will be required to undergo a conversion course, to gain appropriate foundation in accountancy and related subjects, before they are eligible for admission to the CPA examination.

Professional body, universities and commercial companies provide professional education. Necessary expertise and resources are available. Providers are recognized by the government and the professional body.

Public universities and colleges of advanced education are regulated and administered by the Ministry of Education. Private sector providers of general and professional education must obtain the prior approval of government. MACPA undertakes the evaluation of courses provided by both public and private education institutions for purposes of admission or exemption from the CPA examinations.

Practical training content

Practical training is normally 3 years full-time employment under the supervision of a member of MACPA in an approved training organization in public practice, commerce, industry or the public sector. Practical experience must include accounting/auditing and at least two of the following categories: Taxation, Financial Management, Insolvency, Information Technology. Admission requirements before the start of practical training are the same as for admission to professional education. Practical training is constantly monitored by the principal or training supervisor. Details of the training are to be submitted with the application for admission to membership for MACPA's evaluation.

MACPA expects for the near future major developments in professional qualification requirements

MACPA has recently undertaken a major review of its examination structure and training system. The new structure, which will be implemented at the end of 2002, consists of two levels of examinations. The first level, the Professional Stage Examination (consisting of 6 papers), covers the principles and concepts which underpin accountancy in all its disciplines. This is followed by the Advanced Stage Examination, consisting of 3 advanced papers, in taxation, financial reporting and business management.

A new basis of assessment will be introduced for the Advanced Stage Examination. It will consist of two assessment components - assessment in workshops (30%) and in final examination (70%). Greater flexibility will also be introduced in meeting the practical experience requirements.

Overview MIA

Professional Body	**Malaysian Institute of Accountants (MIA)**
Professional Title	**Chartered Accountant of Malaysia C.A. (M)**
Respondent	**Albert Wong Mun Sum, Council Member, MIA**
Country	**Malaysia**

For additional information refer to MIA at www.mia.org.my, or Albert Wong Mun Sum at wjzuntze@tm.net.my.

Malaysian requirements on accounting rules are based on the Companies Act 1965 and on the standards of the Malaysian Accounting Standards Board. The Malaysian Accounting Standards Board uses IASs as the basis for developing accounting standards.

The accountancy sector in Malaysia is regulated by law and by professional self regulation. The Malaysian Institute of Accountants (MIA) is recognized as a regulatory body and a disciplinary body. MIA is a member of IFAC, CAPA and AFA

> The members of MIA are allowed to call themselves Chartered Accountants of Malaysia C.A.(M) as defined in the Amendments of the Accountants Act 2001. MIA is not a professional body; it is a regulatory body. Membership of MIA is through qualification of members from various professional bodies and graduates from local universities. Regulated by law in that only members of MIA are allowed to call themselves an accountant. To be able to practise as an auditor an accountant needs to be a member of the MIA. Professional bodies also regulated their members through their individual articles. Under the Act members of MIA can be disciplined for wrongdoings in public practice.

Members of MIA work in public practice, industry and commerce, government and in other areas. MIA membership is mandatory. Continuing professional education is mandatory under the By-Laws of the Act in Malaysia.

> Membership in MIA is mandatory if you want to continue to practice in public practice or hold a position with the title "accountant".

Admission requirements are based on professional qualifications

> MIA is a regulatory body as such admission to MIA is based on the members qualification in recognized professional bodies or graduates with degrees from a local recognized university with the prerequisite working experience. The various professional bodies providing the professional education and practical training are located in Malaysia and as such they provide their necessary expertise and resources for their students.

> Government has a National Accreditation Board to accredit local universities. Local universities then have to apply to MIA to be accepted as one of those accredited universities for the Govt. to incorporate into the Act.

International standards: MIA follows IFAC IEG 9 and 11.
International recognition of qualifications

> No recognition of the MIA membership qualification in other countries This is mainly because MIA is a regulatory body and thus its membership qualification is recognized currently in Malaysia only.

> Qualifications from other countries are recognized in Malaysia, for example Australia - achieve the CPA exam and become a full member of CPA Australia; UK - achieve the ACCA / CIMA / ICAS / ICAI/ ICAEW exams and become a full member of the respective bodies; other countries like India, Pakistan, NZ

MIA expects for the near future major developments in regulation of the profession, professional qualification requirements, professional education and practical training

In Malaysia, the regulatory body, MIA, will take on a more visible role in its attempts to enhance the economic environment in Malaysia due to the Government's call for greater transparency and corporate governance in the market place by placing the main responsibilities on these areas on the accountants' shoulders.

There will be an increasing need for accountants to enhance their qualifications. The KLSE listing requirements has made it mandatory now for only qualified accountants to be authorised to sign financial accounts presented and the requirement for at least one qualified accountant to sit on the respective boards of plcs.

Professional education will take account of the current development in ICT and other respective local requirements. The recognition by the public on the wider role that an accountant actually plays will help to develop future professional educations. The emphasis on corporate governance has taken centre stage highlighting that the auditors' role in any company is not limited to an annual evaluation of the performance of the organisation. The need for a more wholesome accountant is emphasised in Malaysia.

Practical training will involve exposure to ICT and new local statutory requirements.

Overview IMCP

Professional Body	**Instituto Mexicana de Contadores Publicos (IMCP)**
Professional Title	**Contador Publico (CP) or Licendiado en Contaduria (LC)**
Respondent	**Salvador Ruiz-de-Chavez, Accounting Examinations Director, Ceneval**
Country	**Mexico**

For additional information refer to IMCP at www.imcp.com.mx, or Salvador Ruiz-de-Chavez at contaduria@ceneval.edu.mx.

Mexican requirements on accounting rules are based on the standards issued by the Mexican Institute of Public Accountants, Bulletin A-8 of which requires that IAS must be followed on a supplementary basis when Mexican requirements are silent. The IASC standards are considered in Mexico as supplementary standards in the absence of any accounting rule or principle issues by the Mexican Institute of Public Accountants.

The accountancy sector in Mexico is regulated by law and by professional self-regulation. IMCP is recognized as a regulatory body and a disciplinary body. IMCP is a member of IFAC and of the Asociacion Interamericana de Contabilidad.

Members of IMCP work in public practice, industry and commerce, government and education. IMCP membership is mandatory if in public practice. Continuing professional education is mandatory and is regulated by IMCP.

> Contador Publico (CP) and Licenciado en Contaduria (LC) are the professional titles. Accounting graduates receive not only a certificate from the university but also the professional licence from the Ministry of Education, without further requirements.

> Public accountancy is one of the professions that requires a professional title in Mexico, as stipulated in the Law Regulating Article 5 of the Constitution (LRA5), concerning the practice of professions in Mexico. The Directorate-General of Professions, of the Ministry of Education (SEP) registers all university certificates and issues the appropriate professional licence. The professional licence is issued by the Ministry of Education to a person who has completed the university studies and demonstrated the necessary skills in accordance with the above-mentioned law and other applicable provisions.

Admission requirements as a Certified Public Accountant of the IMCP include a uniform final examination of professional competence university education and practical training.

International standards: IMCP follows IFAC standards.
International recognition of qualifications

> There are no automatic recognition agreements. The Mexican Committee of International Accounting Practice (COMPIC), in the framework of the NAFTA, is working with its counterparts in the United States and Canada mutually acceptable standards and criteria for recognizing their respective licences (education, ethics, examination, professional experience). Negotiations with other countries, particularly those with which Mexico has signed free trade agreements, are also under way.

> Foreigners are subject to compliance with the requirements set out in Mexican law, including revalidation of studies, completion of community service and possession of the qualification, together with reciprocal treatment for Mexicans at the applicant's place of residence. Foreign educational qualifications are recognized by the process of the revalidation of studies (Article 15 of the LRA5).

Final examination core programme

Since 1999 the IMCP implemented a 12 hours uniform accounting examination, in order to certify those accountants that already have an accounting certificate issued by the university and also the professional licence issued by the Ministry of Education. The examination includes Financial Accounting, Taxation, Business Law, Finance, Auditing, Ethics and Managerial Accounting.

Objective final examination: to test theoretical knowledge; the ability to apply knowledge in practice; intellectual skills and professional ethics.

The professional body is the provider of the final examination. The examinations are subject to external review

The IMCP is cofounder along with the Ministry of Education and other organizations of the National Center of Evaluation for Higher Education (CENEVAL). CENEVAL is in charge of the technical development of the uniform accounting examination and also of its administration under adequate security conditions.

Admission requirements cover professional education, practical training and general education

In order to take the uniform accounting examination, the candidates are required to have three years of professional experience, after finishing their professional university education.

Professional education core programme

Accounting, Managerial Accounting, Taxation, Business Law, Auditing, Finance, Economics, Information Technology, Quantitative Methods and Statistics, Organisational Behaviour and Operations Management. A typical accounting university programme is 4 to 5 years, 200 hours and 40 to 50 courses. In order to get the university accounting certificate the students must write a dissertation or take a national accounting examination developed by Ceneval (note that this examination is different from IMCP's Uniform Accounting Examination) or take additional postgraduate courses.

Admission requirements for professional education: university entrance level. Mexican universities provide professional education, starting the first semester.

Practical training content

In order to take the uniform accounting examination, the candidates are required to have at least 3 years of practical experience under the supervision of a Certified Public Accountant. The professional experience period starts when the candidates get the accounting certificate from the university and the professional licence from the Ministry of Education.

IMCP expects for the near future major developments in regulation of the profession and in professional qualification requirements

The certification process will be compulsory for any accountant working in public practice (Auditing), but will remain voluntary for all other accountants. IMCP has already been working with AICPA and the CICA for mutual recognition of the professional licence for over 10 years. It is expected that we can eventually reach an agreement in 2003.

Overview NIVRA

Professional Body	**Koninklijk Nederlands Instituut van Registeraccountants (Royal NIVRA)**
Professional Title	**Registeraccountant (RA)**
Respondent	**Jeroen Buchel, Education Manager, NIVRA-Nyenrode**
Country	**The Netherlands**

For additional information refer to Royal NIVRA at www.nivra.nl, or Jeroen Buchel at j.buchel@nivra-nyenrode.nl.

Dutch accounting requirements can be found in the Civil Code as amended by EU Directives and in Guidelines of the Council for Annual Reporting. Although the guidelines are not mandatory, they should not be departed from without good reason. However, departure is required if application of the requirements does not provide a true and fair view of the state of affairs and results of the enterprise.

The accountancy sector in the Netherlands is regulated by law and by professional self-regulation. The 'Koninklijk Nederlands Instituut van Registeraccountants' (Royal NIVRA) is recognized as a regulatory body and a disciplinary body. NIVRA is a member of IFAC and FEE.

Members of NIVRA work in public practice, industry and commerce, government and other areas. NIVRA membership is mandatory to use the title. Continuing professional education is mandatory and is regulated by NIVRA.

Admission requirements as member of Royal NIVRA include a formal final examination of professional competence, prescribed programmes of professional education and practical training.

> The Government is responsible for legal standards as regulated in the Law on the Registeraccountant. Royal NIVRA is responsible for accountancy education and examination for registeraccountants. There is an Examination Board RA for the accountancy examination under control by the Curatorium. The members of the Examination Board RA and the Curatorium are appointed by the Minister of Economic Affairs.

International standards : EU 8th Directive and IFAC Education Guidelines.
International recognition of qualifications

> Recognition inside the EU according to EU Directives and for other countries on an individual bases. USA – Dutch RA's with a university degree have a masters degree and followed more than 150 hours of education, so they can sit for the CPA Examination.

> Accountants from EU countries (and non EU countries that have signed the Treaty of Oporto on the European Economic Area - Norway, Iceland and Liechtenstein) must submit evidence that they are authorized to carry out audits in their own country in accordance with the requirements of the Eighth EU Directive. Accountants from countries outside the EU must possess an accountancy qualification that is equivalent to the Dutch Registeraccountant qualification. The foreign accountant who fulfils the first condition can take a Special Examination (in Dutch!). This examination tests the knowledge of the candidate in Dutch civil law with special regard to accountancy. i.e. company law; Dutch fiscal law; Dutch accounting rules as laid down in the law; Dutch professional rules and rules of conduct

Final examination core programme

> The final examination consists of a theoretical and a practical part. For both parts a separate thesis must be written and defended.

Objective final examination: to test theoretical knowledge; the ability to apply knowledge in practice; intellectual, interpersonal and communication skills; ICT applications; professional values

Students have to make a case study and defend this case to other students and examiners

NIVRA examinations and examinations by six universities with a postgraduate accountancy programme are subject to external review by the Examination Board.

Admission requirements cover professional education, practical training and general education

Preparation for the theoretical part of the final examination can start after all the required subjects of professional education have been passed. Preparation for the practical part of the final examination can start after admittance to the third year of practical training.

Professional education core programme

Main areas of accountancy: Financial Accounting and Management Accounting, Accounting Information Systems, Auditing. The majority of the students start after a four year degree education at a university (masters degree in accounting or economics) or an institute of higher economic education. there is also a seven year part time programme that starts directly after secondary education.

Admission requirements for professional education

Possession of a university or higher education degree in accounting or economics or a diploma of the first four years NIVRA-Nyenrode part time professional education.

Professional body and universities provide professional education. Necessary expertise and resources are available.

Royal NIVRA in co-operation with Nyenrode University offers a complete programme of accountancy education. Six other universities in the Netherlands also offer complete programmes of accountancy education. In general these programmes are divided in a graduate part and a postgraduate part, which is combined with practical experience. Professional education is offered by a combination of university staff and practicing accountants and auditors.

Practical training content and admission requirements

Candidates for membership require a minimum of 3 year's practical experience. Experience can be obtained after possession of a university or higher education degree in accounting or economics or a diploma of the first four years NIVRA-Nyenrode part time professional education. Practical training is almost full time, four days a week with one day available for classes. The objective of practical training is the application of theoretical knowledge. The areas of practical training are specified in relation to statutory audit. Practical training can be followed in public practice or related fields on the condition that the actual work is comparable to and relevant for statutory audit. Practicing registeraccountants (in the areas distinguished) are responsible as mentor for at least two out of three years practical training. Under government statute providers are recognized by the Board for Practical Training appointed by Royal NIVRA.

NIVRA expects for the near future major developments in regulation of the profession, professional qualification requirements, professional education and practical training

Renewal/evaluation of the accountancy law, introduction of a bachelor-masters system for university qualifications. More ICT in professional education and practical training. Introduction of e-learning.

Overview ICANZ

Professional Body	**Institute of Chartered Accountants of New Zealand (ICANZ)**
Professional Title	**Chartered Accountant (CA)**
Respondent	**Bill Robertson, Director Admissions, ICANZ**
Country	**New Zealand**

For additional information refer to ICANZ at www.icanz.co.nz, or Bill Robertson at bill_robertson@icanz.co.nz.

New Zealand requirements on accounting rules are based on the Financial Reporting Act 1993 and accounting standards issued by the Institute of Chartered Accountants of New Zealand.

The accountancy sector in New Zealand is regulated by law and by professional self regulation. The Institute of Chartered Accountants of New Zealand (ICANZ) is recognized as a regulatory body and a disciplinary body. ICANZ is a member of IFAC and CAPA.

> The Institute of Chartered Accountants of New Zealand has recognized legal status. The Institute has three membership colleges: Chartered Accountants, Associate Chartered Accountants and Accounting Technicians. The premium qualification is Chartered Accountant, the responses relate to this qualification.

Members of ICANZ work in public practice, industry and commerce, government and in other areas. ICANZ membership is mandatory for use of the CA title. Continuing professional education is mandatory for all CAs and is regulated by ICANZ.

Admission requirements include a formal final examination of professional competence, prescribed programmes of professional education and practical training under the responsibility of ICANZ.

> The Institute awards the professional qualifications for all three colleges, determines the admissions requirements and the academic study requirements, accredits tertiary education institutions to deliver recognized programmes, determines the experience requirements and accredits employers to deliver these. The Institute runs its own professional competence programme (professional accounting school and examinations) in accordance with its own policy specifications.

International standards: ICANZ follows IFAC IEG 2, 9, 10 and 11.
International recognition of qualifications

> The Institute currently has reciprocity arrangements with Institutes in Scotland, Ireland, and England & Wales. Mutual recognition agreements with the Institutes in Australia, Canada, and South Africa are currently being reviewed. Institutes in other countries may recognize the Institute by offering exemptions from their own qualifying requirements. In addition, the New Zealand Government permits certain persons from overseas to act as an auditor of NZ companies. Specific professional bodies recognized for this purpose by the NZ government include the Institutes of Chartered Accountants in Australia, England & Wales, Scotland, and Canada. Also recognized for this purpose are CPA Australia, ACCA, and AICPA.

Final examination core programme

> The Professional Competence Programme is required to develop within candidates a range of relevant attributes covering knowledge; technical skills; organisational skills; personal skills; interpersonal skills; analytical and constructive cognitive skills; synthetic, appreciative, and judgemental cognitive skills; and professional values.

Objective final examination: to test theoretical knowledge; the ability to apply knowledge in practice; intellectual, interpersonal and communication skills; ICT applications; professional values.

Because the emphasis in the academic programme is on the essential theoretical and technical accounting knowledge and skills (as well as business and general education), the Professional Competence Programme concentrates on developing the higher level professional skills.

The professional body is the provider of the final examination. ICANZ examinations are subject to external review

The final examination is delivered by Advanced Business Education Limited (ABEL), a subsidiary company of the Institute set up for this purpose. The entire Professional Accounting School and final examination (PCE 2) are moderated externally. Further, the processes are subjected to the scrutiny of an Academic Board. As an added quality assurance measure, the professional competence programme is subject to regular review (academic audit) by an independent panel appointed for that purpose.

Admission requirements cover professional education, practical training and general education

To sit the final exam candidates must have completed the academic requirements , over two years of experience and have completed the first professional exam (PCE 1) followed by success at the professional accounting school (PAS). The last year of professional education coincides with the third year of practical experience.

Professional education core programme

Academic study covers financial accounting, management accounting, auditing, taxation, business finance/treasury, information technology/accounting information systems, economics, organisational management, commercial law and statistics. At least 20% of the required four years of bachelor's degree level study must be in (non-specified) general studies. The professional programme deals with the structure and authority of the profession, professional ethics, current non-technical topics relevant to the profession, professional skills, business environment, compliance (i.e. external reporting, audit, taxation), financial management and business strategy.

Admission requirements for professional education

To sit PCE 1, candidates must have completed a recognized four-year academic programme and one year of experience. To sit PCE 2, candidates must have passed PCE 1, completed over two years of experience (including over one year of tightly specified experience) and passed the Professional Accounting School.

Professional body and universities provide professional education

Professional Accounting School (PAS) is delivered by the Institute. For the CA College, general and professional education programmes are provided by Institute-approved universities.

Practical training content

The first year of experience is not specified and can begin at any time. The (minimum) two years of specified experience cannot begin until the Institute's academic requirements have been satisfied. Candidates must cover three areas of accounting out of six (external reporting, management accounting, audit (internal or external), taxation, finance/treasury, and insolvency/reconstruction). The practical experience and training programmes are provided by Institute-approved employers.

ICANZ expects for the near future major developments in professional qualification requirements, professional education and practical training.

Overview ICAP

Professional Body	**Institute of Chartered Accountants of Pakistan (ICAP)**
Professional Title	**Chartered Accountant (CA)**
Respondent	**Yusuf M Siddiqi, Director of Education and Training, ICAP**
Country	**Pakistan**

For additional information refer to ICAP at www.icap.org.pk or Yusuf Siddiqi at yusuf.siddiqi@icap.org.pk.

Pakistan statutory requirements on accounting rules are based on the Companies Ordinance 1984, regulations issued by the Securities and Exchange Commission of Pakistan (SECP) and those IASs adopted by the SECP for listed companies only.

The accountancy sector in Pakistan is regulated by law and by professional self-regulation. The Institute of Chartered Accountants of Pakistan (ICAP) is recognised as a regulatory body and a disciplinary body. ICAP is a member of IFAC, CAPA and SAFA.

Members of ICAP work in public practice, industry and commerce, government and other areas. ICAP membership is not mandatory. Continuing professional education is mandatory for members in all areas and is regulated by ICAP.

Admission requirements as member of ICAP include a formal final examination of professional competence, prescribed programmes of professional education and practical training.

International standards : international standards on accountancy education are followed.
International recognition of qualifications

> Mutual recognition on qualification and training exists with Bangladesh. Exemptions are given from examination papers by some accountancy bodies such as ACCA, CIMA. Recognition of qualifications from other countries by ICAP : Australia, Canada and the United Kingdom.

Final examination core programme

> Objective of the examinations is to test the knowledge and skills of candidates which they have gained through studies and during training with registered CA firms. The syllabus covers subjects that will enable the candidates to be proficient in the current trends and developments in the profession and to assume leadership roles. Subjects examined are : 1.Advanced Auditing; 2.Advanced Accounting & Financial Reporting; 3.Corporate Laws; 4. Business Management; 5.Management Accounting; 6.Business Finance Decisions; 7.Advanced Taxation; 8.Information Technology Management, Audit and Control.

Objective final examination : to test theoretical knowledge; the ability to apply knowledge in practice; intellectual, interpersonal and communication skills; ICT applications; professional values

ICAP is the provider of the final examination with recognition by the government. Examinations are not subject to external review. ICAP examiners are Chartered Accountants and academics.

Admission requirements cover professional education and practical training.

> Students can either enter if they are graduates or post graduates or have higher secondary education (A level) after which candidate's undergo a two-year full time course. The course is offered by selected Registered accountancy schools which are appraised and monitored regularly by ICAP. Candidates after passing Foundation and Intermediate examinations have to undergo four to five years practical training with registered CA firms during which they have to prepare and sit in Final examination.

Professional education core programme

Auditing, Accounting and Reporting, Business & Commercial Lows, Taxation, IT.
objectives are given in the syllabus of each paper which can be found at the ICAP website.

Professional body and commercial companies provide professional education. Necessary expertise and resources are available. Teachers are Chartered Accountants for core subjects and Masters for support subjects. Syllabi are reviewed by a standing Task Force on a continuing basis. Study material is updated on a yearly basis.

Professional education is mostly full time and consists of a Modular Full Time Course (2 year duration), a Private Study Course in which classes are not mandatory for candidates (2 years for examinations) and Final Private study (4/5 years). Refresher Courses are organised by the Institute and private education providers. Chartered Accountants are teachers for the core subjects and Masters with 5 years teaching experience for the support subjects.

The CA program tests candidates in English, Mathematics Logic, General Knowledge before a student can enter for CA education and training. Such education is given at schools and colleges. There are also special schools which prepare students to complete their general education requirements for entrance tests of ICAP.

Practical training content

Practical Training in Auditing, Taxation, IT and Corporate/Secretarial Work with a duration of four to five years depending on the scheme of entry. Candidates who pass all ICAP's modular examinations (for Modules A, B, C and D), or obtained exemptions from Modular Foundation and Intermediate examinations or their equivalent, will register training arrangements with Principals at CA Firms. University graduates with First Division (or equivalent grades) and Post Graduates with 2nd Division (or equivalent grades) from recognized Universities will register training arrangements with Principals and CA Firms, upon obtaining exemption from Pre-entry Proficiency Test (PPT). Graduates with 2nd Division (or equivalent grades) from recognized Universities will register training arrangements with Principals at CA firms upon passing PPT, for a five year training period.

A trainee at a public practice may request for secondment for training in industry. This is approved by the Council subject to certain specified conditions being met by the industrial/commercial concerned.

In case of experience gained at one of the other Institutes whose examinations and training are recognized by ICAP, the training period completed is exempted. In case of a qualification from CIMA, ACCA, AICPA and ICMAP the training period is reduced to 3 years.

ICAP expects for the near future major developments in professional education and practical training

Tutorial classes for Final level students will be starting shortly. Training organisation and programmes are being revisited though interactive Workshops on training regulations with members of the Institute to revamp the training/experience requirement.

Overview ICMAP

Professional Body	**Institute of Cost and Management Accountants of Pakistan (ICMAP)**
Professional Title	**Associate Cost and Management Accountant (ACMA)**
Respondent	**S. M. Zafarullah, Member National Council, ICMAP**
Country	**Pakistan**

For additional information refer to ICMAP at www.icmap.com.pk, or S.M. Zafarullah at smztzk@comsats.net.pk.

Pakistan requirements on accounting rules are based on the Companies Ordinance 1984, regulations issued by the Securities and Exchange Commission of Pakistan (SECP) and those IASs adopted by the SECP for listed companies only.

The accountancy sector in Pakistan is regulated by law and by professional self-regulation. The Institute of Cost and Management Accountants of Pakistan (ICMAP) is recognized as a regulatory body. ICMAP is a member of IFAC, CAPA and SAFA.

Members of ICMAP work in public practice, industry and commerce, government and in other areas. ICMAP membership is mandatory to use the title. Continuing professional education is mandatory for members and is regulated by ICMAP.

Admission requirements include a formal final examination of professional competence, prescribed programmes of professional education and practical training

> There are five stages of examinations. Exam are held every six months. Three years practical training is required before admission as Associate member. Membership applications have to be supported by three members. The Institute (ICMAP) sets its own standard for education and exam.

International standards: ICMAP follows IFAC IEG 9 and 11.
International recognition of qualifications

> The ICMAP qualification is recognized by CIMA, ACCA, SMA & others
> ICMAP recognizes – CIMA, ACCA, ICAP, SMA & others.

Final examination core programme (see professional education core programme and syllabus)

> Institute examinations and courses cover Foundation I and II; Professional I, II, III, IV and V.
> Levels of competency are defined for all course outlines with a distinction between general education, conceptual and theoretical knowledge, specialized knowledge and skills, professional knowledge and skills

Objective final examination: to test theoretical knowledge; the ability to apply knowledge in practice; intellectual, interpersonal and communication skills; ICT applications; professional values

The professional body is the provider of the final examination. ICMAP examinations are not subject to external review. Necessary expertise and resources are available

> External examiners are experts from universities and the profession who prepare and evaluate the papers – such as senior fellow members in industry, well equipped computer labs, own buildings and libraries.

Admission requirements cover practical training and general education

A graduate degree is required.

Professional education core programme

Foundation-1: Principles of Accounting, Computer Systems & Applications, Business English, Economics & Business Environment. Foundation-II: Financial Accounting, Information Technology, Industrial & Commercial Laws. Professional-I: Management Science Applications, Cost Accounting, Business Communication & Report Writing, Quantitative Methods. Professional-II: Advanced Financial Accounting, Operational Cost Accounting, Business Taxation, Corporate Laws & Secretarial Practices. Professional-III: Financial Reporting, Strategic Management Accounting, Organisational Behaviour Strategic Management, Auditing. Professional-IV: Strategic Financial Management, Corporate Performance Audit & Evaluation, Marketing Management, Information Management.

The completion of each stage shall require a period of six months, which shall include 120 days for coaching and 60 days for self-study and examination. The candidate has to clear Foundation as well as two parts of Prof 1 and 2 before sitting in the final exam. Education takes place by attending regular classes provided by ICMAP or fulfilling correspondence requirements and on the job training and bi-annual exam. About three years is required in total.

Admission requirements for professional education

To qualify for enrolment as a student of the Institute, the candidate shall have to take an entry-test or qualify for exemption from the test. The basic qualification required for appearing in the entry-test is graduate (B.Com, B.Sc, B.A).

The professional body provides professional education. Necessary expertise and resources are available.

Practical training content

Three years working experience in public practice/industry/commerce/government job relevant for accountants under supervision of a qualified professional accountant as a condition for membership. Exemptions based on previous experience outside Pakistan are possible under the supervision of the professional body. There are no exemptions possible based on previous experience inside Pakistan. Members of the professional institutes are working in all fields and are available for training.

ICMAP expects for the near future major developments in professional education and practical training

It is planned to shift all tests on computers and make maximum use of the latest Info technology. Presentation and communication skill case studies and panel discussion; practical experience during on the job training and specially designed courses will be introduced.

Overview SKWP

Professional Body	**Accountants Association in Poland (SKwP)**
Professional Title	**Accountant**
Respondent	**Zygmunt Korzeniewski, Director Professional Training Center, SKwP**
Country	**Poland**

For additional information refer to SKWP at www.skwp.org.pl, Zygmunt Korzeniewski at skwp@skwp.org.pl.

Polish requirements on accounting rules are based on the Commercial Code, the Law on Accounting and decree on consolidation rules. The format of the financial statements and disclosure for public companies are regulated by the Polish Securities and Exchange commission.

The accountancy sector in Poland is regulated by law and by professional self-regulation. SKWP is recognized as a regulatory body and a disciplinary body. SKWP is a member of IFAC and EFAA.

Members of SKWP work in public practice, industry and commerce, government and in other areas. SKWP membership is not mandatory. The title of 'accountant' is not regulated and its use is not restricted to any particular group of people. Continuing professional education is not mandatory.

Admission requirements are based on professional qualifications.

> Entrance regulations of the Accountants Association in Poland are set out in our Articles of Association. According to them our body can be joined only by individuals possessing appropriate qualifications in the field of accounting and finance. It is recognized that this requirement is fulfilled by employees of financial and accounting departments; employees of accounting data processing departments; auditors, chartered accountants, accountants and others responsible for financial and business control; lecturers and academics specialising in finance, accounting, data processing, economics and similar areas; bank employees; tax authorities officers and tax advisors. Membership can be also obtained by employees of organisational units of the AAP, students of finance, accounting and related disciplines.

> Admittance of an ordinary member is subject to submitting a declaration supported by two ordinary members. This is a sort of measure to prevent people from outside the profession joining the Association. Admittance of an ordinary member is decided by the regional board of the AAP. It is possible to appeal against its decision to the Main Board of the AAP.

International standards: SKWP follows IFAC International Education Guidelines on a voluntary basis. International recognition of SKWP qualifications has not been achieved.

Final examination core programme, professional education core programme and practical training are not applicable.

SKWP expects for the near future major developments in regulation of the profession, professional qualification requirements, professional education and practical training

> Regulation of the profession: While regulating the professional qualification requirements, the profession should be recognized as a liberal profession. Professional qualification requirements: As the minimum requirements for the admission to the profession there should be :- at least secondary school (A Level) education- 3 years of practical experience- final examination. Professional education: Already existing voluntary forms of education should be made mandatory. Practical training: 3 years of practical experience should be obligatory.

Overview KIBR

Professional Body	**National Chamber of Statutory Auditors (KIBR)**
Professional Title	**Auditor**
Respondent	**Dr Danuta Krzywda, Vice President, KIBR**
Country	**Poland**

For additional information refer to KIBR at www.kibr.org.pl, or Danuta Krzywda at kibr@pagi.pl.

Polish requirements on accounting rules are based on the Commercial Code, the Law on Accounting and decree on consolidation rules. The format of the financial statements and disclosure for public companies are regulated by the Polish Securities and Exchange commission.

The accountancy sector in Poland is regulated by law and by professional self-regulation. The National Chamber of Statutory Auditors (KIBR) is recognized as a regulatory body and a disciplinary body. KIBR is a member of IFAC.

> KIBR is awaiting the decision concerning its full membership in FEE. Starting from November 2001 KIBR representatives have started participating in the activities of 3 FEE Working Parties (Accounting, Auditing and Ethics).

Members of KIBR work in public practice, industry and commerce, government and in other areas. KIBR membership is mandatory. Continuing professional education is mandatory for all members and is regulated by KIBR.

Admission requirements include a formal final examination of professional competence, prescribed programmes of professional education and practical training

> Admission to the final exam will be granted only to those candidates who meet the general requirements, who have passed all the professional exams and who have successfully finished a three-year practice in Poland, including at least two years of practice under an auditor's supervision which has been approved by Examinations Committee.

International standards: KIBR follows the EU 8th Directive.
International recognition of qualifications

> No recognition has been achieved of the KIBR qualification in other countries. Qualifications gained in the UK (ICAEW, ICAS, ACCA), in Denmark (Beskikkelse Som Statsutoriseret Revisor), in Australia (Australian Institute of Certified Public Accountants), in the US (Massachusetts Society of Certified Public Accountants, Oregon Board of Accountancy) have been recognized in Poland. Candidates had to pass the Polish Economic Law exam (in the Polish language).

Final examination core programme

> The final exam is an oral exam and tests the experience gained during practice as well as theoretical knowledge in the areas of financial accounting, economics and management, civil law, labour law, economic law, tax law, finance, cost accounting and management accounting, financial statements and analysis of financial statements, auditing and other services rendered by auditors.

Objective final examination: to test theoretical knowledge and the ability to apply knowledge in practice; intellectual, interpersonal and communication skills; ICT applications; professional values.

The professional body is the provider of the examination. KIBR examinations are not subject to external review

Final examination is organised by Examinations Committee (established by National Council of Statutory Auditors). Members of the National Council of Statutory Auditors can participate in the exam as observers.

Admission requirements cover professional education, practical training and general education.

Professional education core programme

The core programme of professional education includes 10 subjects: financial accounting - part 1; economics and management; civil law, labour law, economic law; tax law - part 1; finance; tax law – part 2; financial accounting – part 2; cost accounting and management accounting; financial statements and analysis of financial statements; auditing and other services rendered by auditors.

Admission requirements for professional education

In order to be allowed to take professional exams candidates must have a university degree. Exemptions are possible from the following subjects included in the core programme of professional education: financial accounting - part 1; economics and management; civil law, labour law and economic law; tax law - part 1; finance; cost accounting and management accounting. The candidate must have passed the university exam
with at least the mark 'good' and the Examinations Committee must have approved the curriculum as containing all important professional education curriculum issues; the exams must have been written and marked anonymously.

Professional body, universities and commercial companies provide professional education. Necessary expertise and resources are available.

Practical training content

Candidates must have three years of practice in Poland, including at least a two-year practice under an auditor's supervision. They can start the first year of practical experience straight away; practice under supervision of an auditor can be started only after a candidate has finished the first year of practical experience and after he/ she has passed 7 out of 10 professional exams. The first year of practical training includes independent book-keeping, computerised system of book-keeping in accordance with the Accounting Law regulations, knowledge of internal regulations. The two-year practice includes reviewing
audit documentation with regard to the documentation's completeness, correctness and consistency; technical work and selected audit work together with audit documentation and preparing lists of documents; participating in auditor's activities connected especially with audit planning, choice of methods and sampling, analysis of company's equity, company's financial and income position and checking whether the company acts in compliance with law regulations; participating in auditing of at least two annual financial statements and independent documenting of all activities assigned to the candidate by auditor, preparing proposals of audit report and of auditor's opinion; full audit of an annual financial statement under supervision of an auditor, preparing complete audit documentation, preparing proposals of auditor's opinion, audit report and letter to management of the company audited.

KIBR expects for the near future major developments in regulation of the profession, professional education and practical training

Overview of the role of enterprises; managers' interpersonal capabilities; better introduction to becoming a listed company; modern means of management. Better training and education; globalisation issues. Preparing better quality training materials for candidates for auditors; including international and globalisation issues. The role of enterprises in economy; banking systems; insurance systems.

Overview IPA Russia

Professional Body	**Institute of Professional Accountants of Russia (IPA Russia)**
Professional Title	**Professional Accountant**
Respondent	**Oleg Moiseevich Ostrovsky, General Manager IPA Russia**
Country	**Russian Federation**

For additional information refer to IPA Russia at www.ipbr.ru, or Oleg Moiseevich Ostrovsky at oom@ipbr.ru.

Russian requirements on accounting rules are based on the government program of reformation of the accounting system in accordance with IAS/ISA.

> According to GAAP 2000 the Russian requirements for commercial non-banking companies are based on the Civil Code, Law on Accounting, some other laws, and incorporate accounting regulations and standards of the Ministry of Finance of the Russian Federation. Although Russian requirements are mandatory, the Law on Accounting allows departures from them when a fair presentation can not be achieved through their application.

The accountancy sector in Russia is regulated by law and by professional self-regulation. The Institute of Professional Accountants of Russia is recognized as a disciplinary body. IPA Russia is a member of the Eurasian Federation of Accountants.

Members of IPA Russia work in public practice, industry and commerce, government and in other areas. IPA Russia membership is not mandatory. Continuing professional education is mandatory for members and is regulated by IPA Russia.

Admission requirements as a member of IPA Russia include a formal final examination of professional competence, a prescribed programme of professional education and practical experience

> In 1994 a new three-staged system of higher education was adopted. The duration of each stage is two years. In order to be a student of the second or third stage it is obligatory to graduate from the previous stage. The first stage is completed by passing state exams. The second and third stage are completed by passing state exams and by defending a special thesis. A successful graduate is awarded a bachelors degree (after 4 years) or a masters degree (after 6 years).

> For accounting education the first stage has a purely practical orientation and its graduates would be professional bookkeepers, the second stage allows graduates to occupy positions in business demanding comprehensive knowledge of accounting, financial analysis and auditing and knowledge of planning and control aspects, the third stage allows graduates to occupy top management positions in businesses as well as any position in auditing firms.

International standards on accountancy education are not followed.
International recognition of the IPA Russia qualification in other countries and recognition of qualifications from other countries in Russia has not been achieved .

Final examination core programme

> The certification of professional accountants confirms the conformity of the specialist to the requirements of professional competence (level of special training, skills, experience in the corresponding type of business)
> Auditor certification is possible for persons with economic or legal (higher or intermediate special) education who have worked for not less than three years out of the last five years as either an auditor, specialist of an auditing organisation (auditing firm), accountant, economist, inspector, manager of an enterprise, member of staff of a scientific body, or teacher in an economics field.
> Requirements for financial directors are very close to the requirements for chief accountants but for the big enterprises.

Objective final examination: to test theoretical knowledge, the ability to apply knowledge in practice, intellectual skills; ICT applications; professional values.

IPA Russia is the provider of the examination.
Admission requirements cover professional education, practical experience and general education

> Higher or secondary economic education with experience in economic specialties (or in managing positions requiring knowledge of accounting) not less than five years, or the diploma of candidate (doctor) of economic sciences with experience in economic activity (or in managing positions requiring knowledge of accounting) not less than three years. The certificate of additional professional training according to the program of certification and training of the professional accountants (IPA). Practical training in the meaning of practical experience.

Professional education core programme: accounting, economic analysis, law, taxation

> The accountancy curriculum at the universities follows four educational cycles: 1) Humanities and social Disciplines 2) Mathematical and general naturally-scientific disciplines 3) General professional disciplines 4) Special disciplines. The 'special discipline cycle' is the professional training of a student, which reflects the specifics of a particular branch and its advanced training. It assumes professional activity of the specialist in different areas of the economy.

> Only institutions authorised by the State can give a special graduation diploma to their graduates. These diplomas are: Diploma of higher education, given after graduation from any institute if higher education (university, academy, institute); Diploma of professional secondary education in bookkeeping, given after graduation from a college; having earned this diploma a graduate has the right to take the entrance exam to the third year of a university program; Diploma of professional secondary education given after graduation from a vocational training school; this diploma is ranked lower because it gives the right to take the entrance exam to the first year of a university program.

Admission requirements for professional education: diploma of higher education.
Professional body, universities and commercial companies provide professional education. Necessary expertise and resources are available.
Practical experience in economic functions based on higher education is required; there is no practical training

> Certification of the professional accountant: not less than 5 years of practical experience in economic functions (not less than 3 years for the candidate (doctor) of economic sciences).
> Auditor certification: not less than three years out of the last five years as either an auditor, specialist of an auditing organisation (auditing firm), accountant, economist, inspector, manager of an enterprise, member of staff of a scientific body, or teacher in an economics field.

IPA Russia expects for the near future major developments in regulation of the profession, professional education and practical training

> Regulation of the profession: familiarization with IAS
> Professional qualification: toughening requirements to examinations
> Professional education: implementation of the new training programs
> Practical training: extension of the seniority required to 5 years.

Overview SOCPA

Professional Body	**Saudi Organization for Certified Public Accountants (SOCPA)**
Professional Title	**Certified Public Accountant (SOCPA)**
Respondent	**Ahmad Almeghames, Deputy Secretary General (SOCPA)**
Country	**Saudi Arabia**

For additional information refer to SOCPA at www.socpa.org.sa, or Ahmad Almeghames at ahmadatheer@yahoo.com.

Saudi Arabian requirements on accounting rules are based on governmental Regulations for Companies and on accounting standards issued by the Saudi Organization of Certified Public Accountants (SOCPA). The accounting standards issued by SOCPA are a comprehensive basis for accounting. In situations where no Saudi standard is available, companies are required to use the American accounting standards with some modification to suit the Saudi environment.

The accountancy sector in Saudi Arabia is regulated by law and by professional self- regulation. The Saudi Organization of Certified Public Accountants (SOCPA) is recognized as a regulatory body. The Ministry of Commerce is the disciplinary body. SOCPA is a member of IFAC and of the regional organisation called GCC Accounting and Auditing Organisation (established in 1998).

Members of SOCPA work in public practice, industry and commerce and in government. SOCPA membership is mandatory for those who want to have a license to practice. It is optional for those who have passed the fellowship examination. Continuing professional education is mandatory for full members and in public practice; CPE is regulated by SOCPA.

Admission requirements as a member of SOCPA include a formal final examination of professional competence, prescribed programmes of professional education and practical training.

> The government will issue the certificate to practice the profession and professional body will conduct the CPA exam which is mandatory to pass to apply for certificate of practicing, and the certificate will be not active if the holder does not meet the body's condition like the CPE requirements and so on.

International standards on accountancy education are not followed.
International recognition of the SOCPA qualification in other countries has not been achieved. Qualifications from other countries (USA, UK, Canada) are considered for those who want to apply for the SOCPA fellowship examination.

Final examination core programme

> The exam consist of five subjects: 1- Accounting (all areas); 2- Auditing; 3- Tax and Zakah (Islamic due); 4- Commercial laws; 5- Figh almamalat (how to conduct operation in Islam).

> SOCPA fellowship examination rules include professional, practical and scientific aspects of the audit profession and applicable regulations.

Objective final examination: to test theoretical knowledge; the ability to apply knowledge in practice; intellectual, interpersonal and communication skills; ICT applications; professional values.

The professional body is the provider of the final examination. SOCPA examinations are subject to external review. Necessary expertise and resources are available

> SOCPA has a committee that is called Exam Committee in charge of administrating the exam (admission, making the exam , correcting the exam) and the committee is using many consultations in its process. SOCPA is using hundreds of experts in conducting its operation and this includes the exam.

Admission requirements cover professional education

The professional education has to be at least with 30 credit hours of accounting subjects covering accounting area , auditing and tax and it has to be on an university level.

Professional education core programme

SOCPA offers courses covering SOCPA fellowship examination. The aim of these courses is to enable the trainee to be acquainted with the theoretical and practical aspects of accounting and auditing and to apply it skilfully. Each course consists of a number of training materials and each training material covers one or more topics of SOCPA fellowship exam subjects, which include accounting, auditing, zakat and tax, jurisprudence and business law. Each training material includes a discussion of the objectives and elements of the topic, a sufficient explanation of each element, and the same is connected to the relevant professional standards. It also includes problems and application cases.

Admission requirements for professional education

The education has to be on a university level; the applicant has to have a four year undergraduate degree in accounting or any subjects with at least 30 credit hours in accounting subjects. Those who are holding a non accounting degree from an undergraduate school can be admitted to the exam by providing finishing of 30 credit undergraduate hours of accounting courses.

Universities provide professional education. Necessary expertise and resources are available in the universities. Providers of professional education are recognized by the government. There is no periodic review of professional education.

Practical training content

To be a Certified Public Accountant one has to have an experience in CPA firms or commercial or governmental sectors with a job related to accounting or auditing. There is no requirement for the content of practical training but experience. Practical training takes place in public practice, industry and commerce and in government. Each sector has its own expertise. Providers of practical training are recognized by the government and the professional body as each practical training provider has to have a license.

Overview SAICA

Professional Body	**South African Institute of Chartered Accountants (SAICA)**
Professional Title	**Chartered Accountant SA (CA (SA))**
Respondent	**Adri Kleinhans, Project Director Pre-qualification, SAICA**
Country	**South Africa**

For additional information refer to SAICA at www.saica.co.za, or Adri Kleinhans at adrik@saica.co.za.

South African reporting requirements are based on Statements of Generally Accepted Accounting Practice (GAAP) issued by the Accounting Practices Board of the South African Institute of Chartered Accountants, the disclosure requirements of Schedule 4 to the Companies Act and where applicable, the Johannesburg Stock Exchange Listing Requirements.

The accountancy sector in South Africa is regulated by law and by professional self regulation. The South African Institute of Chartered Accountants (SAICA) is recognized as a regulatory body and a disciplinary body. SAICA is a member of IFAC and ECSAFA.

Members of SAICA work in public practice, industry and commerce, government and in other areas. SAICA membership is not mandatory. Continuing professional education is not mandatory.

Admission requirements include a formal final examination of professional competence, prescribed programmes of professional education and practical training. The professional body is solely responsible for the setting of the professional qualification process.

International standards: SAICA follows IFAC IEG 9 and 11.
International recognition of qualifications

> Recognition of the SAICA qualification in other countries: New Zealand, Australia, Canada, England and Wales, Scotland, Ireland. Recognition of the qualification from other countries by SAICA: New Zealand, Australia, Canada, England and Wales, Scotland, Ireland. All have to write conversion examination. SAICA is working closely with the neighbouring countries in the Southern African region, and a number of reciprocity agreements have been put in place. Regional accreditation of education and training programmes continues to play an important role in the economic development of the region and to uplift and ensure the implementation of international standards.

Final examination core programme

> Auditing, Financial Accounting, Taxation, Managerial Accounting & Financial Management, Information Technology. Other supportive courses, including company law, communication skills, human resource management, marketing, etc.

Objective final examination: to test theoretical knowledge; the ability to apply knowledge in practice; intellectual and communication skills; professional values

> The examination is deemed to be a test of professional competence to the extent possible in a written Examination.

The professional body is the provider of the final examination (SAICA sets the qualifying examination). Admission requirements cover professional education and practical training.

The providers for the education qualification required for entry to the professional qualifying (final) examination are accredited for that purpose by SAICA. There is a shortage of adequately experienced, qualified lecturers at education institutions.

Professional education core programme

Financial Accounting, Auditing, Managerial Accounting & Financial Management, Taxation, Information Technology.

Admission requirements for professional education

The education institutions determine the admission requirements into the education programme.

Universities and commercial companies provide professional education. Necessary expertise and resources are available. Providers of professional education are recognized by the professional body (SAICA accredits the providers)

The academic and training resources are generally available, but could be increased. Education and training providers are submit to continuous and regular monitoring processes. Education and training providers are accredited by SAICA, and SAICA determines the syllabus to be covered during the education process.

Coupled with the accreditation of universities offering the education component SAICA has registered the CA (SA) qualification on the national framework.

Practical training content

The same core areas as for education must be covered in the training period, which could be either 36, 48 or 60 months, depending on the level of education of the trainee. There are no admission requirements before the start of practical training. Regulations for practical training cover training contract with core experience hours, core work attendance hours, core experience topics and supervision.
From 2002, SAICA will conduct regular training office reviews. This accreditation will be conducted for training in public practice and outside public practice.

SAICA expects for the near future major developments in regulation of the profession, professional qualification requirements, professional education and practical training

The legislation regulating the profession in South Africa is being amended. We are in the process of revisiting our competencies, flowing from that our education and training requirements, as well as our accreditation and monitoring of education and training providers.

As from 2003, SAICA will be introducing 'limited source' open book examinations. Candidates will be given access to copies of the relevant legislation and the Members' Handbook for use during the examination.

Overview IA-CJCE

Professional Body	**Instituto de Auditores-Censores Jurados de Cuentas (IA-CJCE)**
Professional Title	**Auditor de Cuentas (Auditor)**
Respondent	**Enric Vergés, Technical Department, IA-CJCE**
Country	**Spain**

For additional information refer to IA-CJE at www.iacjce.es, or Enric Vergés at everges@auditors-censors.com .

Spanish requirements on accounting rules are mainly based on the Code of Commerce, the General Accounting Plan, the Companies Act and on standards issued by the Official Institute of Accounting and Audit (ICAC). The methodology for evaluation of post-retirements benefits is governed by the Insurance Regulatory Authority (DGS).

The accountancy sector in Spain is regulated by law. The Instituto de Auditores-Censores Jurados de Cuentas (IA-CJCE) is recognized as a disciplinary body. IA-CJCE is a member of IFAC and FEE

> The professional title of accountant does not exist in Spain. Accountancy is not a regulated profession. Since the Audit Law, a candidate has to be approved auditor to be a member of a professional body (that means comply with the requirements of 8th EC Directive and be a member of the Official Register of Auditors (ROAC-Public Register)). Members of the professional body are approved auditors and can practice as auditors. The ROAC is dependent of the Instituto de Contabilidad y Auditoria de Cuentas (ICAC), the regulatory body, also dependent of Ministry of Economy.

Members of IA-CJCE work in public practice, industry and commerce, government and in other areas. IA-CJCE membership is not mandatory. Continuing professional education is mandatory for members in public practice and is regulated by IA-CJCE

> The statutory rules include the compulsory formation for exercitants only. When a not exercitant member pass to exercitant situation, needs the justification of his formation about accounting and auditing matters in the previous years.

Admission requirements include a formal final examination of professional competence, prescribed programmes of professional education and practical training

> Government (ICAC -see before) is the responsible for the rules of matters object of the education. The professional body organize, with the supervision of ICAC the training courses.

International standards: IA-CJCE follows the EU 8th Directive.
International recognition of qualifications

> Recognition of the IA-CJCE qualification in EU countries and recognition of qualifications from EU countries according to EU regulation.

Final examination core programme

> Exam about audit matters, for confirm: - practical experience - profitability of professional training.

Objective final examination: to test theoretical knowledge; the ability to apply knowledge in practice; professional values

The practical exam includes usually case studies about audit practice. It can also include open question and multiple choice questions, for the person which needs to pass the theoretical exam also, in particular cases in which the formation is not recognize for direct access to practical exam.

IA-CJCE is the provider of the final examination. The examinations are subject to external review

The exam is prepared by professional body, and reviewed by the ICAC.

Admission requirements cover professional education, practical training and general education.

Professional education core programme

Accounting, Taxation, Legal, Audit. Lecture: 5 days per week/15 hours. Self: 10 hours per week. More or less three years for graduates.

Admission requirements for professional education

Depending on type of general education: Education in finance and business degree or graduation is more appropriate to comply easily with the requirements. The general programmes for education in the financial and business areas are designed by a period since 3 and 5 years.

Professional body and universities provide professional education. Necessary expertise and resources are available.

ICAC recognizes the education in accordance with its rules before the examination. Periodic review of professional education takes place in order to update the training objectives of the matters.

Practical training content

Three years full time or part time (200 days per year) in accordance with the possibilities and needs of the student and auditor or firm. No requirements on practical training content. No admission requirements before the start of practical training. Providers of practical training are recognized by the professional body by professional certificate of auditor, firm or company if appropriate.

IA-CJCE expects for the near future major developments in regulation of the profession, professional education and practical training

Regulation of the profession: Changes in: - Independence - Government control - Responsibility
Professional education: Increase in training time about engagements of non statutory audits
Practical experience: Increase in time of experience. One year more on present three years.

Overview FAR

Professional Body	**Föreningen Auktoriserade Revisorer (FAR)**
Professional Title	**Revisor**
Respondent	**Björn Markland, Secretary General of FAR**
Country	**Sweden**

For additional information refer to FAR at www.far.se, or Björn Markland at bjorn.markland@far.se .

Swedish requirements on accounting rules are based on the Annual Accounts Act incorporating EU Directives, and on the accounting standards of the Redovisningsrädet (RR). In rare circumstances, a RR standard can be departed from if the departure is disclosed and adequately justified. Full adherence to the RR standards is not required for unlisted companies, although the adoption of the standards is becoming increasingly common.

The accountancy sector in Sweden is regulated by law and by professional self-regulation. FAR is recognized as a regulatory body. FAR is a member of IFAC and FEE.

Almost all members of FAR work in public practice, relatively few work in government. FAR membership is not mandatory. Continuing professional education is mandatory for members and is regulated by FAR.

Admission requirements include a formal final examination of professional competence, prescribed programmes of professional education and practical training

> There are two official qualifications: Auktoriserad Revisor or Authorised Public Accountant (advanced qualification) and Godkänd Revisor or Approved Public Accountant (basic qualification). The requirements for qualification as an Authorised Public Accountant or an Approved Public Accountant include both academic studies and a period of practical training. Approved Public Accountants and Authorised Public Accountants are qualified to carry out statutory audits for all companies. The Auditors Act states the minimum requirements. FAR issues guidance as to the practical training and in certain cases requires supplementary examinations for voluntary membership.

International standards: FAR follows primarily the EU 8th Company Law Directive.
International recognition of qualifications

> Recognition of the FAR qualification in other countries has been achieved; statistics are not available Recognition of qualifications from other countries includes the UK, France, the Netherlands with an EU-style aptitude test for admission.

Final examination core programme

> *Approved Public Accountant*: Passing the examination of professional competence as approved public accountant (*revisorsexamen*) to ensure the necessary level of theoretical knowledge (to the extent that this does not follow from the academic degree) and the ability to apply the knowledge in practice. *Authorised Public Accountant*: passing the examination of professional competence as authorised public accountant (*högre revisorsexamen*).

Objective final examination: to test theoretical knowledge; the ability to apply knowledge in practice; professional values.

The government and the professional body are the providers of the final examination. Necessary expertise and resources are available.

Examination for qualification: Government. Examination for membership (for applicants who qualified under previous rules): FAR. Separate Examination Boards of the Government and FAR provide resources and expertise.

Admission requirements for the final examination cover professional education, practical training and general education.

Professional education core programme in accordance with the EU 8ᵗʰ Directive

The basic qualification level consists of 3 years academic studies and 3 years of practical training. For the higher qualification the answer is 4 + 5 years. The theoretical studies up to graduation are full time. During practical training 350 hours of classes is recommended for the first three years and another 100 for the last two years to the higher qualification.

Basic qualification: Bachelor degree in finance and accounting (3 years). Advanced qualification: Master degree (4 years) or bachelor with 1 additional year of free subjects. Immediately after primary and secondary education or later in life under an adult education programme.

There are no specific admission requirements for professional education

As a rule, of course, firms will not accept students for practical training unless their theoretical degree will be sufficient for entering the final examination.

Professional body, universities and commercial companies provide professional education. Necessary expertise and resources are available. Providers of professional education are recognized by the government.

The university degree must have been awarded by a publicly recognized university. Professional education is mostly provided by the accounting firms and the universities. Practical training is tested in the final examination; no questions are asked as to who provided it.

Practical training content and duration

Law requires individual training programmes, containing at least 1500 hours of audit experience. Qualified investigations and experience of solving ethical problems must be included. FAR has issued supplementary guidance. Duration is three years for the basic level of qualification. For advanced qualification another 2 years are required. Part time work is possible, but then the time requirements must be converted pro rata, whereby full time is to be considered as at least 1600 hours per year.

Practical training takes place in public practice. Necessary expertise and resources are available

The large firms have their own training departments. FAR has a separate entity, IREV, providing all sorts of training, both to students and as CPE to members. Providers have to hold a professional qualification, issued by the government. Minimum framework requirements are issued by the Government and supplementary guidance by FAR. Auditors Act (SFS 2001:883) Auditors Ordinance (RNFS 1996:1).

FAR expects for the near future major developments in regulation of the profession

Harmonisation with the EU recommendation on quality control and introduction of ISA as mandatory standards. Possible effects of the Enron case.

Overview TURMOB

Professional Body	**Union of the Chambers of Certified Public Accountants of Turkey (TURMOB), Expert Accountants Association of Turkey (EAAT)**
Professional Title	**Certified Public Accountant (CPA) or Serbest Muhasebeci Mali Müþavir (SMMM)**
Respondent	**Recep Pekdemir, Professor of Accounting, Istanbul University**
Country	**Turkey**

For additional information refer to TURMOB at www.turmob.org.tr , EAAT at www.tmud.org.tr, or Recep Pekdemir at pekdemir@turk.net or pekdemir@istanbul.edu.tr.

Turkish requirements on accounting rules are based on accounting standards issued by the Finance Ministry of Turkey and by the Capital Markets Board. Regulations for the finance sector are made by the Treasury Department. Finally there is also a standard setter body within the TURMOB, whose name is the TMUDESK, the Turkish Accounting and Auditing Standards Board.

> There are certain financial accounting standard setters, consequently it is possible to meet certain financial reporting sets in Turkey: The Finance Ministry of Turkey has been most dominant factor. The Ministry launched the Uniform Chart of Accounts, which must be used by all enterprises and firms, not including financial institutions such as banks, finance leasing corporations, factoring companies, etc. This regulation covers all aspects of financial reporting and financial statements. This regulation has been far away from the Turkish Taxation Procedures. In regarding of evaluation of assets and liabilities, the Turkish Taxation Procedures have affected on financial reporting. The Capital Markets Board has been second standard setter on financial accounting and reporting. It has its own standards, which must be applied by the listed companies of the Istanbul Stock Exchange Market. The Treasury Department is the unique one having authority to make regulations for the finance sector. All financial institutions mentioned above have been submitting two financial sets: first one has been coming from either the Ministry's regulation or that of the Board, second one must be complied with the Department's regulation. These regulations are almost the same the International Accounting Standards of the IASB. Finally there is also a standard setter body within the TURMOB, whose name is the TMUDESK, the Turkish Accounting and Auditing Standards Board.

The accountancy sector in Turkey is regulated by law and by professional self-regulation. The Union of the Chambers of Certified Public Accountants of Turkey (TURMOB) is recognized as a regulatory body and a disciplinary body. TURMOB is a member of IFAC and of the Federation of the Expert – Comptable Associations of the Mediterranean.

> There are two member bodies of IFAC: The Expert Accountants Association of Turkey (EAAT) and the Union of the Chambers of Certified Public Accountants of Turkey (TURMOB). The EAAT is one the founding organizations of IFAC. The EAAT is a voluntary organization of expert accountants. The TURMOB is the regulatory professional body in accountancy, and also it is a member body of IFAC. The accountancy law was enacted in 1989. Therefore the accountancy sector in Turkey is regulated by law and by professional self-regulation. The answers in the questionnaire concern the Union of the Chambers of Certified Public Accountants of Turkey (the TURMOB), as the regulatory professional body.

Members of TURMOB work in public practice, industry and commerce, government and in other areas. Membership is mandatory. Continuing professional education is not mandatory.

> Serbest Muhasebeci Mali Müþavir can be translated as Certified Public Accountant (CPA). Turmob distinguishes three levels: - level 1: independent accountant; - level 2: Certified Public Accountant; - level 3: sworn in CPA (State Auditors). Accountants of level 2 and 3 can become member of EAAT by preparing and defending a colloquium paper.

Answers in the questionnaire concerning qualification, education and training in general reflect the CPA Level. Due to a general assembly decision in 1999 mandatory CPE will start for all members of TURMOB in public practice and industry beginning June 2002.

Admission requirements include a formal final examination of professional competence, prescribed programmes of professional education and practical training

Professional body (TURMOB) and Ministry of Finance set standards together.

International standards: TURMOB follows IFAC IEG 9 (not completely).
International recognition of qualifications

Recognition of the qualification from Turkey in other countries and of qualifications from other countries in Turkey has not been achieved, but it is possible on the basis of mutual recognition.

Final examination core programme

Financial Accounting, Cost and Management Accounting, Financial Statement Analysis, Business Law, Taxation, Auditing, Accounting Law

Objective final examination: to test theoretical knowledge; the ability to apply knowledge in practice; intellectual, interpersonal and communication skills; professional values.

The professional body is the provider of the final examination. Examinations are not subject to external Review. They are open to the juridical affairs (courts)

An independent committee prepares the exam questions and a division of the member body provides the examination, but supported and audited by the Finance Ministry.

Admission requirements cover practical training and general education.
Professional education core programme

Accounting fields, Finance Fields, Law, Tax, Business Administration.

Admission requirements for professional education

Admission requirements for professional education are university graduate (4 years) and practical experience (2 years).

Professional body and universities provide professional education. Necessary expertise and resources are not (necessary) available. Providers of professional education are recognized by government agencies.

Practical training content

2 year practical experience (on the job training) is required under the supervision of a member. There is an exam to start for practical experience. First, a 4 year university degree is required. Then an entrance exam is needed for the practical experience. After completing practical experience, the final exam is taken.

TURMOB expects for the near future major developments in regulation of the profession, professional qualification requirements and professional education

There is a draft regulation on the Parliament changing professional regulations and educational programs. Entrance requirements can be changed. CPE might be necessary.

Overview ACCA

Professional Body	**Association of Chartered Certified Accountants (ACCA)**
Professional Title	**Chartered Certified Accountant (ACCA)**
Respondent	**Michael Walsh, Director, ACCA**
Country	**Global including United Kingdom**

For additional information refer to ACCA at www.accaglobal.com, or Michael Walsh at mike.walsh@accaglobal.com.

UK statutory requirements on accounting rules are based on the Companies Act 1985, and comply with EU Directives. The Act states that disclosure should be made as to whether accounts have been prepared in accordance with applicable accounting standards. Accounting standards issued by the Accounting Standards Board and its Urgent Issues Task Force are applicable for the purposes of this Act.

The accountancy sector in the UK is regulated by law and by professional self-regulation. The Association of Chartered Certified Accountants (ACCA) is recognized as a qualifying body and a supervisory body. ACCA is a member of IFAC and FEE and an associate member of CAPA, ECSAFA and AFA.

Members of ACCA work in public practice, industry and commerce, government and other areas. ACCA membership is mandatory to use the designatory title. Membership is also mandatory if candidates wish to be Registered Auditors and hold a Practising Certificate from ACCA. Continuing professional education is mandatory for practising certificate holders and is regulated by ACCA.

Admission requirements as member of ACCA include a formal final examination of professional competence, prescribed programmes of professional education and practical training

ACCA's examinations have to be at least at degree level in regard to Registered Auditors. ACCA in fact sets the same standard for all its members. ACCA operates under a Royal Charter granted by the Privy Council. This covers the holding of examinations. The examinations are also recognized under the Companies Act in respect of Registered Auditors (in other countries national statutes may apply

International standards: EU 8th Directive, IEG 9 and 11, UNCTAD Guideline
International recognition of qualifications

> ACCA is recognized under the European Union's Mutual Recognition Directive. The ACCA qualification is also fully recognized in the legislation of many other countries around the world e.g. in Hong Kong, Malaysia, Singapore, the Caribbean, and many countries in Africa. ACCA is also recognized for the purpose of registration as an auditor or liquidator under Australia's Corporation Act and enjoys reciprocal membership arrangements with the Institute of Chartered Accountants of New Zealand.

> Recognition of qualifications from other countries: EU Member States plus Iceland, Norway and Switzerland. Also Australia, Canada, Hong Kong, New Zealand, South Africa, Zimbabwe, and certain States in the US. Various conditions apply.

Final examination core programme

> ACCA's membership qualification includes 14 written examinations divided into three parts. The final part consists of three core papers plus two papers chosen from four options.

Objective final examination: to test theoretical knowledge; the ability to apply knowledge in practice; intellectual, interpersonal and communication skills; ICT applications; professional values

Key skills are examined as part of the written examinations and training programme.

ACCA is the provider of the final examination. Examinations are subject to external review

All the examinations are organised by ACCA. ACCA's examiners sets the standards of the examinations on a uniform basis world-wide and assesses all candidates on the same criteria.

Admission requirements cover professional education, practical training and general education

To register as a student of ACCA's professional scheme a candidate must be at least 18 years of age and hold the minimum qualification for entry to a UK degree programme. Holders of higher qualifications may attract exemptions from some of ACCA's examinations (not for Part 3 - the final part of 5 papers).

Professional education core programme

The examinations papers cover the following: 1.1 Preparing financial statements; 1.2 Financial information for management; 1.3 Managing people; 2.1 Information systems; 2.2 Corporate and business law; 2.3 Business taxation; 2.4 Financial management and control; 2.5 Financial reporting; 2.6 Audit and internal Review; 3.1 Audit and assurance services; 3.2 Advanced taxation; 3.3 Performance measurement; 3.4 Business information management; 3.5 Strategic business planning and development; 3.6 Advanced corporate reporting; 3.7 Strategic information management.

Universities and commercial companies provide professional education. Necessary expertise and resources are available.

Students study at public and private sector colleges, by distance learning, or by home study. ACCA publishes a textbook and a distance-learning programme through one of the private sector colleges. There are about 250 colleges which offer tuition for ACCA courses in the UK and a comparable number outside the UK. ACCA also has a virtual learning site at ACCAdemy.com. Tuition is provided by qualified academics. Outside the UK there are shortages of qualified teachers in some developing countries.

Practical training content

Candidates require a minimum of 3 year's practical experience. This can be obtained before, during or after the examinations and in any (combination of) employment sector - industry, commerce, public practice or the public sector. ACCA lays down standards of competence for membership in a Students Training Record. Assessments by supervisors are subject to a sample check by ACCA. For Registered Auditors: 3 years experience in a company audit environment including 2 years after membership in an approved training office under a qualified principal (other national legislation may apply outside the UK).
ACCA's latest competency framework covers: Financial information, Business analysis and measurement, Taxation, Statutory audit, Internal review and consultancy, Asset management, Business growth and development, Manage information systems, Manage people. A separate training record for Registered Auditors covers: Audit, Accountancy, Taxation and Business Advice.

ACCA expects for the near future major developments in regulation of the profession, professional qualification requirements, professional education and practical training

There will be developments in all these areas mainly driven by market demand and the demands of regulators. The Accountancy Foundation in the UK and the Public Oversight Board within IFAC will lead to more independent regulation of the profession in the UK and more global regulation internationally. Market demand will lead to an expansion of accountancy qualifications to include both more generalist subjects as well as more specialist options but based on the traditional accounting core. Accountancy training will become more uniform internationally.

Overview ICAEW

Professional Body	**Institute of Chartered Accountants in England & Wales (ICAEW)**
Professional Title	**Chartered Accountant (CA)**
Respondent	**Michael Payne, Education Development Executive, ICAEW**
Country	**United Kingdom**

For additional information refer to ICAEW at www.icaew.co.uk, or Michael Payne at michael.payne@icaew.co.uk .

UK requirements on accounting rules are based on the Companies Act 1985, as amended for EU Directives. The Act states that disclosure should be made as to whether accounts have been prepared in accordance with applicable accounting standards. Accounting standards issued by the Accounting Standards Board and its Urgent Issues Task Force are applicable for the purposes of this Act.

The accountancy sector in the UK is regulated by law and by professional self-regulation. The Institute of Chartered Accountants in England & Wales (ICAEW) is recognized as a regulatory body and a disciplinary body. ICAEW is a member of IFAC and FEE

Members of ICAEW work in public practice, industry and commerce, government and in other areas. ICAEW membership is mandatory to use the title and letters. Continuing professional education is mandatory in public practice and is regulated by ICAEW. CPE in other sectors is not mandatory, but the same number of hours is recommended.

Admission requirements as member of ICAEW include a formal final examination of professional competence, prescribed programmes of professional education and practical training under the responsibility of the government and the professional body.

> UK Dept of Trade and Industry approves examination structure and syllabus.

International standards: EU 8th Directive, IEG 9 and 11.
International recognition of qualifications

> All EU States recognize the ICAEW qualification under EU 8th Directive. Australia, Canada, New Zealand, South Africa, Zimbabwe through reciprocal arrangements. Most other countries with developed accountancy professions recognize the ICAEW qualification through custom and practice.

> All EU States, Australia, Canada, New Zealand, South Africa, Zimbabwe are recognized by ICAEW through reciprocal arrangements.

Final examination core programme

> Integrated business case study and associated technical subjects.

Objective final examination: to test the ability to apply knowledge in practice; intellectual and communication skills; professional values.

ICAEW provides its own examinations. ICAEW examinations are subject to external review

> The ICAEW Assessment Committee includes independent members.

Admission requirements cover professional education, practical training and general education.

Professional education core programme

Professional (First) Stage aims to provide knowledge and understanding of concepts and principles. Examinations are: Accounting, Financial Reporting, Auditing and Assurance, Taxation, Business Finance, Business Management, Business and Company Law. Advanced (Second) Stage provides an integrated approach to the giving of business and financial advice. There are two Tests of Technical Competence plus an Advanced Case Study that include Audit and Assurance, Financial Reporting, and Taxation.

Admission requirements for professional education

Minimum admission requirements are the same as for UK university entrance although in practice 90% of trainees already have university degrees.

Professional body and commercial companies provide professional education. Necessary expertise and resources are available.

ICAEW provides learning materials to recognized companies who are recognized by employers as providing the best available tuition. Internal annual review by ICAEW of syllabus and learning materials which includes representatives of employers and tutorial organisations. Normal duration of professional education is three years part time integrated with work experience.

Practical training content

3 years under a training contract which includes 450 days technical work experience of which accounting and auditing must occupy a minimum of 100 days. Firms of Chartered Accountants and approved employers offer practical training. Providers are authorised by ICAEW following an approval process carried out by ICAEW training advisors. Regulations include authorised employer, supervision by ICAEW member, training contract, breadth and length of experience, training in professional ethics.

ICAEW expects for the near future major developments in regulation of the profession, professional qualification requirements, professional education and practical training

Regulation of the profession: Increased emphasis on public interest
Professional qualification requirements: Adapting to market trends especially in ICT and business advice.
Professional education: Increased emphasis on higher skills of advice as well as technical know-how
Practical experience: Increased emphasis on client and business needs as technical work is done by ICT and other staff.

ICAEW expects for the near future major developments in regulation of the profession, professional qualification requirements, professional education and practical training

Regulation of the profession: Increased emphasis on public interest
Professional qualification requirements: Adapting to market trends especially in ICT and business advice
Professional education: Increased emphasis on higher skills of advice as well as technical know-how
Practical experience: Increased emphasis on client and business needs as technical work is done by ICT and other staff.

Overview ICAS

Professional Body	**Institute of Chartered Accountants of Scotland (ICAS)**
Professional Title	**Chartered Accountant (CA)**
Respondent	**Professor C. Mark Allison, Director of Education, ICAS**
Country	**United Kingdom**

For additional information refer to ICAS at www.icas.org.uk, or Mark Allison at mallison@icas.org.uk.

UK requirements on accounting rules are based on the Companies Act 1985, as amended for EU Directives. The Act states that disclosure should be made as to whether accounts have been prepared in accordance with applicable accounting standards. Accounting standards issued by the Accounting Standards Board and its Urgent Issues Task Force are applicable for the purposes of this Act.

The accountancy sector in the UK is regulated by law and by professional self-regulation. The Institute of Chartered Accountants of Scotland (ICAS) is recognized as a regulatory body and a disciplinary body organised under a Royal Charter. ICAS rules must be approved by the government of the UK. ICAS is a member of IFAC and FEE.

Members of ICAS work in public practice, industry and commerce, government and in other areas ICAS membership is mandatory. Continuing professional education is mandatory in public practice and is regulated by ICAS. In industry and commerce continuing professional education is mandatory for members working for a public interest body (a PLC, charity or bank); this is not regulated by ICAS.

Admission requirements as member of ICAS include a formal final examination of professional competence, prescribed programmes of professional education and practical training

> A CA Student shall be eligible for admission to membership after completion of the prescribed period of approved service as a CA Student; fulfilment of his obligations under Rule 28; passed the various parts of the Institute's Examination; applied for admission within one year from the date of passing his final examination, or from the date of completion of service under Training Contract whichever is the later.

> ICAS is organised under a Royal Charter. ICAS rules must be approved by the Government of the UK. ICAS operate under bye-laws approved by the Council, representing the members; applying these rules. Responsibility of the Professional Body: education provider, training organisation, examination setter.

International standards: ICAS follows EU 8th Directive and IFAC IEG 9 Guideline.
International recognition of qualifications

> Recognition through reciprocal agreements with England, Ireland, New Zealand, Australia, Canada, South Africa and through EU mutual recognition directive.

Final examination core programme, see syllabus and past examination papers
Objective final examination: to test theoretical knowledge and the ability to apply knowledge in practice

> 50% technical and 50% communicative in a case study format.

ICAS is the provider of the examination. Examinations are subject to external review

> Annual syllabus review and consequent impact on examination approach. Must meet UK Company Law requirements for auditors.

Admission requirements cover professional education, practical training and general education

Prospective CA Students will have established the Preliminary Qualification for registration to the satisfaction of the Council. They must produce evidence that they are: holders of a "fully-accredited" degree; or holders of a "qualifying" degree; or members or student members who have passed all the relevant examinations, of the following accountancy bodies - The Association of Chartered Certified Accountants, The Chartered Institute of Management Accountants; individuals who have satisfied membership requirements of the Association of Accounting Technicians; have worked in a financial environment for at least three years; and have their work experience attested by a Member of the Institute.

Professional education core programme

Attendance at compulsory ICAS classes and completion of education programme. This requires a three/four-year university degree plus a three-year training contract during which students follow up to 26 weeks of full time ICAS classes.

Admission requirements for professional education

Qualifying Degree holders will be required to take the Institute's Test of Competence Course and Examinations during the first year of their Training Contract before proceeding to the Test of Professional Skills and Test of Professional Expertise. Exemptions will be given for individual Test of Competence Examination subjects accredited within the degree. Candidates may not attempt the Institute's Examination unless they are serving under a Training Contract, or have completed their required service thereunder, in an ATO.

Professional body, universities and commercial companies provide professional education. Necessary expertise and resources are available as all ICAS education is delivered by accountants.

There is a three level system: At Level 1 education is offered by each of the professional body, university and commercial company. At Levels 2 and 3 education is only offered by the professional body.

Practical training content

At least 450 days experience excluding study holiday and administration. Minimum 43 days in three subject areas. Achievement of competency standards in communication and technical areas per the Achievement Log. The minimum period of Approved Service shall be three years for holders of "fully accredited" degrees, holders of "qualifying" degrees, members of the Association of Chartered Certified Accountants and of the Chartered Institute of Management Accountants and for student members of the two with all the relevant examinations of their own body while working in a training office authorised by ICAS. Four years for others.

ICAS expects for the near future major developments in regulation of the profession, professional education and practical training

A new body, The Foundation, incorporating an independent review board has been set up in the United Kingdom. The profession has funded this independent structure. Future regulation of the profession will come from the Foundation and its operations.
Changes to professional education requirements will come from technical and commercial developments rather than regulatory developments. The two most apparent areas at the moment are e-commerce and internationalisation, whether it be accounting standards or business practices.
The competency format has been developed and implemented over the last three years. It is likely this will continue to be enhanced and close attention will be paid to the IFAC pronouncements, particularly in the areas of information technology through the competency approach to IEG11.

Overview AICPA

Professional Body	**American Institute of Certified Public Accountants (AICPA)**
Professional Title	**Certified Public Accountant (CPA)**
Respondent	**Charles H. Calhoun, Professor of Accounting,**
	University of North Florida
	Bea Sanders, Director Academic & Career Development, AICPA
Country	**USA**

For additional information refer to www.aicpa.org, Charles Calhoun at ccalhoun@unf.edu, or Bea Sanders at bsanders@aicpa.org.

The USA has a very detailed framework of generally accepted accounting principles (US GAAP), based on accounting standards and guidance of the Financial Accounting Standards Board, statements from the AICPA and consensus reached by the Emerging Issues Task Force. Listed companies must follow the rules, regulations and releases of the Securities and Exchange Commission SEC.

The accountancy sector is regulated by law and by professional self-regulation. The American Institute of Certified Public Accountants (AICPA) is recognized as a disciplinary body for its members. AICPA is a member of IFAC. Licenses to practice are the responsibility of the State Boards of Accountancy.

Members of AICPA work in public practice, industry and commerce, government and in other areas. AICPA membership is not mandatory. Continuing professional education is mandatory for all CPA's and is regulated and monitored by the State Boards of Accountancy.

Admission requirements as a CPA include a formal final examination of professional competence, prescribed programmes of professional education and (in certain jurisdictions) practical training.

> Passage of the uniform CPA examination and being licensed by one of the 54 jurisdictions (education & experience requirements differ by jurisdiction). Admission to the CPA examination depends on possession of a degree recognized by the State Board of Accountancy. The Uniform Accountancy Act requires 150 semester hours with a focus on accounting, auditing and related subjects. Around 40 out of 54 jurisdictions have implemented this requirement. There is no formal requirement to have a university degree (masters or bachelors). According to the UAA 1 year of practical training is required.

> State, by law and rules, sets the standards but in actuality adopts the uniform CPA examination prepared by the AICPA. Standards of accounting and auditing practice are also issued by the AICPA and adopted by law and/or rule by the States. The AICPA, NASBA (National Association of State Boards of Accountancy) and State Boards work together in determining the standards, qualifications, etc.

International standards: IEG 9 and 11.
International recognition of qualifications

> NASBA uses the standard of substantial equivalency to facilitate interstate practice and free movement of practitioners between states. This standard is also used for foreign applicants on the additional condition of reciprocity. IQAB (International Quality Assurance Board) has international reciprocity agreements with Australia (CA and CPA) and Canada (CA).

Final examination core programme

> The CPA examination consists of four parts. See AICPA Information to Candidates brochure: Examination Content Specifications. Subjects: Business Law, Auditing, Financial Reporting, Accountancy & Reporting

Objective final examination: to test theoretical knowledge; the ability to apply knowledge in practice; intellectual, interpersonal and communication skills; ICT applications; professional values
ICAA expects for the near future major developments in practical training.

> The examination tests application and includes to a limited extent intellectual skills, communication skills (essays) and ICT applications. Ethics is part of the examination.

The government and the professional body are the providers of the final examination. AICPA examinations are subject to external review.

> State Boards of Accountancy administer the examination in 54 jurisdictions (50 States, Washington D.C., Guam , Puerto Rico, US Virgin Isles). The examinations are recognized under State Law. The AICPA is responsible for preparation and grading of the examination. The AICPA has an Examination Division, NASBA has an Examination Committee and NASBA has an Examination Review Board.

Admission requirements cover professional education and general education.

> BS in Accountancy or its equivalent and an additional 30 semester hours; in total to include 36 hours of 'upper' level accountancy and 39 hours of business (including 6 business law).

Professional education core programme

> Principles of Financial & Managerial Accountancy, Intermediate Financial Accountancy, Cost, Tax, Auditing, Accountancy Systems. AACSB requires that general education makes up 50% of an undergraduate accounting degree programme. Foundation knowledge also has to include basic financial and managerial accounting, behavioural science, economics, mathematics and statistics plus operations and technology management. The standards include coverage of written and oral communication. Specialised skills cover concepts of financial reporting, managerial accounting, information systems, auditing and taxation. Topics on not-for-profit/governmental accounting should also be covered.

Admission requirements for professional education

> High school diploma, national examination required. Scores vary by selectivity of the academic institutions.

Universities provide professional education. Necessary expertise and resources are available

> Most academic faculty have relevant experience. Part time or adjunct faculty teach while working full time.

Practical training content

> In States where practical training is required the minimum for employment is usually a degree in accounting or equivalent. In most states 1-2 years after degree. Licenses to audit can also require experience. Practical experience is gained on the job, provided by employers; no courses or examinations. Public accounting largely, some government, education allowed in most states. Degree of monitoring varies from state to state.

AICPA expects for the near future major developments in regulation of the profession, professional qualification requirements and professional education

> Regulation of the profession: competence approach of CPE. Professional qualification: drastic change of the CPA examination (computerised examination aimed at higher level skills). The examination structure will (probably?) include two independent, one-day sessions. One session will focus on assessing the fundamental knowledge required for newly-licensed CPA´s. The second section will focus on assessing the fundamental skills that newly-licensed CPA´s must demonstrate to be able to practice at entry-level competency. Professional education: Integrating IT in accountancy education with support for faculty development from AICPA, major accountancy firms and individual schools.

Annex 4 Statistical Review

Annex 4.1 Frequency Tables

Cluster 1 Country Profile

1.1 Country Size

Female % of labor force								var13
frequency	mininum	mean	maximum	1e quartile	median	3e quartile	sd	sd/mean
29	15,0%	39,8%	49,0%	37,0%	42,0%	45,0%	7,5%	0,2

Total labor force/Population								var12/var11
frequency	mininum	mean	maximum	1e quartile	median	3e quartile	sd	sd/mean
29	25,9%	47,5%	75,0%	40,9%	50,0%	52,6%	9,6%	0,2

Cluster 2 Regulation and Recognition

2.4 Mandatory CPE

Mandatory Number of hours CPE in public practice								var225
frequency	mininum	mean	maximum	1e quartile	median	3e quartile	sd	sd/mean
30	0	35	100	30	35	40	19	0,5

Mandatory Number of hours CPE in industry and commerce								var227
frequency	mininum	mean	maximum	1e quartile	median	3e quartile	sd	sd/mean
23	0	27	50	15	32	40	15	0,6

Mandatory Number of hours CPE in government								var229
frequency	mininum	mean	maximum	1e quartile	median	3e quartile	sd	sd/mean
24	0	25	50	11	30	40	17	0,7

Mandatory Number of hours CPE in other areas								var2211
frequency	mininum	mean	maximum	1e quartile	median	3e quartile	sd	sd/mean
23	0	28	55	15	35	40	16	0,6

C3 Professional Body

3.1 Frequency of Members

Female members (%) on 01/01/2001   var2139

frequency	mininum	mean	maximum	1e quartile	median	3e quartile	sd	sd/mean
33	1	30	94	15	25	38	22	0,7

3.2 Composition of Members

Percentage public practice   var2135

frequency	mininum	mean	maximum	1e quartile	median	3e quartile	sd	sd/mean
35	5,0%	44,8%	100,0%	25,0%	40,0%	60,0%	27,2%	0,6

Percentage industry and commerce   var2136

frequency	mininum	mean	maximum	1e quartile	median	3e quartile	sd	sd/mean
29	5,0%	42,4%	75,0%	30,0%	45,0%	50,0%	18,0%	0,4

3.3 Frequency of New Members

New female members (%) in 1995   var2311

frequency	mininum	mean	maximum	1e quartile	median	3e quartile	sd	sd/mean
31	0,0%	26,8%	80,0%	12,0%	24,0%	43,0%	19,7%	0,7

New female members (%) in 2000   var2310

frequency	mininum	mean	maximum	1e quartile	median	3e quartile	sd	sd/mean
32	0,0%	37,9%	79,0%	25,0%	39,0%	49,0%	19,7%	0,5

New female members (%) in 2005   var2312

frequency	mininum	mean	maximum	1e quartile	median	3e quartile	sd	sd/mean
32	4,0%	41,9%	70,0%	30,0%	46,5%	50,0%	17,4%	0,4

3.4 Composition of New Members

Percentage in public practice   var235

frequency	mininum	mean	maximum	1e quartile	median	3e quartile	sd	sd/mean
31	8,0%	49,4%	100,0%	20,0%	36,0%	85,0%	32,4%	0,7

Percentage in industry and commerce   var236

frequency	mininum	mean	maximum	1e quartile	median	3e quartile	sd	sd/mean
24	1,0%	42,6%	96,0%	27,5%	43,0%	59,5%	23,8%	0,6

Cluster 4 Professional Qualification and Background

4.1 Education Background

% with accounting, finance and business university degree								var2315
frequency	mininum	mean	maximum	1e quartile	median	3e quartile	sd	sd/mean
28	0,0%	65,1%	100,0%	46,5%	67,5%	92,5%	30,1%	0,5

Cluster 5 Examination, Education and Training

5.3 Examination Standards

Pass mark								var336
frequency	mininum	mean	maximum	1e quartile	median	3e quartile	sd	sd/mean
29	0	53	80	50	50	60	17	0,3

Pass rate								var337
frequency	mininum	mean	maximum	1e quartile	median	3e quartile	sd	sd/mean
30	5	53	98	35	59	70	25	0,5

5.9 Providers, Expertise and Resources Training

Percentage practical training in public practice								var359
frequency	mininum	mean	maximum	1e quartile	median	3e quartile	sd	sd/mean
24	15,0%	70,2%	100,0%	39,0%	80,0%	100,0%	33,0%	0,5

Percentage practical training in industry and commerce								var3510
frequency	mininum	mean	maximum	1e quartile	median	3e quartile	sd	sd/mean
16	1,0%	32,4%	85,0%	10,0%	29,5%	52,5%	24,7%	0,8

Percentage practical training in government								var3511
frequency	mininum	mean	maximum	1e quartile	median	3e quartile	sd	sd/mean
12	1,0%	15,3%	35,0%	5,0%	16,0%	22,5%	11,3%	0,7

Annex 4.2 Cross Tables

var110 versus var19

| | | var19 | | |
		common law	civil	total
var110 industrialised	frequency	7	6	13
	expected	5,38	7,62	
	Cell X2	0,49	0,34	
	percent	24,1%	20,7%	44,8%
var110 in transition/emerging	frequency	5	11	16
	expected	6,62	9,38	
	Cell X2	0,40	0,28	
	percent	17,2%	37,9%	55,2%
total	frequency	12	17	29
	percent	41,4%	58,6%	100,0%

X2	1.51
DF	1
p-value	0,2192

There is no association between the variables.

var110 versus var111

| | | var111 | | |
		small	large	total
var110 industrialised	frequency	9	4	13
	expected	5,38	7,62	
	Cell X2	2,44	1,72	
	percent	31,0%	13,8%	44,8%
var110 in transition/emerging	frequency	3	13	16
	expected	6,62	9,38	
	Cell X2	1,98	1,40	
	percent	10,3%	44,8%	55,2%
total	frequency	12	17	29
	percent	41,4%	58,6%	100,0%

	X2	7,53
	DF	1
	p-value	0,0061

There is association between the variables.

var110 versus var112

			var112		total
			weak	strong	
var110	industrialised	frequency	9	4	13
		expected	6,28	6,72	
		Cell X2	1,18	1,10	
		percent	31,0%	13,8%	44,8%
var110	in transition/ emerging	frequency	5	11	16
		expected	7,72	8,28	
		Cell X2	0,96	0,90	
		percent	17,2%	37,9%	55,2%
total		frequency	14	15	29
		percent	48,3%	51,7%	100,0%

	X2	4,14
	DF	1
	p-value	0,0418

There is association between the variables.

var111 versus var112

			var112		total
			weak	strong	
var111	small	frequency	9	3	12
		expected	5,79	6,21	
		Cell X2	1,78	1,66	
		percent	31,0%	10,3%	41,4%
var1	large	frequency	5	12	17
		expected	8,21	8,79	
		Cell X2	1,25	1,17	

		17,2%	41,4%	58,6%
	percent			

total	frequency	14	15	29
	percent	48,3%	51,7%	100,0%

X2	5.85
DF	1
p-value	0,0155

There is association between the variables.

ANNEX 5   **ABBREVIATIONS**

AAA	American Accounting Association
ACCA	Association of Chartered Certified Accountants
AECC	Accounting Education Change Commission
AFA	ASEAN Federation of Accountants
AICPA	American Institute of Certified Public Accountants
CAPA	Confederation of Asian and Pacific Accountants
CACR	Chamber of Auditors of the Czech Republic
CGA-Canada	Certified General Accountants Canada
CHA	Chamber of Hungarian Auditors
CIA	Central Intelligence Agency
CICPA	Chinese Institute of Certified Public Accountants
CMA-Canada	Society of Management Accountants of Canada
CNAM	Conservatoire National des Arts et Métiers
CPA Australia	Certified Public Accountants, Australia
CPE	Continuing Professional Education
ECSAFA	Eastern, Central and Southern African Federation of Accountants
EFAA	European Federation of Accountants and Auditors for SME's
EIASM	European Institute for Advanced Studies in Management
EU	European Union
FAR	Föreningen Auktoriserade Revisorer
FASB	Financial Accounting Standards Board
FEE	Fédération des Experts-Comptables Européens
FIDEF	Fédération Internationale des Experts-Comptables Francophones
GAAP	Generally Accepted Accounting Practice
GATS	General Agreement on Trade in Services
GNP	Gross National Product
HKSA	Hong Kong Society of Accountants
IAAER	International Association for Accounting Education and Research
IACJCE	Instituto de Auditores-Censores Jurados de Cuentas de España
IAS	International Accounting Standards
IASB	International Accounting Standards Board
IASC	International Accounting Standards Committee
IBRACON	Instituto Brasileiro de Contadores
ICA Alberta	Institute of Chartered Accountants of Alberta
ICA Australia	Institute of Chartered Accountants in Australia
ICAC	Institute of Chartered Accountants of the Caribbean
ICAI	Institute of Chartered Accountants of Ireland
ICAEW	Institute of Chartered Accountants in England and Wales
ICANZ	Institute of Chartered Accountants of New Zealand
ICAS	Institute of Chartered Accountants of Scotland
IASCF	International Accounting Standards Committee Foundation
ICA India	Institute of Chartered Accountants of India
ICAP	Institute of Chartered Accountants of Pakistan
ICJ	International Court of Justice
ICMAP	Institute of Cost and Management Accountants of Pakistan
ICPAK	Institute of Certified Public Accountants of Kenya
ICT	Information Communication Technology
ICWAI	Institute of Cost and Works Accountants of India
IDW	Institut der Wirtschaftsprüfer in Deutschland
IEG	International Education Guideline
IES	International Education Standards for Professional Accountants
IFAC	International Federation of Accountants
IFAD	International Forum on Accountancy Development

IFRSs	International Financial Reporting Standards
IMCP	Instituto Mexicano de Contadores Públicos
IPA Russia	Institute of Professional Accountants
ISA	International Standards in Auditing
JICPA	Japanese Institute of Certified Public Accountants
KIBR	National Chamber of Statutory Auditors in Poland
LACPA	Lebanese Association of Certified Accountants
MACPA	Malaysian Association of Certified Public Accountants
MIA	Malaysian Institute of Accountants
NAFTA	North American Free Trade Association
NIVRA	Koninklijk Nederlands Instituut van Registeraccountants
OECD	Organisation for Economic Co-operation and Development
Ordre	Ordre des Experts-Comptables
SAFA	South Asian Federation of Accountants
SAICA	South African Institute of Chartered Accountants
SEC	Securities and Exchange Commission
SKWP	Association of Accountants in Poland
SOCPA	Saudi Organisation for Certified Public Accountants
UNCTAD	United Nations Conference on Trade and Development
TURMOB	Union of Chambers of Certified Public Accountants in Turkey
WTO	World Trade Organisation

ANNEX 6　　　**TABLES AND GRAPHICS**

ANNEX 7   GLOSSARY OF TERMS

The IFAC Education Committee in its May 2002 *Guiding Principles for International Education Statements* has defined a glossary of terms. This glossary comprises a collection of defined terms, many of which have been specifically defined within existing Education Committee statements. Some of the existing terms may be modified, and other terms added to the glossary, as they are (re)defined in future publications. The Committee acknowledges that terms may be understood to have different nuances of meaning, and may have different applications, among the various countries in which member bodies operate. The glossary does not prescribe the use of terms by member bodies. Rather, the glossary is a list of defined terms *as they are used within the Standards, Guidelines and Papers* produced by the Education Committee. Words marked with an asterisk (*) indicate terms that are defined elsewhere in the glossary.

<u>IFAC International Education Standards for Professional Accountants</u> prescribe standards of generally accepted "good practice" in education and development for professional accountants.
<u>IFAC International Education Guidelines for Professional Accountants</u> assist in the implementation of generally accepted "good practice" in the education of professional accountants by providing advice or guidance on how to achieve "good practice" or current "best practice".
<u>IFAC International Education Papers for Professional Accountants</u> promote discussion or debate on education issues affecting the accounting profession, present findings, or describe situations of interest relating to education issues affecting the accounting profession.

For the use of the glossary in the research project a limited number of definitions is added.
<u>Accountancy Education</u> refers to the system of qualification*, professional accounting education*, practical experience* and general education* for professional accountants*, including auditors.
<u>Auditor</u> as used by the European Union is defined as a professional accountant* who is entitled to carry out statutory audits of accounting documents.
<u>Directives</u> as used by the European Union set standards that must be implemented in member country legislation.
<u>Harmonisation</u> refers to the process to standardise elements of accountancy education* between countries.
<u>Mutual recognition</u> refers to recognition of elements of accountancy education* between countries even when these are not equal.

Assessment	Refers to all forms of tests of professional competence*, whether in writing or otherwise, including examinations.
Best practice	Refers to practices considered to be exemplary, of the highest order, the most advanced, or leading in a particular area in the education* of professional accountants*. Explanation: "Best practice" refers to the best examples of established practice in the preparation of professional accountants. "Best practice" will often go beyond "good practice" and, as such, is at a higher level than the considered minimum requirements. Statements and examples of "best practice" are essential for the advancement of accounting education* and provide useful guidance to member bodies for the continual improvement of their education* programs.

Candidate	Refers to any individual who is presenting themselves for assessment as part of an education* program in preparation to become a professional accountant*.

Capabilities

Are the professional knowledge*, skills and professional values* required to demonstrate competence*.

Explanation:

Capabilities include content knowledge, technical and functional skills, behavioural skills, intellectual abilities, and professional values and attitudes.

[Based on Competence-based Approaches to the Preparation and Work of Professional Accountants, 2001]

Competence

Is being able to perform a work role to a defined standard, with reference to real working environments.

Explanation:

Competence may be assessed by a variety of means, including work place performance, work place simulations, written tests of various types and self-assessment.

[Competence-based Approaches to the Preparation and Work of Professional Accountants, 2001]

Continuing professional development (CPD)

Refers to learning* activities for developing the capabilities* of individuals to perform competently within their professional environments.

Explanation:

Continuing professional development is aimed at the post-qualification maintenance or enhancement of professional competence*. It involves the development of capabilities* through either formal, structured and verifiable learning programs (sometimes referred to as "continuing professional education" – CPE) or informal, unstructured learning activity.

[Based partly on IEG-2: Continuing Professional Education, 1998]

Development

Is the acquisition of capabilities*, which contribute to competence*.

Explanation:

Development refers to the growth of attributes that contribute to competence*, however achieved. Individuals may develop their abilities through a wide range of processes such as learning, including education* and training*; experience; reflection; observation or receipt of information; other structured and unstructured learning activities; or through natural growth over time.

Education	Refers to a systematic act or process aimed at developing knowledge, skills, character, or other abilities and attributes within individuals. It includes developmental activities commonly referred to as "training" *.

Explanation:
Education is a formal, structured learning process whereby individuals develop attributes considered desirable by society. Education is usually characterized by the growth of an individual's mental and practical abilities, as well as maturing in attitude, resulting in an enhanced ability of the individual to function and contribute to society, in either specific or non-specific contexts. While often conducted in academic environments, education also includes formal learning processes in other environments, such as on-the-job and off-the-job training. Education is, by nature, formal and therefore excludes informal, unstructured learning and developmental processes. Valuable learning, training, and development can also take place in less formal environments through processes that are not formal or structured enough to be considered "education".

Ethics	Refers to the professional values* and principles of conduct applying to professional accountants* as well as to students* and trainees* associated with IFAC member bodies.

General education	Consists of subjects drawn from the arts, sciences, social sciences and humanities that are outside the discipline areas of accounting and business.

Explanation:
General education covers a broad range of subjects of which the content is not primarily concerned with business matters. The knowledge gained from general education underpins a professional education, although it is not directly related to, or required for, conducting business activity. It contributes to professional competence* by imparting knowledge of the world, broadening the candidate's mind, and providing a more rounded education than that gained by business study alone.

Good practice	Refers to those elements considered essential to the education* and development* of professional accountants* and performed at a standard necessary to the achievement of competence*.

Explanation:
"Good practice" relates not only to the range of content and processes of education and development programs, but also to the level or standard at which they are performed (i.e., the depth and quality of the programs). The IFAC Education Committee is conscious of the wide diversity of culture; language; and educational, legal, and social systems in the countries of the member bodies and of the variety of functions performed by accountants. Different factors within these environments may vary the ability of member bodies to adopt some aspects of "good practice". Nevertheless, member bodies should continuously aspire to "good practice" and achieve it wherever possible.

Higher education	Refers to education* beyond secondary school level, usually at universities or colleges.

Underline: Explanation:

Primary and secondary education refers to the mainly compulsory element of schooling required by the governments of many countries. "Higher" education refers to a third order of education, which succeeds secondary education and for which a secondary education qualification (or equivalent) is often a prerequisite. It is at a higher level than "higher secondary" or "upper secondary" education and is sometimes referred to as "tertiary education".

Higher education institution

Is an institution recognized (usually by a government) as delivering post-secondary education* programs.

Explanation:

Primary and secondary education refers to the mainly compulsory element of schooling required by the governments of many countries. "Higher" education includes tertiary education, which refers to a third order of education that succeeds secondary education and for which a secondary education qualification (or equivalent) is often a prerequisite. Higher education institutions offer programs ranging from technical and vocational-based courses (aimed in many cases at preparing students for entry to the labour market) to theoretical and research-oriented courses (aimed in many cases at preparing students for entry to the professions or other highly skilled vocations).

Information technology

Refers to hardware and software products, information system operations and management processes, and the human resources and skills required to apply those products and processes to the task of information production and information system development, management and control.

[Exposure draft of IEG-11: Information Technology for Professional Accountants, 2001]

Learning	Refers to a broad range of processes whereby an individual develops capabilities*, including skills* and attitudes, in the application of knowledge. <u>Explanation:</u> Learning can be achieved by formal processes such as education (including training) or informal processes such as day-to-day work experience, reading published material, passive observation, and reflection.
Post-qualification	Refers to the period after qualification* as an individual member of an IFAC member body. <u>Explanation:</u> The term "post-qualification" is usually associated with activities and requirements relating to the professional development of those who have already obtained a professional qualification. It is often associated with action relating to the maintenance or further development of professional competence*.
Practical experience (or professional experience)	Is work experience, undertaken by a trainee* that is relevant to the work of professional accountants*. The program of experience is aimed at developing professional competence* (including values) within trainees and provides a means whereby trainees can demonstrate the achievement of professional competence*. <u>Explanation:</u> Practical experience refers to the on-the-job execution of tasks that are relevant to the field of accountancy. The practical experience component of the qualifying process is intended to develop candidates through the direct application of knowledge, skills, and professional values. Ultimately, it is through practical experience that trainees will demonstrate their competence* to perform the roles of professional accountants. Practical experience is sometimes referred to as "professional experience" and is synonymous with that term. [By reference to the Discussion Paper, Practical Experience, 1998]
Pre-qualification	Refers to the period before qualification* as an individual member of an IFAC member body. <u>Explanation:</u> The term "pre-qualification" is usually associated with activities and requirements relating to the development of those who have not yet obtained a professional qualification. It refers to the developmental period, or any part of the developmental period, between the time at which an individual begins their professional development and the time at which they achieve initial professional competence*, as recognized by qualification.
Professional accountant	Refers to those individuals, whether they be in public practice (including a sole practitioner, partnership or corporate body), industry, commerce, the public sector or education, who are members of an IFAC member body. [IFAC Code of Ethics for Professional Accountants, 2001]
Professional accounting education	Refers to education* that builds on general education* and imparts professional accounting knowledge*, skills*, and values*. It may or may not take place in an academic environment.

Professional knowledge	Refers to those topics that make up the subject of accountancy as well as other business disciplines that, together, constitute the essential body of knowledge for professional accountants*

Professional values   Are the attitudes that identify professional accountants* as members of a profession. They comprise principles of conduct generally associated with, and deemed essential in defining the distinctive characteristics of, professional behaviour.

Explanation:

Professional values include technical competence*, ethical behaviour (e.g., independence, objectivity, confidentiality, and integrity), professional demeanour (e.g., due care, timeliness, courteousness, respect, responsibility, and reliability), pursuit of excellence (e.g., commitment to continual improvement and life-long learning), and social responsibility (e.g., awareness and consideration of the public interest).

Qualification   Qualification as a professional accountant* is recognition that, at a given point in time, an individual is deemed to have met the requirements for recognition as a professional accountant.

Explanation

Qualification is the formal recognition of an individual as having attained a professional designation, or having been admitted to a class of professional membership, that signifies the individual is a professional accountant. Qualification implies that the individual has been deemed competent in terms of meeting the requirements prescribed for obtaining professional accountant status. While the term "qualification" can be applied to various stages of professional development and classes of membership, its usage in IFAC Education Committee documents (unless otherwise indicated) relates to the benchmark for recognition as a professional accountant.

[Based on IEG-9: Pre-qualification Education, Assessment of Professional Competence and Experience Requirements of Professional Accountants, 1998]

Relevant experience   Refers to participation in work activities in an environment appropriate to the application of professional knowledge*, skills*, and values*.

[IEG-9: Pre-qualification Education, Assessment of Professional Competence and Experience Requirements of Professional Accountants, 1998]

Skills   Refer to the various types of abilities required to apply knowledge and values appropriately and effectively in a professional context.

Explanation:

Professional accountants are required to possess a range of skills, including technical and functional skills, organizational and business management skills, personal skills, interpersonal and communication skills, a variety of intellectual skills, and skills in forming professional judgments.

Specialization   Is the formal recognition by a member body of a group of its members possessing distinctive competence* in a field, or fields, of activity related to the work of the professional accountant.*

[Discussion Paper: Specialization in the Accounting Profession, 1992]

Structured learning	Is measurable, verifiable activity designed to impart specific knowledge and skills*. Explanation: Examples of structured learning include courses and presentations; individual study programs that require some completion by the individual; and participation in formal conferences, briefing sessions, or discussion groups. Structured learning is usually, in some respects, not totally within the control of the individual undertaking the learning. For example, a third party may determine the scope or design of the activity, or when or how the learning takes place. [Based on IEG-2: Continuing Professional Education, 1998]
Student	Is an individual following a course of study, including trainees* and apprentices. Explanation: In the context of professional education, a student is an individual undertaking a course or program of study deemed necessary for the education of professional accountants, whether general or professional in nature.
Technical accounting staff	Is staff engaged in technical accounting work who are directed by or support professional accountants.* Explanation: "Technical accounting staff" includes staff customarily known as "accounting technicians" but does not include trainees who are in the process of qualifying as professional accountants. [Advisory on Education and Training of Technical Accounting Staff, 1999]
Trainee	Is an individual undertaking pre-qualification* professional development* within the work place. Explanation: A trainee is an individual who is undertaking a practical experience or work-place training program for qualification as a professional accountant.
Training	Refers to pre- and post-qualification* developmental activities, within the context of the work place, aimed at bringing a student* or professional accountant* to an agreed level of professional competence*. Explanation Training includes work place-based education and experience activities for developing an individual's competence* to perform tasks relevant to the role of the professional accountant. Training may be undertaken while performing actual tasks (on-the-job training) or indirectly through instruction or work-place simulation (off-the-job training). Training is conducted within the context of the work place, with reference to the specific roles or tasks performed by professional accountants. It can include any activity purposefully designed to improve the ability of an individual to fulfil the practical experience requirements for qualification as a professional accountant.

LITERATURE

- Standards, Guidelines and Directives
- General and Development of Accountancy Education
- Classification and Research Method
- Country Information: Profession
- Country Information: Accountancy Education

Standards, Guidelines and Directives

EU, (1984), *Eighth Council Directive of 10 April 1984*, European Union, Directive

EU, (1988), *Council Directive of 21 December 1988 on a general system for the recognition of higher-education diplomas*, European Union, Directive

IFAC, (1992), *14th World Congress*, International Federation of Accountants

IFAC, (1994), *2000 and Beyond: A Strategic Framework for Prequalification Education for the Accountancy Profession in the Year 2000 and Beyond*, IFAC Education Committee

IFAC, (1998), *Advisory on Examination Administration*, IFAC Education Committee, Study

IFAC, (2002), *Assessment of Professional Competence*, IFAC Education Committee, Proposed International Education Standard, June

IFAC, (2002), *Assistance Project in Accountancy Education and Development*, IFAC Education Committee, Study, February

IFAC, (1998, Rev. 2001), *Competence Based Approaches to the Preparation and Work of Professional Accountants*, IFAC Education Committee, Exposure draft Discussion Paper

IFAC, (2002), *Content of Professional Education Programmes, Proposed International Education Standard for Professional Accountants*, IFAC Education Committee, Proposed International Education Standard, June

IFAC, (2002), *Continuing Professional Education and Development*, IFAC Education Committee, Proposed International Education Standard, June

IFAC, (2002), *Entry Requirements*, IFAC Education Committee, Proposed International Education Standard, June

IFAC, (2002), *Experience Requirements*, IFAC Education Committee, Proposed International Education Standard, June

IFAC, (1998), *Guidance on the Formation and Organisation of a Professional Accountancy Body*, IFAC Membership Committee, April

IFAC, (2002), *Guiding Principles for International Education Statements*, IFAC Education Committee, May

IFAC, (1995, Rev. 1998 & 2002), *IEG 11, Information Technology for Professional Accountants*, IFAC Education Committee, International Education Guideline 11

IFAC, (1982, Rev. 1998), *IEG 2, Continuing Professional Education*, IFAC Education Committee, International Education Guideline 2

IFAC, (1991, Rev. 1996), *IEG 9, Prequalification Education, Assessment of Professional Competence and Experience Requirements of Professional Accountants*, IFAC Education Committee, International Education Guideline 9

IFAC, (2002), *Introduction to the Education Committee of the International Federation of Accountants*, IFAC Education Committee, June

IFAC, (1998), *Practical Experience*, IFAC Education Committee, Discussion Paper

IFAC, (2002), *Professional Skills and General Education*, IFAC Education Committee, Proposed International Education Standard, June

IFAC, (1995), *Recognition of Professional Accountancy Qualifications*, International Federation of Accountants, Statement of Policy of Council

IFAC, (1992), *Specialisation in the Accounting Profession*, IFAC Education Committee, Discussion Paper

IFAC, *Towards the 21st Century. Strategic Directions for the Accountancy Profession*, International Federation of Accountants

United Nations, (1998), *Guideline for a Global Accounting Curriculum and Other Qualification Requirements*, UNCTAD

United Nations, (1998), *Global Curriculum for the Professional Education of Professional Accountants*, UNCTAD

General and Development of Accountancy Education

AAA, (1986), *Future Accounting Education: Preparing for the Expanding Profession*, American Accounting Association, Bedford Committee Report

AECC, (1993), *Improving the Early Employment Experience of Accountants : Issues Statement N° 4*, Accounting Education Change Commission, Issues in Accounting Education, Vol. 8, N° 2, Fall

AECC, (1990), *Objectives of Education for Accountants*, Accounting Education Change Commission, Position Statement N° 1, September

AECC & AAA, (1995), *Assessment for New Curriculum : A Guide for Professional Accounting Programs*, Accounting Education Change Commission & American Accounting Association, Accounting Education Series, Vol. 11

AICPA, (1998), *CPA Vision Project*, American Institute of Certified Public Accountants

AICPA, (1998), *Assurance Services*, American Institute of Certified Public Accountants, Special Committee on Assurance Services, International Journal of Accounting

AICPA, (2001), *The Global Business Credential*, Journal of Accountancy, Special Report

Albrecht W.S., Sack R.J., (2000), *Accounting Education : Charting the Course through a Perilous Future*, Accounting Education Series, Vol. 16

Baker e.a., (1999), *Internet Uses in Accounting Education : Survey Results*, Journal of Accounting Education

Barefield R.M., (1991), *A Critical View of the AECC and the Converging Forces of Change*, Issues in Accounting Education, Vol. 6, N° 2, Fall

Beaver W.H., (1982), *Challenges in Accounting Education*, Issues in Accounting Education, Vol. 7, N° 2

Big 8, (1989), *Perspectives on Education: Capabilities for Success in the Accounting Profession*, Arthur Andersen & Co, Arthur Young, Coopers & Lybrand, Deloitte Haskings & Sells, Ernst & Whinney, Peat Marwick Main & Co, Price Waterhouse, Touche Ross

Birkett, (1993), *Competency Based Standards for Professional Accountants in Australia and New Zealand*

Brennan W.J., (1979), *The Internationalization of the Accountancy Profession*, Canadian Institute of Chartered Accountants

Burns J.O., Needles, Jr. B.E., (1994), *Accounting Education for the 21st Century: The Global Challenges*, IAAER

Calhoun Ch., Walsh M., (2000), *Comparative Accounting Curricula*, Accounting & Business, September

Chandler R.A., (1992), *The International Harmonization of Accounting : In Search of Influence*, International Journal of Accounting, Vol. 27, pp. 222-233

Choi F.D.S., (1993), *Accounting Education for the 21st Century : Meeting the Challenges*, Issues in Accounting Education, Vol. 8, N° 2, Fall

Elliot R.K., (1997), *Assurance Service Opportunities: Implications for Academia*, American Accounting Association, Accounting Horizons, Vol. 11, N° 4, December, pp. 61-74

Enthoven A.J.H., (1985), *Mega Accountancy Trends(Extended Accountancy Dimensions in Changing Societal Patterns)*

Enthoven A.J.H., (1984), *Accounting Education in Economic Development Management*

Enthoven A.J.H., (1982), *Accounting Education. Its Importance and Requirements (An Economic Development Focus)*, Fifth International Conference on Accounting Education, October

Harding F., (2000), *What is the Role of Europe in an Increasingly Harmonized World ?*, The European Accounting Review, Vol. 9, N° 4, pp. 593-602

Heaston P.H., (1990), *A Systematic Approach to Improving Experience Requirements for Licensure*, Accounting Horizons

Heeter, (1994), *The GATT Treaty : Issues and Implications for Accountants*

Hoarau Chr., (1995), *International Accounting Harmonization: American hegemony or mutual recognition with benchmarks?*, The European Accounting Review, Vol. 4, N° 2, pp. 217-233

Holstrum G., (1998), *The Internet and Distance Learning in Accounting Education*,

Holstrum G.L., Hutton, (1998), *New Forms of Assurance Services for New Forms of Information : The Global Challenge for Accounting Educators (IAAER 8th Congress)*, International Journal of Accounting, Vol. 33, N° 3, pp. 347-358

Hulle Van K., (1993), *Harmonisation of accounting standards in the EC. Is it the beginning or is it the end ?*, The European Accounting Review, Vol. 2, pp. 387-396

IAAER, (1997), *8th World Congress*, International Association for Accounting and Education Research

ICAA, (1998), *Vision 2020*, Institute of Chartered Accountants in Australia

ICAEW, (1993), *Chartered Accountant - The Future of our Qualification*, Institute of Chartered Accountants in England & Wales

ICAEW, (1996), *Future Shock for Accountants?*, Institute of Chartered Accountants in England & Wales, November

ICAEW, (1986), *Effective Education & Training for the 21st Century*, Institute of Chartered Accountants in England & Wales, Accountancy, September

ICAEW, (1981), *Education and Training: a policy framework for the future*, Institute of Chartered Accountants in England & Wales

ICAEW, (1990), *Accountancy in a Free-market Economy*, Institute of Chartered Accountants in England & Wales

ICAS, (1985), *The CA in the 1990s: An Educational Profile*, Institute of Chartered Accountants in Scotland

Johnson G.F., (2001), *Preparing Students to Thrive in the New Economy : Do Accounting Curricula Reflect IFAC Education Recommendations ?*, November

Mathews M.R., (1994), *An Examination of the Work of the Accounting Education Change Commission 1989-1992*, Accounting Education, an International Journal, Vol. 3, N° 3, pp. 193-204

May G.S., Windal F.W., Sylvestre J., (1995), *The Need for Change in Accounting Education : An Educator Survey*, Journal of Accounting Education, Vol. 13, N° 1, pp. 21-43

Melancon B.C., (1998), *The Changing Strategy for the Profession, the CPA and the AICPA : What This Means for the Education Community*, American Accounting Association, Accounting Horizons, Vol. 12, N° 4, December, pp. 397-406

Monroe G.S., (2001), *Educating Accounting Students to Cope with a Rapidly Changing Business Environment - Asia Pacific Conference Brazil*

Mueller G.G., Simmons J.K., (1989), *Change in Accounting Education*, Issues in Accounting Education, Vol. 4, N° 2

NASBA, (1997), *NASBA Board Reviews Joint Committee's Proposals*

NASBA, (1998), *IQAB Seeks single IQEX*

Needles, Jr. B.E., (1999), *Global Guidelines for Accounting Education: Regulation, Reciprocity and Implications*

Needles, Jr. B.E., (1990), *Standards for International Accounting Education : A Consideration of the Issues*

Nelson I.T., (1995), *What's New about Accounting Education Change? An Historical Perspective on the Change Movement*, American Accounting Association, Accounting Horizons, Vol. 9, N° 4, December, pp. 62-75

Nelson I.T., Bailey J.A., Nelson A.T., (1998), *Changing Accounting Education with Purpose : Market-Based Strategic Planning for Departments of Accounting*, Issues in Accounting Education, Vol. 13, N° 2

OECD, (1997), *World Trade Organization Promotes Trade in Accountancy Services*

Olivier H., *Pre-qualification, education, experience and assessment requirements, implications for reciprocity*

Olivier H., (2000), *Challenges Facing the Accountancy Profession*, The European Accounting Review, Vol. 9, N° 4, pp. 603-624

Pacter P., (1998), *International Accounting Standards : The World's Standards by 2002*, CPA Journal, July

Paisey C., Paisey N.J., (2000), *Comparative Study of Undergraduate and Professional Education in the Professions of Accountancy, Medicine, Law and Architecture*, Institute of Chartered Accountants of Scotland

Patten R.J., Williams D.Z., (1990), *There's Trouble-Right Here in our Accounting Programs: The Challenge to Accounting Educators*, Issues in Accounting Education, Vol. 5, N° 2

Pekdemir R., (2001), *Accounting Education in the Next Century*, Union of Chambers of Certified Public Accountants in Turkey

Rezaee Z., Szendi J.Z., Elmore R.C., (1997), *International Accounting Education : Insights from Academicians and Practitioners*, International Journal of Accounting, Vol. 32, N° 1, pp. 99-117

Saemann G.P., Crooker K.J., (1999), *Student Perceptions of the Profession and its Effect on Decisions to Major in Accounting*, Journal of Accounting Education, Vol. 17, pp. 1-22

Siegel G., Sorensen J.E., (1994), *What Corporate America Wants in Entry-Level Accountants*, The Institute of Management Accountants & The Financial Executives Institute, August

Solomons D., Berridge T.M., (1974), *The Report of the Long Range Enquiry into Education and Training for the Accountancy Profession*, Advisory Board of Accountancy Education

Sundem G.L., (1999), *The Accounting Education Change Commission : Its History and Impact*, American Accounting Association, Accounting Education Series, Vol. 15

Van der Plaats E., (2000), *Regulating Auditor Independence*, The European Accounting Review, Vol. 9, N° 4, pp. 625-638

Velayutham S., Perera H., (1996), *Recent Developments in the Accounting Profession in New Zealand: A Case of Deprofessionalization ?*, International Journal of Accounting, Vol. 31, N° 4, pp. 445-462

Walsh M., (1998), *The Global Approach to an Accounting Qualification*, The Association of Chartered Certified Accountants

Williams D.Z., (1991), *The Challenge of Change in Accounting Education*, Issues in Accounting Education, Vol. 6, N° 1, Spring

Wilson R.M.S., (1992), *Accounting Education : a Statement of intent and a tentative agenda*, Accounting Education, an International Journal, Vol. 1, N° 1, pp. 3-11

WTO, (1998), *Accountancy Services. Background Note by the Secretariat*, Council for Trade in Services, World Trade Organization, December

Classification and Research Method

AAA, (1977), *Committee on International Accounting Operations and Education*, American Accounting Association, Suppl. Vol. 52

Agrawal S.P., Jensen P.H., Meador A.L., Sellers K., (1989), *An International Comparison of Conceptual Frameworks of Accounting*, International Journal of Accounting, Vol. 24, pp. 237-249

Apostolou B., Watson S.F., Hassell J.M., Webber S.A., (2001), *Accounting Education Literature Review (1997-1999)*, Journal of Accounting Education, Vol. 19, N° 1, Spring, pp. 1-61

Benke R.L., Jr., Street D.L., (1992), *Accounting Education Research Methodology*, Accounting Education, an International Journal, Vol. 1, N° 1, pp. 33-45

Berman Brown R., Guilding C.J., (1995), *Research and the Academic Accountant*, Accounting Education, an International Journal, Vol. 4, N° 2, pp. 121-135

Chong A., Zanforlin L., (2000), *Law Tradition and Institutional Quality : Some Empirical Evidence*, Journal of International Development, Vol. 12, N° 2, pp. 1057-1068

CIA, (2002), *Legal Systems*, Central Intelligence Agency, factbook

Cushing B.E., (1987), *Accounting and Culture*, American Accounting Association

David, Brierley, (1985), *Major Legal Systems in the World Today*

Doupnik T.S., Salter S.B., (1995), *External Environment, Culture and Accounting Practice : A Preliminary Test of a General Model of International Accounting Development*, International Journal of Accounting, Vol. 30, pp. 189-207

Fechner H.H.E., Kilgore A., (1994), *The Influence of Cultural Factors on Accounting Practice*, International Journal of Accounting, Vol. 29, pp. 265-277

Frederikson J.R., Pratt J., (1995), *A Model of the Accounting Education Process*, Issues in Accounting Education, Vol. 10, N° 2

Gray S.J., (1988), *Towards a Theory of Cultural Influence on the Development of Accounting Systems Internationally*, ABACUS

Gray S.J., (1989), *International Accounting Research : The Global Challenge*, International Journal of Accounting

Juchau R., (1997), *Cultural Imperatives for the Accounting Education Process*, International Association for Accounting and Education Research, IAAER 8th Congress

La Porta R., Lopez-de-Silanes F., Shleifer A., (1998), *Law and Finance*, University of Chicago, Journal of Political Economy, Vol. 106, N° 6

Magerison J., (1996), *Auditor Licensing in the EU*, The European Accounting Review

Mahoney P.F., (2000), *The Common Law and Economic Growth : Hayek Might be Right*, University of Virginia School of Law, Working Paper 00-8, January

Maijoor S., Meuwissen R., Quadackers L., (2000), *The Effects of National Institutions on Audit Research : Evidence from Europe and North America*, The European Accounting Review, Vol. 9, N° 4, pp. 569-588

Mock T.J., Pincus K.V., Andre J.M., (1991), *A Systems Approach to Accounting Curriculum Development*, International Journal of Accounting, Vol. 6, N° 2

Needles, Jr. B.E., (1997), *International Accounting Research : An Analysis of Thirty-Two Years from the IJA*, Issues in Accounting Education, Vol. 32, N° 2, pp. 203-235

Needles, Jr. B.E., (1989), *International Auditing Research : Current Assessment and Future Direction*, Issues in Accounting Education, Vol. 24, pp. 1-20

Needles, Jr. B.E., (1995), *A Profile, Annotated Bibliography, and Index of Accounting Research on Developing Countries : 1965-1990*, International Journal of Accounting, pp. 7-28

Nobes Chr., (1998), *Towards a General Model of the Reasons for International Differences in Financial Reporting*, ABACUS, Vol. 34, N° 2

Nobes Chr., (1998), *Comparative International Accounting*, Prentice Hall

Perera M.H.B., (1989), *Towards a Framework to Analyze the Impact of Culture on Accounting*, International Journal of Accounting, Vol. 24, pp. 42-56

Rebele J.E., Apostolou B.A., Buckless F.A., Hassell J.M., Paquette L.R., Stout D.E., (1998), *Accounting Education Literature Review (1991-1997), Part I : Curriculum and Instructional Approaches*, Journal of Accounting Education, Vol. 16, N° 1, pp. 1-51

Rebele J.E., Apostolou B.A., Buckless F.A., Hassell J.M., Paquette L.R., Stout D.E., (1998), *Accounting Education Literature Review (1991-1997), Part II : Students, Educational Technology, Assessment, and Faculty Issues*, Journal of Accounting Education, Vol. 16, N° 1, pp. 179-245

Roxas M.L., Stoneback J.Y., Tulin P.S., *Culture and Accounting Values: Hofstede and Trompenaars*, International Association for Accounting and Education Research, IAAER 8th Congress

Stephan P.B., (1999), *The Futility of Unification and Harmonization in International Commercial Law*, University of Virginia School of Law, Working Paper 99-10, June

Therry L., Tower G., (1997), *A Critical Examination of Published Accounting Education Research (1991 to 1995)*, IAAER, 8th International Conference on Accounting Education, October

University of Ottawa, (2002), *World Legal Systems*, web version

Zweigert K., Kötz H., *Introduction to Comparative Law*

Country Information : Profession

AICPA, (1994), *The Accounting Profession in China*, American Institute of Certified Public Accountants

AICPA, (1975), *Professional Accounting in 30 Countries*, American Institute of Certified Public Accountants

AICPA, (1994), *The Accounting Profession in Argentina*, American Institute of Certified Public Accountants

AICPA, (1990), *The Accounting Profession in Australia*, American Institute of Certified Public Accountants

AICPA, (1994), *The Accounting Profession in the United Kingdom*, American Institute of Certified Public Accountants, Vol. 4, November

AICPA, (1988), *The Accounting Profession in Japan*, American Institute of Certified Public Accountants, September

AICPA, (1991), *The Accounting Profession in South Africa*, American Institute of Certified Public Accountants, Vol. 14, June

Bailey D., (1995), *Accounting in transition in the transitional economy*, The European Accounting Review, Vol. 4, N° 4, pp. 595-623

Baker C.R., Mikol A., Quick R., (2001), *Regulation of the Statutory Auditor in the European Union : a Comparative Survey of the United Kingdom, France and Germany*, The European Accounting Review, Vol. 10, N° 4, pp. 763-786

Bloom R., Naciri M.A., (1989), *Accounting Standard Setting and Culture : A Comparative Analysis of the United States, Canada, England, West Germany, Australia, New Zealand, Sweden, Japan, and Switzerland*, International Journal of Accounting, Vol. 24, pp. 70-97

Bychkova S., (1996), *The Development and Status of Auditing in Russia*, The European Accounting Review, Vol. 5, N° 1, pp. 77-90

Enthoven A.J.H., Sokolov Y.V., Kovalev V.V., Bychkova S.M., Smirnova I.M., Semenova M.V., (1998, Rev. 2001), *Accounting, Auditing and Taxation in the Russian Federation*, University of Texas and St. Petersburg State University

Evans, Nobes C., (1998), *Harmonization relating to auditor independence: the Eighth Directive, the UK and Germany*, The European Accounting Review

Favere M., (1998), *Audit Quality in ASEAN*, IAAER, Chicago, October

FEE, (1994), *Survey of the Activities of Professional Accountants in Europe*, Fédération des Experts-Comptables Européens

Hulle Van K., *Harmonisation of Accounting Standards. A View from the European Community*, The European Accounting Review

Hussein M.E., (1996), *A Comparative Study of Cultural Influences on Financial Reporting in the US and the Netherlands*, International Journal of Accounting, Vol. 31, N° 1, pp. 95-120

Lin, Chan, (2000), *Auditing Standards in China, a Comparative Analysis with Relevant International Standards and Guidelines*, International Journal of Accounting

Mueller G.G., (1968), *Accounting Principles Generally Accepted in the US Vs. Those Generally Accepted Elsewhere*, International Journal of Accounting, Vol. 3, N 2

Nobes Chr., (2000), *GAAP 2000, A Survey of National Accounting Rules in 53 Countries*

Ollier C., (1998), *Accounting Standards in Africa*, Accounting & Business, March

PricewaterhouseCoopers, (2000), *International Accounting Standards in Europe. 2005 or now ?*, PricewaterhouseCoopers, November

Schoenfeld H.M.W., *Current Developments and Trends in International Accounting*

Vieten H. R., (1995), *Auditing in Britain and Germany Compared : Professions, Knowledge and the State*, The European Accounting Review, Vol. 4, N° 3, pp. 485-511

Country Information : Accountancy Education

Abdeen A.M., (1985), *Current Status of Accounting Education in Saudi Arabia*, International Journal of Accounting

Agami A.M., Alkafaji U.A., (1987), *Accounting Education in Selected Middle Eastern Countries*, International Journal of Accounting, Fall

AICPA, (1995), *International Qualifications Appraisal Board (IQAB) Procedures*, Institute of Certified Public Accountants, NASBA

AICPA, (1988), *Requirements for Entry into the Accounting Profession : A Statement of AICPA Policies*, Institute of Certified Public Accountants

AICPA, *The 21st Century Exam. Uniform CPA Examination*, Institute of Certified Public Accountants

Albrecht W.S., Clark D.C., Smith J.M., Stocks K.D., Woodfield L.W., (1994), *An Accounting Curriculum for the Next Century*, Issues in Accounting Education, Vol. 9, N° 2, Fall

Chau G., Chan T., (2001), *Challenges Faced by Accountancy Education during and beyond the Years of Transition - Some Hong Kong Evidence*, Journal of Accounting Education, Vol. 19, N° 3, Fall, pp. 145-162

Coenenberg A.G., Haller A., Marten K-U., (1999), *Accounting Education for Professionals in Germany - Current State and New Challenges*, Journal of Accounting Education, Vol. 17, pp. 367-390

Cumming J., Rankin J., (1999), *150 Hours : A Look Back*, Journal of Accountancy, April

Dunn J., Walters D., (1992), *A Survey of Auditing Education in the UK*, Managerial Auditing Journal, Vol. 7, N° 3, pp. 3-11

FEE, (2002), *The Admission to the Profession of Accountant and Auditor. A Comparative Study*, Fédération des Experts-Comptables Européens, FEE Survey 2001, Third Draft, March

FEE, (1988), *Training for the Profession, a Comparative Study*, Fédération des Experts-Comptables Européens

Ferguson C.B., Richardson G.D., Wines G., (2000), *Audit Education and Training : The Effect of Formal Studies and Work Experience*, Accounting Horizons, Vol. 14, N° 2, June, pp. 137-167

Fogarty T.J., (1997), *The Education of Accountants in the US : Reason and its Limits at the Turn of the Century*, Critical Perspectives on Accounting, Vol. 8, pp. 45-68

Francalanza C.A., (1997), *Accounting Education and Change in Financial Accounting*, Journal of Accounting Education, Vol. 15, N° 1, pp. 109-122

Garrett N.T., Moffie R.P., Sweeney K., (1998), *A New Course for the CPA Examination*, The CPA Journal, July

Hay D., Maltby H., (1997), *A New Approach to Accounting Examinations : the Final Qualifying Examination in New Zealand*, Journal of Accounting Education, Vol. 15, N° 2, pp. 169-179

ICAEW, (1996), *Education and Training : Survey of Members*, Institute of Chartered Accountants in England and Wales, Accountancy, October

ICAEW, (1996), *Safeguarding the Future. An Education and Training Consultation Document*, Institute of Chartered Accountants in England and Wales, Accountancy, October

ICAS, (1995), *Education Review 1994-95*, Institute of Chartered Accountants in Scotland

IFAC, (1995), *Bilateral Reciprocal Recognition Arrangements for Accounting in the ASEAN Region*, International Federation of Accountants

IFAC, (1995), *The United-States-Canada Bilateral Agreement on Reciprocity from a US Perspective*, International Federation of Accountants, IFAC Newsletter

Knechel W.R., (2000), *Behavioral Research in Auditing and Its Impact on Audit Education*, Issues in Accounting Education, Vol. 15, N° 4, November

Krausz J., Schiff A.I., Schiff J.B., VanHise J., (1999), *The Effects of Prior Accounting Work Experience and Education on Performance in the Initial Graduate-Level Accounting Course*, Issues in Accounting Education, Vol. 14, N° 1, February

Loft A., Jeppesen K.K., (2001), *Harmonising the Education and Qualification of Auditors? Implementing the EU's Eight Directive in Denmark*, Paper EAA

Marten K-U., Köhler A.G., Klaas H., (2001), *Zugangswege zum Beruf des Wirtschaftsprüfers im europäischen Vergleich*, Die Wirtschaftsprüfung, Vol. 20

Meuwissen R., Vaassen E., (1996), *Audit Education in Europe and the United States*, Maastricht Accounting and Auditing Research Center, Summer

Moores K., MacGregor A.C., (1992), *Accounting Education in New Zealand*, International Journal of Accounting, Vol. 27, pp. 69-79

Nikolai L.A., (1994), *An Approach to Developing a 5-Year Integrated Accounting Program*, Journal of Accouting Education, Vol. 12, N° 2, pp. 141-160

Nikolai L.A., (2001), *Evaluation of an Approach Used to Develop, Implement, and Monitor a 5-Year Integrated Accounting Program*, Journal of Accounting Education, Vol. 19, pp. 87-102

Novin A.M., Fetyko D.F., Tucker J.M., (1997), *Perceptions of Accounting Educators and Public Accounting Practitioners on the Composition of 150 -Hours Accounting Programs : A Comparison*, Issues in Accounting Education, Vol. 12, N° 2

Novin A.M., Tucker J.M., (1993), *The Composition of 150-hour Accounting Programs : The Public Accountants' Point of View*, Issues in Accounting Education, Vol. 8, N° 2

Read W.J., Raghunandan K., Brown C., (2001), *150-Hour Preparation Improves CPA Exam Performance*, The CPA Journal, March

Smirnova I.A., Sokolov J.V., Emmanuel C.R., (1995), *Accounting Education in Russia Today*, The European Accounting Review, Vol. 4, N° 4, pp. 833-846

Stolowy H., Tenenhaus M., (1998), *International Accounting Education in Western Europe*, The European Accounting Review, pp. 289-314

UNEAS, (1994), *European Accountancy Education & Training Report*, Union of European Accountancy Students

UNEAS, (1989), *The Education and Training of the Statutory Auditor in the EEC*, Union of European Accountancy Students, June

Walker K.B., McClelland L.A., (1994), *Accounting Education in New Zealand : A Model for Reforming the American System ?*, Journal of Accounting Education, Vol. 12, N° 4, pp. 343-357

CURRICULUM VITAE

Gert H. Karreman, born August 7, 1937, Blora, Indonesia, Dutch nationality
Secondary education 1949-1954 HBS-B, Huygens Lyceum, Voorburg, The Netherlands
Masters degree in mathematics, 1967, Leiden University, The Netherlands

Professional career

Teacher of mathematics, Christelijke Scholengemeenschap Voorburg
Secondary school administration, Christelijke Scholengemeenschap Voorburg
1972-1979   Deputy director, National Academy of Traffic Sciences, Tilburg
1979-1998   Director of education, Royal NIVRA, Amsterdam
1999-2002   Programme director, European Institute for Advanced Studies in Management

Gert Karreman was director of education with Royal NIVRA (1979-1998) and programme director, Royal NIVRA* Nyenrode University (1993-1998). Royal NIVRA is the professional body of 'registeraccountants' in the Netherlands. It operates the major education and training programme for accountants and auditors in the Netherlands, cooperates with the government in setting the overall examination standards and oversees mandatory practical experience. Together with Nyenrode University a master's degree in accounting and auditing is made available to future accountants.

Responsibilities of Gert Karreman included the management and development of the NIVRA part-time accountancy education programme, co-operation with universities and institutes of higher economic studies in the Netherlands and NIVRA post-qualifying education. International experience includes implementation of the European Union 8th Directive and the EU Directive on the Mutual Recognition of Higher Education Diploma's, contribution to the development and implementation of International Guidelines on Accountancy Education as technical advisor to the IFAC Education Committee (1995-1998) and participation in European Union and OECD projects in Eastern Europe (1990-1999).

From 1998 onwards emphasis in the work of Gert Karreman is placed on international research into the development of accountancy education. As project director for the European Institute for Advanced Studies in Management (EIASM, Belgium) he is responsible for a research project on the Impact of Globalisation on Accountancy Education. The research project has as its general objective to contribute to the understanding of the present position and the possible future development of accountancy education in various parts of the world.

Professional accountancy bodies participate in the project, share their expertise and give a financial contribution towards the coverage of the costs of the research project. Major accountancy firms sponsor the project. A close co-operation is maintained with the IFAC Education Committee and with the International Association for Accounting Education and Research. The International Accounting Standards Board is a co-sponsor of the project. Contacts have been established with international organisations, including the European Union, the Organisation for Economic Co-operation and Development, the World Bank and the United Nations Conference on Trade and Development.

Contact information

Gert H. Karreman   Tel: +3123 528 00 63
Sportparklaan 59   Fax: +3123 529 79 05
2103 VS Heemstede   E-mail: g.karreman@inter.nl.net
The Netherlands